Canadians
are not
Americans

Canadians are not Americans

Myths and Literary Traditions

Katherine L. Morrison

Second Story Press

NATIONAL LIBRARY OF CANADA CATALOGUING IN PUBLICATION
Morrison, Katherine L., 1925-
Canadians are not Americans : myths and literary traditions /
Katherine L. Morrison.

Includes bibliographical references.
ISBN 1-896764-73-8

1. Literature, Comparative—Canadian and American. 2. Literature,
Comparative—American and Canadian. 3. Canadian literature—History and
criticism. 4. American literature—History and criticism. I. Title.

PS8097.A4M69 2003   C810.9   C2003-900554-2
PR9185.3.M67 2003

Cover design by James Kirkpatrick
Text design by Lancaster Reid Creative

Printed and bound in Canada

*Second Story Press gratefully acknowledges the support of the Ontario Arts
Council and the Canada Council for the Arts for our publishing program.
We acknowledge the financial support of the Government of Canada
through the Book Publishing Industry Development Program, and the
Government of Ontario through the Ontario Media Development
Corporation's Ontario Book Initiative.*

ONTARIO ARTS COUNCIL
CONSEIL DES ARTS DE L'ONTARIO

The Canada Council | Le Conseil des Arts
for the Arts | du Canada

Published by
SECOND STORY PRESS
720 Bathurst Street, Suite 301
Toronto, Ontario, Canada
M5S 2R4

www.secondstorypress.on.ca

For Russell and our family:
Donna, Leslie, Rob,
Mark, Tony,
Charlotte, Elliot, Ben and Laura

Contents

Acknowledgements

AMONG THE MANY PEOPLE that have contributed to the development of this book, none deserves my gratitude more than the late Professor John M. Robson. In poor health and working on the papers of Northrop Frye, he asked to read the manuscript. His words of praise and encouragement helped sustain me through revisions and the inevitable frustrations of seeing a work through to publication.

Particular appreciation goes to Ann Schabas, Mary McDougall Maude, and Rosemary Shipton. These three women went well beyond editing to give invaluable help with structure, context, and the balance of history and literature.

Those who read the manuscript at an early stage and made helpful suggestions include Barrie Hayne, W. J. Keith, and Dennis Duffy; also Ruth and the late Claude Isbister.

My thanks to David Staines, who generously read and commented on the manuscript of an unknown writer. I was much too slow in recognizing the best of his advice. My thanks also go to Ian Montagnes, Ann Robson, and Ruth Bradley St-Cyr, for their many helpful suggestions.

A special thanks to my publisher, Margie Wolfe, and her staff, especially Laura McCurdy, whose eagle eye caught many an error.

My husband, Russell, has been a strong support and severe critic, while our daughters read and commented on the manuscript. The rest of the family has been a steady source of encouragement. My thanks to all.

Canadians are not Americans

Myths and Literary Traditions

My interest [in Canada] has stemmed in large measure from a desire to understand the United States better ... [It] is precisely because the two North American democracies have so much in common that they permit students of each to gain insights into the factors that cause variations.

Seymour Martin Lipset, *Continental Divide*

In the beginning the Americans created America, and America is the beginning of the world ... one can still hear the confident tones of its Book of Genesis: "We hold these truths to be self-evident." At least a Canadian can hear them, because nothing has ever been self-evident in Canada.

Northrop Frye, *Divisions on a Ground*

Preface

TWO PREDOMINANTLY ENGLISH-SPEAKING NATIONS share the vast expanse of North America. To most Americans — and to much of the rest of the world — the two nations differ little except in climate, for they share a common British heritage and similar patterns of immigration. Subtle cultural differences appear insignificant to most Americans, but not to Canadians or to a small but growing number of Americans seeking insight into their own national character.

My interest in cultural differences between the United States and Canada developed gradually. I moved to Ontario as a young adult, an American with a Canadian husband and an expected first child. Having lived in Michigan, Illinois, and Tennessee during the previous five years, I was prepared for a slightly colder climate, but not for social or cultural changes other than what I would find moving from one American state to another. The transition was easy; neighbors were friendly and there were other recent arrivals, some from the United States and many from the United Kingdom. I never felt out of place, yet something was unsettling. Jokes about when Canada would become the next American state seemed in poor taste; also, there was a sense of having moved backward in time. There was more churchgoing than I was used to and my new friends did old-fashioned things like collecting flowery china cups and saucers. These habits seemed rather quaint, but hardly slowed my transition to becoming a Canadian. I gradually absorbed the mythology and began to see the United States through the eyes of an outsider.

As my family grew, this outsider's perspective continued to interest me. I began graduate work in nineteenth-century American literature, which brought the United States and its development into sharper focus, but did little to advance my understanding of Canada. In the late 1970s I was hired to teach early American literature at a Canadian university, but the course was cancelled because of poor enrollment. Perhaps, I thought, Canadians are as indifferent to American cultural history as was clearly the opposite case.

When I developed a course comparing the works of nineteenth-century writers in the two countries, interest ran high. Although I had done much work preparing the Canadian material, there was still a lack of understanding of this country that had been my home for so many years. It was clear that I needed to go back to my books and learn more about the history and literature of Canada.

Looking at the histories of the two nations, I came to appreciate that the American Revolution, as Canadian historian J.M.S. Careless says, "created modern Canada no less than it created the American republic."[1] The forefathers of many of today's English Canadians were the Loyalists who fled the American colonies and settled in Nova Scotia or Quebec,[2] the two colonies that remained in the British Empire. Those two colonies bore little resemblance to the future nation called Canada, and the leaders of the new United States believed that only mistakes and incompetence had prevented a clean sweep of the colonies. Surely, they thought, time and good sense would correct the situation.

Manifest Destiny[3] was a vaguely remembered term from a history book for me, but I came to appreciate what an intensely held conviction it was to nineteenth-century Americans, who believed that it was their destiny to expand across the entire North American continent. For over a century, this belief prevented American acceptance of a second English-speaking nation, even though Canada's Confederation took place in 1867. As late as 1919, some American senators suggested that Britain pay its World War I debt by turning Canada over to the United States. The American government finally recognized Canada as a separate country in 1920. Historian W.L. Morton notes that the first Canadian diplomats puzzled the Americans, who behaved "as though the former provincials were a parody, somehow vaguely irrelevant, of the Americans themselves."[4] Some of my own memories began to have greater meaning. For example, I recalled a series of radio talks given by Robert McCormick, publisher of the *Chicago Tribune*, outlining a plan for Canada to become part of the United States. My own father was puzzled by Canada's failure to join the United States. Neither McCormick nor my father could fathom that Canadians had strong objections to becoming Americans.

My study of Canadian/American political relations spanning more than two centuries sparked the idea of tracing the development of other ideas through the literature of the two nations. Cultural mores are often ephemeral, but when they are entrenched by traumatic events — usually wars — they tend to spawn the creation of myths in national cultures. The more traumatic the event, the more deeply the myth is embraced and passed down to succeeding generations. These myths can be traced through the literature of each country and provide paradigms of Canadian and American intellectual development. As Northrop Frye says, "Literature is conscious mythology."[5] The United States and Canada, seemingly so much alike, have some very distinct myths. In his sociological study of both countries, Seymour Martin Lipset notes that Canada and the United States are "formed around sharply different organizing principles. Their basic myths vary considerably, and national ethoses and structures are determined in large part by such images."[6] Lipset does not elaborate on the basic myths, leaving unanswered the questions of how and why such differences have developed. The strength of various myths and how much they influence both ideas and ideals in the populace will always remain something of a mystery. But after much thought I settled on seven themes for purposes of comparison: a sense of the past; nature; a sense of place; religion and the church; gender, ethnicity, and class; violence; and humor.

No doubt it is the Canadian in me that seeks to examine differences. At a conference on American and Canadian western literature in 1978, Canadian critic Rosemary Sullivan noted that "the American scholars were concerned with similarities and the Canadian scholars with differences."[7] Perhaps Manifest Destiny still lingered in the American mind, but the Canadians, most of whom were seeking a "Canadian identity" at that time, could only find satisfaction in examining differences.

Making cultural comparisons using two bodies of literature is a challenge. My most difficult problem was deciding how to structure this study. Many comparative literary studies have been tackled by Canadian scholars — Americans have shown little interest — most in essays that compare one or more works by a Canadian and an American writer. This was not what I had in mind, for my interest was in tracing the development of ideas, not in comparing authors and works. I therefore decided to sacrifice the immediacy gained by direct comparisons in order to show the chain of development in each country. I trace each theme through American literature first, because of its longer history, and make direct literary or cultural comparisons in the sections on Canada.

This strategy solves another problem: changing cultural mores. The major works of Hawthorne, Melville, Thoreau, and Whitman appeared in the early 1850s, when the future Canada was just a scattering of British colonies in a pioneer state of development. Few of the colonists had the time or inclination to write. Those who did looked to Britain or France for standards of excellence, and could offer far fewer insights into their burgeoning society than America's early literary greats were providing for the United States. However, writers in both countries partook of the romanticism prevalent before the American Civil War and Canada's Confederation, and both moved toward realism afterward, the Americans with greater enthusiasm.

My research turned up two surprising discoveries. First, canonized male writers outnumber women writers by more than four to one in the United States. This figure is unbalanced, for while men and women writers are almost evenly divided today, there was a paucity of notable women writers in the nineteenth century. Many literary historians include Emily Dickinson as the sole woman writer of note, although Harriet Beecher Stowe is important historically for *Uncle Tom's Cabin* (1852), and Louisa May Alcott's children's novels have endured. There were women writers — Hawthorne complained about a "damned mob of scribbling women"[8] — but their sentimental romances were soon forgotten. Women writers have always held their own in Canada. Frances Brooke's *The History of Emily Montague* (1769), set largely in Quebec, is the first published novel written in North America. Some of Canada's most important pre-confederation writings were by women and the Canadian canon is much more evenly balanced between the sexes.

The second surprise came with the realization that the large body of Canadian literature in French could be included as a source of examples. French Canadians and English Canadians have never considered themselves

alike, particularly in the early days when religion and natio
more important than they are today. Their challenge w
peacefully, and the relative success of this venture is at least pa...y
similar conservative tendencies. Frye speaks of the American Revolution as a
civil war between the Whigs and the Tories.[9] The Tories, who called
themselves Loyalists, swelled the populations of Nova Scotia and Quebec.
They were forced to join the French — their former enemies — who had been
defeated in the Seven Years' War only two decades earlier. The Loyalists found
that, despite obvious differences in religion and language, the *Canadiens* had
important traits in common with them: a desire to maintain continuity with the
past, a strong attachment to the local community, a belief that the church was
a vital part of civilized society, and a bent toward passivity. These common
traits have made it possible to draw Canadian selections from both French and
English literature.

It is common knowledge that early American and Canadian writers had
different attitudes to the past and to nature, that there has been much more
violence in American life and literature, and that Americans have elevated
many more heroes than Canadians. Most differences between the nations can
be traced from their beginnings, some back to the first English and French
settlements in North America. However, all were in some way affected by the
three wars that did so much to establish borders in the northern part of the
continent: the Seven Years' War (1756–1765), known as the French and Indian
War in the United States; the American Revolution (1775–1783); and the War
of 1812 (1812–1814).

This book is divided into nine chapters. The first chapter establishes the
context and explains the ideological differences that sprang up with the
American Revolution. The seven themes occupy one chapter each, and a final
chapter draws the material together and offers thoughts on trends that have
brought the countries closer together and traits that remain distinctive.

My choice of examples from the literatures of the two countries is
necessarily arbitrary and personal. I have tried to use works that are familiar
to the general reader, but that is not always possible. The choice from
nineteenth-century Canada is limited, while the late twentieth century offers
a dizzying array in both countries. The examples are presented chronologically

and are continued almost to the present, in order to demonstrate the tenacity of national myths. Any type of qualitative analysis of the works selected would be inappropriate.

This is a "history of ideas" study. A.O. Lovejoy, in *The Great Chain of Being: A Study of the History of an Idea* (1936), says, "it is to literature we must look," in tracing ideas through a culture. He adds that the "tendencies of an age appear more distinctly in its writers of inferior rank than in those of commanding genius."[10] In order to understand national myths, one must see the world through the eyes of those who lived at the time, so many of the examples used were once popular, but are no longer considered canonical. Finally, the terminology used for linguistic, racial, and ethnic minorities may appear inconsistent. It seems appropriate to use terminology of the period when discussing early works, but to use the preferred modern terms in a general discussion. There is no simple language for discussing Native North Americans, nor is there a simple way to distinguish French Canadian literature from Quebec literature.

It is my hope that a work of this nature will inspire further study, for anything so broadly based will inevitably leave important matters unexamined. However, my primary objective is to improve understanding between Canada and the United States, and to promote greater and more profound self-knowledge in both nations.

Notes

1 J.M.S. Careless, *Canada: A Story of Challenge*, 3rd ed. (Toronto: Macmillan, 1974), 114.

2 These large colonies included what would later become New Brunswick and Ontario.

3 The term Manifest Destiny gained currency in the 1840s and had wide popular appeal throughout the nineteenth century. It was used to justify the annexation of Texas, the war with Mexico, the dispute with Britain over the Oregon territory, and the purchase of Alaska. The concept implied the eventual annexation of Canada.

4 W.L. Morton, *The Canadian Identity*, 2nd ed. (Toronto: University of Toronto Press, 1972), 72.

5 Northrop Frye, *The Bush Garden: Essays on the Canadian Imagination* (Toronto: Anansi, 1971), 232

6 Seymour Martin Lipset, *Continental Divide: The Values and Institutions of the United States and Canada* (New York: Routledge, 1990), 225.
7 Rosemary Sullivan, "Summing Up," in Dick Harrison, ed., *Crossing Frontiers: Papers in American and Canadian Western Literature* (Edmonton: University of Alberta Press, 1979), 144.
8 *Letters of Hawthorne to William D. Ticknor, 1851–1864.* Vol I (Newark, NJ: The Carterett Book Club, 1910), 75.
9 Northrop Frye, *Divisions on a Ground: Essays on Canadian Culture* (Toronto: Anansi, 1982), 45.
10 Arthur O. Lovejoy, *The Great Chain of Being: A Study of the History of an Idea* (New York: Harper Torchbooks, 1960), 17, 20.

Chapter One

The Launching of National Myths

"THOSE WHO KNOW ONLY ONE COUNTRY KNOW NO COUNTRY," writes Seymour Martin Lipset, arguing that it is impossible to understand any nation unless it is compared to another.[1] Canada and the United States are particularly suited for throwing light on each other's differences. On the surface, they appear much alike, have a long common border, and have faced essentially the same obstacles as they developed westward to the Pacific Ocean. Canada, with a larger land mass but only one-tenth the population of the United States, has never ceased struggling to remain free of its powerful neighbor, a struggle that has always mystified Americans. This has led to an unusual relationship, like no other "in the world," according to Northrop Frye.[2]

Forces Dividing the Continent

THE FORCES THAT DETERMINE A NATION'S BOUNDARIES, characteristics of a people, and distinctive qualities of the literature that they produce are so numerous and complex that only the most dramatic can be isolated. Migration patterns and the wars that often result from struggles over land are primary determinants. In the case of Canada and the United States, different ideologies turned the American Revolution from an argument over rights to a demand for independence. British Whigs and Tories living in the American colonies, disagreed over independence, so they fought a civil war. The defeated Tories were expelled and the majority of them forced to move north to colonies that remained British. They came from every colony, a splitting of the American population, exiles burdened with anger and bitterness. Such early opposing ideologies sparked national myths that have lasted for generations and found expression in two bodies of literature.

Geography plays a vital role in the development of nations, no less in North America than in the rest of the world. Canada is a northern country, made known to European cultures by the Vikings and John Cabot; the United States was explored by the followers of Columbus. The St. Lawrence river system and Hudson Bay opened the interior of the continent to outside explorers and traders before settlers reached the Alleghenies in what is now the United States. J.M.S. Careless views the St. Lawrence as a "broad funnel" through which people poured into the heartland of the continent.[3] There they established a trading system that set the pattern for the settlers' relations with the Native people of North America.

Economist Harold Innis has made a strong case for Canada as a geographically natural country, one that developed along river basins that run predominately east-west. These were the routes of the fur traders, who gradually moved west along the edges of the Canadian or Precambrian Shield. "It is no mere accident," he says, that the present borders of Canada coincide roughly with "the fur-trading areas of northern North America."[4] When the fur trade died out it was replaced by lumbering and mining, resources found in the same east-west wilderness. There was enough arable land in the St. Lawrence river basin, southern Ontario, and the prairies to support these activities. W.L. Morton speaks of "alternate penetration of the wilderness and return to civilization" as the "basic rhythm of Canadian life" that forms the "Canadian character whether French or English."[5]

According to Innis, the continent was divided into three areas at the time of the American Revolution: a northern area that was dependent on the fur trade, a southern area where cotton and tobacco were grown, and a central diversified area that was beginning to industrialize. Because of the enormous distances and harsh climate of the fur-trading area, central organization was thought necessary. Centralized paternalism was traditional in New France, which, along with the tight organization of the Hudson's Bay and later the North West Companies, influenced the "institutional development of Canada."[6] The cotton-and-tobacco-growing states of the American south were forcibly reunited with the central industrializing area after the American Civil War, at which time the United States expanded rapidly westward, not bothering to capture the northern area. Americans believed that the northern colonies would willingly join the Union in due course; instead, those colonies formed a confederation to try to protect themselves against an expected invasion from the Americans. John A. Macdonald, Canada's first prime minister, wrote to a friend in India in 1867 with news of the British North America Act, which would bind the colonies into a confederation: "A brilliant future would certainly await us were it not for these wretched Yankees ... War will come someday."[7]

Canadians and Americans seem unaware of how much geography has shaped their lives, their borders, and their institutions, for mountain ranges and prairies running north and south give the continent an appearance of a natural unit. Americans embraced Manifest Destiny early in the nineteenth century, certain that they were fated to take over the entire continent, while Canadians were not nurtured by this kind of guiding principle. The popular belief is that the borders of Canada and the United States were formed solely by three rapidly succeeding wars in the latter half of the eighteenth and early years of the nineteenth centuries: the Seven Years' War (1756–1765; U.S. French and Indian War, 1754–1765), the American Revolution (1775–1783), and the War of 1812 (1812–1814). Besides the American struggles with Spain and Mexico, these three North American wars largely settled control of the continent.

Three North American Wars

THE FALL OF NEW FRANCE TO THE BRITISH in the Seven Years' War remains a pivotal event in the history of the French-Canadian people. Since then they have struggled to survive and to resist assimilation into the English-speaking culture surrounding them. To the residents of the American colonies, the British success in this war was a great relief, for the French in North America had been a dangerous enemy for a century and a half. Catholics and Protestants still hated and feared each other in most of Europe, and the hostility was even stronger between solidly Catholic New France and Puritan New England. The New England clergy described Catholic Quebec as "the last bastion of evil" in North America, and predicted a "golden age of peace and prosperity" following a "protestant American victory."[8]

The Americans had been happy to be British subjects as long as France remained a threat, but barely ten years after the elimination of that threat they turned hostile. The British parliament began taxing the colonies in order to help with its huge war debt and the cost of defense in North America. The colonial legislatures reacted angrily. The dispute continued for ten years, during which the British, needing their most skilled officials in other fields, left incompetent administrators in charge of the Colonial Office.[9] The thirteen colonies, which had had little to do with each other during their long history, formed the Continental Congress in order to negotiate as a unit with their new adversaries.

During the ten years before the outbreak of war, the American colonists wanted their grievances addressed and only a tiny minority thought in terms of independence. When fighting broke out in 1775, Washington's officers were still toasting the King. Pauline Maier points out that even "the most radical members of Congress professed a strong preference for remaining in the empire."[10] The Declaration of Independence came a year later and resulted in internal fighting as well as battles with the British. Those who favored independence called themselves Patriots, while those opposed were Loyalists — called Tories by the Patriots, who considered them traitors. There were many Loyalists in the colonies, including such notables as George Washington's mother and Benjamin Franklin's son.[11]

The Declaration of Independence, based on Enlightenment ideals, is effectively the first written statement of the American Dream. It was designed to present the colonists' case to the world, to "furnish a moral and legal justification" for rebelling. Troubles in the colonies are blamed on the king, and there is no mention of parliament or the "rights of British subjects."[12] The Declaration was more effective in launching a myth and uniting the colonists than it was in persuading the rest of the world that the Americans were suffering under a tyrant. There was need for a communal myth because there was no effective government. The Continental Congress was no more than a gathering of delegates, representing a barely acquainted group of colonies with widely divergent interests.

The last straw for the British came in December 1773 with the Boston Tea Party, and the final outrage for the colonists was the Quebec Act of 1774, which extended the borders of Quebec to include the Ohio valley, closed the valley to settlement, disallowed a legislative assembly, and gave official recognition to the Roman Catholic religion. The Act was not intended to punish the colonists. Guy Carleton, British Governor of Quebec, admired the orderly French Canadian society and regarded it as a "valuable stronghold against disloyalty and violence in America."[13] He pressed for a recognition of French institutions in order to bind the people to the empire. The members of Parliament listened. The empire now encompassed many diverse peoples, and legal protection for its minorities was high on the agenda.[14] Pontiac's uprising of 1763 to 1765 had alarmed the British, who planned to make the Ohio valley a huge Native reserve to protect the fur trade and prevent Indian wars. Because France remained a serious and ongoing threat, the British considered it politically wise to allow the French in North America to retain their religion and their civil code. The British also hoped to divert settlement northward and dilute French and Catholic influences. Such arguments did not carry weight with the irate colonists to the south. They had little involvement in the fur trade, pressure for western land was becoming explosive, and "popery" was seen as the work of the devil. Of the thirteen colonies, only Maryland and Pennsylvania tolerated Catholics, and even there they were denied a franchise. To the American colonists, the Quebec Act was an act of tyranny, directly attacking their liberty.[15]

The American invasion of Quebec in 1775 was a failure. The *Canadiens* fought to defend their homes, but showed no interest in joining a dispute between the colonists and Great Britain. As Governor Carleton had predicted, the Catholic bishop decided that his people were far safer in the empire where the Quebec Act was in force than in joining rebelling colonists who had little tolerance for Catholicism. The situation in Nova Scotia was more ambiguous. Many of the settlers were from New England, but, being largely uneducated, they were out of touch with the news, "a people in a state of confusion."[16] Between the strength of the British navy at Halifax and the unwitting services of a traveling evangelist, Henry Alline, who turned the people's attention from politics to religion, Nova Scotia remained in British hands.

Once fighting broke out, openly declared Loyalists were in considerable danger. A civil war broke out in New York, and as the war turned gradually against the British, masses of Loyalists were besieged in the port and had to be evacuated. About 30,000 were taken to Nova Scotia, which tripled the population of the colony. About 10,000 made their way by land to Quebec, where they joined the French and the few merchants and government authorities who spoke English.

Fighting ended when Cornwallis surrendered at Yorktown in October 1781, but a peace treaty was delayed for two years, a terrible period for the Loyalists. The Continental Congress openly encouraged the confiscation of Loyalists' property and investment of the proceeds in continental loan certificates. Slaves, the most valuable property, were grabbed, loaded onto ships and sent to the West Indies for sale to plantation owners. At Charleston twenty-four prominent Loyalists were hanged on the waterfront "in sight of the retreating [British] fleet." Bills of attainder were passed by local legislatures naming individuals who could be "libeled, slandered, insulted, blackmailed or assaulted" without legal recourse. This practice was later outlawed in the first paragraph of the Bill of Rights. Mob rule was so widespread that it became acceptable behavior. Walter Stewart claims that the Ku Klux Klan and the lynch mob, "the [American] penchant for home-brewed justice," had their roots in that period.[17]

The negotiations were long and rancorous, mainly over issues of compensation for the Loyalists. Benjamin Franklin suggested that Britain turn over the northern colonies as an act of goodwill. The suggestion was "not thought audacious,"[18] for Britain was heartily sick of the American situation and saw value in future good relations. The King was opposed and a place was needed for the Loyalists, so Quebec, Nova Scotia, and Newfoundland were retained. Britain agreed to relinquish the Ohio valley, but continued to press for compensation for the Loyalists. The Continental Congress agreed in principle, but had no authority to do more than recommend compensation to the individual states, all of which ignored the recommendation.

Relinquishing the Ohio valley was, in effect, a desertion of Native allies, so merchants in Quebec feared an uprising. They persuaded the British to retain their western forts, using the American failure to compensate the Loyalists as an excuse for violating the treaty. This protected the fur trade, but was a major irritant to the Americans. Western posts in the United States were given up with Jay's Treaty of 1793; then the Natives were defeated at Fallen

Timbers in 1794. When the Napoleonic wars broke out in 1803, tensions rapidly increased. The British blockade of France interfered with American trade, and searching American ships for deserters from the Royal Navy led to the impressment of American merchant seamen. In addition, the suspicion of frontiersmen that the Natives were being armed led to considerable pressure to invade the northern colonies. Thomas Jefferson, president from 1800 to 1808, resisted the pressure, but his successor, James Madison, was successfully pushed into declaring war by western "hawks" in Congress.

The War of 1812 was widely unpopular in the United States, particularly in New England, but there was no backing out, and easy victories could be won in the west. The western Natives, who had made another stand against the Americans under the Shawnee chief, Tecumseh, were defeated at the battle of Tippecanoe in 1811. "A war against Canada would finally break the Indians, and might be used to 'liberate' the Canadians," was the general American attitude.[19] Lieutenant Governor Simcoe of Upper Canada had lured so many Americans to the colony by promising free land, safety from Indian attacks, and no military service, that they outnumbered the Loyalists. However, the Loyalists were in control and they made it clear that they did not wish to be liberated, so Upper Canadians fought beside British soldiers to repel the invasion. The French were now fully aware of the danger to their religion and institutions in the United States, so they successfully repelled invasions into Lower Canada. The fighting ended with no change of borders, which was considered a victory by both sides. Much of the war had gone against the Americans — the city of Washington was captured and burned — so retention of their original borders was a relief. The war boosted nationalism on both sides of the border.

The War of 1812 was a footnote to the Napoleonic wars and an addendum to the American Revolution, but to the Loyalists it was of considerable significance and it looms large in Canadian history. The Loyalists were Americans who still hoped to reunite the empire, a hope that was dashed with the 1814 Treaty of Ghent. On the other hand, they had escaped capture and annexation, and could proudly claim that they were still British, living in an outpost of the empire. Since that time Canadians have had a secondary identity; they became "not Americans," a myth that lingers. In his book *Yankee*

Go Home, J.L. Granatstein traces Canada's fluctuating anti-Americanism from the arrival of the Loyalists to the end of the twentieth century and claims that it is as much a "buttress" of the national identity as the "French-English duality."[20] Canadian politicians can still draw a following with some variation on the threat that the Americans are coming.

Different Concepts of Liberty

THE BRITISH DISPUTE WITH THE AMERICAN COLONISTS began with the Stamp Act of 1765, intended to help pay for American defense and to reduce the huge debt left from the Seven Years' War. The colonists' outrage over the Stamp Act sparked an intellectual dispute over moral and legal rights. Having always considered themselves loyal British subjects, the colonists had to find solid reasons to violate an act of Parliament. According to Carl L. Becker, this meant defining colonial rights in such a way as to make the Stamp Act, "not merely an inexpedient measure, but an unconstitutional" one, which the "British Parliament had no 'right' to pass."[21] In the same year, the first *Commentaries* of the great legal scholar Sir William Blackstone appeared, asserting that an "absolute despotic power ... must in all governments reside somewhere," and for the British it resides in Parliament.[22]

This was the age of the "rights of man," when the works of John Locke and Jean Jacques Rousseau were being widely discussed throughout the western world. These works made a strong impression among the educated in the colonies, where important figures such as James Otis, James Wilson, Thomas Jefferson, and John Adams began proposing, as a natural law, that Britain and its colonies were a voluntary association of equals. Wilson asks rhetorically: "Do you quote your Blackstone in support of the sovereignty of the British Parliament? ... I in turn quote him in support of the superior sovereignty of the law of nature," for Blackstone does in fact say "the law of nature is superior in obligation to any other." By assembling axioms of the natural rights philosophy — such as "All men are, by nature, equal and free"; "all lawful government is founded in the consent" of the governed; the "happiness of the society is the first law of every government"; and the inhabitants of the English colonies in North America are "entitled to life, liberty and property" — a case was made against the authority of Parliament to tax its colonies.[23] This was a radical idea that did not conform to the British constitution or the traditions of the empire. Other colonial contentions, such as "no taxation without representation," were not so extreme, and many members of Britain's Parliament agreed with them. A number of taxation bills were repealed, but others followed, and Parliament never wavered in its insistence that it had absolute authority to govern the British Empire.

As the dispute heated up, Patriots and Loyalists clung to sharply different concepts of liberty. The Loyalists remained convinced that Parliament was the ultimate legal authority and that threats to liberty came from the mob. To the Patriots, liberty was threatened by government, particularly traditional institutions such as monarchy, aristocracy, and an established church. Taking many of the most high-flown ideas of the Enlightenment seriously, they held that humans were basically good and only needed freedom from tyrants and oppressive institutions to act virtuously. This *a priori* or deductive approach to governing led them to create a tripartite federal government, no part of which was to have authority over the others: Americans firmly denied Blackstone's contention that every government must have an "absolute despotic power." "History has informed us," says Jefferson, "that bodies of men as well as of individuals, are susceptible of the spirit of tyranny."[24] His famous remark, "that government is best which governs least," was no idle comment; it was the very core of American ideology. This ideology remained strong throughout the nineteenth century, when to call someone a monarchist or "aristocratical" was the most damning of indictments.

The Loyalists, who saw threats to liberty coming from the mob, spoke of the new American democracy as a mobocracy and "anarchy set loose."[25] British institutions, in their view, had evolved over time and had become the most civilized and advanced in the world. The Loyalists suffered much hardship in the northern colonies, but tried to be patient as they had had enough of unruly crowds and populist demands for instant solutions. The British certainly had a mess on their hands. Nova Scotia, which went from about 17,000 inhabitants to nearly three times that number, had to be divided, which meant the creation of new colonies. In Quebec, the 10,000 Loyalists who had lost their homes fighting for British institutions found themselves in a French-speaking colony with no legislature and a French civil code.

Believing that the American Revolution was a result of the failure to establish British institutions, the authorities were determined not to make the same mistake again. So, in haste, the Constitution Act of 1791 was passed, dividing Quebec into Upper and Lower Canada, providing a legislative assembly for each, and setting one-seventh of the land aside for the Protestant clergy. These clergy reserves were widely interpreted as Anglican, in preparation for an established church. New Brunswick and Cape Breton Island had been separated from Nova Scotia in 1784. There was much bickering in New Brunswick as some ultra-conservatives had drawn up plans to pattern the new colony after the feudal Quebec system of a landed gentry, tenant farmers, and no legislative assembly. Due to fierce opposition, the plan was never enacted, but it created "blighted hopes, economic distress, and embittered politics."[26] In fact, British aristocrats, many of them absentee landlords, milked the colonies of Nova Scotia and New Brunswick so shamefully that "it is hard to escape the conclusion that the Loyalists' experience had conditioned them to put up with almost anything to avoid the scourge of mob rule."[27]

Residents of the newly formed United States and the Loyalists with their French compatriots had very different ideas, not just about how nations should be governed, but about human nature itself. To the Americans, humans were fundamentally good and merely needed freedom from institutional restraints to do right by their fellow men. This love affair with the natural rights philosophy made it impossible for most people to think in terms of collective rights for slaves or Natives. The free individual would be virtuous, and any problems would gradually melt away. Lipset claims that the "American creed can be subsumed in four words: antistatism, individualism, populism, and egalitarianism."[28] The powerful nationalism and optimism that followed the American Revolution blinded the Americans to the fundamental paradox in that combination of ideals — that unrestrained liberty of the individual does not result in an egalitarian society. As Lipset writes, there is "a deep contradiction ... at the core of the American creed."[29] The British and Loyalist view that true freedom could exist only under laws that protected minorities and minority opinions was anathema to Americans, then and throughout the nineteenth century. Only recently has the paradox been addressed, as minority groups, particularly Blacks and Native Americans, are demanding compensatory treatment. Collective rights had little part in America's traditions.

The Loyalists, who desired to reunite the empire, strongly disagreed with the Americans' untested concepts. Instead, they held the Burkean view that society is "a partnership between the generations," and that historical experience is "the only reliable guide in human and national affairs." Carl Berger, discussing the "pragmatic and evolutionary" development of Canada, argues that the "preservation of continuities, the respect for tradition, and the slow building of precedents upon established precedents molded Canadian political culture and the country's national character."[30] These traits cannot be attributed solely to British traditions; the French Catholic heritage was even more inclined toward vital institutions, orderly living, and respect for authority. With such opposing initial ideologies, it was inevitable that the United States and Canada would develop along different lines — one revolutionary, the other evolutionary — thus spawning "basic myths" that "vary considerably."[31]

Inherited Problems

THE TWO YOUNG NATIONS had fundamental problems that remain unresolved to this day: slavery and enraged Native tribes in the United States and French-English antagonism in Canada. French and English Canada were and remain, as Dominique Clift says, "like twin stars rotating around each other," unable to pull apart or to merge into a single entity.[32] With differences in language, culture, and religion, the French and the English were uncomfortable compatriots, but the challenge to survive was great and the law required toleration. Linden Macintyre comments that Canada began as "an exercise in practical ethics. It was founded as a partnership among mortal enemies …[who] arrived at a rough consensus that we were all going to die in the wilderness if we didn't learn to get along."[33] French Canada, even further away from the American ideology than the Loyalists, was just getting used to such British inventions as juries and legislative assemblies when émigré priests began arriving from France with horrifying news of the anticlericalism of the French Revolution. With this news, desertion by France was complete, and French Canada became, in effect, a ward of the Papacy. Authority came from the Church, and British laws were to be passively obeyed. With European national ties broken, the French became the first authentic Canadians, a people that could "never be swallowed up."[34] Thus, Canada emerged as counter-revolutionary in a dual sense: the Loyalists opposed the American Revolution and the *Canadiens* the French Revolution.

After Cornwallis's surrender at Yorktown, the only American federal body available to negotiate with the British was the Continental Congress. The Acts of Confederation, drafted in 1777 but not ratified until 1781, provided no federal taxing power, no national courts, and no executive. Congress was unable to regulate trade or raise an army, the individual states retaining full control over such customarily federal matters. State "after state explicitly reserved to itself ... 'the sole and exclusive right of forming a Constitution and Laws.'"[35] It was clear to members of Congress that this situation could not continue, so in 1787 a group of men — principally James Madison, Alexander Hamilton and John Jay — began to draft a federal constitution. The northern states were opposed to slavery, but the southern states' adamant refusal to even consider emancipation, coupled with the necessity of unification for the nation's survival, left Congress no option but to hope that such differences would resolve themselves. The southern states were guaranteed their human property, and northern states were obliged to return fugitive slaves. The tripartite federal government, no part of which was to have authority over the other, was allowed only specified authority. Since all residual powers were left to the states, the authors of the Constitution saw no need for a bill of rights.

The public was not pleased with the proposed constitution, which it saw as granting too much power to a central government. A major campaign of persuasion was launched,[36] and Jefferson convinced Madison that a bill of rights was needed. The Federalist era, spanning the administrations of George Washington and John Adams (1788 to 1800), proved to be a disputatious period; much was accomplished but the political future of the new country remained unclear.

Two political parties formed during Washington's administration, one around Jefferson, the Secretary of State, the other around Hamilton, the Secretary of the Treasury. These were called, respectively, the Republicans and the Federalists. Hamilton, who called his opponents Anti-Federalists, sought a strong central government, increased business and industry, and negotiated trade with Britain. John Jay, a somewhat more moderate Federalist, wanted the western lands sold and orderly settlement. Jefferson, foreseeing a nation of virtuous yeoman farmers, wanted minimal government, no central bank, army, or navy, and close relations with France. Hamilton and Jefferson were archenemies. In *The Federalist Papers*, Hamilton speaks of mankind as "ambitious, vindictive, and rapacious" and founded this judgment on the "accumulated experience of ages." His comment that "there are still to be found visionary or designing men, who stand ready to advocate the paradox of perpetual peace" is clearly aimed at Jefferson.[37] The dispute became so heated that Jefferson resigned after the first presidential administration. Vituperative accusations between members of America's two political parties have probably never since been so heated. Politics in the Federalist era was marked by slander.[38]

An Alien and Sedition Act was passed during Adams's administration, which led Jefferson and Madison to draft the Kentucky and Virginia resolutions, claiming that individual states had the authority to negate a federal act. Gradually, Jefferson emerged as the peoples' champion, so, after the turbulent election of 1800, the Federalist Party passed into history. The irony of this historical fact is that Republican leaders Jefferson and Madison were both Virginia slaveholders. One "of the most striking anomalies" of American history is that the "great slaveholding planters of the South" led the party that "prided itself upon its liberalism, its devotion to republican institutions, and its concern for the welfare of the masses." This recalls Samuel Johnson's famed remark that "the 'loudest yelps' for liberty came from the drivers of Negroes."[39]

It is a commonplace today that Americans fought for their own liberty but were not prepared to extend it to Blacks or Native Americans. This is not entirely true. Though a slaveholder, Jefferson often advocated against slavery. In *A Summary View of the Rights of British America,* he blames the British monarch for introducing it into the colonies and for failing to stop the slave trade. His original draft of the Declaration of Independence contained "a 'philippic' against the slave trade," which Congress removed. None of the members of Congress "objected to the abstract doctrine of natural rights, [but] many of them were naturally ... sensitive to a concrete example of its violation so pointedly relevant as to be invidious."[40] Jefferson tried unsuccessfully to introduce a bill for gradual emancipation in Virginia and Congress voted down his proposed federal law to bar slavery from the western territories. Other thoughtful southerners detested slavery but they were in the minority, for slaves were considered property. The original "holy trinity" of the Enlightenment was life, liberty, and property, and Jefferson's substitution of "the pursuit of happiness" was an attempt to blur the obvious contradiction between liberty and human property. Conscientious slaveholders were at a loss what to do. Jefferson educated his slaves to a trade, but failed to follow Washington's example of freeing them when he died.[41]

The British, like the French, made allies of the Natives, a necessity for conducting the fur trade. Fur traders often took Native wives, something they did openly, unlike the clandestine sexual relations practiced by many southern whites with their slaves. Although the British ignored their commitments to the Natives during the peace negotiations following the American Revolution, they purchased blocks of land from them when Upper Canada was created. The price paid was low, but the disorder of the American frontier was avoided. The 2000 Loyalist Natives were guaranteed a large tract of land.[42]

Madison explains in *The Federalist Papers* how minorities were to be protected in the new nation: "society ... will be broken into so many parts" that the "rights of individuals, or of the minority, will be in little danger from interested combinations of the majority."[43] Madison clearly did not include slaves among his "minorities," and it is doubtful that he had Native Americans in mind. The Americans assumed that the northwest tribes had forfeited any rights when they fought with the British in the Revolution. Pacification of the Natives was American government policy from the beginning. How this was to be accomplished is not clear, but the Republican faith in human goodness allowed them to hope that the Natives would settle down to farming and that frontiersmen would respect the numerous treaties that the government made with different tribes, although many of them had already been breached.

Jefferson never abandoned his faith in the goodness of mankind. He deemed his election as president "the revolution of 1800." His program was to "dethrone 'tory' politics, [which were] elitist, privileged, distrustful of the people, centralizing and monarchical in tendency."[44]

Literary Traditions and the Lack of Objectivity

THE NORTH AMERICAN COLONIES, except those of New England, had little in the way of literary traditions. The intelligentsia left New France after the British conquest and although there were minor poets and storytellers in the other colonies, most writing was done by travelers reporting their experiences to the reading public in Europe. The Puritans brought scholarship across the Atlantic and maintained it by promptly establishing Harvard College and insisting on a school in every village. Although most of their writings are religious tracts, the Puritans left a tradition of learning that spawned America's first literary art.

Objectivity — that is, the sense of distinguishing the interests of one's own group from the interests of others — was lacking in both the early United States and the British colonies. At the time of the Seven Years' War, there was not even a printing press in New France. The upper classes were shipped back to France, and since education among the masses was minimal, a French-Canadian literature built slowly and dwelled almost exclusively on themselves as a conquered people. English-Canadian colonists clung to British conventions and, quite understandably, believed that their early literary efforts failed to measure up to British standards. This emphasis on quality and foreign standards probably delayed the development of Canadian literature by many years. David Staines argues that in relying on foreign standards "critics are unable to recognize the value of the original and the native."[45] Yet British standards were not foreign to the colonists. Their disdain for the Americans prevented them from looking south of the border for originality, although this, too, would have been a reliance on foreign standards. They were a long way from thinking of themselves as a separate nation.

The fiery patriotism of American writers of the early nineteenth century — exemplified by George Bancroft (1800–1891), who wrote patriotic history espousing Manifest Destiny — has made Alexis de Tocqueville's *Democracy in America* (1835) an exceptionally valuable commentary on life and thought in the early days of the United States. His famous phrase, "the tyranny of the majority," gave great comfort to the Loyalists and the British Tories. De Tocqueville visited the United States during the administration of Andrew Jackson (1828–1836), when he was "surprised to find so much distinguished talent among the subjects, and so little among the heads of the Government." He saw corruption as endemic to American democracy, because the rulers are "almost always exposed to the suspicion of dishonourable conduct, [so] they in some measure lend the authority of the Government to the base practices of which they are accused." He found that "subduing the exigencies of the moment, with a view to the future" was not to be found in American political life, but added hopefully that truth could be obtained "as the result of experience."[46]

Ralph Waldo Emerson (1803–1882) was in the early stages of his career at the time of De Tocqueville's visit and was fully conscious of the need to find the original and the native. Relying on British standards was anathema to American writers of the day, so they actively sought something original on their own ground. This proved a fruitful enterprise, as the major works of Nathaniel Hawthorne, Herman Melville, Henry David Thoreau, and Walt Whitman appeared two decades later.

Henry Adams (1838–1918) was probably the first American to attempt scientific history.[47] He aspired to be the Gibbon of North America with his nine-volume history of the Jefferson and Madison administrations, the first six chapters of which were subsequently published as *The United States in 1800*. Adams agreed with de Tocqueville on corruption in public life. In a "new society," he says, "ignorant and semi-barbarous ... demagogues" were inflaming people's worst appetites, so that greed for "wealth, lust for power," and a yearning for a "savage freedom ... were the fires that flamed under the caldron of American society." Adams was not just interested in debunking myths; he sought to get at something elusive, at the "nature" of the "national character." What was it that "turned the European peasant into a new man within half an hour after landing in New York?" While no "foreigner of that day — neither poet, painter, nor philosopher — could detect in American life anything higher than vulgarity," the immigrant saw "copper, silver and gold," "magnificent cities" and "cornfields rustling and waving in the summer breeze." If the visitor sneered and said he saw nothing but "swamps and forests" and people "scalped by savages," the new American was angered, for "his dream was his whole existence." It was not just the poor immigrants who saw a "glowing continent." Adams recounts a 1796 debate in the House of Representatives on whether to reply to President Washington's speech with a remark that the "nation is 'the freest and most enlightened in the world,' — a nation as yet in swaddling clothes, which had neither literature, arts, sciences, nor history." The American Dream bloomed early and was of an intensity that can hardly be overemphasized.[48]

Growth and Development in the British Colonies

THE TREATY OF GHENT (1814) ended the recurring wars between France and England that had had such a profound effect on settlement patterns in North America. Both the United States and the British colonies began to grow. Their most basic myths had taken root, and, as thousands of immigrants poured in, they absorbed the mystique and became Americans or Canadians without being particularly aware of the conflicts behind the culture.

The British and Loyalist distress over the American Revolution and distrust of the mob led to widespread hostility toward any perceived excess of democracy. Although the future Canadians were to enjoy the rights of British subjects, they were not to interfere with governing. A governor was appointed for each colony, who in turn appointed his own council. There was an assembly, made up of elected locals, but a legislative council — with members appointed for life — was established above the assembly, which amounted to a backwoods House of Lords. This made it more difficult for the assembly to control the governor by withholding money. It also delayed the development of self-government — known as "responsible government." Reformers were demanding a system like that in Britain, where the governor and his council were responsible to the elected representatives of the people rather than to colonial authorities. It took until the end of the 1830s for responsible government to be achieved.

The lack of responsible government was bound to lead to conflict, particularly in Lower Canada, where the French, an overwhelming majority, controlled the assembly, with a British governor and Loyalists dominating the governing oligarchy, known as the Chateau Clique. The assembly refused to allow land taxes or the construction of roads and canals, and insisted on taxing commerce, which outraged English merchants. Officials were sent from England periodically, always with instructions to conciliate; the British wanted no more rebelling colonies. Many of the newly appointed governors were military men who disobeyed instructions and engaged in confrontational tactics with the French. At that time, the French were living a semi-feudal lifestyle and the English devotion to the British Empire did not encourage them to modernize. French-English relations were an intractable problem. Various panaceas were adopted, generally attempts to force the French into a minority position so that they could be outvoted and eventually assimilated. Assimilation was the great fear of the French, a fear that exists today.

Growth was hardly peaceful in the other colonies. British governors and the more conservative Loyalists, who were determined to develop an aristocracy and establish the Anglican Church, were up against a wall of resistance. The Colonial Office was not in favor of backwoods barons, or "dukes pitching hay,"[49] and other sects far outnumbered the Anglicans. John Graves Simcoe, the first lieutenant governor of Upper Canada, had a three-fold plan: establish the Anglican Church, develop an aristocracy, and entice more settlers to clear the land. He made no headway with the church, succeeded in drawing settlers, and gave the largest land grants to those he considered aristocrats. These made up the Upper Canada oligarchy, known as the Family Compact. Simcoe has been called a "fathead" and other unflattering terms, but he had plenty of energy and left his mark on the province.[50]

The oligarchy in Nova Scotia was called the Council of Twelve. Similar frustrated plans for an aristocracy and an established church took place in all of the Maritime colonies. In Prince Edward Island, the situation was exacerbated by large blocks of land held by absentee landlords, mainly British aristocrats.

G.M. Craig says that Canadians who think of themselves as "moderate, law-abiding, and cautious people" should look again at the 1830s.[51] There were ferocious political debates and open rebellions broke out in both Upper and Lower Canada. In Upper Canada, fear of disloyalty caused the majority of settlers to turn against the rebels; in Lower Canada the Catholic Church frowned on rebelling against the civil authorities. There was also continued fear of the Americans in both colonies. The rebellions did not completely fail, however, because the British finally agreed to responsible government.

The Loyalists trusted their governments and, by and large, the trust was rewarded. Whatever favoritism went on between members of the oligarchies — the "real power" lay in their hands — British law was clear and it was enforced. Members of the oligarchies were often "public-spirited citizens," who believed it was their duty to govern wisely. They "distrusted the wisdom of the 'mob'," but pioneer conditions with availability of arable land bred equality and resentment was certain to arise.[52] Modern commentators, with varying degrees of irony, note that Canadians are deferential to authority, a trait that stems from the anti-populist bent of the Loyalists. At the end of his comparative study of Canada and the United States, Lipset notes that Canada's parliamentary system of government is less protective of civil rights than America's constitutional system.[53] Canadians have always been less concerned with rights than Americans. For example, with the 1982 patriation of the Canadian Constitution, the Charter of Rights and Freedoms was appended at Prime Minister Pierre Trudeau's insistence, not because the public demanded it. At the end of the twentieth century, many Canadians still objected to the Charter, claiming that it gives power to the courts that rightfully belongs to Parliament.[54]

Prelude to the War Between the States

THE FEWEST LOYALISTS CAME FROM Massachusetts and Virginia, two colonies that were the hotbeds of the American Revolution, the most outraged over British policies, and the first to embrace independence. They had no love for each other, however, and the early years of the American republic could be subtitled "Massachusetts versus Virginia." Puritan New England was not convinced of the innate goodness of humankind and strongly supported national unity and an effective central government. Many of the Federalists came from New England, but before 1800 their greatest asset was the Virginian

George Washington. Republican Virginia controlled the federal government from 1800 to 1824. Presidents Jefferson, Madison, and Monroe tried, with varying degrees of success, to put their theories of minimal government into practice. By the end of the twenty-four years the federal government had been strengthened, due largely to the decisions handed down by Chief Justice John Marshall, Jefferson's second cousin and archenemy.[55] Jefferson's purchase of Louisiana in 1803 was opposed by the Federalists on the grounds that the Constitution gave the President no such powers. A way was found, for "Jefferson believed deeply in what succeeding generations ... were to call 'Manifest Destiny'."[56]

Despite the hold that Virginia had on the federal government, its days were numbered, for the populace was uneducated and there was no tradition of democracy. New England, with its long history of town meetings and a school in every village, was the intellectual capital of the nation. Early nationalism originated there, as did opposition to slavery and the belief in a strong federal government. New England nationalism had its roots in religion — the Puritans' belief that they were God's chosen people, which found its focus in the concept of America as God's favored nation. De Tocqueville recognized that since colonial days, "politics and religion contracted an alliance which has never been dissolved," and Lipset notes that Americans must always have God on their side.[57] Sentiments of national unity were vital in a nation with such a weak central government.

Disputes over slavery and states' rights intensified as new states were formed in the west and immigrants chose to settle in free states or territories. The southern states, with a highly profitable agricultural lifestyle dependent on slavery, were determined to keep their grip on the federal government. Free states were to be balanced with slave states. Federal concessions to the south boosted the abolition movement in the north, and the Underground Railroad to Canada provided an escape route for runaway slaves. Few runaways were returned to their owners, so when a judge ordered a slave returned, as in the famous Dred Scott Decision (1857), citizens of the free states were outraged. The words of the Declaration of Independence, "all men are created equal," were being ridiculed in the South, but were causing increasing moral discomfort in the North. The prolonged hegemony of Virginia, represented by the Democratic Party — the party founded by Jefferson but renamed by Andrew Jackson — came to an abrupt end with the election of Abraham Lincoln, the first president from the new Republican Party.

This new Republican Party stood for the superiority of the Union — that is, the federal government — over the authority of the states. The slave states rapidly seceded as soon as Lincoln's election was confirmed. The bloody war that followed was probably inevitable; the seeds of the conflict had been planted at the time of the Revolution when the union of the colonies was necessary in order to achieve independence from Britain. The exaggerated faith in the goodness of the unencumbered individual and a weak central government, preached by Jefferson and the first Republican Party, contributed to southerners' continuing belief in the right of individual states to disallow federal statutes. Some southerners still claim that the Civil War was fought over states' rights, but the fundamental issue was slavery. Slavery could not be reconciled with the New England-inspired image of America as the most virtuous and innocent nation in the world, a new Garden of Eden.

Conclusion

THERE WAS A CLOSE RELATIONSHIP between the American Civil War and Canada's Confederation, which came just two years after the end of that war. Canadians had watched the Civil War anxiously, fearful that when the contentious issues were settled, the northern colonies would be the next object of American expansionism. Confederation had been considered for many years, mainly as a technique for resolving French-English and aristocratic-democratic tensions, but now it was a matter of defense. Irish Fenians living in the United States launched invasions into Upper and Lower Canada in 1866. This attempt to promote war between the United States and Britain, and thus deflect Britain from Ireland, was the trigger that led to the British North America Act, uniting the colonies. The federal government was to predominate, with no nonsense about provincial rights; all residual rights were to reside with the federal government. The only individual rights guaranteed were religious and linguistic.

The contrast between Canada's founding and that of the United States is stark. Those who drafted the British North America Act assumed that British traditions would prevail, and thus the Act is businesslike without proclamations of "high sounding principles" or expressions of faith in "human reason."[58] As Tamara Smith says, "devotion to the British Empire combined with a marriage contracted largely for business and political reasons did not inspire the passionate, heartfelt nationalism in Canada that the Revolution inspired in the United States."[59] English Canada continued to think of itself as British, while French Canada showed little interest in modernizing and remained principally loyal to the Catholic Church. The church, in fact, "became increasingly aggressive in demanding the subordination of the State to the Church."[60] English Canada's continued identification with the empire was demonstrated in the important election of 1891, when the Liberal party was promoting a commercial union with the United States. John A. Macdonald, a Conservative, won that election with the ringing cry, "A British Subject I was born, A British subject I will die."

The long slow development of Canadian nationalism by its English population was a constant irritation to the French, who considered themselves the original and only Canadians. For many years the term referred only to the French, and, consequently, the English were reluctant to assume the designation. The French watched with disgust as long-term politicians and government officials — some of them born in the colonies — happily moved to England or Scotland on retirement. Perhaps North American nationalism was anathema to the English colonists who sat on the sidelines and watched the Americans glorify their country, agreeing with de Tocqueville that it is "impossible to conceive a more troublesome or more garrulous patriotism."[61]

The basic myths of both Canada and the United States were in place by the early years of the nineteenth century. Myths that are formed with the founding of a nation are amazingly tenacious, able to adapt to changing mores while still retaining their grip on the public psyche. Changing conditions that conflict with the original myth can lead to an outraged reversal. For example, the view of antebellum Americans that their country was "the freest and most enlightened in the world"[62] has been reversed by many people, who, in the late twentieth century, began calling the United States the world's most evil, corrupt, and vulgar nation. Neither attitude is objectively true, but the strength of the feelings involved testify to the strength of the myth. French Canada's myth of being a conquered people has survived over two centuries, and English Canada's reluctance to embrace the nation as home spent a long time dying. The prolonged discussion of "the Canadian Identity" is ending; its roots surely rest in the Loyalist inspired devotion to the British Empire.

It is now more than two centuries since the American Revolution and well over one century since the founding of Canada, long enough for two bodies of literature to mature. Writers in Canada and the United States have picked up national myths and adapted them to the current zeitgeist. The results of this process of retention and adaptation provide today's reader with a comparative history of ideas of the two nations.

Notes

1   Seymour Martin Lipset, *American Exceptionalism: A Double-Edged Sword* (New York: W.W. Norton, 1996), 17.
2   Northrop Frye, "Levels of Cultural Identity," *The Eternal Act of Creation: Essays, 1979–1990*, ed. Robert D. Denham (Bloomington: Indiana University Press, 1993), 179.
3   Careless, *Canada,* 12.
4   Harold A. Innis, *The Fur Trade in Canada: An Introduction to Canadian Economic History*, rev. ed. (Toronto: University of Toronto Press, 1999) 392.
5   Morton, 5.
6   Innis, 390.
7   John A. Macdonald, unpublished letter to Sir Henry James Sumner Maine in Calcutta, 9 April, 1867, National Archives of Canada.
8   Sacvan Bercovitch, "The Rites of Assent: Rhetoric, Ritual, and the Ideology of American Consensus," *The American Self: Myth, Ideology, and Popular Culture*, ed. Sam B. Girgus (University of New Mexico Press, 1981), 12.
9   Walter Stewart speaks of the "series of blunders" that marked the British effort. Lord North, the Earl of Sandwich, and Lord George Germain were in charge of the Colonial Office; all were incompetent and shared a "contempt" for colonials. *True Blue: The Loyalist Legend* (Toronto: Collins, 1985) 63.
10 Pauline Maier, *American Scripture: Making the Declaration of Independence* (New York: Vintage Books, 1998), 21.
11 William Franklin was the last royal governor of New Jersey. He quarreled bitterly with his father, was imprisoned in Connecticut for two years, and spent the rest of his life in England.

12 Carl Becker, *The Declaration of Independence: A Study in the History of Political Ideas* (New York: Vintage Books, 1958), 7, 19–20.
13 Careless, *Canada*, 102.
14 Edmund Burke, who defended the American colonists, would soon lead impeachment proceedings against Warren Hastings, Governor General of India, for abusing the prescriptive rights of Hindus.
15 The Declaration of Independence contains a direct reference to the Quebec Act: "For abolishing the free system of English laws in a neighbouring Province, establishing therein an arbitrary government, and enlarging its boundaries so as to render it at once an example and fit instrument for introducing the same absolute rule into these Colonies."
16 Gordon Stewart and George Rawlyk, *A People Highly Favoured of God: The Nova Scotia Yankees and the American Revolution* (Toronto: Macmillan, 1972), 73.
17 W. Stewart, 102–104, 8.
18 Morton, 22.
19 *Ibid.*, 27.
20 J.L. Granatstein, *Yankee Go Home: Canadians and Anti-Americanism* (Toronto: HarperCollins, 1996), 4.
21 Becker, 85.
22 Max Beloff, ed., *The Debate on the American Revolution, 1761–1783: A Sourcebook* (New York: Harper Torchbooks, 1963), 90.
23 Becker, 108–109, 122.
24 Beloff, 90, 163.
25 Bercovitch, "Rites," 15.
26 S.F. Wise, "The 1790s," in *Colonists and Canadiens: 1760–1867*, ed. J.M.S. Careless (Toronto: Macmillan of Canada, 1978), 82.
27 W. Stewart, 242. R.P. Kerans claims that to this day Americans find Canadians "almost maddeningly complacent." "Two Nations Under Law," *Canada and the United States: Differences that Count,* ed. David Thomas (Peterborough, ON: Broadview Press, 1993), 221.
28 Lipset, *Divide*, 26.
29 Lipset, *Exceptionalism*, 128.
30 Carl Berger, *The Writing of Canadian History: Aspects of English-Canadian Historical Writing since 1900*, 2nd ed. (Toronto: University of Toronto Press, 1986), 233, 53.
31 Lipset, *Divide*, 225.
32 Dominique Clift, *The Secret Kingdom: Interpretations of the Canadian Character* (Toronto: McClelland & Stewart, 1989), 93.
33 Linden Macintyre, "All the News That's Fit to Sell," *Queen's Quarterly* 108.1 (Spring 2001), 42.
34 Careless, *Canada*, 71.
35 Maier, 94.
36 *The Federalist Papers* were written pseudonymously by Alexander Hamilton, James Madison, and John Jay and published in American newspapers with the express purpose of promoting the new constitution.
37 Clinton Rossiter, ed. *The Federalist Papers: Alexander Hamilton, James Madison, and John Jay* (New York: New American Library, 1961), 54, 56.

38   For a fictionalized account, see William Safire, *Scandalmonger* (New York: Harcourt, 2000).

39   John C. Miller, *The Federalist Era: 1789–1801* (New York: Harper Colophon,1960), 105, 107.

40   Becker, xiii.

41   Recent DNA evidence indicates a strong probability that Jefferson fathered five children by his slave Sally Hemings. These children and Sally were gradually freed, some before and some after Jefferson's death. None of his other slaves were so favored.

42   One of Canada's major problems today is that ancient treaties made by the British with the Native peoples are still on the statute books.

43   Rossiter, 324.

44   Merrill D. Peterson, ed., *The Portable Thomas Jefferson* (New York: Penguin Books, 1975), xxxii.

45   David Staines, *Beyond the Provinces: Literary Canada at Century's End* (Toronto: University of Toronto Press, 1995), 76.

46   Alexis de Tocqueville, *Democracy in America*, 2 vols. Trans. Henry Reeve (New York: Schocken Books, 1961), I: 220, 228, 262, 267–68.

47   Henry Adams, *The Education of Henry Adams* (Boston: Houghton Mifflin, 1974), 382.

48   Henry Adams, *The United States in 1800* (Ithaca: Cornell University Press, 1955), 128, 126, 121, 119, 124–125, 113.

49   Careless, *Canada*, 120.

50   W. Stewart, 187.

51   G.M. Craig, "The 1830s," in *Colonists*, ed. Careless, 173.

52   Careless, *Canada*, 166–7.

53   Lipset, *Divide*, 227.

54   Canadians rely almost exclusively on unwritten rules. The prime minister of a majority government has relatively few restrictions compared to an American president.

55   See James F. Simon, *What Kind of Nation: Thomas Jefferson, John Marshall, and the Epic Struggle to Create a United States* (New York: Simon & Schuster, 2002).

56   Kenneth McNaught, with John C. Ricker and John T. Saywell, *Manifest Destiny: A Short History of the United States* (Toronto: Clarke Irwin, 1963), 62.

57   De Tocqueville, I: 355; Lipset, *Exceptionalism* 20.

58   Clift, 189.

59   Tamara Palmer Smith, "Melting Pot and Mosaic: Images and Realities," in *Canada and the United States,* ed. Thomas, 306.

60   Clift, 45. See "Pastoral Letter of the Bishops of the Ecclesiastical Province of Quebec, September 22, 1875." Thomas Thorner, ed. *"a country nourished on self-doubt": Documents in Canadian History, 1867–1980* (Peterborough, ON: Broadview Press, 1998), 138.

61   De Tocqueville, II: 268.

62   Adams, *1800*, 113.

Chapter
Two

A Sense of the Past

1
Beginnings

THE FIRST CITIZENS OF THE UNITED STATES set out to rid themselves of the past. The pre-Revolution desire to be free of particular British laws and customs turned into a generalized rejection of Old-World institutions such as monarchy, aristocracy, and an established church, which were seen as monuments to an evil past. According to Henry Adams, "every American" from the president to the "poorest squatter, seemed to nourish an idea that he was doing what he could to overthrow the tyranny which the past had fastened on the human mind."[1] More recently, Richard Slotkin points to an ambivalence about the idea of a national mythology, claiming that there is a "strong antimythological stream" in American culture, deriving from "the utopian ideals of certain of the original colonists and of the revolutionary generation, which asserts that this New World is to be liberated from the dead hand of the past."[2]

The American's belief in a sinful European past quickly shifted into a broader concept — that the past itself was evil. In a 1789 letter to James Madison, Jefferson questioned whether "one generation of men has a right to bind another." He called it a "question of such consequences" as to merit a place among the "fundamental principles of every government." His famous conclusion, "I set out on this ground, which I suppose to be self evident, '*that the earth belongs in usufruct to the living*,' that the dead have neither powers or rights over it," was held by Jefferson for the rest of his life. In his second inaugural address in 1805, he rebuked his political opponents as "ancestor-worshiping Federalists." Speaking of the Native Americans, who were "liberally furnished" with "the implements of husbandry and household use" and "covered with the aegis of the law," he claimed that their troubles are primarily due to their "sanctimonious reverence for the customs of their ancestors." Jefferson's rejection of the past was shared by the American people and remained axiomatic to the general public throughout the nineteenth and early twentieth centuries.[3]

The adoption of the Garden of Eden as the image of the new nation perfectly mirrored the prevailing sentiments of a fresh start in an uncorrupted world. The place was a virgin land, potentially free of sin, and the archetypal American was Adam before the fall. Belief in the goodness of the unencumbered individual meant that God had shown Americans the way to avoid a second Fall of Man. The twofold implications of this image — that the nation was free of sin and that it had no past — contained seeds of future trouble, as did the emphasis on the rights of man in a country that guaranteed slavery.

Clearly the nation was not free of sin, but the enthusiasm of the times led to the belief that it soon would be, and a rejection of the past would help bring it about. In 1783, while speaking at the opening of the Philips Exeter Academy, the Reverend David McClure asserted that "Paradise, long lost to the children of Adam, shall be found in this western world; and become the residence of the favorites of Heaven"; America would "flourish as the garden of God."[4] The new nation was awash with such rhetoric: America is the "wonder and blessing of the world," which is meant to "promote *the perfection and happiness of mankind,*"; it is to be "His vineyard," the seat of His "glorious kingdom," for the "benefit of the whole world."[5]

The Loyalists, with their Burkean view of society as a partnership between the generations, found all of this offensive. Their contempt helped to offset a sense of loss, a realization that life would be much more comfortable in the land from which they had been expelled. It also gave them a sense of cultural and moral superiority, a feeling that they were above such naive expectations. Many generations later, Northrop Frye expressed the distaste that Canadians have felt for the early American love affair with Edenism: "In the beginning the Americans created America, and America is the beginning of the world." This attitude, he says, resulted in a modern American conception of progress that is "anti-historical. Washington, Franklin, Jefferson" appear in "the popular consciousness ... as deceased contemporaries" rather than "ancestors living among different cultural referents." To Americans, the past is "assimilated to the present," and one can still hear the "confident tones" of America's "Book of Genesis; 'We hold these truths to be self-evident.' At least a Canadian can hear them, because nothing has ever been self-evident in Canada."[6]

The Loyalists would have appreciated Frye's irony, for in coming years they were careful not to accept American innovations and to stick closely to British cultural standards. They had paid a terrible price by refusing to become Americans, so to adopt any New World designation would have meant taking on an identity without a usable past. Forcedly cut off from their American past, the Loyalists gradually adopted the impressive North American past of the *Canadiens*. In fact, they already had a past in the northern part of the continent. The Hudson's Bay Company, founded in 1670, had been competing with the French and trading with the Native peoples for over a century. The settlers of New France, wholly supported by the fur trade, had been dependent on the Natives for survival techniques as well as for furs. When the British took over the colony, they continued the French practices. Thoughts of a virgin land never occurred to them. Many of the fur traders, French and English, married Native women, and the presence in Canada of numerous descendants of these marriages testifies to a very different past from that in the United States.

The Loyalists saw themselves as exiles from a British homeland, forced to live in a northern wilderness. The *Canadiens* also felt like orphans. Their dwindling hope of being returned to France was dashed with the French Revolution, when the monarchy and the authority of the church, the things they had held most dear, were discarded by their former nation. Consequently, their lifeline became the Catholic Church.

Both Perry Miller and Sacvan Bercovitch have argued that the American identification of their new nation with the Garden of Eden had its roots in Puritan ideology. The New England Puritans were the only colonists in pre-Revolutionary America who had no economic motives for emigrating, but were strictly on a mission for God. As the most fervent of the English Puritans, they went to America to establish the "complete reformation," which those left behind would be able to impose if they had "a working model to guide them." The travelers held an "assumption," in their "errand of 1630" that God would "bless the new land," which was free of "established (and corrupt) institutions, empty of bishops and courtiers," and they felt assured that "the eyes of the world" were on them.[7] The rhetoric of the Revolution clearly derived from this earlier period.

The Puritans found passages in the Bible that confirmed their assumptions that their mission was not only blessed but preordained, so early troubles were attributed to God, who was testing his people, or the devil, who inhabited the wilderness, mainly in the form of Natives or French Catholics. As faith weakened over the years, ministers ranted against backsliding, and "Indian wars" were explained as God's way of chastising his people. When the Enlightenment dawned, anxiety among the clergy led to increased predictions of the fulfillment of God's prophecy. A 1710 sermon, "*Providence Declare[s] That Wonderful Revolutions Are Near*," was part of a concerted effort to show that the establishment of God's kingdom was imminent. In 1690, Cotton Mather, a member of the fourth generation of Puritans, wrote that an "*Age of Miracles* ... is now Dawning upon ... this *New-English Israel*," and in his history of the colony, he proclaimed "New England the holiest country in the world."[8] With such predictions, it is not surprising that early nationalism and the idea of the United States as a second Garden of Eden originated in New England. Bercovitch claims that during the Revolution "rebels and loyalists, federalists and republicans urged their audiences to remember the Puritan 'fathers.' "[9] The state of Virginia had no ties to Puritan fathers, so Jefferson's accusation that his opponents were "ancestor-worshipping" had some substance. Of course, such thoughts implied another paradox: if the new country was a Garden of Eden with no past, the people had no ancestors to remember.

The contrasting attitudes toward the past of Americans and future Canadians have had long-term implications. Discarding the past as a time of evil became an American myth. As the United States developed a past of its own, it became easy to assume that everything about that past was sinful, an invitation to excessive feelings of guilt and disillusionment among the populace. T.D. MacLulich notes that "American society is pervaded by the after-effects of a collective slaying of the European father," and each generation "must repeat" the "original disavowal."[10] Living in a Garden of

Eden also contributed to a sense of isolation. To this day, many Americans seem unmindful that other peoples' experiences might be useful to them.

The Canadian determination to maintain ties with the past — the British empire for the Loyalists and the fall of New France in the Seven Years' War for the French — helped to delay the colonies' development into a nation. J.M.S. Careless emphasizes the colonist's rejection of "the ideas behind the American Revolution." The colonists stressed "traditional ties, not a break with the past," and they "feared the power of the new United States and trusted Britain."[11] This tenacious attachment to Britain helped deepen the French-English division, for the French persistently looked upon the British as their conquerors. Each move toward self-government carefully avoided any revolutionary overtones. Dominique Clift notes that "Confederation was not seen as a break with the past but as a way of building on its foundations."[12] Building on the foundations of the past has always been fundamental to Canadian thinking, while discrediting the past as evil and overthrowing it in order to achieve a virtuous freedom has been equally axiomatic in the United States.

2

American Genesis

AMERICA'S EARLY WRITERS, who lived almost exclusively in New England or New York, encountered many problems. They were proud of colonial ancestors who had brought scholarship across the ocean and opposed the importation of British ways, but preferred to forget the cruelty, religious intolerance, and preoccupation with the devil that was so characteristic of the Puritans. A more serious problem for early writers was the glaring presence of slavery, corruption, and urban poverty, which gave the impression that a Garden of Eden was far in the future.

This situation encouraged experimentation in both style and content, for America's early writers were not certain how to handle the past. Almost invariably they romanticized the North American past and vilified Europe. Henry Wadsworth Longfellow (1807–1882) wrote rhyming narratives about colonial history. A more imaginative writer, James Fenimore Cooper (1789–1851), attempted to construct a romantic past, using the wilderness and colonial history rather than the ancient castles and British warfare of Sir Walter Scott, Cooper's main literary inspiration. Edgar Allen Poe (1809–1849) stressed the dark and evil underpinnings of this optimistic young country in his tales and poems. This might have assured him unpopularity except that the gothic novel was in vogue and many of his identifiable settings are European, suggesting a sinful European past.

Such influential writers as Ralph Waldo Emerson (1803–1882), Henry David Thoreau (1817–1862), and Walt Whitman (1819–1892) dismissed the past and glorified the new nation, telling the people what they must do to make the reality conform to the dream. Nathaniel Hawthorne (1804–1864), Herman Melville (1819–1891), and Emily Dickinson (1830–1886), all more difficult to classify, tried to bridge the gap between the glorious dream and the horrors evoked by the Puritan concept of evil. The temper of the times did not appreciate their moral paradoxes, and only Hawthorne was able to hold a wide readership. He had a deep understanding of the New England mind and his deceptively simple plots contained many elements of the popular gothic romance.

De Tocqueville took note of the American passion for newness and an uncorrupted future. The "tie which unites one generation to another is relaxed or broken," he said, with the result that every man loses the "ideas of his forefathers." He commented, too, on the significance of this for the nation's future writers: "Democracy shuts the past against the poet, but opens the future before him."[13] De Tocqueville was able to foresee the essence of Emerson's philosophy and the basics of Whitman's poetry, but he did not predict Poe's dark tales, the sin and guilt prevalent in the writings of Hawthorne and Melville, or the obsession with death in Dickinson's poems.

Of all these early writers, Emerson had the greatest influence on the works of others. He was a true son of New England; his distant ancestors were fanatical Puritans and his more recent forebears Unitarians. Himself a Unitarian minister, he resigned his pulpit in 1833 over a symbolic sacrament, pursued a career as a lecturer, and became known as the "Sage of Concord." In 1836, he began informal meetings of what was to become the famous Transcendental Club.[14]

In his first book, *Nature* (1836), Emerson asks why we should "grope among the dry bones of the past?" He claims that the individual should seek inspiration directly from God or nature — essentially synonymous in Emersonian thought — rather than delving into the past. "Books," he says, are merely a record of another's "act of creation." He argues that "books are for the scholar's idle times. When he can read God directly, the hour is too precious to be wasted in other men's transcripts." In a later essay, Emerson writes that history is an "impertinence and an injury if it be anything more than a ... parable of my being." If "you have life in yourself ... you shall not discern the footprints of any other," and will "gladly disburden the memory of its hoarded treasures as old rubbish." Again and again Emerson insisted that the individual must learn from the world around him, not from examining the past. "He should see that he can live all history in his own person ... there is properly no History."[15]

All American historians have stressed the importance of Emerson's work, for he articulated the most exotic ideals of the new nation, as well as confirming, in secular terms, the reasonableness of proceeding as if the nation had no past. Richard Poirier says: "Emerson's traces are said even by his detractors to be everywhere in American thought." There have certainly been detractors, primarily because of the "assurances" with which "he justified jettisoning history," but early American writers generally found his ideas inspiring.[16] Most would have agreed with the critic who appears to glory in this "escape from the rigidities of habits in action, from dogmas in religion, from academic imitation in art, from colonialism in culture, [and] from idolatry to the past."[17] A generation of New Englanders succeeded in replacing sinfulness — the main preoccupation of the Puritans — with innocence as the distinctive characteristic of the American.

Emerson's hypothetical individual without a past became the typical hero of early American literature, the Emersonian hero, or what R.W.B. Lewis calls "the American Adam."[18] Natty Bumppo, protagonist of Cooper's Leatherstocking series and the narrator of Whitman's *Leaves of Grass,* are outstanding examples. Whitman's narrator is a "liberated, innocent, solitary, forward-thrusting personality,"[19] who ignores the past. Natty Bumppo's adventures take place in the American past, but he takes pride in his innocence. Cooper, like Longfellow, set out to glorify the American past, and to offer the new nation some homegrown myths. Their writings were very popular in their own day and are still seen as at least historically significant. It was Hawthorne, however, who set the stage for America's treatment of the past.

Hawthorne's interest in history was focused on his own ancestors, for he was uncomfortably conscious of being a direct descendant of one of the judges at the Salem witch trials. In "The Custom House," his introduction to *The Scarlet Letter* (1850), Hawthorne imagined his ancestors' opinion of his chosen profession: " 'What is he?' murmurs one grey shadow of my forefathers to another. 'A writer of storybooks! What kind of business in life … may that be? Why, the degenerate fellow might as well have been a fiddler!' "[20] Hawthorne's attitude toward the past was ambiguous. Although he admired the Puritan fathers for their courage and high morality, he condemned their brutalities, their belief in predestination, and their conceit in thinking that they were able to recognize God's elect.

Hawthorne's ambiguity toward the Puritans is particularly apparent in his story "Endicott and the Red Cross," a kind of prelude to *The Scarlet Letter.* Set in Salem in the early seventeenth century, the story tells of news from England that Charles I is planning to send a governor-general to New England and to establish "English Episcopy." Endicott, the town's leader, is so incensed that he refers to the King as this "son of a Scotch tyrant — this grandson of a Papistical and adulterous Scotch woman," then slashes the British flag, called the Red Cross, with his sword. The story contains many details of Puritan brutalities — the whipping post, pillory and stocks, permanently marked sinners with branded cheeks or cropped ears, and a woman with a scarlet "A" on her bosom — but ends with the author's praise for the Puritan leader: "And forever honored be the name of Endicott! We look back through the mist of ages, and recognize in the rending of the Red Cross from New England's banner the first omen of that deliverance which our fathers consummated."[21] Any hostility to the British was to be praised.

The Scarlet Letter is far less ambiguous, for here the past is treated as a time of oppression, a "sins of the fathers" approach. The novel is set in Boston in the early seventeenth century and centers on the consequences of an adulterous act. The most significant events take place on the gallows, where Hester Prynne is condemned to stand in shame for her adultery, and where the adulterer Dimmesdale tries to expiate his guilt. The three main characters represent three levels of sin: Hester, the acknowledged adulteress; Dimmesdale, the unacknowledged adulterer; and Chillingworth, the wronged husband. Movement within the novel is primarily of a moral nature. The significance of the "A" on Hester's bosom changes from "adultery" to "admirable" to "angelic" and, as Hawthorne scholars have argued, to "American."[22] Dimmesdale's guilt is unaffected by self-punishment and is deepened by the townspeople's tenacious perception of him as a saint. Chillingworth becomes a devil or Faust figure, as he commits the unforgivable sin of violating "in cold blood, the sanctity of a human heart."[23] This "sanctity of a human heart" preoccupied Hawthorne, who wrote in his preface to *The House of the Seven Gables* (1851) that "truth of the human heart" is essential in a writer's work.[24] Henry Nash Smith claims that the "truth of the human heart that Hawthorne discovered was not perfectibility but guilt," and it is now generally agreed that Hawthorne introduced guilt into American literature.[25] *The Scarlet Letter*, the first great work of American fiction, presents a harshly judgmental society as part of the nation's past, thus undermining the Emersonian world picture and the concept of America as a Garden of Eden.

Hawthorne must have been unaware of his subversion, for each of his three other novels has an Emersonian heroine, fair and innocent, who is usually countered by a dark heroine who, like Hester Prynne, is burdened with a sinful past.[26] Hawthorne never resolved his ambiguous attitude toward the past, for in the preface to his last novel, *The Marble Faun* (1860), he speaks of the "difficulty of writing a romance about a country where there is no shadow, no antiquity, no mystery, no picturesque and gloomy wrong, nor anything but a commonplace prosperity, in broad and simple daylight, as is happily the case with my dear native land."[27] *The Marble Faun* is set in Italy, with a dark heroine, Miriam, who has a mysterious and sin-laden past that is never explained. She is a close friend of the American heroine, Hilda, who has a nature of "white shining purity" that God had made of "undefiled material." The Puritan ancestors would have been horrified, for in their view man was fallen and nobody was made of undefiled material. Hilda walks through crime-ridden Rome "altogether unconscious of anything wicked." Thus, "innocence continues to make a paradise around itself, and keep it still unfallen."[28] Hilda's "purity" causes her to reject Miriam, who is in serious trouble, feeling that she must protect her own virtue by keeping evil at bay.[29] Kenyon, a sculptor and the novel's American hero, also turns away from Miriam when she seeks to confide in him. This act and Miriam's retort that he is "as cold and pitiless" as his own marble,[30] seems to parallel Hawthorne's unresolved thoughts on the past expressed in the Preface.

In *The Marble Faun*, Italy represents the past. Hawthorne was extending the theme of rejecting the past by placing American heroes in a decadent European setting. Kenyon advises an Italian friend to return with him to the United States, for in that "fortunate land, each generation has only its own sins and sorrows to bear. Here, it seems as if all the weary and dreary Past were piled upon the back of the Present."[31] The Italian commits an impulsive murder and symbolically "falls." He becomes profoundly depressed, but, instead of turning to the Catholic Church as any sensible Italian would do, he takes Kenyon's advice and devotes himself to a life of guilt and remorse. In a dramatic twist, it is Hilda who turns to the Catholic Church, boldly entering a confessional and blurting out her story of the crime she had witnessed and of Miriam's complicity. Kenyon is alarmed, but she is in no danger of conversion for, as critic Murray Krieger argues, "since she can live only in 'the pure, white light of heaven,' ... [h]er direct relationship to God can never be finally threatened."[32] Kenyon gingerly suggests the possibility of a "fortunate fall," but Hilda will have none of it.[33] Hawthorne had almost no understanding of Old World culture or of Catholicism. He was, himself, an American innocent.

Henry James (1843–1916) was profoundly influenced by the writings of Hawthorne, although in a somewhat ironic way. He admired Hawthorne's deep understanding of the New England mind, but was aware of his blindness in dealing with Europe and the Europeans. In his biography, *Hawthorne* (1879), James expresses admiration for the character of Hilda, who appears to be the literary ancestress of James's own Emersonian characters: Christopher Newman, Isabel Archer, and Milly Theale. Malcolm Bradbury argues that James's international theme — that is, the balance of "American futurism with the European past, American innocence with European experience" — clearly originates with *The Marble Faun*.[34]

In his early years, James was an ardent enough American to find many aristocratic Europeans and Old-World institutions objectionable and, like Hawthorne, used the European setting as symbol of an evil past. He understood European culture much better than Hawthorne, so was able to pinpoint many of the institutions and practices of the Old World that had so angered the founders of the United States. In his early novel *The American* (1877), the hero, an innocent American with the significant name of Christopher Newman, is self-made, handsome, wealthy, and good natured. During an extended trip to France, he meets and proposes to Claire de Cintré, daughter of the aristocratic Bellegarde family. Madame de Bellegarde and her eldest son are arrogantly determined to maintain the conventions of the past. Though Newman has no pedigree, they need his money, so they consent to the engagement. When a more suitable candidate for Claire's hand comes along, they order her to reject Newman and marry the other man. Newman is not able to understand why Claire, a widow from an earlier arranged marriage, is not free to defy her family. He angrily demands to know what means her mother and brother have used to persuade her. "We have used authority," Madame de Bellegarde answers.[35] Claire, unable to defy her family, takes her only recourse. She flees to an institution with higher authority and becomes a Carmelite nun, in a convent as gloomy and forbidding as any European institution in American literature. Newman shows no more understanding of Old World traditions than Hawthorne did in *The Marble Faun.*

James came to appreciate Old World institutions as he grew older, and he later laughed at his own naive treatment of the Bellegardes.[36] He repeated his theme of the innocent American abroad in *The Portrait of a Lady* (1881) and in his last three novels, *The Wings of the Dove* (1902), *The Ambassadors* (1903), and *The Golden Bowl* (1904). His later American characters still enter the Old World with their pasts discarded, a dangerous condition that makes them fair game for the unscrupulous. They eventually come to understand that world, but usually too late to save themselves from unhappiness.

James's contemporary, Mark Twain, is often considered the true originator of the nation's literature.[37] In *The Adventures of Tom Sawyer* (1876) and *The Adventures of Huckleberry Finn* (1885) he created two innocents who are unmistakably American. *Huckleberry Finn* is now considered Twain's finest work, but his contemporaries gave higher praise to *A Connecticut Yankee in King Arthur's Court* (1889). Satires on America's pre-Revolutionary rulers were still very much in vogue, and *Yankee*, another past-is-evil novel, has a strong anti-British and anti-feudal theme. Inspired by Thomas Malory's *Morte d'Arthur* and Twain's combined fascination with and distaste for the European past, the novel makes no pretence of historical accuracy. The author explains that the "ungentle laws and customs touched upon" are historical, but do not apply to any particular time and place.[38] Bradbury calls *Yankee* Twain's "burlesquing satire on the Arthurian wonderland, the cult of medievalism, feudalism, chivalry and other fabulous flummery."[39] Twain assumed that the more remote the time, the worse the laws and customs, and was so hostile to any monarchy or aristocracy that he wanted to include an appendix showing the depravity of pre-nineteenth-century English society, an addition opposed by his English publishers.

Hank Morgan, the Connecticut technocrat who finds himself, magically, in the England of King Arthur, sets out to replace all the observed horrors with the wonders of nineteenth-century America. Of course, the sixth-century characters see his technical know-how as magic, so Hank carefully prepares for his "miracles," taking particular glee in embarrassing the famous magician Merlin. Initially saved by a timely solar eclipse, Hank becomes "the Boss," the chief minister to King Arthur, and is thus in a position to carry out his plans of reform. He will modernize the place with mechanical marvels and, at the same time, educate the people to abandon their cruel and antiquated ways and embrace democracy, freedom, and equality. Therein lies the paradox, for Twain combined his humorist's imagination of the ancient world — the discomforts of wearing armor and the gullibility of the people — with thoughtful observations of the world around him. Somehow "the people" did not measure up to the Edenic ideals Emerson had so successfully promoted.

Unlike Huckleberry Finn, Hank Morgan does not stand alone as a character. Throughout the novel the author intrudes and Twain himself clearly speaks through Hank. His defense of the French Revolution, tirades against the Roman Catholic Church, and disgust with titled, inherited nobility gradually expands into anger at the entire human race. Early in the novel, Hank sees the sixth-century people as "animals" that do not "reason," and says it "was pitiful for a person born in a wholesome free atmosphere to listen to their humble and hearty outpourings of loyalty toward their King and Church and nobility." As the Boss, he is "a giant among pigmies." By the end of the novel, Hank speaks of the common people as "human muck," for all of his trainees have deserted except fifty-two, and even those have to be persuaded to kill only the nobility. Hank sees no solution except extermination, which he executes with Gatling guns, dynamite, electrified fences, and diverted flood waters. He proudly states that in "ten short minutes after we had opened fire ... [t]wenty-five thousand men lay dead around us."[40]

Slotkin has written about how much the American Frontier Myth, modified by the Civil War, influenced Twain's thinking. The sixth-century English society of *Yankee* is much like the antebellum South where Twain was born, with its slaves and its poor whites who toady to the upper classes and help to keep the slaves down. Near the end of the novel, Hank accepts a challenge to fight a tournament. Instead of appearing in armor, he comes dressed like a cowboy, with lariat and two six-shooters. Fighting a single knight, Hank merely lassoes him and drags him from his horse, but when he is attacked en masse, he guns them down. A "central theme of the Myth of the Frontier" was that the only way to get rid of the "savages" was "extermination."[41]

The American public was not ready for such a dour outlook, so the popularity of *Yankee* rested on delight in a humorous satire on the Old World past. Justin Kaplan argues that Twain often convinced himself that he had written another "blameless 'literary' tale." Kaplan notes that W.D. Howells called it "charming, original, wonderful — good in fancy, and sound to the core in morals."[42]

The undervaluing of history by the American people — what Frye called a tendency inherent in countries founded on a revolution[43] — was solidly established in the early twentieth century. In *The Education of Henry Adams* (1907), Adams wrote that America "stood alone in history for its ignorance of the past."[44] His own historical writings were almost totally ignored by his contemporaries. Americans who read history preferred George Bancroft's patriotic histories or Frances Parkman's romantic adventures in the wilderness. Henry Ford's 1916 comment that "history is more or less bunk" expressed a popular attitude in the United States.[45]

William Dean Howells (1837–1920), the most respected and influential author and critic in the United States at the beginning of the twentieth century, was the first president of the American Academy of Arts and Letters, and the Dean of American Letters. A close friend of both James and Twain, he pronounced *Yankee* to be Twain's masterpiece. In his own extensive writings, Howells was often a social critic and reformer. Such important novels as *The Rise of Silas Lapham* (1885) and *A Hazard of New Fortunes* (1890) emphasize that America was no Garden of Eden. However, the next generation of writers was thoroughly disrespectful toward Howells. Henry F. May claims that Howells, in spite of his almost radical ideas, became a symbol of America's "rejected past" to the post–World War I generation.[46]

By the 1920s American literature had turned grim. T.S. Eliot's *The Waste Land* (1922) and F. Scott Fitzgerald's valley of ashes in *The Great Gatsby* (1925) illustrate what these authors thought of the Garden of Eden myth.[47] There were still many American innocents, but they were no longer virtuous, and signs of the "ugly American" were beginning to appear. Sinclair Lewis's George F. Babbitt in *Babbitt* (1922) and Fitzgerald's Jay Gatsby in *The Great*

Gatsby (1925) are good examples. The world of Clyde Griffith in Theodore Dreiser's *An American Tragedy* (1925) is the polar opposite of a Garden of Eden. These novels, however, do not deal directly with the past. Rather, they imply a guilty nation, one that corrupts and then destroys its innocents. According to May, it was the devastation of World War I that "explains the period's rejection of the past." He adds that it is still the custom in many quarters to speak of "overthrowing of the dead past, the opening of doors to the future, [as] a process not only heroic but almost without cost."[48]

The novels and stories of William Faulkner (1897–1962) are in the tradition of Hawthorne, where a sin-riddled past casts a dark and destructive shadow on the present. Faulkner's major novels are set in the Mississippi of his time, when the Civil War and slavery hung over the region and the characters like a sword of Damocles. Faulkner was not troubled by ambiguities like Hawthorne or the bitterness of disillusionment like Twain. The sins of the fathers in Faulkner's world are so powerful that their descendants seem helpless in their grip. In *Light in August* (1932), a complex novel with several important characters, the fictional town of Jefferson speaks for the past and can be read as the principal character; narrow-minded, suspicious, and determined to maintain its backward thinking regardless of how destructive it is to the present. The town drives away dissenters, or, if that fails, it isolates them, or "wall[s] them off," according to Cleanth Brooks.[49] The theme of the novel is race relations in the rural South between the two World Wars. With the exception of Lena Grove, whose story frames the central action, all of the principal characters are preoccupied with the past. The past of slavery is reinforced by Calvinism, with its conceit of knowing God's expectations.

Joe Christmas, an orphan, is haunted by the suspicion that he has "Negro blood," although he has no proof and nothing in his appearance would seem to suggest this. The two men who dominate his childhood — Doc Hines, his grandfather, who works as a janitor in order to watch over him at the orphanage, and Joe's foster father, McEachern — are rigid Calvinists, whose lives are dominated by "God's will." Hines, responsible for the rumor of Joe's Negro heritage, killed his daughter's lover and then let her die in childbirth because of his suspicions. "[It's] God's abomination of womanflesh!" the crazed old man shouts. "[I] should have knowed the walking shape of bitchery and abomination already stinking in God's sight. Telling old Doc Hines, that knowed better, that he was a Mexican."[50] Alfred Kazin points out that Faulkner "saw his native South reflected in the Old Testament." Joe is all victim, and his "maniacally obsessed" grandfather is the man who casts him off "in the name of religion."[51]

The Jim Crow era is at its peak in the rural South and the least suspicion of "Negro" blood is enough to rigidly classify an individual or endanger his life if he steps out of line. Joe is so gripped by his ill-kept secret that he is driven to homicide and suicide. He murders Joanna Burden, the daughter and granddaughter of carpetbaggers, after she tries to mother him, thus threatening the hard outer shell that protects his alienated self. The town has failed to drive Joanna away, but she has been shunned and taunted with cries of "Nigger lover! Nigger lover!"[52] Her grandfather and brother were shot by a planter and buried secretly. She will not leave their unmarked graves.

Percy Grimm is the most extreme representative of the town's rigidly backward beliefs. His frustration at having been born too late to serve in World War I is partly offset when he becomes a town vigilante. He has "a sublime and implicit faith in physical courage and blind obedience, and a belief that the white race is superior to any and all other races and that the American is superior to all other white races." Grimm kills and castrates Joe Christmas, then remarks, "[n]ow you'll let white women alone, even in hell."[53] Grimm would never have spoken to Joanna Burden while she was alive. He is a horrific example of "American innocence."

The evil past of slavery is a main theme in American literature, but the nation's writers find other reasons to vilify the past. In Shirley Jackson's famous story, "The Lottery," the residents of a small town hold an annual lottery, a tradition they maintain although no one can remember the reason. The loser is stoned to death.[54]

Postmodern novels, which treat history as just another form of fiction, still tell us much about an author's attitude toward the past. John Barth's *The Sot-Weed Factor* (1960) is loosely based on the state of Maryland's colonial past. The protagonist is a historical figure, a minor poet named Ebenezer Cooke. A clear distinction cannot be made between historical events and the author's fictions. As Tony Tanner says, Barth has "dissolved and reerected" history in "an ironic form," which is "a gesture of freedom from imposed historical patterning." Most of the characters and events are historical, but Barth approaches the characters and documents as "versions." Tanner notes that an "important sub-plot is concerned with tracking down fragments of a document which has different versions written on each side, suggesting that history is, at the very least, two-faced."[55]

The character of Henry Burlingame illustrates Barth's ambiguous approach to history. Burlingame pops up throughout the novel in several roles and disguises. He is worldly rather than naïve like Cooke. Burlingame dons so many masks that Cooke wonders if there is any reality to the man. Burlingame encourages Cooke's confusion: "your true and constant Burlingame lives only in your fancy ... [W]hether 'tis we who shift and alter and dissolve; or you whose lens changes color, field, and focus; or both together. The upshot is the same." Burlingame's only consistent behavior is his search for his own parentage. "A man's father is his link to the past," he is told, and he pursues this link with a single-mindedness that anchors him in the story.[56] In the character of Burlingame, "Barth has summarized an age-old debate about America's relation to history and the old world."[57]

The Sot-Weed Factor is a worthy descendant of Twain's *Yankee*. Both are works of humor set in a brutalized past. Humans are cruel, devious, and self-serving, while history — American history for Barth — is built on the basest of human motives. Next to the ambiguities of the past, the core of the novel is a satire on the Edenism and myths of innocence in early American thought. Ebeneezer Cooke is a parody of an Emersonian hero. He is gullible and hence reminiscent of Twain's sixth-century Englishmen. Burlingame tries to enlighten him: "'tis Adam's story thou'rt re-enacting ... Ye set great store upon your innocence, and by reason of't have lost your earthly paradise ... Your father ... will not lose this chance to play the wrathful God and turn ye out o' the Garden." Finally Cooke admits that the paradisal colony he had planned to immortalize in an epic poem to be called the "Marylandiad" is more like hell than heaven. "Here's nought but scoundrels and perverts, hovels and brothels, corruption and poltroonery," he writes, and proceeds to pen a bitter satire entitled "The Sot-Weed Factor." Finally, he decides that he stands "indicted" for "the crime of innocence, whereof the Knowledged must bear the burthen."[58] His is a fortunate fall, a theme that Hawthorne was unable to do more than mention in *The Marble Faun* a hundred years earlier.

It may be that the traditional American attitude toward the past is a partial explanation for the enthusiasm with which American writers have embraced postmodernism. What could be more attractive in a nation that traditionally disdains the past and now finds it excessively painful than an avant-garde movement that treats history as fiction?

Interest in the past and searching for roots is very much a part of the current literary scene. As a result, more American writers are choosing historical settings for their works — many taking a post-colonial approach — which demonstrates their fascination with guilt as the nation strives mightily to come to terms with its heritage of slavery, Jim Crow, and Native genocide. An apparent exception is Gore Vidal, whose fictional treatment of the American past has a non-judgmental appearance. His American political novels have carefully reconstructed history where fictional characters blend smoothly with historical ones.[59] Vidal claims that when he introduces a historical figure in his novels, "whatever he says and does he actually said and did." Vidal, himself, is as critical of the United States as the most fervent post-colonial writer. Speaking of the American Constitution, he says: "just throw the whole goddam thing out except the Bill of Rights."[60] Vidal's characters do not usually betray the author's prejudices, a markedly different approach to that of Twain and Barth. Richard Poirier says that Vidal has a sense of national proprietorship and that he mixes "inextricably the fictive and the historical, the social and the legendary."[61]

Vidal's novel *Empire* (1989) centers on American imperialism from the end of the Spanish-American War through most of the presidency of Theodore Roosevelt, when Manifest Destiny was at its peak. Characters include a fictional heroine, major political figures of the day, plus Henry James, Henry and Brooks Adams, and William Randolph Hearst. A conversation between Henry James and Henry Adams brings Theodore Roosevelt to center stage. Adams sees him as a promising new politician. James has recently reviewed a book by Roosevelt, which James calls a "paginated printed nullity." "I cannot, dear Adams ... endure your white knight, Theodore." Adams protests that

Roosevelt "embodies the spirit of our race, as we now move onto the world stage, and take our part, the leading part, which history's law requires." "What law ... is that?" asks James. "That the most efficient will prevail." "Ah, your brother's law!" says James. Henry's brother, Brooks Adams, was a close friend of Roosevelt, who admired Brooks' *The Law of Civilization and Decay* (1896). Brooks was an ardent imperialist, who was elated when he received news of McKinley's death. "Teddy's got it all now ... He will have the opportunity — and the means — to subjugate all Asia, and so give America the hegemony of the earth, which is our destiny, written in stars!"[62]

John Hay, Secretary of State to McKinley and Roosevelt and a close friend of Henry Adams, is not eager for war. He is trying to avoid a war with England over Canada, a place he always refers to as "Our Lady of the Snows." He asks Henry how much influence Brooks has on Roosevelt. Henry has become disillusioned with his brother and admits that he sees Brooks "as little as possible ... He is the most bloodthirsty creature I have ever known."[63]

Vidal claims that it is not possible to be a "just and democratic society and be an empire."[64] In the novel, he locates the American imperialism of the turn of the century in the conjunction of "Roosevelt's jingoism with Hearst's yellow journalism."[65] Hearst is a significant character in the novel, and, like Roosevelt, approved of imperialism. Hearst wanted to be president, but the two men despised and tried to destroy each other. Through scandals, Roosevelt succeeded in ending Hearst's political ambitions. A meeting between the two men did occur but was never recorded, so Vidal did not always quote his historical characters exactly and, in this case, imagines the conversation. Hearst says that Roosevelt is safe for now, then Roosevelt wonders if Hearst is. Hearst replies: "It's my story, isn't it? This country. The author's always safe. It's his characters who better watch out." Roosevelt replies, "history invented me, not you." Hearst has the last word: "True history ... is the final fiction. I thought even you knew that."[66] Because of Vidal's concern for historical accuracy, a similar conversation may well have taken place.

Gore Vidal deplores the American lack of interest in its history. He claims that, except for Thornton Wilder, he "can think of no contemporary American who has any interest in what happened before the long present he lives in." Vidal is "interested in history for its own sake," not for lessons it might teach the present, and warns that a "society without a recollected" past is in danger. He sees "Caesars moving in upon the forum."[67] These words were published in 1980, his dire predictions have not come to pass, and Americans are showing greater interest in their own past. He is correct, however, that Americans rarely examine their past for its own sake.

3

The Canadian Search for a Past

THE BITTERNESS OF THE COLONISTS, both English and French, prevented them from considering innovative ideas coming from the United States. Cultural standards were set in Britain and, therefore, English Canada's colonial literature is mostly derivative, "formula-writing," according to Frye. Far from seeking new styles and genres, pre-Confederation writers seemed to strive to be old fashioned. One of their favorite genres was the long narrative poem, numerous examples of which can be found throughout Canadian literary history. In the United States, Longfellow wrote narrative poems about incidents in America's colonial history, but Whitman and the Transcendentalists decried such traditional poesy. Frye finds something distinctively Canadian in these early narrative poems and compares them to Old English poems with their "feeling of the melancholy of a thinly-settled country under a bleak northern sky, of the terrible isolation of the creative mind in such a country."[68] He implies that such narratives were inspired by geography and isolation, but the prevailing attitude toward the past must have been important, too, for the need to build a history paralleled the need to populate this bleak northern land. Unlike the Americans, Canadians, both English and French, felt that their past had been somehow abducted. The long narrative poem has remained a popular genre in Canada, primarily used to immortalize past events.[69]

In order to grow roots in their new land, English Canada's early writers began treating the French colonial past as their own. The first important body of writings north of the Canada-US border came from Nova Scotia in the early nineteenth century. Oliver Goldsmith (1794–1861) — great nephew and namesake of the author of "The Deserted Village" — plus Joseph Howe (1804–1873) and Thomas Chandler Haliburton (1796–1873), both offspring of Loyalists, were the most notable. In his narrative poem, "Acadia," Howe pays tribute to French forefathers, speaking of them as though they were his own ancestors.

Haliburton was famous in his own day for his Sam Slick stories, satiric portraits of a Yankee peddler and clockmaker. Haliburton simultaneously admired Americans for their efficiency and high energy and despised them for their braggadocio and shortsightedness. His disgust was the stronger because he was a fervent Loyalist. His ultra-Tory sentiments were a century out of date in England, but his wit and skill as a humorist made his Sam Slick books as popular in the United States and England as they were in the colonies.

Haliburton enlivened the Nova Scotia past with a collection of stories, *The Old Judge or Life in a Colony* (1849), which includes interpretations of important historical events, tales of courage and disaster, ghost stories, and comic tales. These contrast sharply with most American fiction of the period, for disasters occur because of a failure to understand the past, not because the past itself is evil. One of his best stories, "Horse-Shoe Cove; or, Hufeisen Bucht," tells of successive inhabitants of the lovely wooded Horse-Shoe Cove near Lunenburg, who are struck by disaster: a French Acadian family evicted by the British; a German, Nicholas Spohr, whose family is murdered and scalped by "Indians" because he had desecrated their burial ground; and Captain John Smith, who is unjustly convicted of a murder by his hostile neighbors. Nicholas Spohr does not trouble himself to learn that desecrating a burial ground is a serious offence to the nearby Natives, and Captain Smith fails to befriend — and thus understand — his superstitious neighbors.

Almost everything about modern life offends the Old Judge, who narrates Horse-Shoe Cove to illustrate his distaste for individualism, which leads people to leave their ancestral communities and live in isolation. At the end of the story, he scolds the present generation for its failure to preserve the past: "The story of Nicholas and Captain Smith is only known to a few old men like myself, and will soon be lost altogether, in a country where there is no one likely to found a romance on the inmates and incidents of the 'Hufeisen Bucht.'"[70] Haliburton, a contemporary of Emerson, found many occasions to berate his countrymen for paying insufficient attention to the past.

A number of historical romances were written in pre-confederation Canada. Major John Richardson's *Wacousta or the Prophecy* (1832) is firmly in the tradition of the gothic romance so popular in the early nineteenth century. Richardson claimed a debt to Cooper's *The Last of the Mohicans*, but the novel is closer to those of Sir Walter Scott.[71] Set in Fort Detroit and the surrounding wilderness in 1763 — the time of Pontiac's uprising — the besieged fort is not unlike an Old World castle. There is no virtuous innocent among the characters, and the British military is a commanding presence. Karl F. Klinck claims that Richardson "made too much of the worst conventions of the sentimental novel," and produced a work of "treachery, hatred, vengeance, and murder."[72] The plot hinges on a curse, revenge for a treacherous act that occurred in Scotland around the time of the defeat of the Scottish Jacobites in 1715. Because of its sense of defeat, Dennis Duffy finds *Wacousta* closer to the French-Canadian romances of the nineteenth century. The execution of the curse leaves the novel with as many dead bodies as a Shakespearean tragedy, and the underlying theme becomes the doomed resistance of a backward people following the intrusion of a powerful empire that seems remote and irrelevant to the Canadian landscape. Duffy finds a "unique sense of Canadian history" in this novel.[73]

There are two curses in the novel — the curse of Wacousta, a former British officer disguised as a Native, and that of Ellen Hathaway, the wife of a soldier summarily executed for a minor infraction of duty. Colonel de Haldimar, commander at Fort Detroit, maintains rigid discipline. When his son, Captain Frederick de Haldimar, is found to have left the fort during the night, the guard at the gate is put on trial by a drumhead court. Class distinctions are as important as military rank in this novel. In his defense, the soldier tells the court that he is "a gentleman by birth," disowned by his family for marrying the daughter of a poor clergyman and forced to serve as a common soldier. At the Battle of Quebec, the soldier argues that he saw an opportunity to perform a deed of valor that would earn him a promotion to "that rank ... which by birth and education I was so justly entitled."[74] He took a bullet intended for Frederick. The colonel will have none of this and orders the execution to proceed. The victim's distraught wife screams a curse on the colonel and all of his family. However, the far more serious curse — a sworn act of revenge — comes from Wacousta, whose great love and fiancé had been stolen by the colonel when both were junior officers. Wacousta, whose real name is Reginald Morton, had been dishonorably discharged, then convicted as a traitor on charges led by de Haldimar.

The colonel adores his children, but is first and foremost the disciplined soldier. Near the end of the story, he is an unwilling witness to the murder of his daughter and younger son, and assumes his older son is dead. He "gazed upon the murder of his child, but heaved not a sigh, he shed not a tear ... 'It is done, gentlemen,' he at length remarked. 'The tragedy is closed, the curse of Ellen Hathaway is fulfilled, and I am — childless!'" He orders Captain Blackwater to "pay every attention to the security of the garrison," retires to his room, and dies, unaware that his son Frederick and niece Madeline have survived to fulfill the marriage requirements of the gothic romance.[75]

Duffy claims that Richardson depended more on experience than on his imagination for his material. His grandmother was at the siege of Detroit, and he himself fought in the War of 1812, was taken prisoner, and witnessed some of the bloody incidents he describes. There was not a large enough audience in the colonies to support a writer, so Richardson tried to adapt his material for American readers. His world, which was dominated by the British army and was full of Natives and those of mixed race,[76] did not offer him Emersonian optimism or the traditions of a successful revolution. The best he could do was demonize the Natives — something at which he was not very successful — and avoid any hint of miscegenation. Richardson, tragically, starved to death in New York.

Given the sense of defeat experienced by the Loyalists, it is hardly surprising that English Canada's early writers glorified British military triumphs in America. Other more subtle and distinctly Canadian attitudes are also apparent. Howe's poetic tribute to his French forefathers has its counterpart in a number of romances set in Quebec at the time of the French defeat by the British. William Kirby's *The Golden Dog* (1877) and Gilbert Parker's *The Seats of the Mighty* (1896) show careful historical research and actual historical figures. François Bigot, the last intendant of New France, who nearly ruined the colony with his embezzlements, is a villain in both novels. Neither Kirby nor Parker treat New France as an alien culture; there is an absence of anti-Catholicism and a warmth and sympathy shown in the depiction of the French colonists. Both novels demonstrate the English colonists' desire to appropriate the French North American past. Duffy notes some Edenic imagery in *The Golden Dog*,[77] but Kirby spent his teens in the United States, when the influence of Emerson would have been difficult to avoid. When he moved to Upper Canada and married the daughter of a Loyalist, he enthusiastically embraced the colonial sentiments he found there, including the desire to reconstruct the past.

It was common for Canadian writers of fiction in the nineteenth and early twentieth centuries to explain in a preface that their purpose was to preserve the past. A French romance, Philippe-Joseph Aubert de Gaspé's *Canadians of Old* (1863) is, in the words of the author, a recording of "a few episodes of bygone days, a few memories of youth, alas! long past," and meant to illustrate the "manners and customs of the old Canadians."[78] In a 1974 preface to the novel, Clara Thomas says that it preserves "the lore and legend of pre-conquest Quebec which then was Canada entire and whose history we can all claim as Canada's."[79] The Rev. Charles W. Gordon (1860–1937) who, under the pseudonym of Ralph Connor, wrote many best-selling novels, expressed similar sentiments in his preface to *The Man From Glengarry* (1901): "The solid forests of Glengarry have vanished, and with the forests the men who conquered them.... It is part of the purpose of this book to so picture these men and their times that they may not drop quite out of mind."[80] There is nothing in any of these works to imply that the present generation should feel guilty. Whatever horrors are described, they are not sins of the fathers, and are understandable in the context of their day.

The long narrative poem, so prominent in nineteenth-century Canada, was dramatically reintroduced by E.J. Pratt (1882–1964), a Newfoundland poet. His early writings are about Newfoundland and the sea, but his long sojourn as both graduate student and teacher at the University of Toronto awakened his interest in the Canadian past. His most famous narrative, *Brébeuf and His Brethren* (1940), recounts the events leading to the martyrdom of a group of Jesuit priests on the shores of Georgian Bay in 1649. A great deal of scholarship, including the entire *Jesuit Relations,*[81] went into its preparation. The poem is as long as a novella and the author does not intrude on his story. Told from the point of view of the priests — the only written record — Pratt in no way condemns either the religious enthusiasm of the priests or the Iroquois custom of torturing their captives.

The poem opens in the 1620s — before the Puritans founded Boston — when the "winds of God were blowing over France." Such was the fervor of the Counter-Reformation that ambitious young men and women dreamed of martyrdom. Young Brébeuf is on his knees with the voice of God in his ears, while "[f]orests and streams and trails thronged through his mind, / The painted faces of the Iroquis, / Nomadic bands and smoking bivoacs / Along the shores of western inland seas." Incredible hardships, including torture, fail to daunt the ardor of the priests, who keep returning to their western missions: "from the monastic calm / To the noise and smoke and vermin of the lodges, / and the insufferable sights and stinks." The growing strength of the Iroquois, plus an epidemic among the Huron, which they blame on the Blackrobes, lead to an end that the priest anticipates. Brébeuf knows that he has failed and that his death is near. He celebrates his last mass "before as rude an altar / As ever was reared within a sanctuary, / But hallowed as that chancel ... [at] Saint Peter's." He prays for the strength to endure his suffering: *"Grant that / I may so bear it as to win Thy grace."*[82] Such intense religious faith can be difficult for the modern reader to appreciate, but Pratt's sympathy for his protagonist gives us another example of the English Canadian determination to treat the French past as a common ancestry, one in which all Canadians can take pride. His views about history are startlingly different from those of Hawthorne and Pratt's contemporary, Faulkner.

The narrative poem was almost universally considered antiquated. The American critic Winfield Townley Scott, reviewing Pratt's *Collected Poems* in 1945, found Canada's "major poet" to be "a hundred years out of date" by American standards.[83] Northrop Frye found such an attitude amusing. In his Introduction to the second edition of Pratt's *Collected Poems*, he says that Pratt "worked unperturbed while the bright young men of the twenties, the scolding young men of the thirties, the funky young men of the forties, and the angry young men of the fifties, were ... riding off rapidly in all directions."[84]

There were historical novels written in the period between the two World Wars, but realism was then the accepted literary mode, and thus there was a strong tendency for critics and academics to dismiss the nation's historical romances as potboilers. Duffy argues that university "course outlines canonize ... grey" works, and "do not revel in the grand opera of [Parker's] *The Seats of the Mighty*."[85] Canada's tenacious interest in its past could not be restrained indefinitely by critics preoccupied with realism. Duffy claims that the "appearance of Anne Hébert's *Kamouraska* in 1970 began a rebirth of the historical novel in Canada."[86]

The adoption of the French North American past by numerous English-Canadian writers was merely one step in what appears to be a national trend.

The editors of *Canadian Literature in the 70s* suggest that Canada's "quest for a past often took the form of a search for the voices of Indians ... as ancestors."[87] Margaret Laurence wrote about the prairie Natives as "other people's ancestors who become mine."[88] This phenomenon is barely perceptible in the United States, where the present guilt-induced rewriting of western history from a Native perspective does not try to merge ancestries. In addition, only Black people look on the slaves as ancestors.

Rudy Wiebe's *The Temptations of Big Bear* (1973) shows the lengths to which a serious writer in Canada will go to bring the nation's past alive. This complex novel, with its many characters and shifting points of view, is set on the Canadian prairies between 1876 and 1888, a time when the government was making treaties with the Natives, the surveyors were mapping the land, and the first transcontinental railroad was being built. There are no fictional characters, and events are firmly grounded in history. Although Wiebe's sympathies are with the Natives, he does not pass overt moral judgments on any of his characters. Ignorant whites are balanced by unimaginative Natives who cannot recognize the inevitability of the coming changes.

In this novel, Big Bear, chief of the Plains Cree, attempts to unite other chiefs and their tribes into a confederation to resist the white intruders. His failure, coupled with the disappearance of the buffalo and impending starvation for his people, force him to sign a treaty with the Canadian government; he is the last Native chief to do so. Wiebe, who spent six years researching his story, could find no written records of the events from the Natives' point of view. Big Bear, he found, lived beneath "the giant slag heap left by the heroic white history of fur trader and police and homesteader and rancher and railroad builder." Wiebe found that he had to rely primarily on his own imagination and five senses to flesh out the story. He describes the process: "Through the smoke and darkness and piled up factuality of a hundred years to see a face; to hear, and comprehend, a voice whose verbal language he will never understand; ... [to] touch, to learn the texture of leather, of earth; [to] smell, the tinct of sweetgrass and urine; [to] taste, the golden poplar sap or the hot, raw buffalo liver dipped in gall."[89] Much of the complexity of this novel can be attributed to Wiebe's attempts to give Big Bear a voice.

Edward Dewdney, an intelligent and perceptive white man employed by the Department of Indian Affairs, writes to Prime Minister Macdonald about Big Bear and his remarkable ability to present the Natives' point of view. Dewdney and Big Bear agree that there is one God and that He has made "Indians" and whites what they are. Why then, asks Big Bear, "must Indians change?" Dewdney writes that Big Bear has a voice that would be "unbelievable in Parliament," and adds that "oddly enough in argument the mind of this stubby native seems as logical, almost civilized as any Oxford debater." Dewdney's letter ends with a meaningful statement: "I feel I must disagree with you Sir John: all Indians are *not* alike."[90] Such an attitude was unusual anywhere in North America in the late nineteenth century.

When the buffalo disappear, the Plains Cree are faced with starvation and forced to submit to terms set by the Canadian government. Although Big Bear tries to keep the negotiations peaceful, some of the young Cree kill eleven white people at Frog Lake in 1885. Big Bear is put on trial, convicted, and sentenced to three years in prison. During the trial, he gives a moving speech: "My people are hiding in the woods, terrified — those are my children, and they are starving, driven from the land which was our great inheritance ... Have you no children? Have they never asked you for food? Is there nothing but punishment in the Grandmother's law? ... This land belonged to me. When I had it I never needed your flour and pork ... But you have taken our inheritance and our strength." The judge who sentences Big Bear corrects him: "This land never belonged to you. The land was and is the Queen's. She has allowed you to use it."[91] W. J. Keith has written, "the whites ... were incapable of appreciating the fact that the Indians looked at the land with totally different preconceptions from their own."[92]

Canadians today agree with Wiebe that Big Bear was "a noble individual destroyed by the inexorable clash of cultures."[93] Wiebe seems to believe that Canadians should feel remorse — even guilt — not so much for their treatment of the Natives as for their failure to preserve the nation's past. The true story of Big Bear, hidden under that "slag heap" of white history, is an essential part of the past for all Canadians, he claims. Wiebe traveled to the American Museum of Natural History in New York to find the ultimate artifact: "the sacred bundle of Big Bear." He explains that the "Cree believe that a person's soul comes to him at birth and resides along the back of the neck." Big Bear wore the important part of this bundle, a skinned and sewn bear paw, on the back of his neck, in order to be in the "assured, perfect relationship with the Great Bear Spirit." Wiebe speaks of this artifact as if it had been stolen from the grave of his own ancestor. To a Canadian today, this bundle is "a priceless historical item, but a museum is great," he adds, because it "never gives up anything it has once ransacked the world to get."[94]

An interesting contrast to Rudy Wiebe's approach to the past is that of Robert Kroetsch. His novel *Badlands* (1975) is a postmodern work that treats the past as a fiction that can be readily dismissed or rewritten at will. The narrative follows three characters: William Dawe, a paleontologist who spends his days hunting dinosaur bones; Anna, his neglected daughter who is obsessed with her father's work; and Anna Yellowbird, Dawe's mistress on his first expedition into the badlands of southern Alberta. Each of these characters has a distinctive attitude toward the past. Dawe's commitment to his work never wavers, although it requires near total absence from his wife and daughter. "I recover the past," he says unsmilingly to a photographer; "[y]ou reduce it." For the rest of his life Dawe would *"fly into a rage"* when recalling his assistant's *"indifference about the past they were seeking together."* His daughter's obsession is a combination of bitterness for her father's neglect and a need to understand what had driven him. She pores over his field notes and imagines "a past, an ancestor, a legend, a vision, a fate." With both of her parents dead and herself a middle-aged spinster, Anna travels to the badlands in an attempt to recover the essence of that 1916 expedition.[95]

The past for Anna Yellowbird consists of memories of her time with Dawe and her search for the dead. She is a fifteen-year-old widow when Dawe and his men discover her lying in an open grave. A shaman had told her to wait there for the guide who would take her to the place of the dead. She is found later in a tepee made of dinosaur bones, and Dawe hires her, sensing that she can help locate the skeletons. Anna hears an explosion that kills one of the men, an event that she believes is "her confrontation with the dead, the moment for which she had traveled so far, waited so long." When the expedition leaves they again encounter the photographer, who shows Anna a picture of the man who was killed: "Anna stared at the picture ... She turned the photo over and looked at the blank side ... 'But he's dead' ... 'You can bring him back.' " She leaves with the photographer, who will give her photos of the group in exchange for "her youth."[96]

The middle-aged Anna Dawe locates the aged Anna Yellowbird and, carrying the notes and the photographs, the two of them travel toward the site of the 1916 expedition. As they near their goal, they see a supposedly tranquilized bear struggling in a mesh bag that is dangling from a helicopter. This symbol of detachment from the earth releases them from their obsessions, and they laughingly discard notes and pictures. The project to recover dinosaur bones, says Anna Yellowbird, was like *"pissing in the ocean."*[97]

Leon Surette claims that Kroetsch does not permit his characters the "luxury" of inhabiting "the country they have invented," and because of this rejection of the past, the novel is denied a place in the Canadian canon.[98] Surette has a point. Anna Yellowbird does not deny her Native past, and the liberation of the two women is too sudden, too unconvincing. There is nothing ambiguous about Dawe's expedition or the dinosaur bones reclaimed. Kroetsch's efforts to treat the past as fiction pales beside the work of John Barth, where different versions of past events offer characters a choice, if not a mystery. In spite of Kroetsch's efforts, postmodernism has never had the following in Canada that it has in the United States.

Newfoundland did not join Canada until 1949, yet it has a long and turbulent history. Wayne Johnston's *The Colony of Unrequited Dreams* (1998) is a fictionalized biography of Joseph (Joey) Smallwood, the man who led Newfoundland into Canada, and its first Premier. Johnston has liberally mixed fiction with history, and raised the hackles of some Canadian critics who insist that he took unacceptable liberties with Smallwood's life. The book had better reviews in England and the United States, where less is known about Newfoundland but interest had been aroused, largely due to the popularity of E. Annie Proulx's *The Shipping News* (1993). Johnston's novel interweaves Smallwood's story with that of the fictional Sheilagh Fielding, a sharp-tongued and witty journalist, who, some critics argue, represents Newfoundland itself. Newfoundland often appears as the strongest character — turbulent, corrupt, impoverished, and both repelling and attracting its inhabitants — not unlike the character of Fielding. When Smallwood returns to Newfoundland after a failed attempt to succeed in New York he says: "I wondered if I, too, had reached the limits of a leash I had not until now even known I was wearing and was, like my father, coming home not because I wanted to, but because I was being pulled back, yanked back by the past."[99]

Smallwood and Fielding have a love-hate relationship. She makes several attempts to destroy him, but also appears as a guardian angel who rescues him when he is in trouble, once risking her own life to save him when he is caught in a blizzard. Aside from her often hilarious newspaper columns, Fielding is writing a *Condensed History of Newfoundland,* sections of which are interspersed with the chapters of the novel. She also keeps a journal and writes often heartrending letters that are never mailed. A lonely and tortured woman, she is an apt image of the torment that has been inflicted on Newfoundland by men and nature. The novel opens with one of her unsent letters to Smallwood, written six months after Newfoundland joined Canada in 1949. She recalls the city of St. Johns:

> *[H]ow different it used to be, Smallwood, this city, yours and mine ... Animals were every where ... [c]ows, goats, chickens, horses, dogs ... There were so many schooners that when their sails were down, the harbour was a grove of spear-like masts. After it rained, the schooners would unfurl their sails to let them dry, ... the whole harbour a mass of flapping canvas you could hear a mile away ... The city smells. Tar and dust, horse manure and turpentine ... fish and salt and the reek of bilge-water ... It was like that, Smallwood. Not three hundred years ago but twenty. One generation.*[100]

Newfoundland is weighed down with history. The fictional Smallwood makes a winter trip to isolated communities on the southeast part of the island, hoping to organize the fishermen into a union. He hires a small schooner run by a retired fisherman. As they sail down the coast, he finds it hard to believe that Newfoundland is an island; it is "a massive assertion of land ... a great looming, sky-obliterating chunk of rock." They find three-centuries-old cemeteries at the end of fjords. Smallwood carries on in spite of the captain's advice to turn back, and must walk over heaving chunks of ice floes to reach the shore. The people are happy to see him, but are destitute beyond anything he had imagined.

> They had never seen an automobile, a train, a motorized vehicle
> of any kind except a boat ... Most of them did not understand or
> even have a word for the concept of government ... Had only the
> most rudimentary understanding of what a country was ... I was
> able to get across only the notion that I had come to try to help
> them. But as I had with me none of the forms of 'help' they were
> familiar with — no supply boat, no medicine, no clerical collar
> — they regarded me as something of a crackpot ... [y]et if I had
> told the head of any household that from now on I would live
> with him, he would have assured me I was welcome.[101]

The sections of Fielding's *Condensed History* trace the essential events of
Newfoundland's past. Discovered by John Cabot in 1497, fought over by
England and France, mismanaged and exploited, it did not receive its first local
legislature until 1832. Lord Baltimore, the proprietor of Maryland (who is
referred to in Barth's *The Sot-Weed Factor*), began his North American
residency with a large land grant in Newfoundland. One winter there destroyed
his health. The British tried repeatedly to rid themselves of the expensive
colony and helped push it into joining Canada. Johnston may have taken
liberties with the life of Joey Smallwood, but the history of Newfoundland rings
true.

Newfoundland did not experience the same relationship with the past that
the Loyalists did in what is now central Canada. Newfoundlanders clung to
colonial status and resisted entry into Canada for many years. In the novel, a
young Smallwood attends a boy's school, where "[m]ost of the masters were
wittily scornful of Newfoundland, delighted in itemizing its deficiencies and
the many ways it fell short of being England ... We were taught next to nothing
about Newfoundland, the masters drilling into us instead the history and
geography of England."[102] At the end of the twentieth century, there were still
some Newfoundlanders who believed that they could have survived as an
independent country and avoided amalgamation into Canada.

4

Conclusion

ALL NATIONS TEACH HISTORY from their country's perspective and, in most cases, essentially the same history is taught throughout the country. Both Canada and the United States are exceptions. For generations after the Civil War, northern and southern states taught markedly different versions of that bloody conflict. In Canada education is still governed provincially — there is no federal department of education — and Quebec has, understandably, always blocked attempts to set national standards. The student of history, in particular, has suffered. In Johnston's novel *The Colony of Unrequited Dreams*, the boys are taught English history and learn almost nothing about Newfoundland. The English provinces of Canada have stressed British history and the development of English-speaking Canada; in Quebec, the emphasis has been on the fall of New France and the French Canadian struggle against British oppression. Books are appearing in both the United States and Canada exposing student ignorance of their own history, and prompting widespread public concern. In *Who Killed Canadian History* (1998), J.L. Granatstein is particularly outraged that, unlike in the United States, there has never even been an attempt to establish national standards for Canadian history.

The inevitability of any nation becoming reconciled to its past and the worldwide interest of the present generation in exploring its roots are helping to merge Canadian and American literary objectives, at least with regard to national history. In Canada, with no siren song of a land of milk and honey and no American dream, the route has been comparatively straight. Since the 1960s, Canada and the United States have shared many reform movements, particularly the New Left and the various postmodern theories, that have emphasized subversion of the established order. Carl Berger says that reform movements that "seek to change the future have always tried to rewrite the past."[103] It is in the various approaches used by Canadian and American authors to write or rewrite the past that cultural differences can still be detected.

Far from diminishing the national sense of guilt, increased interest in the past among Americans has reinforced it to the point where it is difficult to find an example of American literature that treats the national past with sympathy. Vidal's American history novels and some recent works of John Updike[104] treat the American past dispassionately, but they are the exception. Perhaps the great interest shown by American writers in postmodern concepts is partly due to the freedom it offers writers to play games with history. It also reinforces that American tradition that "history is more or less bunk."

Some Canadian critics lament the fact that post-modernism has not affected Canadian writers as it has American writers. In *Canadian Canons* (1991), several of the contributors claim that works have been canonized not for their literary value, but because of their effectiveness in defining Canada.[105] Walter Pache argues that the "historical novel" has long been regarded as "a quasi-objective medium for recording the past and transforming it into a collective myth."[106] Pache seems to find this deplorable, and happily reports that Kroetsch and Canadian writer George Bowering are correcting the situation with postmodern techniques.

Kroetsch claims that Canadians do not ask "*who* they are," as Americans do, but rather "*if* they are"[107] This idea is not new, but rather another reference to the lingering suspicion in the Canadian psyche that Canada is a historical accident. Despite Innis's convincing case that Canada is a geographically natural country, the general populace remains doubtful, so writers respond to the perceived need to define the nation by bringing its history to life. Under such conditions, postmodernism, with its claim that history is in the eye of the beholder and can be rewritten to suit any individual, is not likely to have wide appeal. Clift argues that the "main objective" of Canadian literature is to "explore the determinants" that have shaped the nation and to "isolate the factors that give the idea of Canada the same inevitability that other countries exhibit in their own history."[108] Such a pursuit does little to subvert the social order, but it is no more likely to suppress artistic excellence than an American writer's drive to vilify the nation's past.

Imaginative reconstructions of Canada's past have sought ever-wider grounds. Jürgen Schäfer, in an article on Wiebe's *Big Bear* and Kroetsch's *Gone Indian* (1973), claims that these novels are not "nostalgic primitivism but an imaginative evocation of the Indian past as a new and significant dimension of Canadian history." He claims that they meet a "national need" by "constructing a usable past on foundations hitherto neglected."[109] Americans have just as great a need. Postmodern techniques that use a liberal amount of humor may be providing the Americans with a mystical past less painful to contemplate than a more direct approach that continually stumbles over evidence of slavery and genocide.

Historical writing in Canada has long been associated with nationalism. Duffy says that "the historical novel as nationalist statement remains a living tradition in French Canada," and recent work confirms the same in English Canada. Americans, whose most fervent nationalism once rested on denying history, are now facing the inevitability of repairing the damage. Duffy's claim that what "the Bible does for the Judeo-Christian tradition, historical fiction and history provide for the yearnings of secular man,"[110] may be only a slight exaggeration.

Notes

1 Adams, *1800,* 126.
2 Richard Slotkin, *Regeneration Through Violence: The Mythology of the American Frontier, 1600–1860* (Middleton, CT: Weslyan University Press, 1973), 3.
3 Peterson, 445, xxxv, 318–19.
4 Qtd in Stewart and Rawlyk, 194.
5 Qtd in Bercovitch, "Rites," 14.
6 Frye, *Divisions,* 76–77.
7 Perry Miller, *Errand into the Wilderness* (Cambridge: Harvard University Press, 1956), 11–12.
8 Qtd by Sacvan Bercovitch, *The Puritan Origins of the American Self* (New Haven: Yale University Press, 1975), 52, 57.
9 *Ibid.,* 88.
10 T.D. MacLulich, "Our Place on the Map: The Canadian Tradition in Fiction," *University of Toronto Quarterly* 52:2 (1982/3), 191.
11 Careless, *Canada,* 118.
12 Clift, 189.
13 De Tocqueville II, 2, 88.
14 The Transcendentalists were ardent followers of Emerson's philosophy, an American form of the Romantic movement that swept Europe early in the nineteenth century. Its better known adherents include Henry David Thoreau, Bronson Alcott (father of Louisa May Alcott), Orestes Brownson, George Ripley, Theodore Parker, Margaret Fuller, Andrew Norton, and Elizabeth Palmer Peabody (Hawthorne's sister-in-law).

15 Ralph Waldo Emerson, *Ralph Waldo Emerson,* ed. Richard Poirier (Oxford: Oxford University Press, 1990), 3, 40–41, 141, 115–16. This theorizing sounds much like contemporary postmodernism. Emerson did not value consistency, so careful selection from his writings can make him sound like most avant-garde movements that stress individual freedom. He was consistent in his belief in a universal soul, however, a position with which postmodernism would not agree.

16 Richard Poirier, Introduction to *Emerson,* ix.

17 Irwin Edman, Introduction, *Emerson's Essays* (New York: Thomas Y. Crowell: 1951), viii–ix.

18 R.W.B. Lewis, *The American Adam: Innocence, Tragedy, and Tradition in the Nineteenth Century* (Chicago: Phoenix Books, 1958), 5–7.

19 R.W.B. Lewis, 28.

20 Nathaniel Hawthorne, "The Custom House," in *The Scarlet Letter* (New York: Signet Classics, 1999), 7.

21 Nathaniel Hawthorne, *Hawthorne's Short Stories* (New York: Vintage Books, 1946), 143, 145.

22 Tony Tanner, *City of Words: American Fiction 1950 – 1970* (New York: Harper and Row, 1971), 24–5; Charles Child Walcutt, "The Range of Interpretations — *The Scarlet Letter* and Its Modern Critics," *Twentieth Century Interpretations of The Scarlet Letter,* ed. John C. Gerber (Englewood Cliffs, NJ: Prentice-Hall, 1968), 71–81; Bercovitch, *Origins,* 177.

23 Nathaniel Hawthorne, *The Scarlet Letter* (New York: Signet Classics, 1999), 177; Ch 17.

24 Nathaniel Hawthorne, Introduction, *The House of the Seven Gables: A Romance* (New York: Signet Classics, 1961), vii.

25 Henry Nash Smith, *Democracy and the Novel: Popular Resistance to Classic American Writers* (Oxford: Oxford University Press, 1981), 21.

26 Fair and dark heroines was a convention of the time which was not limited to the United States. Cooper's *The Last of the Mohicans* (1826) has duel heroines, the dark one, reputed to be of mixed-race, is in love with the Indian Uncas. The American public would not tolerate miscegenation, so the lovers had to be destroyed.

27 Nathaniel Hawthorne, Preface, *The Marble Faun* (New York: Signet Classics, 1961), vi.

28 Hawthorne, *Faun,* 209; Ch 31, 279; Ch 42.

29 Hawthorne did not intend any irony when he created the character of Hilda, for he dedicated her to his beloved wife Sophia.

30 Hawthorne, *Faun,* 99; Ch 14.

31 *Ibid.,* 220; Ch 33.

32 Murray Krieger, Afterword, *The Marble Faun,* 344.

33 Hawthorne, *Faun,* 329; Ch 50.

34 Malcolm Bradbury, *Dangerous Pilgrimages: Trans-Atlantic Mythologies and the Novel* (London: Penguin Books, 1996), 157.

35 Henry James, *The American* (New York: Holt, Rinehart and Winston, 1949), 244; Ch 18.

36 Henry James, *The Art of the Novel* (New York: Charles Scribner's Sons, 1934), 20–39.

37 Hemingway's remark that "all modern American literature comes from one book by Mark Twain called *Huckleberry Finn*" has often been quoted and has achieved wide agreement among critics of American literature (*Green Hills of Africa*, New York, 1935, p. 22).

38 Mark Twain, *A Connecticut Yankee in King Arthur's Court* (London: Penguin Classics, 1986), Preface.

39 Bradbury, *Pilgrimages*, 172.

40 Twain, *Yankee*, 66; Ch 5, 87, 90; Ch 8, 392, 404–5; Ch 43.

41 Richard Slotkin, *The Fatal Environment: The Myth of the Frontier in the Age of Industrialization, 1800–1890* (Norman: University of Oklahoma Press, 1994), 523–30.

42 Justin Kaplan, Introduction, *Yankee*, 19, 23.

43 Frye, *Garden*, 248.

44 Adams, *Education*, 328,

45 Henry Ford, Interview with Charles N. Wheeler, *Chicago Tribune,* May 25, 1916.

46 Henry F. May, *The End of American Innocence: A Study of the First Years of Our Time: 1912–1917* (Oxford: Oxford University Press, 1979), 7.

47 *The Waste Land* is set in Europe after World War I, but the tone of disillusionment is particularly American. See Perry Miller, *Nature's Nation* (Cambridge: Harvard University Press, 1967), 262; and Alfred Kazin, *God and the American Writer* (New York: Vintage Books, 1998), 200.

48 May, x, xiii.

49 Cleanth Brooks, Introduction to *Light in August* by William Faulkner (New York: The Modern Library, 1968), xvii–xviii.

50 Faulkner, *Light in August*, 353; Ch 16.

51 Kazin, *God*, 235–6, 239, 249.

52 Faulkner, *Light in August*, 275; Ch. 13.

53 *Ibid.*, 426, 439; Ch 19.

54 Shirley Jackson, "The Lottery," *The Small Town in American Literature,* Second edition, ed. David M. Cook and Craig G. Swauger (New York: Harper and Row, 1977), 225.

55 Tanner, *City*, 241–43.

56 John Barth, *The Sot-Weed Factor* (New York: Grosset and Dunlap, 1966), 349; II Ch. 22, 42: I Ch. 4.

57 Tanner, *City*, 245.

58 Barth, *Factor*, 423; I Ch. 28, 483; II Ch. 32, 788; III Ch. 21.

59 *Washington D.C.* (1967) (from the New Deal to the McCarthy era); *Burr* (1973) (the early years of the Republic); *1876* (1976) (the Gilded Age); *Lincoln* (1984) (before and during the Civil War); *Empire* (1987) (the turn of the twentieth century); *Hollywood* (1990) (post World War I); and *The Golden Age* (2000) (World War II).

60 Gore Vidal, *Views From a Window: Conversations with Gore Vidal*, ed. Robert J. Stanton and Gore Vidal (Secaucus NJ: Lyle Stuart, 1980), 20, 247.

61   Richard Poirier, *Trying It Out in America: Literary and Other Performances* (New York: Farrar, Straus and Giroux, 1999), 148.

62   Gore Vidal, *Empire* (New York: Ballantine, 1987), 39–40; Ch. 1, 289–90; Ch. 9.

63   *Ibid.*, 153; Ch. 4, 386; Ch. 12.

64   Vidal, *Views*, 116.

65   Poirier, *America*, 152.

66   Vidal, *Empire*, 472; Ch. 17.

67   Vidal, *Views*, 63, 98, 252.

68   Frye, *Garden*, 234, 146.

69   Among the more important nineteenth-century Canadian narrative poems are Oliver Goldsmith's "The Rising Village" (1834), Charles Sangster's "The Saint Lawrence and the Saguenay" (1856), William Kirby's "The U.E.: A Tale of Upper Canada" (1859), Alexander McLachlan's "The Emigrant" (1861), and Isabella Valancy Crawford's "Malcolm's Katie" (1884).

70   Thomas Chandler Haliburton, *The Old Judge or Life in a Colony* (Ottawa: The Tecumseh Press, 1978), 301–02.

71   Dennis Duffy, *A World Under Sentence: John Richardson and the Interior* (Toronto: ECW Press, 1996), 17–19.

72   Carl F. Klinck, Introduction to *Wacousta or The Prophecy* by John Richardson (Toronto: McClelland & Stewart, 1967), xi, v.

73   Dennis Duffy, *Sounding the Iceburg: An Essay on Canadian Historical Novels* (Toronto: ECW Press, 1986), 3–5.

74   Richardson, *Wacousta*, 47.

75   *Ibid.*, 293.

76   Richardson had many mixed race relatives, descendants of fur traders and their Native wives, and may have been part Native himself. Duffy, *World* 47.

77   Duffy, *Iceberg*, 11.

78   Philippe-Joseph Aubert de Gaspé, *Canadians of Old,* trans. Jane Brierley (Montreal: Véhicule Press, 1996), 20; Ch 1. At the time de Gaspé was writing, the term "Canadian" applied only to the French.

79   Clara Thomas, Preface, *Canadians of Old*, by Aubert de Gaspé (Toronto: McClelland & Stewart, 1974), xii.

80   Ralph Connor, *The Man from Glengarry* (Toronto: McClelland & Stewart, 1993), 9.

81   The *Jesuit Relations* is a collection of reports written by Jesuit priests in New France and published annually in France from 1632 to 1673.

82   E.J. Pratt, *The Collected Poems of E.J. Pratt*, Second Edition (Toronto: Macmillan of Canada, 1962), 244, 252, 292.

83   Winfield Townley Scott, Review of *Collected Poems of E.J. Pratt, Poetry,* September 1945: 332.

84   Northrop Frye, Introduction to *E.J Pratt*, xxvi.

85   Duffy, *Iceberg*, ii.

86   Ibid., 54.

87   Paul Denham and Mary Jane Edwards, Introduction, *Canadian Literature in the 70s* (Toronto: Holt, Rinehart and Winston, 1980), xviii.

88   Qtd by George Woodcock, *Northern Spring: The Flowering of Canadian Literature* (Vancouver: Douglas and McIntyre, 1987), 22–23.

89 Rudy Wiebe, "On the Trail of Big Bear," *A Voice in the Land: Essays By and About Rudy Wiebe*, ed. W.J. Keith (Edmonton: NeWest Press, 1981), 134, 132.
90 Wiebe, *The Temptations of Big Bear* (Toronto: McClelland & Stewart, 1976), 113–14; Ch 2:4.
91 *Ibid.*, 397–99; Ch 6:3.
92 W. J. Keith, *Epic Fiction: The Art of Rudy Wiebe* (Edmonton: University of Alberta Press, 1981), 69.
93 *Ibid.*, 63.
94 Wiebe, "Bear Spirit in a Strange Land," *Voice*, 146, 148, 149.
95 Robert Kroetsch, *Badlands* (Toronto: General Publishing, 1976), 128, 162, 3.
96 *Ibid.*, 215, 250.
97 *Ibid.*, 270.
98 Leon Surette, "Creating the Canadian Canon" *Canadian Canons: Essays in Literary Value,* ed. Robert Lecker (Toronto: University of Toronto Press, 1991), 29.
99 Wayne Johnston, *The Colony of Unrequited Dreams* (Toronto: Vintage Canada, 1999), 211.
100 *Ibid.*, 4–7.
101 *Ibid.*, 347, 354–55.
102 *Ibid.*, 34–5.
103 Berger, 264.
104 See particularly *Memories of the Ford Administration* (1992) and *In the Beauty of the Lilies* (1995).
105 Lecker, ed. *Canadian Canons*, 16, 32, 134.
106 Walter Pache, "The Fiction Makes Us Real: Aspects of Postmodernism in Canada," *Gaining Ground: European Critics on Canadian Literature*, ed. Robert Kroetsch and Reingard Nischik (Edmonton: NeWest Press, 1986), 72.
107 Kroetsch, *The Lovely Treachery of Words: Essays Selected and New* (Toronto: Oxford University Press, 1989), 55.
108 Clift, 135.
109 Jürgen Schäfer, "A Farewell to Europe: Rudy Wiebe's *The Temptations of Big Bear* and Robert Kroetsch's *Gone Indian*," *Gaining Ground*, 87–88.
110 Duffy, *Iceberg*, 63, 75.

Chapter
Three

Nature

1
The Commanding Presence of Nature

THE DEBATE THAT PRECEDED the American Revolution centered on the natural rights philosophy, which dated back to the seventeenth-century struggle against arbitrary government. Opponents of the Divine Right of Kings claimed that God's will could be discovered through an understanding of the laws of nature. Gradually, the emphasis shifted from God to nature. Max Beloff notes that appeals to nature became as "omnipresent in the eighteenth century as appeals to the Divine Word" were in the seventeenth.[1] Or, as Carl Becker writes, " 'Nature' had stepped in between man and God."[2] The first sentence of the Declaration of Independence states that Americans claim "the separate and equal station to which the Laws of Nature and of Nature's God entitle them." The study of natural rights had led to a theory of "parliamentary sovereignty" in Britain, but Americans reinterpreted the theory to mean "limited government."[3] Thus, the American interpretation of the law of nature became the colonists' most effective weapon against the British insistence on the supremacy of Parliament. While the Loyalists carried a belief in parliamentary supremacy with them to Canada, the new citizens of the United States were primed to deify nature, on which the legitimacy of their new nation could be said to rest.

Thomas Paine's pamphlet *Common Sense*, published in early 1776, is credited with persuading the American public to push for independence. Paine's implication that "only America was close enough to nature" probably has more merit than his many arguments about British tyranny.[4] Truly, the New World appeared to be a land of milk and honey. To the eighteenth-century mind, freedom from want could come only through the ownership of property, and America had a plethora of fertile land, easily acquired and widely distributed. The European peasant had never before dreamed of owning large tracts of land, and such bounty made it easy for the people to believe that God had chosen them and their land to receive His special blessing. The American Dream, in its original form, was intimately associated with the land.

The same cannot be said of the origins of Canada. Although the settlers were equally convinced that the ownership of property represented the only true freedom, the land itself had little to do with national legitimacy, and it came with some distinct drawbacks. The weather was brutal, the growing season short, and many Loyalists found themselves cultivating land on the Canadian Shield with soil only a few inches deep. The French occupied the land on either side of the St. Lawrence river, on which they had established a seigneurial system. The land belonged to upper-class seigneurs and was farmed by *habitants*. The Loyalists expanded southwest of the Shield to fertile land in Upper Canada. Large sections of this land were reserved for the clergy and for Natives, and newcomers were not permitted to intrude.

Geography predetermined attitudes toward nature in Canada and the United States, for political philosophies did not just arise from theories, but reflected the natural world the two peoples encountered. Morton compares the Mississippi valley's "fertile lands ... gentle slopes and hardwood forests" — the "heartland of the United States" — with the Canadian Shield's "naked granite ridges, its multitudinous waters and sodden muskegs." The Shield covers almost half of all Canadian territory, and is "one of nature's grimmest challenges to man." Jacques Cartier gazed on the Labrador coast of the Shield and said it was the "land that God gave Cain." Morton claims that no Canadian has found it necessary to dispute such a reaction seriously.[5]

The Shield plus the climate of the Arctic gives Canada a permanent northern frontier. In addition, the river systems and the ever-present fear of an invasion from the south led to an east-west orientation. The United States, however, has always had a north-south orientation. It united thirteen different colonies into a nation, faced the fracturing of the Civil War, and, as Robert Kroetsch notes, its writers have felt themselves caught "between the Old World of Europe and the promise of the western frontier."[6] Frederick Jackson Turner's claim that the frontier brought a return to primitive conditions, or a "perennial rebirth" that furnished "the forces dominating American character," suggests that the loss of the frontier would have profound effects on the nation's self-image.[7]

The Romantic period reached its peak in England in the early nineteenth century with the poetry of Wordsworth, Coleridge, Shelley, and Keats. Emerson traveled to Europe in the early 1830s where he met Wordsworth and Coleridge and became a lifelong friend of Thomas Carlyle. He brought the Romanticism of nature back to the United States and turned it into a movement that no European could have imagined. God, the United States, and nature became almost indistinguishable. In effect, Emerson developed a pantheistic religion: America was a second Garden of Eden, and the best method of finding God was through contact with nature. Critics of American history and literature have commented on this worship of nature. "Nature," writes D.H. Lawrence, "I wish I could write it larger than that. NATURE."[8] Perry Miller claims that nature was seen as "the American TEMPLE,"[9] but Sacvan Bercovitch prefers "AMERICA as the temple of nature."[10] Wherever critics wish to place the emphasis, the young nation, with its boundless energy and discarded past, worshiped nature.

Emersonians assumed that contact with nature was the way to human improvement if not perfection. Floods of commentary on the glories of nature in the West compared to the decadence of the East led *The Literary World* to wonder in 1847 "if this tedious declamation was not becoming trite." Do men who go deeper and deeper into the wild "in fact put off false and artificial ways?" The article concludes that: "[u]nfortunately ... some of the fairest portions of the earth are occupied by the most degraded of mankind."[11] Almost half a century later, Turner would describe the return to primitive conditions on the frontier, yet insist that the process was positive, since it removed all vestiges of Europe and produced a complete American.[12] Richard Slotkin, who calls the "Myth of the Frontier" the oldest American myth, adds that prospective settlers in the West were consistently told that the place was "a Garden of Earthly Delights."[13]

The Romantic movement was ubiquitous in the western world, so early Canadian writers expressed their own relationship with nature. Magnificent natural surroundings could be expected to inspire the artist, but few artists in Canada depicted nature as a benevolent force. With few exceptions, early Canadian literary works describe death or near death at the hands of nature alongside lengthy descriptions of the often spectacular beauty of the setting.

In Canada there was no confusing God with nature. Frye was struck by "a tone of deep terror in regard to nature" in early Canadian poetry, not physical fear, but "a terror of the soul."[14] Explorers and settlers of the seventeenth and eighteenth centuries needed the felt presence of God and His approval of their lonely and dangerous undertakings. If, as Becker says, nature "stepped in between man and God" in the eighteenth century,[15] the newcomer in the northern colonies was left "without human and moral values to cling to." The "vast unconsciousness of nature" appeared to be "an unanswerable denial of those values."[16]

There has been much controversy over Frye's contention among Canadian critics. Some have taken a simplistic view and bristled over a presumption of cowardly ancestors. Mary Lu MacDonald read everything published in the Canadas before 1850 and concluded that Frye was wrong; she claims that early attitudes toward nature were positive, and that "sublime" was the most commonly used word.[17] British poets of the early nineteenth century were familiar with Edmund Burke's *A Philosophical Enquiry into the Origin of Our Ideas of the Sublime and Beautiful* (1756), in which the author argues that "sublime" has its origins in "fear," and that whatever "is terrible, with regard to sight, is sublime too."[18] There were educated people among the early settlers in Canada who read Burke but were preoccupied with the poetry of the Romantics. They maintained British literary fashions and praised the real beauties of the landscape, but the sensitive among them faced up to Canadian realities. Donna Bennett notes that a rural tradition in Canadian fiction is not bucolic, but responds to "a world dominated by random forces of nature."[19]

The early love affair with nature in the United States had some undesired consequences. Of greatest concern was that civilization was destroying nature. In 1835, *Knickerbocker* magazine of New York published an essay, widely reprinted, that argued: "God has promised us a renowned existence, if we will but preserve it. He speaks this promise in the sublimity of Nature."[20] Did Americans want unspoiled nature, or did they want civilization, and, if the former, how was the moving frontier to be stopped? Henry Adams describes the frontier in 1800: "From Lake Erie to Florida, in long, unbroken line, pioneers were at work, cutting into the forests with the energy of so many beavers, and with no more express moral purpose than the beavers they drove away."[21] Cooper, Emerson, Thoreau, and Whitman glorified a nature untouched by civilization, but there was no stopping that moving frontier.

While American civilization was destroying nature, it was also destroying the Native peoples. The light and dark pairings of males found in some famous nineteenth-century American novels suggest an early attempt to identify dark-skinned people with nature. The attempt did not last and, by the late nineteenth century, Cooper and Longfellow were strongly criticized for glorifying the Native.[22] In general, Americans, unlike Canadians, did not consider the Native peoples to be a part of nature, since nature was regarded as benevolent. Guilt over slavery can be traced back to pre-Civil War days, but the Native perspective first appeared in American literature a century later. Although Canadians often exploited them, the Natives were looked on as trading partners, a people with knowledge. The women also made ideal wives for men detained in the wilderness. Only the Natives could teach the white man how to survive in a harsh northern wilderness. The challenge was to understand, adapt, and above all, to be wary of the natural world in all of its manifestations.

Canada was built on the exploitation of natural resources: fur, fish, timber, and minerals. Frye claims that "the main focus of guilt in Canada seems to fall on the rape of nature," as though "the screams of all the trapped and tortured creatures who built up the Canadian fur trade were still echoing in our minds."[23] Guilt has been a main theme in western literature since World War II, but in Canada a subtle sense of discomfort over sufferings in the natural world can be traced back to the late nineteenth century, primarily in the form of stories told from the animal's point of view. W.J. Keith claims that "the animal-story can with justice be regarded as the one native Canadian art-form."[24]

Leslie Fiedler's *The Return of the Vanishing American* (1968) divides American literature into the four points of the compass, claiming that "geography in the United States is mythological." In this study, great emphasis is placed on the West, and the vanishing American of the title is the Native, whose image "has haunted all Americans," for it is rooted in "profoundest guilt."[25] The consequences of that moving frontier — which replaced much of the nature worshiped by early Americans with a civilization of doubtful morality and destroyed many Native cultures — rests heavily in the American psyche. It is not surprising that mankind as nature's destroyer became, and remains, a main theme in American literature.

Fiedler's North is identified with New England and human contact with a hostile environment, a theme that suggests the author did not look very far north. T.D. MacLulich has shown that Fiedler's emphasis on an oppressive Puritanical society, rather than nature, clearly distinguishes it from the nature theme in Canada.[26] Sherrill E. Grace adds that only Canadians write "northerns," where the north remains "silent, mysterious and deadly."[27] The "silence of the eternal spaces remained at the bottom of the Canadian psyche" for a long time; perhaps it is still there.[28] Nature in Canada does not respond to prayers or adoration, so the adventurer had better be wary.

2

Romantic Naturalism in the United States

Bercovitch claims that the New England Puritans gave "America the status of visible sainthood."[29] Frequently comparing themselves to the Children of Israel soon to enter the new Jerusalem, Puritans laid the groundwork for deification of the new nation. Such an inheritance, plus the eighteenth-century preoccupation with nature and a seemingly endless supply of fertile land, was almost certain to lead to inflated expectations.

The earliest important American work to idealize nature is Hector St. Jean de Crèvecoeur's *Letters from an American Farmer* (1782). De Crèvecoeur expressed the Jeffersonian ideal of the United States as a nation of yeomen farmers at least as early as Jefferson did, for the book was written before the American Revolution. De Crèvecoeur, a French aristocrat who served under Montcalm in Quebec, moved to the American colonies, married a New Yorker, and became a farmer in the unspoiled land. He also became a Loyalist, who was driven from his farm by American Patriots and later arrested in New York as a spy. He made it back to France, and later became French Consul General to the United States.

De Crèvecoeur's *Letters* were written to Abbé Raynal, FRS. In one of the earliest he says that here "nature opens her broad lap to receive the perpetual accession of new comers, and to supply them with food." In another letter he describes the arrival of a new immigrant who "must greatly rejoice that he lived at a time to see this fair country discovered and settled." "We are a people of cultivators," he writes, "united by the silken bands of mild government." The new immigrant discovers that "his labour is founded on the basis of nature," and that wives and children will "gladly help their father to clear those fields whence exuberant crops are to arise." From being a slave or a servant, the new arrival becomes "a free man, invested with lands." He becomes "an American,"[30] D.H. Lawrence, in his inimitable fashion, notes that de Crèvecoeur discovered "Nature-Sweet-and-Pure ... long before Thoreau and Emerson worked it up."[31]

By the 1830s, the United States was firmly established in the public mind as the new garden of the world. Emerson, having resigned his pulpit and met the principal writers of English Romanticism, took the nature worship of the Romantic movement to undreamed-of heights in America.

In his first book, *Nature*, Emerson describes the human religious experience as an intimate relationship between God, nature, and a single individual. He stresses being "alone" with nature, a nature that "never wears a mean appearance." He claims that he is not alone when he is reading or writing, so prefers looking at the stars and walking in the woods, for outdoors he finds "perpetual youth." He describes his own experience of standing on the "bare ground — my head bathed by the blithe air, and uplifted into infinite space." He writes: "I become a transparent eye-ball" and as "the currents of the Universal Being circulate through me; I am part or particle of God." Nature, he says, "stretcheth out her arms to embrace man." Emerson claims that the "moral law lies at the centre of nature and radiates to the circumference," and adds that "every natural process is a version of a moral sentence." Finally, he assures his readers that the "aspect of nature is devout. Like the figure of Jesus, she stands with bended head, and arms folded upon the breast." The greatest happiness, he claims, is to learn from nature "the lesson of worship."[32]

Emerson insisted that civilization and attention to the past are impediments to human contact with nature. His emotional rendering of man's highest possible religious experience is replete with warnings: country life is to be preferred to "the artificial ... life of cities," but the greatest danger, he claims, lurks within. He writes: "man and nature are indissolubly joined," but the "presence of Reason mars this faith."[33] Danger also comes from tradition. He asks why we should not "enjoy an original relation to the universe ... a religion by revelation to us?" Emerson claims that the teachings of most churches put "an affront upon nature," and "the most ignorant sects" tell people to condemn "the unsubstantial shows of the world" and to seek "the realities of religion." The devotees of such sects, he argues, "flout nature."[34]

The optimism of Emerson and his followers seemed to have no limits. Thoreau speaks of the "indescribable innocence and beneficence of Nature," and describes White Pond and Walden as "great crystals on the surface of earth, Lakes of Light."[35] Whitman's advice to future American writers is that nature "must furnish the pervading atmosphere to poems," not "the smooth walks, trimm'd hedges, poseys and nightingales of the English poets, but the whole orb ... the kosmos."[36] With a serious belief in a beneficent nature that cared for mankind and in human inhabitants who were innately good, that Garden of Eden idea was taken very seriously.[37]

Emerson and his followers were preaching heresy. Christian theology — Catholic or Protestant — could never accept the idea that nature might be substituted for the Bible as the voice of God. Emerson's ideas, however, were widely embraced by the majority of Americans, who seemed unaware of any conflict. Miller notes that nature had somehow "effactually taken the place of the Bible," yet what he found astonishing is that "most of the ardent celebrators of natural America serenely continued to be professing Christians."[38] Pantheism has been a recurrent heresy in the history of Christianity. De Tocqueville found it in the United States and warned that all should "struggle and combine" against it. He states that "[a]mong the different systems by whose aid Philosophy endeavours to explain the Universe, I believe pantheism to be one of those most fitted to seduce the human mind in democratic ages."[39]

That nature taught moral lessons and had emotions that caused it to care for humans were other Romantic ideas that could not stand the test of time or reason. Thoreau claims that the world has such sympathy with our race that "all Nature would be affected and the sun's brightness fade, and the winds would sigh humanely, and the clouds rain tears, and the woods shed their leaves and put on mourning in midsummer, if any man should ever for a just cause grieve." [40] This is romance run rampant; outlandish sentiments that tend to separate humans from nature and to cast them in the role of destroyer. John Ruskin (1819–1900) condemned the practice of attributing human emotions to nature and labeled it the pathetic fallacy.

Americans may not have been disturbed by the Christian paradox, but they were troubled by the rapid destruction of nature, for America's vaunted superiority over Europe, with its moldering old institutions, was based on this great gift of nature. When Thoreau wrote that nature "flourishes most alone, far from the towns,"[41] he opened a national wound that bleeds to this day.

There were some voices raised in protest against this faith in nature's benevolence. Hawthorne was doubtful; sin and its consequences were all too real to him. Melville struggled against optimism in *Moby Dick* (1851) and *Pierre* (1852), and as a result he lost his public. A reaction against the Emersonian position was inevitable. An important tentative reaction came from Emily Dickinson who practiced a degree of solitude unimagined by Thoreau. Dickinson spent her life in the Connecticut Valley, where Puritanism remained strong and continued to try to counter the heresies of Unitarianism and Transcendentalism.

Dickinson grew up during the antebellum period and completed her major works around the time of the Civil War. She admired Emerson and found the world of the Transcendentalists enticing, but her Calvinist heritage was stronger. As Alfred Kazin has made clear, God was never in nature for her; He was a "distant stately lover."[42] She never doubted the existence of God and her major poems deal with death and immortality. Allen Tate, who calls Emerson "the Lucifer of Concord" because he discredited the Puritan drama of the soul, compares Dickinson to the seventeenth-century poet John Donne because of her "morbid concern" with "personal revelation."[43] God seems overwhelmingly vast and inscrutable in lines such as: "Infinitude — Had'st Thou no Face / That I might look on Thee?"[44]

Ivor Winters chose three poems to be Dickinson's finest, all of which reveal an intimate link between nature and death or despair.[45] Here is Winter's first choice:

> There's a certain Slant of light,
> Winter Afternoons —
> That oppresses, like the Heft
> Of Cathedral Tunes ...
> Tis the Seal Despair ...
> Sent us of the Air —
> When it comes, the Landscape listens —
> Shadows — hold their breath —
> When it goes, 'tis like the Distance
> On the look of Death — [46]

His second choice, "A light exists in Spring," suggests that nature at its most hopeful and life affirming is brief and transitory. The third, "As imperceptibly as Grief," has a flow and style that matches the author's sorrows.[47] The cries of pain that resound through the poems of Emily Dickinson are like a prelude to the anger and frustration that began to appear in major American writings after the Civil War. American authors who had accepted the exalted status and grandiose expectations that accompanied the birth and early years of the nation were beginning to find reality a bitter disappointment.

The one indestructible heritage left by the Transcendentalists was an irreconcilable difference between nature and civilization. If the Civil War took much of the benevolence out of nature, it did not turn nature into a dangerous force. The gentle features of Leatherstocking's wilderness are repeated in the river of *Huckleberry Finn*, where the travelers never suffer from cold, insect bites, or hunger. Nature as a threat to mankind is almost unknown in American literature; it is humanity that threatens nature.

Four major American writers came of age during the Civil War: Henry James, William Dean Howells, Henry Adams, and Mark Twain. According to Miller, these four were "intuitively determined to declare unrelenting war on the deification of Nature, [and] to turn from the wilderness to the city."[48] Mark Twain did not attempt to enliven cities, for organized society was a horror to him, so nature is more a refuge than something blessed by the Almighty.

The late nineteenth century saw the rapid movement of the frontier to the Pacific coast. It was during this period that hatred of the Native reached its peak. The concept of Manifest Destiny made it possible for much of the populace to whitewash genocide. Horace Greeley, founder and publisher of the *New York Tribune*, made a trip across the continent in 1859 and published his impressions the following year. He learned to appreciate the "dislike, aversion, contempt, wherewith Indians are usually regarded by their white neighbors" and declares that these "people must die out — there is no help for them. God has given this earth to those who will subdue and cultivate it, and it is vain to struggle against His righteous decree."[49]

Henry Adams led the twentieth-century American outrage over civilization's destruction of nature. Adams, a historian, claims that he had an eighteenth-century education where "God was a father and nature a mother, and all was for the best in a scientific universe." As technology advanced in the late nineteenth century, Adams became interested in science, tried to understand the second law of thermodynamics, and became nearly hysterical about science releasing too much power from nature. "Power leaped from every atom," he says, with enough of it to "supply the stellar universe ... running to waste." The "new American," he adds, is "the child of incalculable" power, and "must be a sort of God compared with any former creation of nature." His despair led him to the conclusion that "Chaos was the law of nature; Order was the dream of man." Adams' message is that man is the culprit; by releasing all of this power he is about to destroy himself and nature too.[50] Miller claims that "only an American" could have written *The Education of Henry Adams*, and adds that "it had to be an American" who wrote "that tremendous revival sermon, [T.S. Eliot's] *The Waste Land*."[51]

In spite of the fact that Eliot (1888–1965) was born and raised in St. Louis, Missouri, that he settled in London in 1915, and that he became a British citizen in 1928, he had roots in New England as deep as Adams'. A scion of the New England Eliots, he was educated at Harvard and steeped in the tradition of that notable corner of the United States. *The Waste Land* professes to depict the condition of Europe at the end of World War I, but the many images of a destroyed nature suggest the most bitterly disillusioned of Americans. His poetry is a complete rejection of Emersonion ideas and the crashing failure of an unrealized ideal. Lines such as "What are the roots that clutch, what branches grow / Out of this stony rubbish? Son of man, / You cannot say, or guess, for you know only / A heap of broken images, where the sun beats, / And the dead tree gives no shelter."[52] In "The Dry Salvages" (1941), Eliot uses the coast of New England as his setting:

> Where is there an end of it, the soundless wailing,
> The silent withering of autumn flowers
> Dropping their petals and remaining motionless;
> Where is there an end to the drifting wreckage,
> The prayer of the bone on the beach, the unprayable
> Prayer at the calamitous annunciation?[53]

Kazin argues that everything in Eliot's poetry goes "back to America."[54]

Adams and Eliot were ahead of their time, both in the intensity of their outrage and in the images used to express it. Mainstream writers in the United States tended to concentrate on the destruction of nature by industry and technology. Leo Marx claims that "it is difficult to think of a major American writer upon whom the image of the machine's sudden appearance in the landscape has not exercised its fascination."[55] In the nineteenth century, the typical scene was the sudden arrival of a railroad train in a pastoral setting. Hawthorne, Thoreau, and Dickinson, among others, made notable use of this image.[56] By the 1920s, when cynicism had entered the imaginations of so many of America's writers, the theme became more complex.

F. Scott Fitzgerald's *The Great Gatsby* (1925) treats nature as either man-made or destroyed and offers a pastoral vision as an indestructible illusion. Nick Carraway, the narrator, who has come to New York from the Mid-west, encounters an American innocent in his next-door neighbor, Jay Gatsby. Gatsby tells Nick the story of his made-up self: a young man born to wealth who went to Oxford and lived like a young rajah in order to persuade Nick to arrange a meeting between him and Daisy Buchanan, a woman for whom he had yearned for five years. Gatsby's story is false and his monstrous house and possessions grossly ostentatious, but he is convinced that he can win Daisy from her playboy husband and realize his dream. Nick gathers that "he wanted to recover something, some idea of himself perhaps, that had gone into loving Daisy." Daisy is a bored and spoiled rich girl, but Gatsby sees her as the incarnation of beauty and innocence. He is an incurable romantic, who has surrounded himself with the artificial. His house is "a factual imitation of some Hôtel de Ville in Normandy, with a tower on one side, spanking new under a thin beard of raw ivy, and a marble swimming pool, and more than forty acres of lawn and garden." Gatsby holds elaborate parties where people come and go "like moths," and, rather than a train invading a forest, "two motor-boats slit the waters of the Sound, drawing aquaplanes over cataracts of foam."[57]

Destroyed nature in *The Great Gatsby* is the "valley of ashes," which both road and railway pass on the way to New York City. This is "a fantastic farm where ashes grow like wheat into ridges and hills and grotesque gardens." Another variation of the "train in the garden" image occurs here: "Occasionally a line of gray cars crawls along an invisible track, gives out a ghastly creak, and comes to rest." Immediately, "ash-gray men swarm up with leaden spades and stir up an impenetrable cloud." This hellish scene is witnessed by an artificial god or the ominous face of "man the destroyer." On a billboard advertisement, the "eyes of Doctor T.J. Eckleburg," which are "blue and gigantic," look out from "enormous yellow spectacles which pass over a non-existent nose."[58] Leo Marx has noted that glimpses of this scene — "the material and human detritus of industrial society" — are fleeting but crucial to the novel, for the "valley of ashes" can have no place in Gatsby's "green vision of America."[59]

Although Gatsby is unable to pass from innocence to experience, Nick Carraway does. As he interacts with Gatsby, the Buchanans, and their decadent friends, he learns to recognize the connection between Gatsby's longing for Daisy, symbolized by a green light at the end of her dock, with the American Dream, the "fresh, green breast of the new world" that had "flowered once for Dutch sailors' eyes." The trees that disappeared to make way for Gatsby's house "had once pandered in whispers to the last and greatest of all human dreams."[60] Marx claims to know of no "work of literature that invests an image of landscape with greater significance."[61] Stripped of its irony, this image could have been expressed by Emerson. Fitzgerald ends his novel with an assertion that the dream is unrealizable yet indestructible. "It eluded us then, but that's no matter — tomorrow we will run faster, stretch out our arms farther ... And one fine morning — So we beat on, boats against the current, borne back ceaselessly into the past."[62] The past is generally a very bad place for an American to be borne to, yet in this novel it is where Gatsby yearns to be, the realization of his five-year-old dream. Unfortunately he is found murdered in his marble pool, and the unconcerned Buchanans carry on with their careless lives.

William Faulkner's story "The Bear" — originally part of the novel, *Go Down Moses* (1942) — was reworked a number of times, finally appearing in an abbreviated form in *Big Woods* (1955). The original story is told in five parts; four of them have a straightforward narrative style and the fifth consists of a complex dialogue between the protagonist, Isaac McCaslin, and his cousin. This dialogue centers on the family history and the relationship between the White and Black descendants of Ike's grandfather, old Carothers McCaslin. Ike explains why he will refuse his inheritance, the plantation that is willed to him: "Don't you see? This whole land, the whole south, is cursed," and all who descend from it, whom it ever nursed, "white and black both, lie under the curse?" Ike continues his impassioned speech on the South, where God "had done so much with woods for game and streams for fish and deep rich soil for seed" and then saw the rich descendants of slave owners passing resolutions about "horror and outrage." This section gives a depth of meaning to "The Bear" that is lacking in the more unified four-part story.[63]

The story takes place in the wilderness, the "big woods, bigger and older than any recorded document" where Ike is taken as a ten-year-old boy. By the age of sixteen, he is a "man's hunter" in a wilderness that is being chipped away by civilization. The man who leads the hunters, who knows the woods, is Sam Fathers, son of a slave and a Native chief. He has been a great teacher to Ike, who calls him "the chief, the prince," yet Sam is forced to live as a "Negro." The bear of the title, Old Ben, is a symbol of the shrinking wilderness. He has ravaged the surrounding farms for many years, has a trap-damaged foot and much buckshot in his body, but has survived all attempts to kill him.[64]

The hunt for Old Ben is a yearly ritual. Ike longs to see the bear, but Sam informs him that Old Ben will not reveal himself until all trappings of civilization are left behind. Sam assures the boy that nature is no danger to him: "Don't be afraid," he says, "nothing in the woods going to hurt you" unless you "corner it" or it smells that you are "afraid."[65] Ike spends a long day without his gun, but, only after he discards his compass, his watch, and even the stick used for killing snakes, does the bear appear to him. When Old Ben is finally killed, Sam Fathers dies mysteriously, as though his life was tied to this symbol of uncorrupted nature.

The death of the bear and Sam signals the end of the wilderness. Ike goes back to the hunters' camp "one more time" before the lumber company moves in and begins to "cut the timber." He rides in the log-train caboose and watches the train's head "vanish into the wilderness, dragging its length of train behind it." To Ike the train resembles "a small dingy harmless snake" that is passing between the walls of "unaxed wilderness." There is much irony in Ike's belief that the snake is "harmless," for it is another image of a machine invading and destroying nature.[66]

Images of nature destroyed pervade contemporary American literature, underlying almost all urban fiction, with its excessive violence and urban decay, and road novels, with their abundant billboards, gas stations, and hot dog stands. Thomas Pynchon, for example, borrows his idea of nature accelerating out of control and yet governed by an impersonal force from Henry Adams.[67] Pynchon, like Adams, has roots among the New England Puritans.[68] This part of the United States, which produced Emerson and his followers, also reacted with particular outrage over the destruction or apparent failure of the American Dream.[69]

Pynchon's *The Crying of Lot 49* (1966) takes the reader into "the plastic megalopolis" of California, and gives cynical expression to attempts by industry to reconstruct natural settings.[70] The heroine — with the significant name of Oedipa Maas — has been named co-executor of the estate of her former lover, Pierce Inverarity, a "real estate mogul who had once lost two million dollars in his spare time but still had assets numerous and tangled enough to make the job of sorting it all out more than honorary."[71] Oedipa is launched on a pilgrimage to discover the truth about the Inverarity holdings. She never finds an answer, but as she picks up clues about a mysterious and threatening communications system, she moves deeper into what may be considered more anti-nature than destroyed nature. The ambiguous communication system is called Trystero, has a muted post horn as a symbol, and uses the acronym W.A.S.T.E. The reference to "waste" recalls Henry Adams.

Oedipa — who sees herself as Rapunzel imprisoned in a tower — encounters her first ominous image before she has even begun her task as executor. She looks down from an expressway "onto a vast sprawl of houses which had grown up altogether, like a well-tended crop ... The ordered swirl of houses and streets, from this high angle, sprang at her." After an ominous beginning, she and her co-executor decide to visit one of the company projects, a place called Fangoso Lagoons. As they drive by "three-bedroom houses rushing by the thousands across all the dark beige hills," Oedipa recalls that she had long believed "in some principle of the sea as redemption for Southern California ... some unvoiced idea that no matter what you did to its edges the true Pacific stayed inviolate." At Fangoso Lagoons they find "earth-moving machines," a "total absence of trees," and a "sculptured body of water." In the middle of the water is a "round island of fill," and on it "squatted the social hall, a chunky, ogived and verdigrised, Art Nouveau reconstruction of some European pleasure-casino."[72] Oedipa never moves far from the redemptive Pacific, but her searches become increasingly horrifying. Harold Bloom speaks of her "vivid descent into the night world of San Francisco," for there is no redemption from the sea or nature in any other form.[73]

By the end of the novel, Oedipa finds herself alone; everyone who might have helped or comforted her has disappeared, died, become addicted to drugs, or gone insane. "She had dedicated herself, weeks ago, to making sense of what Inverarity had left behind, never suspecting that the legacy was America."[74]

Writers such as Pynchon depict an American hell, completely at odds with the heaven of the Transcendentalists. Disillusionment continues to plague the American literary scene, and the images used of destroyed or parodied nature are legion. At the end of the twentieth century most American urban novels at least imply that humans have been guilty of the destruction of nature.

Don DeLillo's novel *Underworld* (1997), with its multiplicity of characters and action covering the second half of the twentieth century, depicts Americans as mass producers of waste. Although much of the action takes place in the desert, there are numerous inner city scenes. Brian Glassic, who works with the protagonist Nick Shay at Waste Containment, visits New York in order to see a "man-made" island. It is "[t]hree thousand acres of mountained garbage, contoured and road-graded, with bulldozers pushing waves of refuse onto the active face." Brian "imagined he was watching the construction of the Great Pyramid at Giza—only this was twenty-five times bigger." DeLillo deals in all types of waste in this novel, from the human waste that modern man often makes of his life to nuclear or other kinds of toxic waste. Matt Shay, a nuclear engineer working in "the Pocket" in New Mexico, is driving with his girl friend when an explosion occurs. They had driven too close to a test site and are "speechless in the wake of a power and thrust snatched from nature's own greatness, or how men bend heaven to their methods." Henry Adams would have thought himself vindicated.[75]

Underworld opens at a New York stadium in October 1951, where the New York Giants win the pennant in a surprise upset. Two types of waste are introduced at this game. Ecstatic fans of the winning Giants throw debris onto the field: "crushed cigarette packs and sticky wrap from ice-cream sandwiches, pages from memo pads and pocket calendars"; this is "happy garbage," by-products of consumerism, that show "the fans' intimate wish to be connected to the event." One of the fans, J. Edgar Hoover of the FBI, receives news of the Soviet's successful detonation of an atomic bomb. Another kind of waste has been spewed into the air, and the Cold War has begun.[76]

Waste disposal is as central to the novel as waste production. The most creative recycling is done by Klara Sax, called "the Bag-Lady," who turns junk into works of art.[77] Her last project is to paint old B-52s from World War II. She and a team of volunteers are creating this massive work of art in the middle of the desert. At the opposite extreme, is a different kind of waste disposal. In Kazakhstan, a Soviet company, Tchaika, disposes of dangerous waste in underground nuclear explosions; the more dangerous the waste, the higher the price.

At a conference in the desert, Nick Shay and an acquaintance come upon a new landfill site. The "enormous gouged bowl lined with artful plastic" is the first sign Nick had that "this was a business of a certain drastic grandeur, even a kind of greatness." He listens to "Sims recite the numbers, how much methane we would recover to light how many homes." Nick turns facetious: "I'll tell you what I see here, Sims. The scenery of the future ... The more toxic the waste, the greater the effort and expense a tourist will be willing to tolerate in order to visit the site ... Make an architecture of waste." Sims is not sure he likes the idea.[78]

The first sentence in the novel — "He speaks in your voice, American..." — assures the reader that this is a novel on American culture. Jennifer Pincott speaks of an "underworld of detritus,"[79] yet the novel is historical and does not appear to be a polemic. *Underworld* is like a closure to the twentieth century, a sense that life goes on and Americans may yet find ways of reconciling modern life with the natural world.

3

Omnipresent Nature in Canada

Since the beginning of settlement in New France,[80] nature has been an awe-inspiring and dangerous presence in Canada, never absent from the minds of the people. The many written and visual depictions of natural beauty and grandeur have not implied — as American literature and art have — that the land was a garden or that it could ever be tamed. No matter how much sublimity appears in American art works, they can usually be distinguished from the mainstream of Canadian art, where the most lauded painters — such as Lawren Harris and Emily Carr — depict a nature that appears indestructible, sending a message that this land cannot be conquered.

The geographical distinctness of Canada — the east-west river systems, the natural and permanent northern frontier, and arable land only outside of the Canadian Shield — has made nature a demanding partner from the beginning. Also, Natives — trading partners who could teach survival techniques — inject a powerful sense of past to the land. The fundamental lesson taught by the Native peoples was that man is a part of nature. Such a simple deduction has always been difficult for Christians to comprehend, but Canadians necessarily reconciled it with their religious faiths, much as Americans kept their Christian faith in some sort of harmony with Emersonian pantheism.

Two important early Canadian writers are Catharine Parr Traill and her younger sister Susanna Moodie, who came from a family of English writers, the Stricklands. They were part of a larger group of upper-class British immigrants, accustomed to the world of Jane Austen and steeped in the poetry of Wordsworth. Both immigrated to Upper Canada in the 1830s and published accounts of their experiences of pioneer living. Traill's *The Backwoods of Canada* (1836) is a series of letters she wrote to relatives and friends in England, while Moodie's emotional memoir, *Roughing it in the Bush* (1852), generally preferred by literary scholars, approaches fiction. Both books describe scenes of grandeur as seen from ships ascending the St. Lawrence River. Moodie's Wordsworthian eyes were "blinded [with tears] by the excess of beauty" she saw at Quebec City, with its surrounding forest, islands, and river. "Nature had lavished all her grandest elements to form this astonishing panorama," she writes.[81] Both families received warnings of severe hardships ahead. Traill recounts an ominous incident: when her husband remarks about "the picturesque appearance of the scene" before them to an officer who had come on board, the officer replies sadly, "[b]elieve me, in this instance, as in many others, 'tis distance lends enchantment to the view."[82]

The Traills and the Moodies experienced nature in Canada, and nature defeated them. They suffered from cold, fires, broken limbs with no doctor available, accidental loss of livestock, and, fairly often, a shortage of food. Too old and genteel to endure the harsh life of the bush pioneer, both eventually settled in towns. Perhaps the least of their hardships was the recognition that any attention to beauty in their woodland homes was an unaffordable luxury. Traveling by wagon to their property, Traill saw smiles on the lips of her fellow travelers when they heard of her "plans for the adornment" of their future dwelling. She had hoped to have some trees around their home, but discovered that the forest trees are not suitable as lawn ornaments and that the easiest and most effective means of clearing the land was by fire. Although she finds it a "magnificent sight to see the blazing trees and watch the awful progress of the conflagration," it left "such scorched mementoes" that "the forest growth" was blasted for years.[83] Traill did not allow such harsh beginnings to destroy her love of nature. She studied botanical specimens and wrote important works on Canadian wildflowers.[84]

Moodie was so wretched in her forest home that her "love for Canada" turned into "a feeling very nearly allied to that which the condemned criminal entertains for his cell." In spite of the series of natural disasters that struck both families, there were some pleasures, including friendships with nearby Natives. Traill recounts two visits that included some small-scale trading and hymn singing, after which she was taken home in a canoe, paddled by the strong arms of a Native woman. Moodie "met them with confidence," and claims never to have met a people "more sensible of kindness," who "in no single instance ever destroyed the good opinion we entertained of them."[85] Such casual neighborliness between Natives and whites would be difficult to find in American literature of the time.

After seven years in the bush, Moodie's husband secured the position of county sheriff, and the Moodies settled in the town of Belleville. Such comfort allowed her to return to the Wordsworthian Romanticism she had brought from England. In *Life in the Clearings* (1853), she describes a boat trip to Niagara Falls: "Next to the love of God, the love of nature may be regarded as the purest and holiest feeling of the human breast. In the outward beauty of his creation, we catch a reflection of the divine image of the Creator." She invites the reader to take a seat with her on the deck of the steamer: "[A]s we glide over the water of this beautiful Bay of Quinte, I will make you acquainted with every spot worthy of note along its picturesque shores."[86]

Traill and Moodie were writing and publishing at the same time as Thoreau, and their woodland homes were not too distant from Walden Pond nor markedly different in climate. The distinction, of course, is that Thoreau had the good fortune to enjoy a patch of wilderness surrounded by a civilization to which he had easy access. Thoreau would have been horrified at the idea of burning trees; Traill and Moodie, on the other hand, faced the necessity of destroying part of nature in order to create conditions in which they could live. This seemingly simple distinction between pioneer and settled conditions pervades the literature of the two countries. Traill and Moodie are two of Canada's most important early women writers.

In nineteenth-century Canadian narrative poetry, descriptions of natural beauty are interspersed with stories of death or near death from cold or accidents. Most are formulaic in their depictions of local settings and situations and follow British literary fashions. There is much attention to generalized grandeur, as was common among writers in the Romantic era.

A reach toward something more original and identifiably Canadian can be found in Isabella Valancy Crawford's narrative poem, *Malcolm's Katie* (1884). It tells the love story of Max, a poor woodsman, and Katie, the only child of Malcolm, a successful farmer and devoted father. The villain, Alfred, longs for Malcolm's wealth but, unable to win Katie's hand, tries to destroy Max and persuade Katie that her love is dead. The imagery in the poem drifts toward tragedy, but the author wrestles the storyline into a happy ending and a final comparison of their woodland home to the Garden of Eden.

In his introduction to a collection of nineteenth-century Canadian narrative poems, David Sinclair writes that "pioneering" is a central theme, "the breaking and settling of the land."[87] In Crawford's poem, Max works with other woodsmen: "the axe stirred waste / In these new days men spread about the earth / with wings at heel .... So shanties grew / Other than his amid the blacken'd stumps." These hard-working and driven people have one overriding incentive: "The lab'rer with train'd muscles, grim and grave, / Look'd at the ground and wonder'd in his soul? What joyous anguish stirr'd his darken'd heart / ... And found his answer in the words, '*Mine own*.'" This does not sound much like de Crèvecoeur gladly clearing his land.[88]

There is much beautiful lyric verse in this poem, with almost an excess of nature images and similes. One feature that raises it above the work of Crawford's contemporaries is the way she has used Native imagery to vivify the coming of a Canadian winter. Native peoples are treated as a part of nature, neither Rousseau's noble savages nor Cooper's good Indians/bad Indians:

> The South Wind crept on moccasins of flame. ...
> Struck maple and struck sumach, and a blaze
> Ran swift from leaf to leaf, from bough to bough,
> Til round the forest flash'd a belt of flame. ...
> From his far wigwam sprang the strong North Wind
> And rush'd with war-cry down the steep ravines. ...
> "Oh, my white squaw, come from thy wigwam grey;
> Spread thy white blanket on the twice-slain dead,
> And hide them, ere the waking of the Sun!"
> High grew the snow beneath the low-hung sky,
> And all was silent in the Wilderness.[89]

"Malcolm's Katie" anticipates the animal stories of Charles G.D. Roberts (1860–1945) and Ernest Thompson Seton (1860–1946) in its depiction of nature "red in tooth and claw." For example: "an eagle with / His angry eyes set sunward ... / And his bald eaglets, in their bare, broad nest, / Shrill pipe their angry echoes: 'Sun, arise, / And show me that pale dove beside her nest, / Which I shall strike with piercing beak and tear / With iron talons for my hungry young'."[90] An Edenic ending hardly suits this majestic poem. Crawford died in her mid-thirties, never able to develop her promising literary talent.

The animal stories of Roberts and Seton are landmarks in Canadian writing. Animal stories were popular around the turn of the century,[91] but the stories of Roberts and Seton are distinctively Canadian and the beginning of a nature writing free of Wordsworthian Romanticism. The two men were contemporaries whose works differ primarily in tone. Seton was a scientist and naturalist and Roberts a literary artist, but both strove to treat animals as animals, not as disguised humans, to avoid emotion and sentimentality, and to suggest an ordered pattern in the amorality of the natural world. Humans are usually classified by occupation — that is, as hunter, trapper, settler, or "the boy" — and are representatives of their species. These stories are strongly Darwinian.

Roberts' "The Young Ravens that Call upon Him" (1907) recalls "Malcolm's Katie." Two adult eagles who are feeding nestlings have had trouble finding food and are "racked with hunger." On a nearby hill, a ewe, having fallen behind the flock when she stopped to give birth during the night, is trying to urge the tiny lamb to move, when there comes "a terrible hissing rush out of the sky." A "great form" falls upon the lamb and the eagle rises, clutching the lamb in his talons, while the ewe runs beneath uttering "piteous cries." Later, the family of eagles rests contentedly in the sun, the "pain of their hunger appeased." Nearby, "hither and thither over the round bleak hill" wanders the ewe, "calling for her lamb."[92] In these stories nature is a surrounding force, not something on a frontier with the safety of civilization behind and a benevolent nature ahead.[93] Traditionally, in Canadian literature, consciousness of danger is deemed necessary for survival.

Seton refers to animals caught in traps when he ends his book, *Wild Animals I Have Known* (1898), with the poignant questions: "Have the wild things no moral or legal rights? What right has man to inflict such long and fearful agony on a fellow-creature?"[94] This plea to humans to remember their place in nature and not to play God with the animal kingdom was ahead of its time. Roberts' and Seton's nameless treatment of their human characters highlights the lesson of the Native peoples, that mankind is an integral part of the natural world.

Louis Hémon's novel *Maria Chapdelaine* (1914) demonstrates how awed the author was by the harsh life and unforgiving nature in the northern fringes of settlement in Quebec. He had come from France, had spent months studying the life and habits of the French-Canadian farmer, but, sadly, was killed by a train before his book was published. The novel became famous throughout the world after it was translated into English in 1921, and is now a Canadian classic. Sir Wilfrid Laurier, Canadian prime minister from 1896 to 1911, suggested that his countrymen were "painted with too dark a brush," but W.H. Blake says critics generally agree that the novel "gives an incomparably true and beautiful picture of the French-Canadian peasant."[95]

Maria Chapdelaine opens in a small town in Quebec. The surroundings betray a "harsh existence in a stern land," with the "gloomy forest edging so close that it seemed to threaten." The Chapdelaine family lives on a primitive farm, many miles into the bush in a sterner and even more threatening setting. It is April, and the ground is still covered with snow. As Maria and her father return home, their sleigh cracks the ice and they narrowly escape a cold and watery death, foreshadowing a later attempt to defy nature. The mother regrets her husband's taste for "moving, and pushing on and on into the woods, and not for living on a farm in one of the old parishes." She throws "a melancholy glance over the scanty cleared fields behind the house, the barn built of ill-joined planks that showed marks of fire, and the land beyond still covered with stumps and encompassed by the forest."[96]

Maria falls in love with a young man who is a true pioneer. He has sold his father's farm and taken up a life as trapper, woodsman, and explorer. On a visit to the Chapdelaines, he tells about his good relations with the Native peoples, who once saved his father's life. The father asked them to visit after his recovery. When they did, "every one carried away a new ax, a fine woolen blanket and tobacco for six months." Each year after that his father "had the pick of their best skins," and when his father died, they trained him in the same way, "because I was his son and bore the same name, François Paradis." On a second visit, François and Maria exchange vows.[97]

At Christmas, François leaves the lumber camp where he is working to visit Maria, becomes lost in the bush, and freezes to death. Maria's father comments on the sadness of the young man's death, for he was "one of the best men of these parts in the woods," although he took a foolhardy risk: "Some there be who think themselves pretty strong — able to get on without God's help in their houses and on their lands … but in the bush." Maria steps outside to try to hide her grief, but "the cold smote her like the hungry blade of a sword and the forest leaped toward her in menace."[98]

Eventually Maria agrees to marry a neighboring farmer, although she has no illusions about the life she faces — one of unending labor. During her brief rests, she will be able to look only on "their scant fields girt by the eternally frowning woods." Always, she thinks sadly, "the inscrutable, inimical forest" will be "closed round them with a savage grip that must be loosened little by little, year by year."[99] Traill and Moodie, earlier arrivals from the Old World, found more beauty and less danger in the Canadian forests than Hémon, but all three agreed that nature in Canada is an awe-inspiring force, not at all like the benign nature still being celebrated in nearby New England.

E.J. Pratt's first collection of poems, *Newfoundland Verse* (1924), and his long narrative poem, *The Roosevelt and the Antinoe* (1930), stress encounters between humans and the elements on or near the coast of Newfoundland. His poem "The Cachelot" (1926) is about an encounter between a giant whale and a whaling vessel. Pratt almost certainly had Melville in mind, but he put a distinctly Canadian stamp on his poem; it is told from the point of view of the whale. Beginning with the whale's ancestors, who "Established the Mammalian lead: / The founder (in cetacean lore) / Had followed Leif to Labrador," the poem continues discussing the size and life of the great sperm whale. An encounter with a giant squid is described: "No Titan with Olympian god / Had ever waged a fiercer fight; / Tail and skull and teeth and maw / Met sinew, cartilage, and claw." Eventually, the whale meets the "*Albatross*," that is captained by "a master-whaler— / New England's pride was Martin Taylor." The attack on the whale proceeds much like the attack in *Moby Dick*; boats are launched, each one led by captain or mate, and each sending its harpoons into the body of the whale. Finally, the Captain's harpoon pierces the heart muscle and the dying whale heads for the ship:

> Made for the port bow of the ship.
> All the tonnage, all the speed,
> All the courage of his breed, ...
> Halliard and shroud and trestle-cheek,
> Of yard and topsail to the last
> Dank flutter of the ensign as a wave
> Closed in upon the skysail peak,

Followed the Monarch to his grave.[100]

W.O. Mitchell's *Who Has Seen the Wind* (1947) has an introductory paragraph that tells the reader that this is "the story of a boy and the wind." Brian O'Connal, age four at the beginning and a much wiser eleven at the end, lives in a prairie town in Saskatchewan during the drought and depression of the 1930s. Nature surrounds and controls an island of civilization. He has an inquiring mind and strange feelings that puzzle him, but seem to be linked to the life cycle. These feelings are particularly strong when an animal dies or when he wanders on the prairie. In Brian's mind "there loomed vaguely fearful images of a still and brooding spirit, a quiescent power unsmiling from everlasting to everlasting to which the coming and passing of the prairie's creatures was but incidental." When his father dies unexpectedly Brian finds that he is unable to cry, until he walks out onto the prairie and listens to the wind: "A forever-and-forever sound it had … Forever for the prairie; never for his father — never again." He thinks of the "dark well of his mother's loneliness" and tastes the salt tears on his cheek. The song of a meadowlark breaks the spell and Brian turns toward home.[101]

In his first year in school Brian is excessively punished by a rigid teacher. Lying in bed that night he listens to "a rising wind … He felt a gathering Presence in his room as the wind lifted high, and higher still, keening and keening again, to die away and be born once more while the sad hum of the weather stripping lingered on in the silence."[102] Brian screams in terror and the next day his mother visits the teacher.

The town has a government building, truancy laws, and cement sidewalks, but ends abruptly at the edge of the prairie. A new teacher comes to town who is sensitive to the children, particularly those who are outside the social core like two Chinese children and Young Ben, son of the town drunk and a creature of the prairie who is like a caged animal in school. Except for his aversion to school, Young Ben is not like Huckleberry Finn. He defends Brian against the abusive teacher, helps bury Brian's dog that has been accidentally killed, and severely beats another boy for torturing a gopher. Young Ben is a loner, nobody's playmate, but something resembling a friendship grows between him and Brian, who senses that the prairie boy is related to the mysterious life-and-death forces that trouble him.

The people of the prairie are much closer to nature than the townspeople. The Bens are said to be "as naked of right and wrong as … the sun cracking the face of the prairie." Saint Sammy, who owns some valuable horses but chooses to live in a piano box and hold conversations with the Lord, has "gone crazy from the prairie." The most significant prairie dweller is Brian's farmer uncle, Sean O'Connal. Sean is uneducated but wise, is experimenting with irrigation and planting techniques, and is elated when he hears that Brian has been writing school papers on agriculture and aspires to be a "dirt doctor." He tells Brian's mother to send him out to the farm next summer. "Be doin' me a favor — have somebody 'round listens to what I say — an' I'll learn him. I'll learn him to be a dirt doctor." *Who Has Seen the Wind* is an essential part of the Canadian canon, written by an author who knew the land he was describing.[103]

Since the 1960s, the theme of nature has remained strong in Canadian literature, in spite of greater urbanization and less sense of nature as something encircling and threatening. Dominique Clift claims that "Canadians have gradually lost their awareness of nature and of the wilderness … But the imprint has remained fixed below the level of consciousness."[104] The realization that Native Canadians are much closer to nature than immigrants and their descendants has come more to the fore, and the world-wide environmental movement has fostered a renewed sense of kinship with the animal world. The works of naturalist writers such as Fred Bodsworth and Farley Mowat broaden the tradition started by Roberts and Seton. Bodsworth and Mowat are more concerned with entire species than with individual animals, but, like Roberts and Seton, they tell many stories from the animal's point of view.

Nature is integral to Mordecai Richler's novel, *Solomon Gursky Was Here* (1989). There are no gardens or crops, for nature in this novel is the arctic, deadly and in no danger from civilization. Richler calls it his most Canadian of novels.[105]

The opening scene is at Lake Memphremagog in Canada East during the terrible winter of 1851. Preceded by a large black raven — the central symbol in the novel — Ephraim Gursky arrives by dog team and builds himself an igloo. The raven is shot by a local man, who is found to have mysteriously hanged himself after Ephraim's departure. Ephraim and his grandson, Solomon, are semi-fantastic characters, who appear and disappear mysteriously and perform astounding feats. Their skills have been honed in the Canadian arctic.

Ephraim, we learn, was the sole survivor of the last Franklin expedition, accomplishing his survival by learning skills from the Inuit, with whom he lived and started a Jewish religious cult — he is the first deity. As an old man of eighty-nine, Ephraim kidnaps Solomon and takes him to the "Far ... north" to learn how to survive. It is assumed that Ephraim dies among the Inuit, for Solomon is forced to find his way home alone.[106]

The central symbol of the raven — the trickster of Haida legend — is repeated as a black Gypsy Moth, piloted by Solomon. Solomon is the better side of Ephraim; his brother, Bernard, the dark side, the "shifty little Jew" stereotype that Richler took such glee in creating. Bernie is skeptical of most of Solomon's tales about his trek to the Polar Sea with his grandfather, but realizes that Solomon has since been blessed with "a certain grace, an inner stillness." He is jealous of his brother, realizing that "he would have to scratch and bite and cheat to get what he wanted out of life ... but that Solomon would sit, expecting the world to come to him, and he would be served."[107]

Bernie's bitterness that Solomon is "Ephraim's anointed one" is nursed over the years and when the opportunity to trap Solomon arises he takes it. The Gurskys have been pursued for years by a junior official, whom Bernie once tried to bribe. When the case comes to trial, the judge tells Bernie that there must be a victim. Solomon can see that a surprise witness, prepared to perjure himself, is coming. It is reported that there was a terrible fight between the brothers that evening and the next morning Solomon takes off in his black Gypsy Moth, refuels in Newfoundland, and takes off again in a whiteout. The wreckage of the plane is found but not the body.

Solomon has a son, Henry, who becomes an orthodox Jew, discovers Ephraim's cult in the arctic, moves to the north and marries an Inuit woman. Henry's son, Isaac, is required to accompany his father on a yearly pilgrimage at Passover. One year "a big menacing black raven" pecking at the window wakes Henry's wife.[108] She sees the raven as an omen and begs him not to go. Henry will not break the tradition. This year, instead of going by dog team, they use snowmobiles that break down. Henry dies, but Isaac survives by eating his father.

Solomon reappears periodically under different names and with different nationalities, but he is officially dead and believed dead by his family. Only

Moses Berger, the narrator and would-be biographer of Solomon, knows better. When Berger — who has had a lifelong fascination with Solomon — starts to write the biography he is interrupted by the sound of a plane buzzing his cabin. He runs outside to see a black Gypsy Moth flying due north.

Solomon Gursky Was Here is Richler's most complex and ambitious novel. It covers one hundred and fifty years and four generations, with a multiplicity of characters and an intricate plot. The novel is a good illustration of Clift's comment about the north staying in the Canadian consciousness in spite of the fact that it is no longer a nearby threat.

Canadians never tire of stories of their northern land, many of them accounts of hubristic individuals who meet defeat at the hands of an unforgiving nature. As Douglas LePan, in his poem "Canoe Trip," says:

> Let whoever comes to tame this land, beware!
> Can you put a bit to the lunging wind?
> Can you hold wild horses by the hair?
> Then have no hope to harness the energy here.[109]

4

Conclusion

Poet Robert Frost (1874–1963) could be called a twentieth-century heir to the Transcendentalists. His devotion to the land and to the United States took a remarkable turn with his famous poem, "The Gift Outright," read at the presidential inauguration of John F. Kennedy in 1961. This commentary on the American Revolution takes an unusual view of the land:

> The land was ours before we were the land's.
> She was our land more than a hundred years
> Before we were her people....
> But we were England's, still colonials,
> Possessing what we still were unpossessed by....
> Something we were withholding made us weak
> Until we found out that it was ourselves
> We were withholding from our land of living,
> And forthwith found salvation in surrender....[110]

Frye claims to have often thought about Frost's line, "The land was ours before we were the land's." However appropriate it may be to the United States, Frye says, it "does not apply to Canada."[111] It is questionable whether Frost's assertion can realistically apply to any one nation, but such sentiments, recalling the deep feelings of the Transcendentalists, tend to counteract the pessimism of many American writers.

Canadian and American attitudes toward nature appear to have come together, as vigorous attempts to preserve ancient forests and endangered species are pursued in both countries. In a sense, this is the opposite of the early nineteenth century romanticizing of nature, also pursued in both countries but with different results. Also, there is a much greater consciousness of the problems confronting Native peoples. Different national approaches to nature tend to be subtle today, the mere residue of past attitudes.

A number of forces should be kept in mind, especially by critics who insist on judging past achievements through the haze of the present zeitgeist. First, the early American concept of the land as a Garden of Eden, its close identification with God, plus a discarding of the past, were powerful influences on America's literary artists. Cooper, Emerson, Thoreau, and Whitman gave expression to an ideology that did not exist in Canada, so could not produce comparable results.

Second, Canadians have something of a mystical feel for the North. As fear of nature weakened, the North became mythologized. It presses "into the Canadian consciousness," according to Kroetsch, who notes a "will toward silence" among Canadian writers. In Kroetsch's view, the painter Tom Tomson is the archetypal Canadian artist, who "lived between south and north" and whose best works are "without people." Kroetsch finds a general leaning toward the North in Canadian literature, a silent and mystical place, and away from the United States, a "world of technocracy ... a world of noise."[112] He also notes that Canadians do not have to go to the North in order to draw sustenance from it, any more than Americans had to go to their frontier when they had one.

The most important result of past attitudes toward nature lies in the depth of guilt and disillusionment found in contemporary American literature. Works by Pynchon, William Burroughs, Robert Coover and others depict the United States as a hell that is at least as exaggerated as the heaven of the Transcendentalists. The disappearance of the frontier completed the conquest of nature and destroyed an early form of the American Dream — no more virgin land. Although politicians still talk of renewing the American Dream, they are referring to material success with only the vaguest implications of a Garden of Eden. There is considerable irony in the assumption that the nation has fallen away from a better past.

Canadians, too, express remorse over past actions. Since the Native peoples were rarely vilified, there was an absence of "Indian wars," and there is a comparatively larger segment of the population of mixed ancestry, the contemporary need to express guilt called for other outlets. Frye's claim that the "main focus of guilt in Canada seems to fall on the rape of nature" is verified by the large body of Canadian literature in which animals are the objects of empathy. [113] As discussed in Chapter II, Natives are often being treated as ancestors. Schäfer argues that in Kroetsch's *Gone Indian* (1973), the protagonist completes "the discovery of the Indian ... in his own person," and Wiebe's *Big Bear* merges the Native "into the Canadian landscape."[114] These works contain sentiments of guilt that are comparatively pallid beside American works seeking to come to terms with attempted genocide.

In the eyes of some American writers, the whole nation is beyond redemption. Canadian literature never depicts the nation as a place that is guilty beyond repair. Such an idea never seems to have occurred to Canada's writers. There is a vague sense of moral superiority in their attitude, reminiscent of the Loyalists looking on the new United States as a "mobocracy."

Notes

1 Beloff, 4.
2 Becker, 37.
3 Beloff, 6.
4 P. Miller, *Nation,* 9.
5 Morton, 4–5.
6 Kroetsch, *Treachery*, 53.
7 Frederick Jackson Turner, *Frontier and Section: Selected Essays of Frederick Jackson Turner* (Englewood Cliffs, NJ: Prentice–Hall, 1961), 38.
8 D.H. Lawrence, *Studies in Classic American Literature* (New York: The Viking Press, 1961), 24.
9 Miller, *Nation*, 159.
10 Bercovitch, *Origins*, 152.
11 Qtd by Miller, *Nation*, 206.
12 Turner, 39.
13 Slotkin, *Fatal Environment*, 34, 39.
14 Frye, *Garden*, 225.
15 Becker, 37.
16 Frye, *Garden*, 225.
17 Mary Lu MacDonald, "The Natural World in Early Nineteenth-Century Canadian Literature," *Canadian Literature* 91 (1981): 49.
18 Edmund Burke, *A Philosophical Enquiry into the Origin of Our Ideas of the Sublime and Beautiful*, ed. J.T. Boulton (Notre Dame: University of Notre Dame Press, 1968), 57.
19 Donna Bennett, "Conflicted Vision: A Consideration of Canon and Genre in English Canadian Literature," *Canadian Canons*, 144.
20 Qtd by Miller, *Nation*, 201.
21 Adams, *1800*, 127.
22 The most famous pairings of light and dark males are Natty and Chingachgook in Cooper's Leatherstocking series, Ishmael and Queequeg in Melville's *Moby*

Dick, and Huck and Jim in Twain's *The Adventures of Huckleberry Finn*. A good example of a late nineteenth century satire of Cooper is Bret Harte's *Muck A Muck: An Indian Novel, after Cooper* (1867).

23 Frye, *Ground*, 68.
24 W.J. Keith, *Charles G.D. Roberts* (Toronto: Copp Clark, 1969), 86.
25 Leslie Fiedler, *The Return of the Vanishing American* (New York: Stein and Day, 1968), 16, 75.
26 MacLulich, 197.
27 Sherril E. Grace, "Comparing Mythologies: Ideas of West and North," *Borderlands: Essays in Canadian-American Relations* (Toronto: ECW Press, 1991), 250.
28 Frye, "Levels," 188.
29 Bercovitch, *Origins*, 108.
30 Hector St. John de Crèvecour, *Letters from an American Farmer* (New York: Fox, Duffield, 1904), 11, 48–49, 55, 79.
31 D.H. Lawrence, *Studies*, 24–5.
32 Emerson, *Emerson*, 5–6, 11, 20, 29.
33 Richard Hofstadter, in his book *Anti-Intellectualism in American Life* (New York: Vintage Books, 1973) 9, notes that Emerson has provided anti-intellectual movements with "a great many texts."
34 Emerson, *Emerson*, 15, 23, 3, 28.
35 Henry David Thoreau, *Walden and Other Writings*, ed. Brooks Atkinson (New York: The Modern Library, 1992), 130, 188.
36 Walt Whitman, *The Complete Poetry and Prose of Walt Whitman,* 2 vols. (New York: Pellegrini and Cudahy, 1948), II: 252.
37 Krista Comer, in her feminist study, *Landscapes of the New West: Gender and Geography in Contemporary Women's Writing* (Chapel Hill: University of North Carolina Press, 1999), 56, claims that "Western places, like women and nature, take care of people."
38 Miller, *Nation*, 202–3.
39 De Tocqueville, II: 36.
40 Thoreau, *Walden*, 130.
41 *Ibid.*, 189.
42 Kazin, *God*, 158.
43 Allen Tate, "Emily Dickinson," *Interpretations of American Literature*, ed. Charles Feidelson, Jr. and Paul Brodtkorb, Jr. (New York: Oxford University Press, 1959), 199, 206.
44 Qtd by Albert J. Gelpi, *Emily Dickinson: The Mind of the Poet* (New York: W.W. Norton, 1971), 38.
45 Ivor Winters, "Emily Dickinson and the Limits of Judgement," *Maule's Curse: Seven Studies in the History of American Obscurantism* (Norfolk, CT: New Directions, 1938), 160–62.
46 Emily Dickinson, *Final Harvest: Emily Dickinson's Poems*, ed. Thomas H. Johnson (Boston: Little Brown, 1961).
47 *Ibid.*, 201, 296.
48 Miller, *Nation*, 262.
49 Horace Greeley, *An Overland Journey* (Readex Microprint Corporation, 1966), 151–52.

50   Adams, *Education*, 458, 494–96, 451.
51   Miller, *Nation*, 282.
52   T.S. Eliot, "The Waste Land," *Poetry in English: An Anthology,* ed. M.L. Rosenthal (Toronto: Oxford University Press, 1987), 889.
53   T.S. Eliot, *Four Quartets* (London: Faber and Faber, 1970), 37.
54   Kazin, *God*, 200.
55   Leo Marx, *The Machine in the Garden: Technology and the Pastoral Ideal in America* (New York: Oxford University Press, 1967), 16.
56   See Hawthorne's story, "The Celestial Railroad"; the chapter, "Spring," in Thoreau's *Walden*; and Dickinson's poem, "I like to see it lap the Miles."
57   F. Scott Fitzgerald, *The Great Gatsby* (New York: Charles Scribner's Sons, 1953), 111; Ch. 6, 5; Ch 1, 39; Ch. 3.
58   *Ibid.,* 23; Ch 2.
59   Leo Marx, "The Puzzle of Anti-Urbanism in American Literature," *The Pilot and the Passenger: Essays on Literature, Technology, and Culture in the United States* (New York: Oxford University Press, 1988), 224.
60   Fitzgerald, 182; Ch 9.
61   Leo Marx, "The American Revolution and the American Landscape," *The Pilot*, 318.
62   Fitzgerald, 182; Ch 9.
63   William Faulkner, *The Bear, Three Famous Short Novels by William Faulkner* (New York: Vintage Books, 1961), 267, 272.
64   *Ibid.*, 185, 215.
65   *Ibid.*, 201.
66   *Ibid.*, 301, 305.
67   See *The Education of Henry Adams*, 455–58.
68   Joseph Pynchon wrote to Hawthorne to protest the characterization of the Pynchon family in *The House of the Seven Gables*.
69   Richard Pearce, Introduction, *Critical Essays on Thomas Pynchon* (Boston: G.H. Hall, 1981), 3.
70   *Ibid.,* 8.
71   Thomas Pynchon, *The Crying of Lot 49* (Toronto: Bantam, 1980), 1; Ch. 1.
72   *Ibid.,* 13; Ch. 2, 36–37; Ch. 3.
73   Harold Bloom, *How to Read and Why* (New York: Scribner, 2000), 253.
74   Pynchon, 134; Ch. 6.
75   Don DeLillo, *Underworld* (New York: Scribner Paperback, 1998), 184, 401, 468.
76   *Ibid.*, 44–45.
77   *Ibid.*, 70.
78   *Ibid.*, 285–86.
79   Jennifer Pincott, "The Inner Workings: Technoscience, Self, and Society in DeLillo's *Underworld.*" *Undercurrent: An Online Journal for the Analysis of the Present*, Number 7, Spring 1999.
80   Champlain founded Quebec City in 1608, one year after the founding of Jamestown, Virginia.
81   Susanna Moodie, *Roughing It in the Bush* (Toronto: McClelland & Stewart, 1989), 37.
82   Catharine Parr Traill, *The Backwoods of Canada* (Toronto: McClelland & Stewart, 1989), 26.

83 Traill, 55, 158.

84 Traill wrote children's stories, guides for immigrants, and several important naturalist works: *Rambles in the Canadian Forest* (1859), *Canadian Wild Flowers* (1869), and *Studies of Plant Life in Canada* (1885).

85 Moodie, *Bush*, 135, 279.

86 Moodie, *Life in the Clearings*, ed. Robert L. McDougall (Toronto: Macmillan of Canada, 1976), 3–4.

87 David Sinclair, Introduction, *Nineteenth-Century Narrative Poems* (Toronto: McClelland & Stewart, 1972), vii.

88 Isabella Valancy Crawford, "Malcolm's Katie," Sinclair, 166–67.

89 *Ibid.*, 162, 174–5.

90 *Ibid.*, 181.

91 Rudyard Kipling and Jack London are among the well-known writers of animal stories from that period.

92 Charles G.D. Roberts, "The Young Ravens that Call Upon Him," *The Last Barrier and Other Stories* (Toronto: McClelland & Stewart, 1970),142, 144–45.

93 Frye speaks of the frontier in early Canadian writings as something that surrounded each isolated settlement. Frye, *Garden*, 220–21.

94 Ernest Thompson Seton, *Wild Animals I Have Known* (Toronto: McClelland & Stewart, 1972), 297.

95 W.H. Blake, Introduction, *Maria Chapdelaine,* by Louis Hémon (Toronto: Macmillan of Canada, 1973), vi.

96 Louis Hémon, *Maria Chapdelaine*, trans. W.H. Blake, 1; Ch 1, 17; Ch. 2.

97 *Ibid.,* 31; Ch. 3.

98 *Ibid.*, 93, 95; Ch 10.

99 *Ibid.*, 121; Ch 13.

100 Pratt, 138, 142, 143, 150.

101 W.O. Mitchell, *Who Has Seen the Wind* (Toronto: Macmillan, 1974), 128–29; Ch 14, 246–47; Ch 26.

102 *Ibid.,* 94–5; Ch. 10.

103 *Ibid.*, 84; Ch. 9, 199; Ch. 21, 295–96; Ch. 32.

104 Clift, 19.

105 Stephen Godfrey, "I really feel I took a lot of risks in this one," *The Globe and Mail,* 8 November 1989: C9.

106 Mordecai Richler, *Solomon Gursky Was Here* (Markham, Ontario: Viking Canada, 1989), 4; Ch. 1, 34; Ch. 5.

107 *Ibid.,* 351–52; Pt 5, Ch 3.

108 *Ibid.,* 523; Pt 8, Ch 4.

109 Douglas LePan, "Canoe Trip," *The Oxford Book of Canadian Verse in English and French*, ed. A.J.M. Smith (Toronto: Oxford University Press, 1965), 313.

110 Robert Frost, "The Gift Outright," *Selected Poems of Robert Frost* (New York: Holt, Rinehart and Winston, Inc., 1963), 299–300.

111 Frye, *Ground,* 79.

112 Kroetsch, *Treachery,* 53–56.

113 Frye, *Ground,* 68.

114 Schäfer, 86, 83.

Chapter
Four

A Sense of Place

1
Conflicting Images of Home

IN THE EARLY DAYS OF THE UNITED STATES, the revolutionary concepts of liberty, Enlightenment ideas about the goodness of the unencumbered individual, and the pull of the frontier combined to create such a fascination with movement that it discouraged a sense of place in American literature. All national literatures have some sense of place, but, in two centuries of American literature, places are generally oppressive and the protagonist has a great need to escape. American heroes are almost always alone, unlike classical heroes who have a mission to save a people. The American myth of the lone wanderer as hero has resulted in a pronounced theme and variations on "the road": the forest path, the wagon trail, the river, the railroad, the highway, and now the expressway.

This restless movement stands in sharp contrast to the situation in pre-Confederation Canada. The Loyalists suffered the traumas of exile and impoverishment. Their reluctant departure from their homes did not inspire wanderlust but rather a grim determination to found new homes and communities. The existing seigneuries of Quebec were tight communities, and in Nova Scotia there were scatterings of equally close settlements of Germans, Highland Scots, and Acadians. These settlements were isolated, with nature a threatening force, or as Frye says, a "frontier" surrounding each one.[1] Nineteenth-century immigrants in both countries normally settled in blocks with people of their own religious and cultural background, but in Canada such clannishness was more acceptable and less likely to cause resentment among settled inhabitants. Such a pattern in Canada led to a social situation that merged the individual into the community and stressed the importance of institutions. Conditions were ripe for a literature with a dearth of heroes and a strong sense of place.

These contrasting outlooks derived from the debate that preceded the American Revolution, particularly the conflict over the nature of liberty (see Chapter I). The British and the Loyalists saw threats to liberty coming from the mob, while to the Patriots, governing institutions were the threat. Americans turned their hostility toward the European past into a rejection of the past in general, which evolved first into a collective distaste for governing institutions, then broadened into suspicion of all institutions, including communities and families.

Frye put considerable stress on what he calls a "garrison mentality" in early Canadian literature, caused by isolation and "a huge, unthinking, menacing, and formidable physical setting." In such a situation the individual's greatest fear is "pulling away from the group," a group that not only sets standards but also provides the only available security.[2] There is little questioning of community standards in pre-Confederation literature, but the general tone is of a nurturing community. By American standards, this atmosphere is complacent, if not cloying.

It is not surprising that the great migration westward became a major theme in American literature. After their successful revolution, the people were at liberty to move west where many of them had been given land as payment for revolutionary war service. The despised Quebec Act was no more, and the Ohio Valley was now available to those brave enough to risk the fury of the Natives. With talk around them of a virgin land, a benevolent nature, and early suggestions of Manifest Destiny, the people rushed to take over the fertile lands west of the Alleghenies. De Tocqueville comments on the "rapacity with which the American rushes forward to secure the immense booty which fortune proffers to him"; it is "a sort of game of chance" that he pursues for "the emotions it excites, as much as for the gain it procures."[3] The Americans found it easy to discount Natives from any lingering ideals of the Rights of Man. Henry Nash Smith argues that, "the *vacant* continent beyond the frontier" impacted on "the consciousness of Americans" [emphasis added].[4] In Canada, although populations were thinly spread, the land was not considered vacant.

When Frederick Jackson Turner's famous essay, "The Significance of the Frontier in American History," appeared in 1893, it increased interest in the effect of the frontier on the American character. Turner argues that conquest of the

frontier takes place in stages: it masters the frontiersman who turns primitive —
"he shouts the war cry and takes the scalp" — then gradually he takes control of
the wilderness — "Little by little he transforms the wilderness, but the outcome
is not the old Europe ... here is a new product that is American."[5] American
historian Howard R. Lamar argues that the negative side of this process has been
largely ignored as most writers saw Turner's stages leading to "the purification
and improvement of the American character and institutions."[6] Richard Slotkin
claims that successful "myth-making in the United States requires bridging or
covering-over ideological dichotomies,"[7] but this is true of any nation to some
extent. There has been some skepticism expressed by twentieth-century
historians, many of whom claim that Turner did more to create a myth than to
contribute to history. However, the myth was already there; Turner's articulation
of it was an important contribution to American self-awareness.

Carl Berger notes that Canadian historians who examined Turner's thesis
saw that "social cohesiveness of French-Canadian settlements ... appeared to
be a major exception to Turner's generalizations." "Nothing could be farther
from the American experience," for the *coureurs de bois* roamed the hinterland
with as much courage and enterprise as any American frontiersman, yet far
from responding to a call for "free land," they returned to "carefully pre-
arranged ... communities."[8] Lamar comments that, unlike the American West,
settlement on the Canadian prairies produced a "sense of place" because of the
absence of "manifest destiny, [and] the burden of theory."[9]

There never was a moving western frontier in Canada. The Canadian
Shield and the Great Lakes are physical barriers that made wagon trains
impossible. The principal difference is that in Canada the law preceded the
settlers. How to save the West from the encroaching Americans was probably
the major problem for the Canadian government after Confederation. Concern
over the diminishing amount of farmland in Ontario and the need to establish
links with settlements in Manitoba were dwarfed by the threat of British
Columbia and the Hudson's Bay lands falling to the Americans. Building the
Canadian Pacific Railway was a matter of urgency.

History or myth, Turner's ideas rang with the American people; the early
form of the American Dream, which was tied to land and glorified farming,
had changed to a complex fascination with movement. Jefferson's ideal of a

nation of yeoman farmers never took root. Roy W. Meyer reports that there was "virtually no real farm fiction" in the nineteenth century, and quotes Henry Nash Smith's comment that the farmer could not be made into "an acceptable hero."[10] Lamar comments on a study of American poetry written between 1870 and 1905, in which "rural and farm topics" strike a consistent note of "failure."[11]

Canadians were aware of the disorder and violence on the American frontier and were determined to avoid such a pattern in Canada. The construction of the railroad was accompanied by treaties with the Natives and the establishment of the Northwest Mounted Police. Settlers traveled by railroad and required a land title before settling. Small homogeneous communities became the pattern in the West much like they were in eastern Canada. A few had been established before the railroad was built: Scottish groups in Manitoba that had come via Hudson Bay, and communities of Métis. Distinct religious or ethnic groups — Mennonites, Ukrainians, and Icelanders — had official sanction to establish their communities according to their own traditions. It is not surprising that Canada's western literature says almost nothing about the journey and everything about the pioneers' struggles to survive.

The rejection of place in American literature has two distinct streams. First, there is the archetypal quest to find a promised land, to live in the wilderness, or to find gold in California. This theme includes wanderlust, which is merely an unfocused quest, closely linked to the American Dream. Second is escape from a situation perceived to be oppressive, with an oppressor that is almost always a group or an institution and rarely an individual. These two themes tend to overlap as the restless individual usually finds that rules and customs are oppressive. Critics have noted that the American western hero, who sheds culture and reverts to the primitive, is going through "a rite of passage to manhood."[12] "Go west, young man" became a ringing cry after it appeared in an Indiana newspaper in 1851.[13] The implication is somewhat ambiguous: go west to make your fortune or go west to get away from home?

It is important to keep in mind that the cry to "go west" is addressed to a young man, for the quest theme in American literature is dominated by male authors and protagonists. Krista Comer says that the "West as a geographical imaginary remains so deeply associated with masculinism that ... any study that ... manages to get a few feminist words in edgewise does the field of western studies a service."[14] Early American fictional heroes frequently form an alliance with a dark-skinned male — such pairings are almost unknown in Canadian literature — while women, both as authors and characters, are far more prominent in Canadian than in American literature.[15] Leslie Fiedler traces the original story of "light" and "dark" male bonding to the adventures of a Canadian fur trader, Alexander Henry, and his Native friend Wawatam, discussed by Thoreau in *A Week on the Concord and Merrimack Rivers* (1849).[16] Thoreau did not launch an American myth, however, since the last of Cooper's Leatherstocking series — all featuring Natty Bumppo with his friend and companion Chingachgook — appeared in 1841. The Lone Ranger and his faithful "Indian" companion Tonto testify to the tenaciousness of the American myth of the West. No one ever asks if the Lone Ranger has a wife or a girlfriend, or where he lives.

Heroes dominate both American literature and American culture. This is not surprising in a society that stresses individualism and is highly suspicious of institutions in general. Military heroes frequently become president of the United States — this has never been the case with a Canadian prime minister — and literary heroes tend to exude individualism. There are no Robin Hoods. American literature with a strong sense of place — the works of Hawthorne and Faulkner are most notable — generally treat the place as a villain, set on destroying anyone who does not fit its rigid preconceptions.

Slotkin claims that myths are built on three elements: a "protagonist or hero," a "universe in which the hero may act," and a narrative. This hardly applies to Canada, which is more at home with Joseph Campbell's definition of myth as "traditional metaphor addressed to ultimate questions."[17] W.H. New notes that outstanding Canadians, "however admirable," are "not worshipped as models of perfection. They are acknowledged to have flaws and limitations, and consequently appear human-sized." He adds that this "process of recognizing ... imperfection produces a greater faith in the community that can cope with adversity than in the individual as mighty hero."[18]

The presence or absence of women is central to a sense of place in literature, as life on the road is the prerogative of men. In Thoreau's *Walden*, which describes a notable place in American literature, women are conspicuously absent. Thoreau was describing a religious experience derived from close contact with nature, so Walden Pond as an image of the natural world was conceived as a memorable place only by later generations. Attempts to escape an oppressive environment can be made by either sex, but in American literature it is often the women who cause the men to flee; as Fiedler says, Americans love "shiftless" males who flee women and domesticity. Since women are traditionally associated with hearth and home, visions of institutions seem to rise in the heads of these shiftless males. Washington Irving's famous story "Rip Van Winkle," in which Rip flees from his nagging wife to virgin land, only lacks a dark-skinned companion to make it the quintessential American story.[19]

To "find oneself" by continual wandering is a powerful American myth. American wanderlust started early, but probably reached its peak in the late 1960s, when both Europe and North America were inundated with hitchhiking youths. It was at this time that a number of Canadian critics expressed outrage at the apparent inability of Canadians to leave home. In *Survival* (1972), Margaret Atwood complains that the choice for Canadian characters is to "stay in the culture and be crippled as an artist; or escape into nothing,"[20] while Ronald Sutherland claims that Canadians, unlike Americans, have "remained enslaved" to their institutions, causing adverse effects on the "intellectual-artistic" life of the country.[21] Canadian culture discourages pointless wandering, so fiction that depicts a protagonist who stays on the family farm or enters into the life of a small town has all too often been judged inferior on that ground alone. Many of these outraged critics buttress their arguments with Frye's comment about a "garrison mentality" in early Canadian literature. Communities do not in themselves hamper the creative process. In a later work Frye says that "culture has something vegetable about it, something that increasingly needs to grow from roots, something that demands a small region and a restricted locale."[22]

George Woodcock sees Canada, like Switzerland, as a nation that was put together in pieces, and where regionalism is a strength, not a hindrance. He notes that "provincialism ... is the word by which its critics so often derogate regionalism," and adds that "the geographical feeling of locality, the historical feeling of a living community, the personal sense of ties to a place where one has been born or which one has passionately adopted" should not be seen to hamper the artistic process.[23]

David Staines claims that Sheila Watson's *The Double Hook* (1959) marks the "beginning of the post-colonial voice in Canadian fiction." He notes that for Watson "her own 'backyard'" was a "breaking with the colonial mentality ... no longer a backyard but the only possible centre."[24] Watson's novel is set on a farm in a remote area of British Columbia.

Since the 1960s, American writers have been taking a greater interest in developing a sense of place in their works. This is partly because of an increasing number of outstanding women writers since World War II. Some male writers — such as John Updike — are bringing distinctive places that are not destructive to individualism more to the fore. Dominique Clift argues that the "tyranny of the tribe" has lost its power in Canada. However, his words were written before the October 1995 referendum, when Quebec came within a hair of voting to separate from Canada.[25] This narrow vote alerted Canada to the continued tribal thinking — a manifestation of garrison mentality — that still threatens the nation.

2

American Wanderlust

A LITERARY IMAGE OF ESCAPE from an oppressive society and the success to be found by traveling west was in place when the United States was born. The first part of Benjamin Franklin's *Autobiography* (begun in 1771) reads like a picaresque novel.[26] The story is of a rebellious boy apprenticed to his brother, a printer in Puritan Boston in the days of Cotton Mather. Mather was outraged at the Franklins' tendency to "blacken and burlesque the virtuous ... ministers of religion,"[27] and, as a result, James Franklin was jailed for three weeks and forbidden to publish his paper except under the supervision of the Secretary of the Province. Benjamin ran away, traveled west, and arrived penniless in Philadelphia with his pockets "stuffed out with shirts and stockings."[28] He achieved success and later world-renown. Although Franklin's *Autobiography* was extremely popular in the early nineteenth century, his story is not typical of the American western hero. Franklin moved from one city to another and practiced a degree of self-discipline that made him the polar opposite of Fiedler's "shiftless" male.

A more significant literary figure in the movement westward is Natty Bumppo, protagonist of Cooper's Leatherstocking series. Slotkin claims that few "writers have so deserved the name of literary pioneer," and adds that historians Bancroft and Parkman "in effect read Cooper's fiction into the historical record." Cooper's contribution, Slotkin says, is two-fold: he put "the Indian and the matter of racial character at the center of his consideration of moral questions, and he represents the historical process as essentially a violent one."[29] Unlike Franklin, Natty seeks freedom, not success.

The first volume in the series, *The Pioneers*, takes place in western New York in the 1790s, when Leatherstocking is an old man and his Native friend Chingachgook is even older, dying near the end of the story. They are living in a hut in the wilderness when Judge Temple, owner of vast tracts of the surrounding land, moves there, draws enough settlers to form a town, and establishes the rule of law. The Judge is serious about the importance of the law, reminding his daughter Elizabeth that society "cannot exist without wholesome restraints ... [The] laws alone remove us from the condition of the savages."[30]

Judge Temple is determined to enforce laws on property rights and seasonal restrictions on hunting. Leatherstocking, who has been living by the law of nature, finds this intolerable. He tells the judge, "it's a hard case to a man to have his honest calling for a livelyhood stopt by laws." Leatherstocking is fined for shooting a deer out of season, but his real trouble with the law comes when he refuses a deputy sheriff armed with a search warrant entry to his hut. For that he is tried, convicted, fined, put in the stocks, and jailed. As the board on the stocks is lowered, someone says that it does no harm. Leatherstocking is incensed: "[I]s it no harm to show off a man in his seventy-first year like a tame bear ... to bring down the pride of an honest man to be the equal of the beasts of the forest."[31] The town of Templeton is as oppressive to Leatherstocking as Boston is to Hester Prynne.

A fundamental moral question underlying this novel is the legal right to own property, making it a forerunner of Faulkner's *The Bear*. Unlike the other Leatherstocking novels, *The Pioneers* has no "bad Indians" among the characters and the Natives' right to the land is suggested but never made specific. Judge Temple insists that all Native rights to the land have been resolved, but he is deeply troubled over the rights of his old friend Major Effingham, a Loyalist, who had entrusted his holdings to the judge's care. When "the estates of the adherents of the crown fell under the hammer by the acts of confiscation," the judge became "the purchaser of extensive possessions, at, comparatively, low prices." A strange young man named Oliver Edwards, who lives with Leatherstocking and Chingachgook, is in the judge's employ. Unbeknownst to the judge, Edwards is the son of Major Effingham and, when he hears that the judge will bring the full force of the law against Leatherstocking, the young man loses his temper: "Walk to that door, Sir, and look out upon the valley ... [and ask yourself] whence came these riches ... and why am I their owner? I should think, sir, that the appearance of Mohegan and the Leatherstocking ... impoverished and forlorn, would wither your sight." Edwards is at least partially thinking of his family, but there is a strong suggestion that the land has been stolen from the Natives. The subject of Native rights is never raised again, but this questioning of the legitimacy of organized society anticipates Emerson.[32]

Leatherstocking cannot bear civilization, speaks of the wilderness as a "second paradise," and after Chingachgook dies and the young people are married, he decides to leave. Elizabeth and Oliver plead with him to stay, but he is resolved: "I love the woods, and ye relish the face of man; I eat when hungry, and drink when adry; and ye keep stated hours and rules ... I'm formed for the wilderness; if ye love me, let me go where my soul craves to be ag'in." Leatherstocking looks forward to the great day "when the whites shall meet the redskins in judgment, and justice shall be the law, and not power."[33] Leatherstocking not only chooses to live like a Native person, but seems to look upon them as equals, something the author may not have fully intended.

The novel ends on a discordant note. Leatherstocking, according to the author, was "the foremost in that band of Pioneers, who are opening the way for the march of the nation across the continent."[34] But Leatherstocking has been arguing against civilization throughout the novel, and as Donald A. Ringe claims, "one cannot picture him as the willing leader in the advance of civilization into the wilderness."[35] According to Robert E. Spiller, Leatherstocking represents a value system that "must always in some way remain an essential part of the American national character."[36]

The literary descendants of Leatherstocking can be found in the hundreds of western novels and movies that pervade American popular culture. Frontiersmen like Daniel Boone, Kit Carson, Davy Crockett, and William F. Cody were turned into mythical heroes alongside fictional heroes such as Deadwood Dick and Seth Jones. There were even a few tough women as heroines, such as Hurricane Nell and Calamity Jane. Smith says that the strongest link between the typical western novel and Leatherstocking is the stereotype of the "benevolent hunter without a fixed place of abode, advanced in age, celibate, and of unequalled prowess in trailing, marksmanship, and Indian fighting."[37] Such a definition precludes women; although, ironically, female characters have a god-like quality as they appear when needed and then magically disappear, much like a fairy godmother.

Eager movement westward in search of more land was spontaneous — it preceded the nation's birth — but its counterpart, the desire to escape from a society deemed oppressive and destructive, had to be taught. Emerson and his followers built on the pre-revolutionary resentment of the British Parliament and established church, which they turned into a generalized rejection of institutional authority. Emerson encouraged the movement westward: "We are willing to see our sons emigrate, as to see our hives swarm. That is what they were made to do, and what the land wants and invites."[38] His principal thrust, however, was the elevation of the individual, who, he claims, reaches his highest potential alone with nature and remains almost a slave as part of society: "Society everywhere is in conspiracy against the manhood of every one of its members. Society is a joint-stock company, in which the members agree" to surrender liberty.[39]

Walt Whitman is as famous a lone wanderer as Leatherstocking, although he did not flee civilization. Whitman is the poet of Manifest Destiny, in love with the United States and all it represents. His later work betrays his outrage at evidence of failed expectations, which makes him a forerunner to Mark Twain. Almost all of the poems in *Leaves of Grass* express movement in some sense, none more than his "Song of the Open Road" (1856). Starting with, "Afoot and light-hearted I take to the open road, / Healthy, free, the world before me," he wanders, inhaling "great drafts of space / The east and the west are mine, and the north and the south are mine." Whitman seems to be echoing Emerson when he writes, "Now I see the secret of the making of the best persons / It is to grow in the open air and to eat and sleep with the earth." Whitman learned a few words of French when he worked as a journalist in New Orleans. His favorite was "Allons," used to begin nine stanzas of "Song of the Open Road."[40] As Kazin says, "Whitman celebrates himself as an individual personifying all he sees and honors."[41]

The Civil War did nothing to reduce American restlessness or urge to escape social restraints. Twain's *The Adventures of Huckleberry Finn* (1884) juxtaposes the two themes of attraction to the natural world and escape from society, although the escape theme is far stronger. Both Huck and Jim are escaping the constraints of society — Sunday school or its equivalent for Huck and slavery for Jim. The oppressor, Miss Watson, is Jim's owner and Huck's guardian. The implied equivalent of their constraints is one of the novel's many ironies. Jim, a grown man with a wife and children, is in constant danger, while Huck, an American innocent, repeatedly threatens to add to the danger by seeing Jim through the eyes of a society that makes him a lesser being than any white person. Huck's conscience tells him it is wrong to help a slave escape: "My conscience got to stirring me up ... until at last I says to it, 'Let up on me

— it ain't too late, yet — I'll paddle ashore at the first light, and tell.' "[42] Jim, however, is so kind and trusting that Huck weakens and makes up a story that saves Jim from being captured. John Seelye says, "the greatest irony in Mark Twain's supremely ironic fiction is the partnership between Huck and Jim."[43] It never occurs to Huck to try to reform society, but repeated contacts with it, and the strengthening of his friendship with Jim, lead him to a final decision to "*go* to hell" rather than tell on Jim.[44] James M. Cox notes that when Huck decides to go to hell he is there in five minutes — hell is "civilization."[45]

Most critics commenting on *Huckleberry Finn* divide the book into three sections. The first and last parts involving Tom Sawyer show the author struggling to write a comic sequel to his earlier *The Adventures of Tom Sawyer* (1876). A long middle section details Jim and Huck floating down the Mississippi River on a raft. The river is a road and on the road they are happy and free, can live like brothers, and enjoy the relaxed life that is Huck's chief ambition: "Other places do seem so cramped up and smothery, but a raft don't. You feel mighty free and easy and comfortable on a raft."[46] At this stage of the novel, Huck lacks the drive to go west like the more traditional American hero.

Huck's encounters with society during his periodic trips ashore are variations on the monstrous. The least of these is the town where the "stores and houses was most all old shackly dried-up frame concerns that hadn't ever been painted," with "little gardens" full of "jimpson weeds, and sunflowers, and ash piles, and old curled-up boots and shoes, and pieces of bottles, and rags, and played-out tin-ware."[47] From the feuding Grangerfords and Shepherdsons who slaughter each other, to Colonel Sherburn's cold-blooded murder of Boggs, to the unscrupulous crooks, the Duke and the King, Huck's encounters with society are tales of horror.

The deepest irony in the novel is that the apparently liberating river down which Huck and Jim are riding is heading deeper and deeper into slave country, toward the notorious slave market in New Orleans. Society threatens at every turn; it even invades the river when men in boats come hunting runaway slaves. This section of the novel drifts toward tragedy, but Twain — famous as a humorist — does not allow that. He reintroduces Tom Sawyer and wrestles the story into a happy ending. Critics agree that the sections of the novel with Tom Sawyer are the weakest, and that Tom's pranks have no place in the world of Huck and Jim. At the end, however, Huck becomes a full-fledged American hero — a son of Leatherstocking — who will "light out for the Territory ... Aunt Sally she's going to adopt me and sivilize me and I can't stand it. I been there before."[48] From Miss Watson to Aunt Sally, women as oppressors frame the novel.

Around 1880, William Dean Howells issued a call to America's writers to use more local color in their fictions.[49] Sarah Orne Jewett and Hamlin Garland are the best known of those who complied. Howells had many critics, however, who accused him of "insisting on the humdrum detail as against the ennobling ideal as the proper material for literature." Henry F. May notes that in the early twentieth century, the "great plains were still almost entirely the domain of the cowboy romancers," and that Willa Cather was the only writer to "treat the Nebraska prairie as a place where actual people lived."[50] Depicting the local community as a place of warmth and beauty hardly suited American aspirations, and the trend toward Howells' local color was essentially terminated by a movement that critic Carl Van Doren calls a "revolt from the village." In particular, Van Doren points to Edgar Lee Master's *Spoon River Anthology* (1915) and Sherwood Anderson's *Winesburg, Ohio* (1919).[51] A sense of place at this period in American literary history seems to have been the prerogative of the few notable women writers.

Sinclair Lewis's *Main Street* (1920) is very much a part of this movement, which criticizes life in small towns. The heroine, Carol Kennicott, a young idealist with grandiose ideas about beauty and culture, is married to a country doctor and trapped in the soul-destroying town of Gopher Prairie, Minnesota. The sense of place in this novel is strong but, like Hawthorne's Boston and Faulkner's Jefferson, it is rigid in its ways and unmerciful to any would-be reformers. Neither Carol nor the town ever change, and the novel is something of a period piece. Mark Shorer wrote in 1961 that *Main Street* could be read as a historical novel, yet claims that Lewis's view of the small town is "pretty much the image of the village that most of us still hold today."[52]

The day Carol arrives in Gopher Prairie, with thoughts of "village charm — hollyhocks and lanes and apple-cheeked cottagers," she finds that the view from her window is the side of the Seventh-Day Adventist Church — "a plain clapboard wall of a sour liver color; the ash pile back of the church; an unpainted stable, and an alley." The vision, reminiscent of the town seen by Huck Finn, leaves her sensing "a forbidding spirit which she could never conquer." Carol is determined, however, so she enters into the town life, meeting every challenge as a self-righteous reformer. Predictably, the people are intractable philistines and social snobs, and Carol soon gets the reputation of being "affected," "patronizing," "eccentric" in her taste, and too "chummy" with her maid.[53]

Lewis's satire is humorous when he depicts a busybody like the neighbor who visits Carol: "I've wanted to call on you so long, dearie ... you must run in and see me, how much did that big chair cost? ... Well, I suppose it's all right for them that can afford it ... [Y]our husband was raised up a Baptist, and ... it's proper for the little bride to take her husband's vessel of faith, so we all hope we shall see you at the baptist Church." The satire loses its humor, however, when attacking snobbery. Carol's maid, Bea, marries and Carol tries to persuade her friends to attend the wedding. The only response she gets is, "Huh? Me go to their Scandahoofian wedding? Not a chance!" There is an "uneasy knot" of only nine guests at the wedding. Humor drains completely from the story with a series of events: Bea and her baby die of typhoid and no one attends the funeral; the teacher is fired over trumped-up charges from a village gossip and her redneck son; and, finally, an agitator is run out of town by a mob led by the sheriff.

Frustrated and angry, Carol tells her husband that she will leave him and take their baby.[54] She moves to Washington, gets a job, and meets other escapees from small towns. Distance allows her to absorb Emerson's still vibrant message that society is "in conspiracy" against the individual.[55] "And why," Carol asks herself, "did she rage at individuals? Not individuals but institutions are the enemies." She notes that institutions "insinuate their tyranny under a hundred guises and pompous names, such as Polite Society, the Family, the Church, Sound Business, the Party, the Country, the Superior White Race."[56] Carol seeks cultured society, not solitude or the wilderness, but the restraints that Gopher Prairie put on her do not differ significantly from those that trouble Leatherstocking and Huck Finn. The attraction theme of the nineteenth century — that is, seeking a paradisiacal land in the west — ended with the disappearance of the frontier. This theme was replaced in the 1920s with unfocused wandering to escape inner torments. Hemingway's restless travelers have a passion for the outdoor life and repeated confrontations with violence that suggest twentieth-century Leatherstockings, but with a major difference: there is no pull toward some vague realm of happiness, no American Dream. In Hemingway's world, the characters seek violence — such as war or bullfighting — and cover their misery with alcohol, sex, and restless traveling. John Steinbeck takes a different approach to the apparent failure of the American Dream in *The Grapes of Wrath* (1939), a bitterly ironic inversion of the western novel. Steinbeck wrote the book in a state of rage for, like Mark Twain, he had believed deeply in American paradisiacal expectations. In his Nobel Prize acceptance speech of 1962, he claimed that "a writer who does not passionately believe in the perfectibility of man has no dedication nor any membership in Literature."[57]

At the end of World War II and the beginning of the 1950s, American wanderlust began throwing off all restraints, including the tone of despair so pronounced in the 1920s and 1930s. Jack Kerouac's *On the Road* (1957) has almost no escape theme, since social conventions no longer have even moral power to constrain the principal characters when the opportunity arises to get behind the wheel of a car and drive. William Burroughs is said to have claimed that the book "sold a trillion levis and ... sent countless kids on the road."[58]

On the Road is an account of the author's experiences traveling back and forth across the country. Kerouac spent seven years on the road and became friends with other notable members of the Beat Generation, including William Burroughs and Allan Ginsberg. The book can hardly be called fiction although the author has given fictional names to the characters, calling himself Sal Paradise and the man with whom he does most of his traveling, Dean Moriarty. The object of all of their travels seems to be to reach the opposite coast as fast as an automobile can take them. Sal says of Dean that his soul is "wrapped up in a fast car, a coast to reach, and a woman at the end of the road."[59] Fiedler's comment about American fondness for "shiftless" males who flee women and domesticity never had a better example.[60]

On the Road is a story of men. Women are sex objects to be abandoned the moment a restless male has the opportunity to hit the road. Dean regularly abandons a wife on the coast he is leaving and meets another on the opposite coast. By the end of the story, he has "four little ones" by various women and "not a cent," but is "all troubles and ecstasy and speed as ever." His wives and girlfriends come to hate him, but when told off he "giggled."[61]

When Sal first meets him, Dean is with his first wife and has a criminal record, which Sal finds a "wild yea-saying overburst of American joy." He sees Dean as "a new kind of American saint," and describes driving with this "mad Ahab" at the wheel and feeling the road under him "unfurling and flying and hissing at incredible speeds." The two men roam the continent, stealing and wrecking other peoples' cars. The author implies something new in this treadmill of joy, and only after Dean abandons him, sick and penniless, in Mexico City does Sal realize "what a rat" the man was.[62]

Ann Charters says that Kerouac was never able to convince his critics that the Beat Generation was basically religious, but his friend John Clellan Holmes understood that the characters in the book are on "a quest," searching for something "spiritual." Charters claims that the book is an "American classic" along with *Huckleberry Finn* and *The Great Gatsby*, exploring the theme of "personal freedom" and challenging "the promise of the 'American dream.'" Charters puts the book in the context of American literary history.[63] Gilbert Millstein reviewed *On the Road* for *The New York Times* and predicted that it would become the testament for the Beat Generation of the 1960s, much like Hemingway's *The Sun Also Rises* (1926) had been the testament for the Lost Generation of the 1920s.[64] John Updike explains in the preface to a limited edition of *Rabbit Run* (1960) what inspired him to write the novel: "Kerouac's *On the Road* was in the air, and a decade of dropping-out about to arrive." Updike set out to show the "price society pays for unrestrained motion."[65] Harry "Rabbit" Angstrom is a lovable oaf, a former high school basketball star, and a child-like man. When personal or domestic problems arise, he runs away. This shiftless male was so popular that Updike eventually turned Rabbit's life into a four-volume series.

On the surface, Toni Morrison's *Paradise* (1997) is neither a road novel nor the story of an oppressive town, yet it contains elements of both. There is no single protagonist and the multiple viewpoints and considerable magic realism make it complex. The story follows a group of racially homogeneous people — descendants of slaves from Mississippi and Louisiana — who wander in search of a promised land, found a paradisiacal town, and defend it against all attempts at change. The place has much in common with the archetypal American town, because the town fathers are prepared to use violence in defense of their perceived Eden. The town turns into an ironic counterpart of Faulkner's Jefferson, Mississippi.

The communal oven, with its motto, "Beware the Furrow of His Brow," was carried in pieces from their previous town and is the central symbol of Ruby, Oklahoma — population 360 and seventeen miles from the next town. The oven is now useless since each house has acquired its own stove, and the ambiguous motto implies religious fundamentalism. When a group of young people, encouraged by a forward-thinking minister, wish to change the motto to "Be the Furrow of His Brow," suggesting individual human dignity, the town fathers gather to put a stop to this heresy. Steward Morgan, the most intractable of the fathers, terminates the meeting with a threat to "blow" the "head off" of anyone who makes any changes to the motto in the "Oven."[66] This seemingly trite issue forecasts the much more serious matter of the attack on the convent.

The convent is a nearby building, originally the hideout of a criminal, then a Catholic school for Native girls, and now a place where a group of homeless women have taken shelter. It is a safety valve for the town. Unpleasant things like abortion, insanity, and death occur there, which spares the town from any suggestion that it is other than a paradise. The town fathers refuse to see the convent in this light, insisting that those loose and perverted women are corrupting their young people. When they attack the convent carrying "rope, a palm leaf cross, handcuffs ... [and] guns," they resemble a southern lynch mob.[67]

Other features make Ruby the counterpart of Jefferson, particularly the struggle for racial purity. The founders of the town are proud and determined. In their wanderings they encountered not just a violent town with the sign "No Niggers," but another town of Blacks who will not accept them because they are too dark. Their pride has inverted these rebuffs into a determination to avoid any white blood. The first one to break the rule is Roger Best, father of the village teacher, Pat Best. Pat is working on a genealogy and history of the founders of Ruby. She calls the founding families "8-rock" for a "deep level in the coal mines." They are tall, graceful and "[b]lue-black." She writes to her father that the townspeople hate them because Pat's mother "looked like a cracker" and was sure to have a child who looked the same. Pat ironically mentions the "one drop law the whites made up" and details family histories suggesting that Ruby is suffering from inbreeding. Pat has a discussion with Richard Misner, the forward-thinking minister, who says he is "an outsider but ... not an enemy." Pat rejoins that "in this town those two words mean the same thing." Pat switches to a defense of the townspeople, but Richard asks if she could imagine having "a true home? ... Not some fortress" that had been built to keep people "locked in or out."[68]

Paradise would seem to have nothing in common with a *roman á clef* like *On the Road*, yet the women who take shelter at the convent are female counterparts to the footloose characters in Kerouac's novel. They are homeless, have been wandering the nation's highways, and are given to petty thievery and casual sex. Connie, the caretaker at the convent, deems them guilty of the "three *d*'s: disorder, deception, and ... drift" that led to "perdition." She becomes a mother figure to the four women and snaps them into order. They become a family shortly before the men of Ruby attack. The men see the women as "witches," and regard the place as a coven not a convent. They claim that before "those heifers" arrived, theirs was a "peaceable kingdom" but now, "the mess" is creeping into their "homes" and "families."[69]

The ambiguous conclusion to the violence — no one is held responsible for the attack on the convent because no evidence is found — is interpreted by the village mystic as God's giving "Ruby a second chance." The mystic is essentially correct, for the novel ends happily. Richard Misner decides to stay, marries a local girl, and the young people change the motto on the Oven to "We are the Furrow of His Brow." Ruby differs from Jefferson and Gopher Prairie in that it is capable of change.[70]

A remarkable novel like *Paradise* is part of a growing trend toward meaningful places in American literature, a trend in which women writers are dominant. However, the road novel is far from dead. In 1993, Francis X. Clines reviewed five new road novels for *The New York Times Book Review*, which he linked to the classics: "[In] their separate careerings in time among American epiphanies, Walt Whitman and Jack Kerouac went beyond self-concoction to achieve an originality that made it all look easy: hit the road, get to the core."

Clines finds it all "indelibly American," and adds that "fresh attempts at wandering the nation and mapping its presumptive soul go forward with the inevitability of book advances."[71] Just as the cowboy novel has been given new life in the work of Cormac McCarthy, the road novel may be immortal.

Smith's claim that the typical descendant of Leatherstocking is "a benevolent hunter without a fixed place of abode, advanced in age, celibate, and of unequaled prowess in trailing, marksmanship, and Indian fighting" is out of date, but still has some validity.[72] Benevolence, advanced age, celibacy, and Indian fighting are now rarely seen. Today, Leatherstocking's descendants are virulent, macho, free of domestic attachments, and fighters of anything vaguely classified as "the establishment." Such characters are still heroes in the American tradition.

3

The Home Base in Canada

THERE IS NOTHING IN CANADA'S EARLY NOVELS even remotely like the Leatherstocking series. Wars and protection of the home are central themes. Frye's comment about a "garrison mentality" in early Canadian literature refers primarily to isolation and a dangerous nature,[73] although the earliest novels frequently have fortress settings. Frances Brooke's *The History of Emily Montague* (1769), Richardson's *Wacousta*, Kirby's *The Golden Dog*, and Parker's *The Seats of the Mighty* are all set in fortresses, and in the last three a war is raging. The Kirby and Parker novels are set in Quebec City around the time of the Seven Years' War and both have French-Canadian heroines, demonstrating that the French past is very much the past of all of Canada.

Aubert de Gaspé's *Canadians of Old* also deals with the fall of Quebec in the Seven Years' War, but is set on a rural seigneury that is charged with emotion, as sentimental as any in nineteenth-century romance. The Seigneury d'Haberville is not a garrison; it is a home. The protagonist, Archibald Cameron of Lochiel, is the son of a Highland Chieftain and a French mother. Like *Wacousta*, this novel harks back to the defeat of the Scottish Jacobites. Archie's father was killed at the Battle of Culloden in 1745 and Archie was raised in France and educated by Jesuits. At college in Quebec, he becomes friends with Jules d'Haberville and is like an adopted son to Jules's family. Both young men have military commissions, but Archie has recovered his ancestral estates, so his is in the British army. They fight on opposite sides in the Seven Years' War.

Archie's knowledge of the language and countryside of New France is valuable to the British, so he is ordered to fight there and commanded on pain of death to burn the homes, including that of the d'Habervilles. Both young men manage to save each other's lives during the fighting, and Archie threatens to resign his commission if the d'Habervilles are forced to leave for France at the end of the war. Forgiveness does not come easily. Although most of the d'Habervilles forgive Archie, the daughter will not; she will not dilute her blood by marrying the enemy.

The life described in this novel is feudal, complete with a noble and kindly seigneur, his gentle wife, devoted *habitants*, and even a slave who, although freed, refuses to leave. When the two young men leave college and travel to Jules's home, he shows deep emotion and confides to Archie: "I've never approached my forefathers' domain without feeling deeply moved ... People may boast all they like about the beauties of the picturesque and the sublime, so plentiful in this lovely land of New France, but there's only one sight that has any meaning for me, and that's the place of my birth!"[74] The novel is today considered a treasure trove of early French-Canadian practices. Dennis Duffy calls it "a septuagenarian's pastoral on the *moeurs* of a bygone era."[75]

Before the young men depart for their respective armies, two traditional celebrations take place: the May-Day festivities and the Feast of Saint-Jean-Baptiste. At the former event two elderly *habitants* ceremonially visit the Seigneur: "[They] bowed with the gracious courtesy that came naturally to Canadians of old, and requested permission to plant a maypole before his door." At the Feast of Saint-Jean-Baptiste, rural "Canadians had preserved a very impressive ritual handed down from their Normandy forefathers. This was the bonfire set alight at dusk on Saint-Jean-Baptiste eve" before the door of the church.[76]

The war leaves the d'Habervilles ruined but the mutual devotion of the people of different classes remains. There was no question of Seigneur d'Haberville asking "his impoverished censitaires for the considerable arrears in rent owed him. On the contrary, he lost no time in coming to their aid by rebuilding his mill." When they were finally able to rebuild the manor house, "the whole parish was quick to volunteer work parties to speed the labour along." This feudal paradise does not seriously exaggerate the living conditions in Quebec, where the system of seigneurial tenure survived until 1854.[77] Duffy cites a *nationaliste* critic, who claims that the novel is more than nostalgia; it presents "a conservative tableau of a post-Conquest, Francophone elite as a model for the good society."[78]

A powerful sense of place established itself on the Canadian artistic landscape long before there was any realization that culture could mature only as a home-grown product. De Gaspé's seigneury is a nurturing community, more medieval, but not different in kind from those in romances written by

English Canadians. Life in a fortress is apt to be beleaguered — it is an environment that cannot permit any questioning of rules or values — but it does not follow that an author treating such a subject suffers from a garrison mentality. The inspiration that led Canada's early writers to pay close attention to place was a necessary prelude to the development of a national literature.

William H. Magee claims that the "local colour" movement was a failure in Canada because writers "generally fumbled their technique." He claims that the movement "gripped Canadian literature" and that Kirby and Parker used it to "flavour pure adventure with a taste of authentic life."[79] Canadian writers were still struggling with technique at the beginning of the twentieth century, but given the established practice of emphasizing place in the national literature and the fact that several works featuring memorable fictional places appeared in the early years of the twentieth century, the movement could hardly be called a failure.[80] Ralph Connor's Glengarry in *The Man from Glengarry* and *Glengarry School Days* (1902), Sara Jeanette Duncan's Elgin in *The Imperialist* (1904), Lucy Maud Montgomery's Avonlea in *Anne of Green Gables* (1908), and Stephen Leacock's Mariposa in *Sunshine Sketches of a Little Town* (1912) are lasting works in Canadian literary history. All of these works are based on rural communities with which the authors had personal connections, and all show a desire to maintain the best of British traditions. This continued attachment to British traditions certainly contributed to the fumbled technique that troubles Magee, but it can be argued that these works are the first serious attempts to resolve the dilemma of local inspiration versus Old World literary standards. In spite of their attachment to a British heritage, the authors disparage or ridicule such things as Scottish blood feuds and British class consciousness, because they threaten the viability of the community and seem so irrelevant in a New World setting.

In Duncan's *The Imperialist,* the town of Elgin is the hero, since no single character can be considered the protagonist. Elgin is alive, rife with political controversy, and is peopled with many intelligent individuals who have strongly held opinions. Although characters leave Elgin for a variety of reasons, they feel no compulsion to escape. Elgin is certainly not a garrison. In fact, it has such vitality that it escapes the author's belief in Imperial Federation, a late nineteenth-century concept that encouraged Britain and its colonies to function almost as one nation. *The Imperialist* is essentially a comic novel, with much humor directed at British snobbishness toward the colonies.

Lorne Murchison, a young lawyer who seeks a career in politics, recognizes that his devotion and ambition are centered on his hometown. Gazing out at the busy town square, a "sense of kinship surged in his heart; these were his people, this his lot as well as theirs." He is dressed "to the standard of Elgin, though he wore his straw hat quite on the back of his head and buried both hands in his trouser pockets." On "Fifth Avenue Lorne would have looked countrified, in Piccadilly colonial," but he has won an important legal case and has been asked to run for Parliament as a Liberal on a platform promoting Imperial Federation.[81] When the members of a trade mission to London are treated like inferior colonials and Imperial Federation is shown to be too expensive, Lorne's political ambitions are dashed. Critic Claude Bissell describes Duncan's views as "shaped in a school that placed truth to human nature above fidelity to private conviction."[82]

There is nothing in Elgin that remotely resembles the societies encountered by Huck Finn, but some comparison can be made with Lewis's Gopher Prairie. Gopher Prairie is turned in on itself, is rigidly set in its ways, and is destructive of individualism. Elgin abounds with individuals and is preoccupied with the outside world, but there is plenty of social snobbery. Lorne's girlfriend has been taught to speak with "an 'English accent.' The accent in general use … was clearly an American product." Church attendance is almost mandatory; "not only a basis of respectability, but practically the only one." " 'They come to our church' was the argument of first force whether for calling or for charity," and a threadbare carpet in your church aisles "was almost as personal a reproach as a hole under the dining room table."[83] Seen through the eyes of the author of *Main Street*, such affectations are a threat; seen by the author of *The Imperialist,* they are amusing, if not lovable. A visitor to the two towns might see little difference.

Mazo de la Roche's *Jalna* series (1927–1960) puts such emphasis on place that it is reminiscent of the prairie in *Who Has Seen the Wind*. People are born and die, come and go, but the old family homestead remains constant. Most critics of this much-maligned sixteen-volume series agree that Jalna is the principal character. It "has a soul," according to Daniel L. Bratton.[84]

.

The *Jalna* series follows several generations of the Whiteoak family, a multi-talented and disputatious tribe, who come and go, but are continually drawn back to the old family estate in southern Ontario. The series begins with the third generation, but after a few volumes the author reached the present, then began filling in the past, from the founding of Jalna by a British officer and his Anglo-Irish wife in the mid-nineteenth century. The one-hundred-year-old grandmother, Adeline, dies in volume two, but her presence is felt throughout the series. Her portrait, hanging in the dining room, casts a continuous judgmental eye on the family.

There is considerable tension between the practical, hard-working members of the family, represented by Renny and Piers, and the artistic ones, Eden, a poet, and Finch, a musician. The author shows considerable sympathy for both sides. All of the characters have redeeming qualities with the possible exception of Meg, Renny's sister, who resembles a small town busybody. Renny, the owner of Jalna, inherited it from his father, although two of the father's brothers are alive and living at Jalna. When Piers elopes with the illegitimate daughter of a neighbor and then returns to face his outraged relatives, Renny walks in on a stormy scene: "This was his family. His tribe. He was head of his family ... [and] took a very primitive, direct, and simple pleasure in lording it over them.... They expected him to lay down the law."[85] Renny announces that Piers will stay; he is needed on the farm and his bride is to be accepted.

The principal outside character is Alayne, a cultured young woman from New York, who marries Eden and later Renny. When she first arrives at Jalna as Eden's wife, Alayne is overwhelmed by the turbulent family. Later she finds that she can no longer distinguish Eden's poems from Jalna and begins seeing the Whiteoaks as animals, "a menagerie." When she leaves after Eden's affair with Piers' wife, she tells Renny that she used to think men and women were equals, but since living at Jalna has decided that women are "slaves."[86]

Alayne returns to nurse a dying Eden in the second volume. She is deeply in love with Renny and has no feelings left for Eden, so wonders if Jalna has "caught her in the coil of its spell." She denies returning because of Renny, so Eden says: "I honestly believe that Jalna drew you back." Alayne never quite fits with the Whiteoaks, but neither can she be happy away from them. These formidable people show their true colors when the grandmother dies and leaves all of her money to Finch. The outraged family wants to challenge the will in court, but Renny says no. It would be a scandal and they would be in the newspapers. They reluctantly agree, for the "wall about them must be kept intact."[87]

The series would probably be seen in a much more favorable light today if the author had stopped with three or four volumes. *Jalna* won the *Atlantic Monthly* $10,000 prize, a prestigious literary award at the time, and the early volumes received praise from many literary professionals, including Hugh Walpole.[88] Canadian critics today seem almost embarrassed by the Jalna series, and have been known to refer to it as soap opera,[89] but a reader can hardly help getting caught up with such dynamic characters and such a vivid setting.

Places in Canadian literature are not always, or even usually, happy. The important difference from places in American literature is that the unhappiness is caused by such things as poverty, a tyrannical father, or nature at its most severe, and rarely by a community or an institution. Three prairie novels from the 1920s illustrate the point. Frederick Philip Grove's *Settlers of the Marsh* (1925), Martha Ostenso's *Wild Geese* (1925), and Robert J.C. Stead's *Grain* (1926) are all set on farms recently started by immigrants, where hard manual labor is the prime virtue. Amundsen and Caleb Gare, the brutal fathers of Grove's and Ostenso's novels respectively, are Scandinavian immigrants, obsessed with expanding and improving their farms. Neither will tolerate any slackening of effort, even when illness strikes. The atmosphere around them is heavy and tense, due to the fear in those under their domination. Both men are accidentally killed, releasing their families from their tyranny. Marriage and happiness are achieved — eventually in *Settlers of the Marsh* and immediately in *Wild Geese* — but the release does not mean leaving the farm. Devotion to the land is shared with the brutal fathers and continues after their deaths. The protagonist of *Grain* is forced to leave his beloved farm because he loves a married woman; it is exile not escape. All three authors vividly recreate the pioneer lifestyle and the harsh climate on the Canadian prairies.

Few Canadian novels surpass the vitality of place in Ernest Buckler's *The Mountain and the Valley* (1952), set in rural Nova Scotia, where past and present seem to merge. Young David Canaan and his loving family live on a farm in the Annapolis Valley. David's favorite place is the top of the mountain that looks over the valley. There he has sought solace since childhood: "He would take happiness there, to be alone with it," or find comfort from "the tick, tick, tick of emptiness." His grandmother, Ellen, is like one of the spinning fates of classical mythology as she ties past to present by hooking rugs made from discarded clothing. Before being torn into rags and woven into an artistic pattern, each item brings forth a memory, a symbol of the ongoing life of the family. The finished rugs provide some of the beauty David's mother continually seeks for her home. There is always joy in the activities the Canaans do as a family, including a picnic outing to clean up the family burial plot. As they wind their way up the log road that ascends the mountain to the cemetery, David picks out places of historic importance: "He could hear the echo of the voices and the movements which had once made this old place young." He finds "the spot on the log road" where his friend's great-great-grandmother was killed and discovers "the cellar of the old house where his grandparents first lived."[90]

David is a brilliant but overly sensitive child, and the intensity of his emotions makes communication with others increasingly difficult. When his city friend Toby visits the farm, David senses that "if Toby found himself alone in the country, it would have no language for him at all." David describes the wonderful view from the top of the mountain, but Toby responds: "Is *that* all we're going way up there for? ... It isn't like it was a *real* mountain." David is crushed and turns around, declining to go further.[91]

David is not strong. After a fall from some scaffolding, he lives with constant pain, but will never admit it. When others try to spare him, his anger mounts. He is rejected by the army in World War II because he has a bad heart, which further intensifies his crippling isolation. Warren Tallman claims that David is "trying to sustain an illusion," and that his brief life is "heroic," due to "the extreme tenacity" with which he "clings to the sources of his suffering."[92]

This novel has an inverted escape theme. David tries several times to leave and pursue a career, but his ties to home always prove too strong to break. After a fight with his father, he starts to walk to Halifax, but turns back, stopping on a bridge where he puts his head into the crook of his elbow and begins to sob: "He sobbed because he could neither leave nor stay. He sobbed because he was neither one thing nor the other."[93] That night, his grandmother gives him a tiny locket containing the picture of a sailor who looks just like David. She understands because she too could never bring herself to leave.

David's beloved mountaintop is a place of death — the location of the graveyard. David's father is killed there by a falling tree, and David, still a young man, dies there of heart failure, having just received the inspiration to write his story. "He stood there, looking down over the mountain and the valley ... I will *tell* it, he thought rushingly." As he makes plans to contact those he loves, "the blackness swam in his head ... And then the blackness turned to grey and then to white ... And then the snow began to fall." The mountain takes possession of him, as his body is quickly buried under falling snow.[94] Tallman says that passages in this novel "read like lyric poems."[95]

The sense of place in Canadian fiction has become varied and complex, but no less prominent in recent works. More and more, place is tied to the past and, even with novels that show the influence of an American writer, a carefree life on the road or a passionate need to leave home are missing.

There are no American-style road novels in Canadian fiction. Jacques Poulin's *Volkswagen Blues* (1984) looks like a French-Canadian version of Kerouac's *On the Road*, but only on the surface.[96] The story follows a young couple — a French-Canadian novelist nicknamed Jack and a young Métis woman called La Grande Sauterelle — who travel across the continent in an aging Volkswagen, hunting for Jack's long-lost brother, Théo. They make only one trip across the continent, and it is a trip into the past, dwelling on the brutal treatment of Native North Americans and, to a lesser extent, discovering the movements of the early French explorers. Their trip begins on the Gaspé Peninsula with references to Jacques Cartier, which sets the tone for this journey into the past. Poulin clearly had *On the Road* in mind, for there are repeated references to Kerouac among the clues they find to Théo's whereabouts. There is also a meeting with Saul Bellow, a hitchhiker who is compared to Hemingway, and a photograph of Allen Ginsberg with Théo. When they finally locate Théo in San Francisco, he is ill beyond help and does not recognize his brother. The travelers are not escaping from home, seeking a better life in the west, or traveling for the joy of movement.

After Théo is found, Jack flies home, but La Grande Sauterelle remains with the car. She has been the perceptive one on the trip, suggesting that Théo may have intended to follow the route of the French explorers, and she fills in the past of the Native tribes along the way. She is also a skilled mechanic who keeps the Volkswagen operational. Her Métis identity gives her a divided heritage that troubles her, so she thinks that she may be able to find more about herself in this city with so many people of mixed heritage. She and Jack kiss passionately, and the implication is that she too will soon return home.

There is considerable anti-American sentiment in *Volkswagen Blues,* for the United States is "built on violence,"[97] and the past that the characters discover is primarily founded on the destruction of Native peoples and their cultures. The word "Blue" in the title has multiple meanings: blue for the Quebec flag, the blues as in jazz, and Jack's periodic depressions. The book stresses oppression of minorities — Natives, Blacks, and French — and far from resembling an American road novel, it parodies the genre.

Place is inextricably tied to the past in Alistair MacLeod's *No Great Mischief* (1999). There are two places that grip the characters: Cape Breton Island, where most of the descendants of a Scottish immigrant have lived for over two centuries, and the bleak coast of the Highlands from which the ancestor, Calum Ruadh MacDonald, set sail in 1779. All the principal characters are members of the MacDonald family and three of them are named Alexander: the narrator, a cousin, and a more distant cousin whose family lives in San Francisco. The San Francisco Alex has lost touch with his roots. When he comes to Canada to escape the Vietnam War draft he immediately asks a French Canadian why he doesn't "speak English," since this is North America.[98] He later steals a wallet, precipitating a clan fight in which a French Canadian is killed by the narrator's eldest brother. This fight occurs at a uranium mine near Sudbury, where the miners live in groups like hostile tribes — the French-speaking Québécois versus the Gaelic-speaking MacDonalds from Cape Breton.[99] As a result of this clash, the narrator's brother, Calum, is sent to prison.

The relationship between Alex, the narrator, and his brother Calum is set on its course when Alex and his twin sister are three and Calum is sixteen. Their father, a lighthouse keeper on a small island off Cape Breton, walks with his family across the ice to the town in March. Calum and two more teenage brothers go to visit cousins and the twins stay with their grandparents, while the father, mother, and eleven-year-old brother return to the lighthouse. The ice gives way under them and all three are drowned, leaving five orphans. The three teenage boys drop out of school, move into an ancient family dwelling, and subsist on fishing and some farming. They speak more and more Gaelic, sleep in their clothes, and drink tea out of jam jars. The twins are raised by the grandparents, go to university, and settle into affluent lifestyles. As children, the twins visit their brothers until the sister asks why there are no tablecloths and napkins; then Alex goes alone. He goes fishing with his brothers, witnessing blizzards and the near loss of the boat. One summer he works as a miner with his brothers rather than take a comfortable research job at his university.

The twins are raised on Gaelic songs and stories of the Scottish past, although their maternal grandfather makes it clear how much suffering and brutality accompanied the clan wars. When the wind is off the sea during visits with their brothers, the twins loved to run to the point to see who could remain standing in the wind's force the longest. The "wind would blow our breath back within us as the spray from the water on the rocks rose and covered us and *Calum Ruadh*'s gravestone with glistening drops." The ancestor who came from Scotland is buried on this point; his grave, covered by a large boulder, is · the central symbol in the novel. The boulder appears to be moving toward the sea, as the coastline is gradually worn away by the waves. Alex sees more of life in the raw than his sister, but she is the one to travel to Scotland with her engineer husband to find the place where the family set out. She is recognized by the Scots and told she is "from here.... You have just been away for a while."[100]

The novel opens near the end of the story. Alex is driving from Windsor to Toronto to visit Calum, now out of prison and a hopeless alcoholic living in a stinking rooming house on Queen Street in Toronto. Alex is an orthodontist, charging high prices to make people beautiful, or "improving on God," as his grandmother would say. He recalls a dramatic incident when he went fishing with his brothers. Everything went wrong that day: the weather was terrible, there was engine trouble, no fish were caught, and Calum was in pain from an infected molar. He tried unsuccessfully to pull the tooth with a pair of pliers, then tied a line to his horse, the other end to his tooth, told his brothers to hold him, and whistled for the horse to pull the boat ashore. "When her weight hit him, his head and the upper part of his body snapped forward but his brothers had braced their feet and set their shoulders and they held him firm as the yellowed infected tooth flew out and over the bow and rolled at the end of its line like a white and yellow seashell." Alex is fully aware of the ironic contrast between his lucrative work and the life led by his older brothers.[101]

One day, Alex receives a call from Calum saying "It's time ... Time to go." It is night and storming outside, but Alex departs, picks up a now sober Calum, and they drive all day and all night. A storm is raging when they arrive on the coast and a policeman tells them that the causeway is flooded and they cannot drive to the island. Calum takes the wheel and drives across the flooded causeway. After Alex resumes driving toward their home, he suddenly realizes that Calum is dead.[102] This powerful return home makes *No Great Mischief* a most Canadian novel.

In an interview, MacLeod speaks of Cape Breton as "the landscape" that he cares most about. He mentions Canadian writers W.O. Mitchell and Alice Munro, who also have a landscape.[103] Many Canadian writers do, for the sense of place in Canadian literature has never weakened.

Some comparisons can be made between *No Great Mischief* and Toni Morrison's *Paradise*, as both novels tie a vivid place to a dramatic past. In *No Great Mischief*, the place maintains a strong hold on the characters, who go elsewhere to earn a living. There is little victimization associated with the past. In *Paradise*, characters feel the need to defend the place against outside threats, essentially trying to shut out forces that had made victims of them in the past.

An important aspect of the Canadian sense of place is a protagonist's need to return home before becoming a fully functioning adult. Examples can be found from the earliest days of Canadian literature, but particularly notable are Ranald MacDonald's return to Glengarry before moving permanently to British Columbia in Connor's *The Man from Glengarry*, Margaret Atwood's unnamed narrator in *Surfacing* (1972), and Morag Gunn's return to Manawaka in Margaret Laurence's *The Diviners* (1974). These returns are like a Canadian version of finding oneself, which in the United States continues to take the opposite approach of hitting the road. There is still a dearth of American-type heroes in Canadian literature, for no matter how dynamic the protagonist, the places they inhabit vie for centrality. This strong sense of place may be the most distinctive feature still separating Canadian from American literature.

4

Conclusion

A SENSE OF PLACE IN LITERATURE tends to be of little significance unless it implies the past. Hence, recent attempts by a number of American writers to give a stronger sense of place to their works must counter two old and tenacious myths: the desirability of overthrowing the past and the urge to wander free of institutional commitments. Merely identifying a string of novels with a particular locale is little more than a beginning. Eleanor Cook identifies a sense of place in literature in two different but related ways: "The first is *place* in the more usual meaning of the sights and sounds, smells and tastes, the textures of a place ... The second is *place* as category — of cultural identity."[104] It is this second sense — a place that implies a past and a culture — that Canadian writers have conveyed so successfully.

Updike's "Rabbit" novels are set in Brewer, Pennsylvania, and the sights, sounds, smells, and tastes of the place are pronounced, but Brewer lacks place in Cook's second sense. American writers like Hawthorne, Faulkner, and Morrison understand this second sense. No matter how oppressive Boston, Jefferson, and Ruby are, they are collective personalities that function like flawed characters, with a past, a future, and an ability to frustrate or control those who operate within their limits. It is as though Lewis's *Main Street* describes a permanent obstacle in the minds of American writers. It is the sense of place as "cultural identity," but without the life-denying features that Hawthorne, Faulkner, and Morrison found necessary, that Canada's best writers are now displaying to the world, none more so than Alice Munro.

Munro has an international reputation; her stories have been read and admired in the United States for several decades. Her short story, "A Wilderness Station" (1994),[105] is historical fiction that shows marked changes in a place at different periods of history. Updike, reviewing her *Selected Stories* for *The New York Times*, was particularly impressed with this story, which evokes "the brutality, stoicism and chaos of the time when God-fearing men and women were improvising their way into the American wilderness." It is somehow incongruous that this story, set in a Canadian wilderness with the same locale turned into small town Ontario in later episodes, is casually compared to American frontier fiction. Updike compares Munro to Tolstoy and praises her "historical imagination," yet fails to come to grips with the essence of her talent.[106] Not so British novelist A.S. Byatt, who claims that Munro's stories are "Canadian, rooted in a particular part of the earth and a particular society, full of precise details that make her world so lively that the foreign reader has the illusion of knowing exactly how those people and places were and are."[107] The British have always had a strong sense of place in their literature, so Canada's long apprenticeship to British culture did have lasting benefit.

For the first time, a work of fiction won prizes and was claimed by both Canada and the United States. Carol Shields, who is a dual citizen, won both the Governor General's Award and the Pulitzer Prize for her novel, *The Stone Diaries* (1993). The novel's protagonist, Daisy Goodwill, whose life spans the twentieth century and who lives in both Canada and the United States, is a very ordinary woman who adapts readily to the society in which she lives. The places that Daisy lives and how they change and mold her is a central theme. Her childhood in Winnipeg is recalled as a happy one, and in Ottawa she marries successfully, has three children, and a career as a garden columnist. In Indiana, she lives as a society belle and has a short disastrous marriage, and in Florida she plays bridge and endures the indignities of a nursing home before her death. Daisy is so adaptable that she achieves happiness wherever she lives. But when her train crosses the border from Michigan to Ontario, she is full of eager anticipation, returning to the "country of her birth and early childhood." She muses: "A cool clean place, is how she thinks of it, with a king and queen and Mounties wearing red jackets and people drinking tea." Daisy believes she has arrived at "a healing kingdom," suppressing her "real memories of the hurly-burly of the Winnipeg schoolyard and the dust and horse turds" of its streets.[108] Carol Shield's earlier works are set primarily in Canada, where she has been known to readers for a number of years and no one perceived anything "American" about her writings. There can be no definitive answer why *The Stone Diaries* and the stories of Alice Munro have achieved such popularity in the United States — both could be called old-fashioned — but the powerful sense of past and place may hint at something that may have been missing for the perceptive American reader.

It has been said repeatedly that when the frontier vanished, the American Dream turned into a nightmare, depicted by Fitzgerald, Nathanael West, Pynchon, and many others. It is America's women writers who have recently made the greatest strides toward creating nurturing communities. Louise Erdrich, a literary heir of Willa Cather, writes about the western plains as a place where people live. Toni Morrison, in her 1993 novel, *Jazz*, brings Harlem in the 1920s vividly to life.

Frye, whose comments about a "garrison mentality" and a "deep terror" of nature have been so widely misinterpreted, distinguished provincial from regional literature in one of his last essays: "The provincial writer assumes that literary standards have been established for him outside his environment." Gradually the provincial writer takes ideas, techniques, and forms from around the world and becomes part of an "international idiom," but is not uprooted from his or her "localized place." Frye sees a "curious law in [literary] culture ... which says that the most specific settings have the best chance of becoming universal in their appeal."[109] A warmth of place in the literature of any nation cannot be long denied.

Notes

1   Frye, *Garden*, 220.
2   *Ibid.*, 225, 226.
3   De Tocqueville, I: 348–49.
4   Henry Nash Smith, *Virgin Land: The American West as Symbol and Myth* (New York: Vintage, 1957), 4.
5   Turner, 39.
6   Howard R. Lamar, "The Unsettling of the American West: The Mobility of Defeat," Harrison, *Frontiers*, 42.
7   Richard Slotkin, *Gunfighter Nation: The Myth of the Frontier in Twentieth-Century America* (Norman: University of Oklahoma Press, 1998), 185.
8   Berger, 119.
9   Lamar, 48.
10 Roy W. Meyers, *The Middle Western Farm Novel in the Twentieth Century* (Lincoln: University of Nebraska Press, 1965), 4, 18. Roy W. Meyers says that only Hamlin Garland and Joseph Kirkland, who are hardly well known today, wrote important rural fiction in nineteenth-century America.
11 Lamar, 42–43.

12 Lamar, 40.
13 This well-known rallying cry is widely believed to have originated with Horace Greeley, publisher of the *New York Herald Tribune.*
14 Comer, 11.
15 MacLulich, 195.
16 Fiedler, *Return*, 109.
17 Slotkin, *Regeneration*, 8, 14.
18 W.H. New, *Borderlands: How we talk about Canada* (Vancouver: University of British Columbia Press, 1998), 44–45.
19 Fiedler, *Return*, 60, 59.
20 Margaret Atwood, *Survival: A Thematic Guide to Canadian Literature* (Toronto: House of Anansi, 1972), 189.
21 Ronald Sutherland, *Second Image: Comparative Studies in Quebec/Canadian Literature* (Don Mills, ON: Newpress, 1971), 68.
22 Frye, *Ground*, 62.
23 Woodcock, *Spring*, 23.
24 Staines, *Provinces*, 16–17.
25 Clift, 226.
26 Franklin's *Autobiography* was written in three installments between 1771 and 1790. It went through 170 editions by 1890.
27 Kenneth S. Lynn, ed., *The Comic Tradition in America* (New York: Doubleday Anchor, 1958), 2.
28 Benjamin Franklin, *Benjamin Franklin: The Autobiography and Other Writings* (New York: Signet Classics, 1961), 38.
29 Slotkin, *Fatal Environment*, 81, 88.
30 James Fenimore Cooper, *The Pioneers* (New York: Penguin Books, 1988), 382–83; Ch. 35.
31 *Ibid.*, 161; Ch 14, 374; Ch. 34.
32 *Ibid.*, 36; Ch 2, 345; Ch 31.
33 *Ibid.,* 454; Ch 41.
34 *Ibid.*, 456; Ch 41.
35 Donald A. Ringe, Introduction, *The Pioneers*, xxii.
36 Robert E. Spiller, Afterword, *The Pioneers* (New York: Signet Classic, 1964), 444.
37 H.N. Smith, *Virgin Land*, 92.
38 Ralph Waldo Emerson, *The Complete Works of Ralph Waldo Emerson*, 12 vols (Boston: Houghton Mifflin, 1904), XII: 207.
39 Emerson, *Emerson*, 133.
40 Whitman, I: 156–66.
41 Kazin, *God*, 108.
42 Mark Twain, *The Adventures of Huckleberry Finn* (New York: Penguin Books, 1985), 98; Ch 16.
43 John Seelye, Introduction, *Huckleberry Finn*, xxviii.
44 Twain, *Huckleberry Finn*, 235; Ch 31.
45 James M. Cox, "Southwestern Vernacular," *Twentieth Century Interpretations of Huckleberry Finn,* ed. Claude M. Simpson (Englewood Cliffs, NJ: Prentice–Hall, 1968), 93.

46 Twain, *Huckleberry Finn*, 128; Ch 18.

47 *Ibid.*, 152–53; Ch 21.

48 *Ibid.*, 321; Ch 43.

49 There was a "local color" movement throughout the English-speaking world in the late nineteenth century, which was most effective in the writings of Anthony Trollope and George Eliot. William H. Magee, "Local Colour in Canadian Fiction," *Twentieth-Century Essays on Confederation Literature*, ed. Lorraine McMullen (Ottawa: The Tecumseh Press, 1976), 77.

50 May, 5, 89–90.

51 Morris Dickstein, Introduction, *Main Street*, by Sinclair Lewis (New York: Bantam Books, 1996), x.

52 Mark Schorer, Afterword, *Main Street* (New York: Signet Classics, 1961), 438.

53 Lewis, *Main Street*, 36, 39; Ch 4, 109–10; Ch 8.

54 *Ibid.*, 80; Ch. 6, 267; Ch. 19.

55 Emerson, *Emerson,* 133.

56 Lewis, *Main Street*, 498; Ch 37.

57 Qtd by Brad Leithauser, Introduction, *The Grapes of Wrath* (New York: Everyman's Library, 1993), viii.

58 Qtd by Ann Charters, Introduction, *On the Road*, by Jack Kerouac (New York: Penguin Books, 1991), xxviii.

59 Kerouac, 230.

60 Fiedler, *Return*, 60.

61 Kerouac, 247, 193.

62 *Ibid.*, 10, 39, 234, 303.

63 Charters, xxx.

64 *Ibid.*, viii.

65 John Updike, *Hugging the Shore: Essays and Criticism* (New York: Vintage Books, 1984), 850.

66 Toni Morrison, *Paradise* (New York: A Plume Book, 1999), 87.

67 *Ibid.*, 3.

68 *Ibid.*, 154, 189, 193, 196, 200, 212, 213.

69 *Ibid.*, 221–22, 276.

70 *Ibid.*, 297, 298.

71 Francis X. Clines, "They See America Rolling," *The New York Times Book Review* May 9, 1993: 1.

72 H.N. Smith, *Virgin Land*, 92.

73 Frye, *Bush Garden*, 225.

74 Aubert de Gaspé, *Canadians of Old*, 94.

75 Duffy, *Iceberg*, 5.

76 De Gaspé, 106, 114.

77 *Ibid.*, 191, 203.

78 Duffy, *Iceberg*, 6.

79 Magee, 77, 81.

80 Local color, which stresses habits, mannerisms, and dialects of a particular people, is distinct from regionalism.

81 Sara Jeannette Duncan, *The Imperialist* (Toronto: McClelland & Stewart, 1990),

81, 83; Ch. 9.

82   Claude Bissell, Introduction, *The Imperialist* by Duncan (Toronto: McClelland & Stewart, 1974), vii.

83   Duncan, 51; Ch. 5, 65–6; Ch. 7.

84   Daniel L. Bratton, *Thirty-two Short Views of Mazo de la Roche* (Toronto: ECW Press, 1996), 92.

85   Mazo de la Roche, *Jalna* (Toronto: Macmillan of Canada, 1947), 81.

86   *Ibid.*, 202, 288.

87   De la Roche, *The Whiteoaks of Jalna* (Toronto: Macmillan of Canada, 1929), 177, 367, 288.

88   Sterling North, *The Writings of Mazo de la Roche* (Boston: Little Brown & Co., n.d.), 4.

89   Dennis Duffy, *Gardens, Covenants, Exiles: Loyalism in the Literature of Upper Canada/Ontario* (Toronto: University of Toronto Press, 1982), 76.

90   Ernest Buckler, *The Mountain and the Valley* (Toronto: McClelland & Stewart, 1991), 7; Prologue 82–83; Ch 12.

91   *Ibid.*, 134; Ch 20, 138; Ch 11.

92   Warren Tallman, "Wolf in the Snow," *Contexts of Canadian Criticism,* ed. Eli Mandel (Toronto: University of Toronto Press, 1977), 238.

93   Buckler, 165; Ch 25.

94   *Ibid.*, 292, 294; Ch 40.

95   Tallman, 238.

96   Kerouac's family was originally French Canadian. He grew up speaking *joual,* a dialect widely spoken in rural Quebec.

97   Jacques Poulin, *Volkswagen Blues*, Trans. Sheila Fischman (Toronto: McClelland & Stewart, 1988), 92.

98   Alistair MacLeod, *No Great Mischief* (Toronto: McClelland & Stewart, 1999), 224.

99   There is a similar fight in Ralph Connor's *The Man From Glengarry*. A Gaelic-speaking Scottish lumbering crew gets into a disastrous fight with a French-speaking crew.

100 MacLeod, *No Great Mischief,* 73, 160.

101 *Ibid.*, 103, 80–81.

102 *Ibid.*, 276.

103 Sandra Martin, "I think you carry a landscape within you," *The Globe and Mail,* 29 April 2000: D9.

104 Eleanor Cook, "A Seeing and Unseeing of the Eye: Canadian Literature and the Sense of Place," *Daedalus* 117: 4 (1988): 217.

105 In *Selected Stories*, by Alice Munro (Toronto: McClelland & Stewart, 1996).

106 John Updike, "Magnetic North," Review of *Selected Stories*, by Alice Munro, *New York Times Book Review*, October 27, 1996: 11+.

107 A.S. Byatt, "Alice Munro: One of the Great Ones," Review of *Selected Stories*, by Munro, *The Globe and Mail*, November 2, 1996: D18+.

108 Carol Shields, *The Stone Diaries* (Toronto: Vintage Books, 1993), 133.

109 Frye, "Levels," 185.

Chapter
Five

Religion and the Church

1
Christianity in North America

THEOLOGICALLY, CANADA AND THE UNITED STATES are much alike, both being predominately Christian with generally the same denominations on both sides of the border. The similarities end there, however, for until the 1960s in Canada, both the government and the people considered the church to be an institution essential to a functioning society. Ecclesiastical differences between the two countries are three-fold: legal separation of church and state in the United States versus a close, if not official, relationship in Canada; the American movement toward fragmentation and innovation versus Canada's struggle to unify; and, largely because of Canada's French population and the Quebec Act, differing attitudes toward Catholicism.[1]

Religion dominated the thinking of the first European settlers in North America. The seventeenth century, burning with the fires of the Reformation and Counter-Reformation, saw the universe as "the manipulations of an intelligent being," and what God expected of them was first in the minds of the people. The United States is the only significant part of the Western Hemisphere where the first European settlers were Protestant, so New France and New England faced each other with hostility. Members of the Virginia Company also considered themselves "first and foremost Christians, and above all militant Protestants," whose primary duty was "converting Indians."[2] None of these colonies had any plans for a future democracy, for fallen man was incapable of governing himself. New France, where Protestants were not allowed, was ruled by a triumvirate — a royal governor, a bishop, and an intendant — that foreshadowed the close association between government and institutionalized religion so characteristic of Canada before the 1960s. Since the 1960s, however, Canada has become more secular than the United States.

139

How the fanatical theocracy of New England fathered the future United States is one of the most intriguing stories in North American history. To the fervent English Puritans of the Massachusetts Bay Company, who looked on themselves as a chosen people on God's errand into the wilderness, God was omnipotent and therefore not subject to time. Since God knew the future, man was predestined.[3] Humans were fallen and therefore born sinful, and only a few, the Elect, could achieve salvation through God's mercy. These first New Englanders were a community of saints who had been struck by the lightning of God. The obvious conundrum — the need for moral effort from humans whose lives were predestined — was a major preoccupation of the learned clergy in both England and New England. Their solution, the Covenant of Grace, was an "adroit and highly legalistic formulation" that was convincing to people of the day.[4]

The Puritans believed that God notified his chosen people with a dramatic emotional experience. The people were therefore put under enormous strain as they searched within for signs of election or damnation. Berkovitch, who has identified aspects of Puritan thought around which American ideology later adhered, found none more central than the individual wrestling within himself to find God — "Self Civil War," he calls it.[5] The tormented clergyman Dimmesdale in *The Scarlet Letter* is the best literary example. Father Laforgue in Brian Moore's *Black Robe* (1985) is told that he is one of God's chosen, perhaps implying that in the seventeenth century the Catholics thought along similar lines.

Religious innovation in New England began as new-world conditions put strains on Puritan preconceptions. First, there was trouble getting later generations to experience salvation. Only the Elect were allowed to join the church so new techniques had to be found to keep up the membership. Second, the Restoration in England led their English brethren to adopt religious tolerance, a horror that they could scarcely believe, for tolerance meant acceptance of evil. Other denominations were looked on as heretical or as encroachments of the devil, who had had his greatest triumph in complete domination of the Roman Catholic Church and was now insinuating his way among the Protestants. Evil in any form was not tolerated in New England, and proscribed acts were severely chastised.[6] Finally, the Enlightenment dawned. Early in the eighteenth century, some English Puritans began preaching that pure Calvinism is "unscriptural, unreasonable ... [and] invalidates all moral effort." The question, "if men are irresistibly predestined, how can you ask them to be good?" began to appear unanswerable.[7] The Scots, ancestors of many of today's Canadians, would have none of such heresy, but several New England clergy picked up the new ideas, and Harvard fell to the forerunners of the Unitarians. New England went through a violent upheaval as Yale and the frontier attempted to hold the line against the heretics now entrenched in the east.

Jonathan Edwards, a learned man from Yale, tried to reinvigorate Calvinism with his own interpretation of Newton and Locke. He was able to induce conversions by preaching hellfire, thus helping to light the fire of the Great Awakening, the American part of a larger movement "known in Germany as Pietism, [and] in England as Evangelicalism and Methodism." The English evangelist George Whitefield arrived in New England in 1740, where he spoke to enormous crowds in open fields, sending the people into convulsions and paroxysms of weeping and screaming. Whitefield was a friend and follower of John Wesley, the founder of Methodism. Perry Miller claims that the evangelical tradition in the United States derives from Wesley via Whitefield rather than from the Puritans of New England.[8] Benjamin Franklin described the enormous "multitudes of all sects and denominations that attended" Whitefield's sermons and the "extraordinary influence of his oratory on his hearers, and how much they admired and respected him, notwithstanding his common abuse of them, by assuring them they were naturally 'half beasts and half devils.'"[9]

Harvard and Boston won the battle for the mind of New England and thus for intellectual and literary authority in the future United States. The victory did not occur overnight: Yale eventually joined Harvard as a liberal institution, but the Connecticut River valley was still struggling with the issue a century later when Emily Dickinson was writing. Enlightenment ideas formed the basis for the case against England before the American Revolution, and the Constitution and governing institutions are monuments to the great liberal thinkers of the eighteenth century.

New England Puritanism, which maintained a high level of piety for three generations, was not to be eradicated. The Great Awakening caused a split in American religious thinking that has continued to this day. The liberal tradition led directly to Emerson and the Transcendentalists, and to the vaunted New England conscience. On the other side, Whitefield was the first of many wandering evangelists to ignore denominational differences and sway huge crowds with blatant emotional manipulations. Today, Billy Graham has gained dignity with age, but, with the assistance of television, religious enthusiasts like Oral Roberts, Jerry Falwell, and Jimmy Swaggart maintain the tradition.

Bercovitch has summed up the long-term effects of Puritan thought in the United States: it gave America "the status of visible sainthood," and contributed to "the anthropomorphic nationalism that characterizes" American literature. "American dream, manifest destiny, [and] redeemer nation," are all derived from it, so its impact "cannot be overestimated."[10] Because the Puritan period and the Great Awakening occurred before the American Revolution, they are part of the Loyalists' heritage, yet none of the effects listed by Bercovitch have taken place in Canada. What the Loyalists did take from their American (as well as their British) heritage was a belief in the importance of the church in human society, for the Puritans had maintained a rigid theocracy and most of the colonies had established churches at the time of the Revolution. The Loyalists joined the French, whose lives were minutely controlled by the Catholic Church, and while few of them had any fondness for Catholicism, they had to accept these well-established people. Also, the Loyalists agreed with the French that an established church was a necessary part of civil society.

The First Amendment to the American Constitution, which states that "Congress shall make no law respecting an establishment of religion or prohibiting the free exercise thereof," was passed in 1791. It took more than forty years for all of the states to comply; Connecticut was the last. The meaning of the First Amendment has always been controversial. In 1833, Justice Joseph Story wrote that its purpose was to "exclude all rivalry among Christian sects, and to prevent any national ecclesiastical establishment." More recently Miller, recalling Story's words, adds that the amendment did not propose any "civil equality of atheism and Christianity," but was intended to prevent the involvement of the state in "the evangelical crusade to make and keep America Christian."[11] Harold Bloom quotes Donald Meyer on the "positive meaning" of the "ban on any establishment of religion": "Americans were free to invent new theologies, new churches, new religions."[12] Americans continue to invent new theologies and religions, and the "evangelical crusade" has never stopped.

The distinction between a camp meeting and a religious revival is not always clear. The camp meeting is held out of doors or in a tent and lasts for several days; a revival is usually under the auspices of a church. Bloom says that the first American camp meeting took place at Cane Ridge, Kentucky in August 1801, but the inspiration came from men like Whitefield.[13] De Tocqueville found men "full of a fanatical and almost wild enthusiasm," and strange sects that endeavored to "strike out extraordinary paths to eternal happiness." He claimed that such things hardly existed in Europe, and concluded that religious "insanity is very common in the United States."[14] Numerous traveling evangelists wandered the hinterland, most of them devoid of any formal theological training. They undercut their critics by quoting the Bible and brazenly holding "the Enlightenment conviction that truth was self-evident."[15] One of the best examples of religious "insanity" occurred on October 22, 1844, when thousands of followers of William Miller gathered in a field in western New York to await the end of the world. The failure of this cataclysmic event to take place — called the "Great Disappointment" — spurred undaunted followers to originate "Seventh-day Adventism and (less directly) Jehovah's Witnesses."[16]

The intellectuals on the eastern seaboard disapproved of such theatrics, just as the liberal clergy at Harvard had frowned on Jonathan Edwards' technique for inducing conversions, but the intelligentsia had more in common with leaders of camp meetings than they cared to admit; both were undermining the institution of the church. Both sought to dispense with church history, which, for the evangelicals, meant a return to the origins of Christianity and immediate personal contact with Jesus. For the intellectuals, it meant disposing of traditional religion in favor of something new and distinctly American.

When the Loyalists fled north, French Catholics were long established and, though conquered by the British, their religion and lifestyle were protected by the Quebec Act. The French looked on the Catholic Church as their primary authority and passively obeyed British law. The English struggled to establish the Anglican Church and thus duplicate British society in the New World. An established church had been the norm for a thousand years of Christendom and was almost universally considered necessary for a smoothly functioning society. It handled education and welfare and stood at the center of "community life," where it was "the core of the whole national system of values."[17] Peaceful, medieval Quebec mirrored many of the Loyalists' own ideas of a virtuous lifestyle.

The British Colonial Office was under the impression that the root cause of the American Revolution was Britain's failure to establish its own institutions in the colonies. It was determined not to repeat the mistake, and so the Constitution Act of 1791, which created Upper and Lower Canada, provided for one-seventh of the land to be reserved "for the support of a Protestant clergy," widely interpreted as Anglican.[18] However, these lands, known as the Clergy Reserves, caused much dissent. Although the colonists may have shared an ideal of a unified society — one in which the church worked in tandem with the state — the majority of colonists were not Anglicans. In the early nineteenth century, saddlebag Methodists took religion to the rural areas, whereas massive immigration from Scotland and Ireland swelled the ranks of Presbyterians and English-speaking Catholics. The population grew rapidly; by the middle of the nineteenth century, Methodists, Presbyterians, and Baptists outnumbered the Anglicans by a wide margin.[19] The struggle for an Anglican establishment was doomed from the beginning, despite the fact that Anglicans maintained an elite status in both government and society.

British law required tolerance, but each colony made its own rules with regard to relations between church and state. In Quebec the ties were close indeed. In Upper Canada in 1837, Bishop John Strachan received a royal charter to open the Anglican King's College. The public outcry over one denomination being favored over the others forced the government to secularize the school. This was the origin of the University of Toronto, now a federation of colleges, many of them church-based. In 1854, the government bowed again to the majority and secularized the Clergy Reserves. But, even though this meant that there was to be no established church, the ideal of some type of religious unification remained. On the practical side, a tiny and widely scattered population could ill-afford a multiplicity of churches.

Because Canadians lacked the anti-historical bias that led American theologians to contemplate a new Christian society to replace one deemed obsolete, the American camp meeting did not enter Canada. Unschooled preachers were not tolerated by church authorities. Instead of inventing new theologies and fragmenting existing denominations, Canadians struggled to unify. Shortly after Confederation, both the Methodists and the Presbyterians formed single nation-wide denominations. In 1908, Methodists, Presbyterians, and Congregationalists began discussions on church union, and in 1925, the United Church of Canada came into being to "foster the spirit of unity," in the hope for a church that could be called "national."[20] Until the 1960s, the vast majority of the Canadian population adhered to no more than six or seven Christian denominations.[21] There are many more in the United States, where mainline denominations have repeatedly split over contentious issues.[22] Alfred Kazin points out, for example, that defending "slavery by Scripture was a great exercise for Southern ministers."[23]

Throughout the nineteenth century, both Canada and the United States considered themselves Christian nations, but to Americans this meant only Protestant. Kazin notes that the "first evangelical zeal of the Reformation was re-created in America with a vengeance ... A masterful all-pervading Protestantism that was to exfoliate into innumerable sects was split on every doctrinal issue except its hostility to Catholicism, the Whore of Babylon."[24] The citizens of the United States had not forgotten their outrage over the Quebec Act's official acceptance of Catholicism. According to David Reynolds, "anti-Catholicism," along with temperance, anti-slavery, and labor conditions, was actually a "reform movement" in antebellum America. Licentious priests are common characters in early popular fiction, and a series of "exposés" appeared in the 1830s that describe "alcoholism, flagellation, prostitution, and infanticide within convent walls." The incoming Irish were greeted with such hostility that they were effectively stranded along the

Atlantic coast. Emily Dickinson heard that her brother, who was teaching in Boston, had many Irish boys among his students. She wrote to him in 1851, saying that she prayed for the souls of the poor Irish, but that, so far as she was concerned, he could "kill some — there are so many now, there is no room for Americans."[25]

The Loyalists were obliged to accept the Quebec Act, so Catholics and Protestants were more or less evenly matched in pre-Confederation Canada. Irish-Catholic immigrants to Canada could settle where they wished, and there was an absence of any scandalous novels about licentious priests or evil doings in convents in Canadian literature. Of much greater importance, however, is the fact that the "redeemer nation" concept of the United States was utterly foreign to Canadian national ideas, and not just because the Loyalists considered themselves British. Catholic theology could not countenance the idea of a nation chosen by God, so no form of the American Dream could be sold to French Canadians, or, indeed, to Irish Catholics.

Catholicism has had a difficult time in the Americas north of Mexico, but because of French loyalty, it had much greater influence in Canada than in the United States. So much influence, in fact, that the Bishops of Quebec issued a Pastoral Letter in 1875, stating that the Church is "constituted by its Divine founder in the form of a Society perfect in itself, distinct and independent of civil society ... Not only is the Church independent of civil society, but it is superior to it ... the State, then, is in the Church, and not the Church in the State."[26] One can hardly imagine the effect of such a publication in the United States.

The Loyalists and the French got along fairly well until large numbers of Protestants from northern Ireland arrived in the early nineteenth century. In Ontario in the 1800s, Protestant Irish outnumbered Catholic Irish by three to one. These fervent Protestants formed numerous Orange societies, with their accompanying lodges, parades, and virulent anti-Catholicism. Clearly, Ontario was a hopeless case in the eyes of the French, but the opening of the West presented "some tantalizing prospects for the Catholic clergy of Quebec. Because of the French population's unusually high birth rate and its tightly knit social organization, it was thought possible to leapfrog Anglo-Protestant Ontario and establish French-Catholic hegemony on the Prairies." The Riel

Rebellion of 1885 made these ambitions look like a "sinister plot" in English Canada, and Manitoba became something of a Catholic-Protestant battleground.[27] The Catholic clergy's opposition to industry and city life spelled its eventual loss of influence.

In Canada, the strength of the Christian denominations and the population's tendency to rely on European social standards meant that authority came from Europe: the Vatican for Catholics and Britain for most Protestants. The resulting cultural climate discouraged theological innovation and mystical imaginings. Canada has never produced a Jonathan Edwards, a Ralph Waldo Emerson, or a Reinhold Niebuhr. By American standards, this is theological rigidity. Denominational authority, plus a strong emphasis on education, led many of Canada's clergy to move into other fields. E.J. Pratt, a doctor of theology, and Northrop Frye, an ordained minister, are two examples of Canadians who have made their major contributions in scholarship and the arts while retaining their religious underpinnings. Several of Canada's political parties were started by members of the clergy, and one still finds ordained ministers running for public office. Frye notes that Canadian philosophy has "a strong emphasis on religion" and that French Canada established a pattern — which English Canada tended to imitate — of "keeping church and state" close together.[28] In Canada's philosophy, education, public life, and literature, religion has always been prominent. Canadian clergy have never lost their social positions as Nathan Hatch claims they did in the United States.[29]

This situation changed dramatically in the 1960s with Quebec's Quiet Revolution. The provincial government of Jean Lesage took control of education, welfare, and other social functions away from the church, the birth rate dropped dramatically, and today Quebec is at least as secular as the other provinces. Church influences have decreased throughout Canada. This is a startling change from the days when the United Church and the Catholic bishops had real political influence with all three levels of government. Before the 1960s, however, the strength of the major denominations, the lack of a love affair with newness and innocence, and the absence of individualist philosophers like Emerson have meant that the Puritan (or Calvinist) ethos has been more tenacious in Canada than in the United States.

Ronald Sutherland claims "there are more clergymen per book in Canadian literature than in the literature of any other country." He finds this equally true in French and in English Canada, and suggests that this nation-wide concern with the ecclesiastic has been a distinct hindrance to the cultural and artistic development of the nation.[30] In the many small communities in both English and French Canadian literature, the church and clergy are prominent; authors stress the importance of church affiliation and the authority and high prestige of the clergy. This is often done with affectionate irony, in contrast to American literature, where the preacher is frequently an object of satire.

2

Religious Innovation in the United States

COTTON MATHER WAS A FOURTH-GENERATION New England Puritan. A descendant of the most notable of Puritan divines, he shared their religious fervor and, like them, wrote extensively. His *Magnalia Christi Americana*, published in England in 1704, was intended to be an *Aeneid* for Americans — what Foxe's *Book of Martyrs* had been to the English. Instead it fell on deaf ears, "a monumental elegy to a defunct corporate ideal." The eighteenth century had dawned, and, although the book was ignored, Mather left something of great value to his descendants: he predicted a great revolution, he used the term "American" in its corporate sense for the first time, and he sanctified the nation that was to be.[31]

The first American edition of Mather's *Magnalia* appeared in 1820 and sold surprisingly well. The theology was ignored, but details about the history of the new country struck a responsive chord. Harriet Beecher Stowe spoke for many of her contemporaries when she exclaimed over such "wonderful stories" about "my own country." They made her feel that the ground under her feet was "consecrated by some special dealing of God's providence." The book contributed to one of those paradoxes that arise periodically in human society: as the Americans were cutting off their past and depicting themselves as Adam before the fall, they were at the same time glorifying their Puritan ancestors. John Adams gave voice to a common platitude of the day when he spoke of the first fleet of Puritan ships inaugurating the "grand scene and Design in Providence, for the illumination of ... Mankind over the Earth."[32]

Bloom notes that a number of commentators have spoken of "the American Religion." If this "religion" had a theologian, he would be Emerson.[33] Emerson was firmly in the American tradition of theological innovation when he founded the Transcendental Club in 1836.[34] He defines a "Transcendentalist" as an "idealist," who places emphasis on "the power of Thought and of Will, on inspiration, on miracle, on individual culture." Emerson contrasts the idealist to the "materialist," who insists "on facts, on history, on the force of circumstances, and the animal wants of man." The

Transcendentalist may safely neglect, even contravene "every written commandment"; he has a "tendency to respect the intuitions," and to give them "authority over ... experience."[35]

Despite the fact that Emerson was himself a Unitarian minister until he resigned in 1838, his individualist philosophy discouraged organized religion and church affiliation. In the year of his resignation, he gave an address to the Harvard Divinity School in which he spoke of Jesus, who alone "estimated the greatness of man." Emerson then shocked his audience by claiming that the "idioms of his language, and the figures of his rhetoric, have usurped the place of his truth; and churches are not built on his principles, but on his tropes." In his 1841 essay, "Self-Reliance," Emerson disparages those who would "maintain a dead church" or "contribute to a dead Bible Society."[36] Kazin argues that, "Emerson's God did not make this world or provide salvation in the next ... He was another side of oneself ... Father, Son, and Holy Ghost were now just beautiful figures of speech."[37] Emerson was, in a sense, closer to his Puritan ancestors than to the Unitarians because of his need to internalize God, but the ancestors would not have recognized any kinship. He turned their theology upside down, arguing for a pantheistic religion, with a concept he called the "Over-Soul" — "that great nature in which we rest, as the earth lies in the soft arms of the atmosphere." It contains, he adds, "every man's particular being," while each being is "made one with all other." Emerson uses God and the soul more or less interchangeably, and stresses the direct communication between the Almighty and each individual. The "soul's communication of truth is the highest event in nature," for it is "an influx of the Divine mind into our mind."[38]

Emerson suppressed his distaste for history sufficiently to make some glowing comments about the New England Puritans and the American Revolution. In his essay "Boston" (1861), he praised the Puritan's "deep religious sentiment" and "culture of the intellect," although the Middle Ages was still "obscuring their reason."[39] He said nothing about Puritan theology or about the brutality with which a rigid code of conduct was enforced. The "redeemer nation" concept in his philosophy is revealed in his essay on the American Revolution, "The Fortune of the Republic" (1863): "When the cannon is aimed by ideas, when men with religious convictions are behind it, when men die for what they live for ... then poets are born, and the better code of laws at last records the victory." He concluded that "these triumphs of humanity" culminated with "the planting of America," and assured his readers that "this country, the last found, is the great charity of God to the human race."[40]

The Transcendentalists were religious enthusiasts in a broad sense, although the term is usually applied to fundamentalists or evangelicals. None was more enthusiastic than Thoreau, whose *Walden*, generally seen today as the work of an early environmentalist, in fact recounts a religious experience. *Walden* is something of a "scriptural parable," and was like a bible to the Transcendentalists.[41] Thoreau tended to make more extreme statements than Emerson did, especially when discussing any institution of society. Traditional religion to Thoreau has corrupted our manners "by communication with the saints. Our hymn-books resound with a melodious cursing of God."[42] The woods, he believed, was the place to find the religious experience the churches failed to provide. Walden Pond can be interpreted as a baptismal font, as a mirror of the soul, and as a window onto the divine creation.[43] Thoreau, filled with religious inspiration, is at his most poetic when he discusses the pond. Describing his famous experience of "fishing from a boat by moonlight," he writes: "It was very queer, especially in dark nights, when your thoughts had wandered to vast cosmogonal themes in other spheres, to feel this faint jerk, which came to interrupt your dreams and link you to Nature again. It seemed as if I might next cast my line upward into the air, as well as downward into this element." As Thoreau moves from summer to winter and from night to day, he makes explicit the image of the pond as a window opened to the creator. Cutting through snow and ice in order to "open a window," he finds that "Heaven is under our feet as well as over our heads."[44]

Thoreau made a visit to Canada in 1850 and described the experience in *A Yankee in Canada*, published posthumously in 1866. The place was full of visible members of institutions — such as soldiers and priests — and Thoreau was horrified. He claimed that the inhabitants were "inferior" to those of New England because they have "no quarrel with Church or State." His conclusion is that the English government is "too good for them" because it permits them to "wear their own fetters."[45] Even voluntary adherence to church and state was considered slavery by Thoreau. He visited a Catholic church during this trip and was "impressed by the quiet religious atmosphere of the place," but could say nothing good about Roman Catholics. He describes them as a people who have "fallen far behind the significance of their symbols. It is as if an ox had strayed into a church and were trying to bethink himself." He concludes that New England's "forests are such a church, far grander and more sacred."[46]

Melville had little respect for the Transcendentalists, and he came to look upon Emerson as a fool, although he could not ignore them. Transcendental ideology appears in his writings, often in a perverse form. Captain Ahab in *Moby Dick* (1851) is not so much a devil as a demonic god, who can be interpreted as a parody of Emerson. Ahab recognizes no god outside himself, and expresses the ultimate in self-reliance; he is prepared to risk the destruction of his ship and crew in order to take revenge on a giant white whale. When his first mate suggests that vengeance on a dumb brute is "blasphemous," Ahab replies, "Talk not to me of blasphemy, man, I'd strike the sun if it insulted me." He muses on his own perverse relationship to nature with a Puritan's preconception about election and damnation: "Gifted with the high perception, I lack the low, enjoying power; damned, most subtly and most malignantly damned! in the midst of Paradise!"[47] Bloom sees Ahab as a tragic hero — akin to Macbeth and Milton's Satan — who appears to have converted from "Quaker Christianity to a Parsee version of Manichaeism, in which the cosmos is in contention between two rival deities."[48] Ahab certainly considers himself one of those deities.

Ishmael, the narrator in *Moby Dick*, has a vision of Emerson's Over-Soul. Sitting on the masthead and staring into the ocean, he is a "sorry guard," for he has "the problem of the universe revolving" in him. He is lulled into an "opium-like listlessness" and "loses his identity," until he takes the "mystic ocean at his feet for the visible image of that deep, blue, bottomless soul, pervading mankind and nature."[49]

Melville's fascination with American religious attitudes is more apparent in *Billy Budd, Foretopman*, written shortly before the author's death in 1891 but not discovered until 1920. Melville's failure to find acceptance as a serious writer in America had led to despair and emotional collapse, and so his sense of irony as he looked back on the myth of Adam before the Fall must have been intense. Billy Budd is certainly an unfallen Adam, a virtuous and innocent youth who is taken from a merchant vessel named "The Rights of Man" and pressed into service on a British warship during the Napoleonic Wars. When he is unjustly accused of treason, Billy is struck dumb and lashes out at his accuser, killing a superior officer. For the sake of naval discipline, he must hang. This Fall-of-Man theme is heavy with both biblical and Emersonian imagery. The body of Billy's accuser is like a "dead snake," which a distraught Captain Vere says was struck dead "by an angel of God. Yet the angel must hang!" The officers of the court wish to spare Billy, whom they believe to be "innocent before God." Captain Vere agrees with their sentiments, for it is "Nature" to do so. He then brings them back to the real world with the reminder that their uniforms do not "attest that our allegiance is to Nature ... No, to the King." The court reluctantly condemns Billy, and the verdict is announced to the entire crew, who listen with a dumbness "like that of a seated congregation of believers in Hell listening to the clergyman's announcement of his Calvinistic text."[50]

Billy's hanging suggests Christ's dying for the sins of the world. Awaiting his fate, Billy is confined in one of several gun bays, "like small confessionals or side-chapels in a cathedral," where he experiences the agony of "a generous young heart's virgin experience of the diabolical." Billy goes to his death calling for God's blessing on the captain who condemned him, a blessing echoed by the mesmerized crew. He is hanged just as the sunrise is "shot through with a soft glory as of the fleece of the Lamb of God," and his ascending body takes "the full rose of the dawn."[51] One wonders what Emerson's reaction would have been had he lived to read Melville's last novel.

Clergy are fairly common in antebellum American literature — Dimmesdale in *The Scarlet Letter* and Father Mapple in *Moby Dick* — but after the Civil War, which was so devastating to the Garden of Eden and "redeemer nation" concepts, members of the clergy began to appear as objects of satire. Hatch notes that clergymen in the nineteenth century "lost their unrivaled position as authoritative sources of information." Millions of people turned to unschooled "upstarts" such as Lorenzo Dow, famous traveling evangelist, Joseph Smith, founder of the Mormons, and William Miller, who predicted that the world would end in 1844.[52] The preacher leading a camp meeting became a favorite subject for satire.

In the early twentieth century, Sinclair Lewis turned his satiric pen to various lowbrow aspects of American life. He was particularly effective savaging the small town in *Main Street,* and nearly as thorough in shooting down the preacher in *Elmer Gantry* (1927). Elmer Gantry is in turn a Baptist, a traveling evangelist, and a Methodist, but he is primarily a hypocrite. His is the story of a rake's progress, for Gantry, who is proud of his ability to sway crowds, is not troubled by faith. At Terwillinger College, he is captain of the football team and nicknamed Hell-Cat. He also has a freethinking roommate, who ridicules religious hysteria at this Baptist college and Gantry generally agrees with him until he goes to a religious revival. Caught up in the emotional hysteria, he emotes: "Oh God, oh, I have sinned! My sins are heavy on me! I am unworthy of compassion! O Jesus, intercede for me!" Those around him are "beating their foreheads," "shrieking," "jerking," and "twitching." Gantry is affected by the hysteria and joins in, realizing that he has found the key to his success. "He had it now — popularity, almost love, almost reverence, and he felt overpoweringly his role as leading man."[53] With the urging of his mother and encouragement of the authorities, he decides to enter the ministry. It is necessary for Gantry to receive a "Call" from God before entering the seminary, a feat he accomplishes with two drinks of corn whiskey. Covering the smell with strong peppermints, Gantry runs to the house of the college president: "he shouted from the door, erect, while they knelt and looked up at him mousily, 'It's come! I feel it in everything! God just opened my eyes.'" They listen, adding "grunts of 'Amen, Brother.'" Gantry is ordained after his third year at the seminary, and is given a small country church, where he is in his element, no longer pestered by courses in Greek or theology. He preaches about love, but "for the benefit of the more leathery and zealous deacons down front, he permitted them to hate all Catholics, all persons who failed to believe in hell and immersion, and all rich mortgage-holders." He is caught enjoying a drunken weekend, and expelled from the college.[54]

Gantry has trouble staying away from liquor and tobacco, but manages to conquer both desires after he gets involved with a woman evangelist, Sharon Falconer, an even more effective crook than he is. He discovers her at a tent big enough to hold three thousand people, with a three-tiered structure at the front: "one for the choir, one higher up for a row of seated local clergy; and at the top a small platform with a pulpit shaped like a shell and painted like a rainbow." Sharon comes forward with her arms outstretched. "The sleeves of her straight white robe, with its ruby girdle, were slashed, and fell away from her arms as she drew everyone to her." Gantry is smitten. Whatever other sins he is able to overcome, he cannot resist women.[55]

Sharon later dies in a fire as she is preaching to thousands on an ancient pier. Gantry finds that he cannot manage alone as an evangelist, so he ingratiates himself with the Methodists, and rapidly moves upward with increasingly better-paying congregations. He has repeated narrow escapes from disgrace, but the more he sins, the louder he preaches against "vice. Booze. Legs. Society bridge." His Sunday evening services are entertainments. One night he hires a juggler, who wears "a placard proclaiming that he stood for 'God's Word' and who showed how easy it was to pick up weights symbolically labeled 'Sin' and 'Sorrow' and 'Ignorance' and 'Papistry.'"[56]

Finally, Gantry is caught in an affair with the church secretary, blackmailed, and faced with a major scandal, but manages to outwit his accusers with the help of a private detective and some blackmail of his own. Facing his enormous adoring congregation, he kneels, sobs, and appeals to them: "do you believe in my innocence, in the fiendishness of my accusers?" After the thunderous hallelujah, Gantry notices the attractive ankle of a new member of the choir, but continues his prayer: "Dear Lord, thy work is but begun! We shall yet make these United States a moral nation!"[57] This novel is not well plotted; as Mark Shorer points out, it is, "a loosely episodic chronicle."[58] It does, however, paint a vivid picture of the contempt that American descendants of the Emersonians felt for overt religious hysteria.

William Styron calls his controversial 1967 novel, *The Confessions of Nat Turner*, "less an 'historical novel' … than a meditation on history." Nat Turner, a slave in southeastern Virginia in the early nineteenth century, led the most "effective, sustained revolt" in the history of American slavery.[59] The revolt was put down and the leaders hanged. Turner's confession before his death is the basis of this novel.[60] Styron stays close to the few known facts about Turner's life, but the fictional treatment of his childhood and the motivations for the revolt comprise one of the most devastating commentaries on slavery in the annals of American literature.

In Styron's novel, Nat Turner is raised as a privileged house servant, given an elementary education, religious instruction, and a Bible one Christmas, his sole possession and his only reading material throughout most of his life. He is trained as a carpenter and plans are made for him to be freed. The soil of Virginia, ruined by tobacco, leaves one plantation after another bankrupt, and sends the displaced slaves to the Deep South to be sold. When Turner's owner loses his plantation, he is left with a Baptist preacher, Reverend Eppes, who, it is understood, is to take him to Richmond to complete his apprenticeship as a carpenter before he is freed. Instead, Eppes — an archetypal southern redneck — nearly works Turner to death by renting him out to members of the dirt-poor congregation, then selling him at the local slave market. Waiting in a slave pen for someone to buy him, Turner recounts his feelings: "I experienced a kind of disbelief which verged close upon madness, then a sense of betrayal, then fury such as I had never known before, then finally ... hatred so bitter that I grew dizzy." He is able to carry on because he hears the Lord speaking to him. It is a voice "booming in the trees: '*I abide.*'"[61]

Nat Turner is both a Christ figure and a Moses figure. He is a skilled carpenter whose life is spent near a town called Jerusalem; his preaching among the slaves is so well known that his white lawyer calls him "Reverend"; he performs several baptisms in the river; and his reading in the Old Testament leads him to the conclusion that he is chosen to lead his people out of slavery. Numerous quotations from the Bible show the logic of Turner's conclusions: "*Go through the midst of Jerusalem ... Slay utterly old and young, both maids and little children.*" He wonders why God should spare some and "slay the helpless; nonetheless, it was His word ... it seemed as if His will and my mission could not be more plain and intelligible: to free my people."[62]

Religion in the rural South is central to the setting. Turner asks permission to go to a camp meeting, where "for four days and nights there would be singing and praying and feasting.... There would be a laying-on of hands and organ and banjo music, and general salvation for all lucky enough to attend." Later he sees Reverend Eppes as "a skinny, big-nosed, pentecostal, Christ-devoured" preacher, who rakes his congregation "through hellfire." He finds Eppes' church services scandalous and degrading: "whooping and shouting and bubbling at the mouth ... falling into a kind of ultimate frenzy, stripping to their underdrawers, male and female, and riding each other bareback up and down the aisles."[63]

When he settles down with a new master and begins to plan his uprising, Turner becomes famous for his knowledge of scripture. When he can get time off, he goes to the woods and fasts, remembering lines from Isaiah: *"To loose the bonds of wickedness, to undo the heavy burdens, and to let the oppressed go free."* After several days of fasting, an enormous black angel appears in the sky and speaks to Turner in a thunderous voice: *"Fear God and give glory to Him for the hour of His judgment is come."*[64]

One day a poor and miserable white man comes to him for help, and Turner agrees to baptize the man after he has spent a week fasting and meditating. Turner goes to a local white minister and asks permission to do the baptism in his church. The minister is outraged and asks where he got his training in divinity. Turner replies that "[I]n God's sight I am a preacher of His word." This further enrages the minister, who aims a kick and says he has "better things to do than be made a fool of by ... an uppity nigger. Your master will hear of this, I promise *you-u-u!"* The trial of Nat Turner is like a psychological crucifixion. The lawyer "defending" him speaks in detail about the "deficiencies of the Negro character." He claims that the "ordinary Negro slave ... will leap to his master's defense" and thus "give proud evidence of the benevolence of a system so ignorantly decried by ... moralistically dishonest detractors." The lawyer predicts that slavery will last a thousand years. Nat Turner goes unrepentant to his death, a sacrificial figure to the end.[65]

A different kind of Christ figure can be found in Anne Tyler's 1991 novel, *Saint Maybe.* The protagonist, Ian Bedloe, is burdened with sin. Believing that he was responsible for his brother's suicide and his sister-in-law's death from a drug overdose, which left three young children in the care of his aging parents, Ian seeks relief from his suffering at several churches. One evening he passes a storefront where he hears a hymn being sung. He joins the group, then laughs at an inappropriate moment and burns with shame. "To laugh out loud at a mother's bereavement. He wished he could disappear." He apologizes to the people and asks them to pray for him to be "good again ... to be forgiven."[66] After the service, the minister boldly asks Ian why he needs to be forgiven. A shocked Ian tells him the story. Reverend Emmett calmly informs him that in order to be forgiven, he must make restitution — that is, he must leave college and help his mother raise the children. As part of his compliance, Ian gets himself apprenticed to a carpenter and becomes a devout member of the Church of the Second Chance.

The setting of *Saint Maybe* is a complete contrast to that of *The Confession of Nat Turner*. Far from being surrounded by religion, Ian lives in contemporary Baltimore with middle-class parents who are casual Presbyterians. When he tells his parents of his decision, his shocked father asks if he has "fallen into the hands of some *sect*." Ian tells them the whole story, leaving them white faced and unquestioning. Ian gradually takes over the household and essentially raises all three children. Twice he tells someone that he is only a carpenter and receives the reply: our Lord "was a carpenter."[67]

All of Tyler's novels are replete with ironic humor. The Church of the Second Chance is a creation of its minister and most of the members are simple and uneducated; they call each other brother and sister using only first names. Rev. Emmett, however, is wise. The son of an Episcopal minister, he was at an Episcopal seminary when he decided that kneeling before a crucifix was idolatry. He decided to found a church "without symbols ... without baptism or communion where only the *real* things mattered and where the atonement must be as real as the sin itself." Emerson would have approved. This church suits Ian, who remains faithful to it. After years of penance Ian wonders why he doesn't feel forgiven, until Emmett tells him that to relieve his "burden" he must forgive his brother and his brother's wife. When Emmett tries to talk Ian into going to Bible college and ultimately taking over the church, Ian is stunned and wants to say, *"you* ARE *the church*," but worries that this sounds blasphemous. Emmett finally realizes that his church is far from perfect and that many of the rules he invented are arbitrary and unreasonable. It will probably die with its minister.[68]

Much of the humor in this novel derives from Ian's comments about God. His fellow carpenters consider him "peculiar" because he once "made the mistake of trying to talk about Second Chance." The children try to arrange a wife for Ian by inviting an attractive teacher to dinner. Ian invites some church members to the same dinner, and, as his disgusted family watches, he proceeds to talk about God: "turning all holy on them." The teacher's "smile was glazing over the way people's always did when the bald, uncomfortable sound of God's name was uttered in social surroundings."[69] *Saint Maybe* shows the touch of a woman writer, one who eschews the caustic humor of a Sinclair Lewis and the tragic irony of a William Styron. The novel has an effective sense of place, an offbeat religion treated with gentle irony, and a sensitivity to the feelings of the protagonist rarely found in novels by men.

At the end of the twentieth century, religion is as pervasive in the United States as it has ever been. Television has given new life to evangelism, so that itinerant preachers can now talk to far larger crowds than could be assembled at any camp meeting. Lipset reported in 1996 that Gallup polls "indicate that Americans are the most churchgoing in Protestantism and the most fundamentalist in Christendom."[70]

3

Striving for Church Unity in Canada

NINETEENTH-CENTURY FICTION WRITTEN IN CANADA almost invariably contains references to the church as a normal part of everyday living, particularly the Catholic Church, which is present to some degree in all fiction set in early Quebec. Novels written in French in this era treat the church and the clergy as integral to daily life; those written in English demonstrate a surprising lack of hostility to Catholicism, considering the strength of the Protestant sects in the English colonies.

Both William Kirby's *The Golden Dog* and Gilbert Parker's *The Seats of the Mighty* are set in Quebec at the time of the Seven Years' War. Both have French-Canadian heroines, and both heroines spend time in a convent. Both convents have kind and understanding Mother Superiors who bend iron rules to help the heroes become reunited with their loves. Dennis Duffy sees this attitude springing from "an imperialist nationalism" that flourished in English Canada in the late nineteenth century.[71] Such sympathetic treatment of Catholic institutions was almost unknown in American literature at that time.

The unadulterated Presbyterianism brought to Canada by Scottish immigrants is best illustrated in Ralph Connor's *The Man from Glengarry*. Connor's work was extremely popular in its day and was often praised by the intelligentsia, but the author never had a very high opinion of his own literary skills and considered the Presbyterian ministry his primary occupation. The community of Glengarry is much like the one in which Connor himself was raised — homogeneous (like a Highland clan), with a rough pioneer lifestyle and the Presbyterian Church at its center, the emotional focal point for the people. The minister is deeply respected and treated as the highest authority, and the church, while not legally an established church, is the only one in the community.

Ranald MacDonald, Connor's youthful hero, receives much of his moral education from the minister's wife, Mrs. Murray. His most important lesson is learning to renounce vengeance, no easy task when Highland tradition calls for vengeance on one's enemy. Ranald's father, Black Hugh, was tricked into a fight and badly beaten, and has sworn to kill his assailant once he recovers. But because he is dying, revenge is expected to be carried out by his son. Mrs. Murray, trying to teach forgiveness, has the help of Hugh's brother, who has been "saved" and who silences his Highland instincts with the biblical phrase, "Vengeance is mine saith the Lord." On his deathbed Hugh forgives his enemy and extracts a promise from Ranald to do the same. Before Hugh dies, he expresses concern that his deceased wife did not have "the marks" of one elected for salvation. Mrs. Murray comforts him with the assurance: "If she loved her Saviour she is with him now."[72]

A more difficult situation arises when a member of the Glengarry lumbering crew is accidentally drowned, and the subject of salvation is raised. An American member of the crew, known as "Yankee," joins the mourners. No one expects him to be religious; he is not a Presbyterian and is "woefully ignorant of the elements of Christian knowledge." At the wake, when he overhears an elder of the church saying that the death of the young man is "a small thing ... when the Lord is speaking in judgment and wrath," he explodes: "I'll be gol-blamed to a cinder! ... They ain't sendin' him to hell, are they?" He expounds on the goodness of the deceased young man, but the elder protests against any "Armenian doctrine of works,"[73] and asks severely: "You would not be pointing to good works as a ground of salvation?"[74] The minister's sermon at the funeral comforts the bereaved, for it is only the strength of the church and the authority of the minister that can soften the harshest aspects of Calvinism.

The church in Glengarry holds a "great revival." This is unlike an American camp meeting, for it is a function of the church and led by the minister, who has "a great fear of religious excitement" and has seen "the dreadful reaction following a state of exalted religious feeling." The inspiration for the revival comes after the opening of a new church and the sermon of a visiting professor who speaks on love. The sternest of the elders is displeased, for the people were there to "lament their Original and Actual sin; and they expected and required to hear of the judgments of the Lord, and to be summoned to flee from the wrath to come."[75] The sermon moves others, however, and one man comes forward to be saved, inspiring the community to agree to a great revival.

The situation in Glengarry is reminiscent of seventeenth-century New England, except that there are no gallows and whipping posts. It was noted earlier that the Scots would have nothing to do with the heresy of Unitarianism and retained their belief in predestination. The Murrays never argue against predestination but do try to steer around it; and since they have such prestige and authority, they are able to do so. The evils they try to counter are both imported from Britain: clan fighting and class snobbery. The latter has no place in Glengarry where they are all members of one class, but outside the village, Ranald must learn to apply the moral lessons taught by Mrs. Murray to the world of business and society at large. He revisits his home and contacts Mrs. Murray before he gains the confidence to reject the social climbing girl he had been pursuing and marry the upright one. Connor attributed the popularity of his books to three things: muscular Christianity, verisimilitude, and the powerful story of Canada itself.[76]

Stephen Leacock satirizes rival churches in *Arcadian Adventures with the Idle Rich* (1914). The tall spire of St. Asaph's Episcopal Church points,[77] the rector says, "to the blue sky" as a "warning against the sins of a commercial age." Businessmen sit before the rector in rows, "their bald heads uncovered and their faces stamped with contrition" as they think of business deals they have failed to make for "lack of faith." Less than a hundred yards away is the rival church of St. Osoph, "presbyterian down to its very foundations in bed rock, thirty feet below the level of the avenue," with its "short, squat tower ... and a gloomy minister with a shovel hat who lectures on philosophy on week-days at the university. He loves to think that his congregation are made of the lowly and the meek in spirit, and to reflect that, lowly and meek as they are, there are men among them that could buy out half the congregation of St. Asaph's."[78]

St. Osoph's has been losing parishioners to St. Asaph's, because the Episcopal rector is going "forward with the times" while the Presbyterian minister is sliding "quietly backwards with the centuries." When St. Osoph's minister has a stroke, the trustees grasp the opportunity to hire a replacement — one who demands a high salary and has "Scotch parentage." In his first sermon, the new minister tells his congregation that at least seventy percent of them are destined for "eternal punishment," which he labels "simply and forcibly 'hell.'" The people are delighted and so many attend the next Sunday that he raises the percentage to eighty-five. "Young and old flocked to St. Osoph's."[79]

Discussions on church union were ongoing during the time Leacock was writing *Arcadian Adventures* and, not surprisingly, became the subject of his humor. Trustees of the rival churches begin to talk of a merger, "to be known as the United Church Limited or by some similar name." One trustee, who had arranged "a merger of four soda-water companies," explains that the two churches "can't live under the present conditions of competition." Likening the situation to that of "two rum distilleries," he recommends a "business solution ... a merger." Both congregations agree and thenceforth "the two churches ... stand side by side united and at peace."[80] There is no Lewis-type satire in Leacock's comic irony, which is indeed comic, as any uniting of churches in Canada would have to be done by the "head office." Ralph L. Curry notes that Leacock's "sense of time and place is so sharp," that he probably "owes a great deal to the influence of the nineteenth-century 'local colour' writers."[81] Leacock was also drawing on Canada's ecclesiastical traditions.

The irony with which Leacock depicts Canadian religious observances does not deny the fact that in Canada's many small towns, the church was both a cultural and a religious center. The town of Horizon in Sinclair Ross's *As For Me and My House* (1941) is too poor to afford much culture. Philip Bentley is a clergyman who longs to be an artist, and Horizon is his fifth small-town congregation. His wife, the narrator and a musician, refers collectively to all of the towns they have served as Main Streets, suggesting Sinclair Lewis' influence. The novel is set in the 1930s, a time of drought and depression on the prairie where nature is at its most challenging: "The town seems huddled together, cowering on a high, tiny perch, afraid to move lest it topple into the wind."[82]

The church is the dispenser of whatever beauty, comfort, and meaning can be added to the bleak lives of the townspeople. The minister and his wife are grindingly poor, but their artistic talents are appreciated and, of course, their social position is unassailable, a recurring theme in Canadian fiction. Mrs. Bentley describes how they are entertained on their first night in town by the president of the Ladies Aid. The meal is good "to an almost sacrificial degree" and is a "kind of rite," at which the Bentleys preside as "priest and priestess." When they have settled into the manse, Mrs. Bentley notices that her neighbor has social ambitions. The neighbor is quick to see that the minister's wife may "be useful," and is lavish in her offers of food and "help." Mrs. Bentley muses on the town's "social hierarchy"; no matter how poorly she is dressed, "the minister's wife goes everywhere, meets everyone," and her "prestige" is second to none.[83]

The Bentleys' unhappiness is due primarily to the fact that the minister has lost his religious faith, feels like a hypocrite, and, in true Puritan fashion, is consumed with guilt. The title of his first sermon, *As For Me and My House We Will Serve the Lord*, is a "stalwart, four-square, Christian sermon." His wife says that the sermon "nails his colors to the mast," but he "handicaps himself with a guilty feeling that he ought to mean everything he says." He believes that he has compromised his conscience and is paying for it in "Main Streets." Philip's only outlet is drawing. His wife recalls that yesterday "he sketched a congregation as he sees it from the pulpit. Seven faces in the first row — ugly, wretched faces, big-mouthed, mean-eyed." He feels that he has not earned even the meager promised salary, and such debilitating guilt prevents him from asking for money owed him from previous congregations.[84]

When the Bentleys take in an abandoned twelve-year-old boy named Steve, the minister starts asking for back pay and angers some of the church members by indulging the boy. Steve was raised a Roman Catholic and insists on keeping a picture of the Virgin and a crucifix over his bed. This worries Mrs. Bentley: "Very fine and broad-minded of us, I have to admit, only what's Horizon going to say?" Before the situation becomes explosive, the bubble bursts. Someone notifies the Catholic authorities, and two priests who are "tactful, kindly enough men" arrive to take him away. The Bentleys do not argue. The priests thank them for everything they have "done for Steve," but "in a sentence or two" let them know they have "no claim on him."[85] Such a low key and tolerant resolution to an emotionally charged situation between Catholics and Protestants in a small town setting would be hard to find in an American novel of the period. Roy Daniells claims that the book is "an exposition of the Puritan conscience."[86] It is much more than that; it demonstrates the centrality of the church in traditional Canadian society.

The struggle to get money for Steve gives Mrs. Bentley the idea of saving a thousand dollars to get her husband out of the ministry — and to get themselves away from Main Street. They overcome their embarrassment, write to former congregations asking for the money owed them, and finally contemplate a new life. There is no bitterness shown and their congregation parts with them reluctantly.

The foregoing literary examples concern Protestant churches in narrow social environments. The respect and authority enjoyed by their ministers pales when compared with the position of priests in rural French Canada, a position that went unchallenged in French-Canadian literature until the publication of Ringuet's *Thirty Acres* (1938). This novel is a devastating commentary on a society that clung to the soil, fostered severe poverty, and encouraged large families and only minimal education. *Thirty Acres* introduced realism to French-Canadian fiction but, far more important, it defied a tradition in the "rural *terroir* novel" of idealizing life in the country. This ideology "proclaimed that only fidelity to the soil held out any hope of future happiness to French Canadians." Antoine Sirois argues that Ringuet created a "tragic hero."[87]

Euchariste Moisan inherits his uncle's farm and becomes engaged to a local girl. Before the wedding, he has a conversation with the parish priest, who is "pastor, judge, and advisor to the whole flock, arbiter of all disputes, intercessor to the Throne of Heaven, which sends good weather or bad; in fact, the real soul of that tightly knit, closed community — the French-Canadian parish." The priest assures Euchariste that he is "marrying a fine girl ... You'll get on well together, and I hope you have lots of youngsters." Moisan replies: "Don't worry about that, Father. And if God's willing I'll try to have one raised for a priest." The thought of raising a son to be a priest had never occurred to him before, but he likes the idea. He imagines his son driving along the road "carrying the Blessed Sacrament while people knelt as he passed ... everyone would look up to him, as is proper; and a little of this glory would be reflected on him, the father of a priest."[88]

Moisan and his wife have many children, but when the oldest son is ready to start studying for the priesthood, Moisan is hesitant. The education would be expensive, and the boy is just becoming helpful on the farm. The priest, who claims that it is his "duty ... to think for everybody in the parish," will not let Moisan forget his impulsive commitment. If he wants his "family to be blessed," he must "pay tithe in children too." The priest then offers to pay half the expenses, for "he was ashamed never to see his parish included in the list of those which sent up pupils."[89]

In addition to the son who becomes a priest, two of Moisan's daughters become nuns, so Moisan thinks that "God would be well pleased and would surely be generous in return." God shows no generosity. The family priest is given a dirt-poor parish, seems a stranger when he comes home, and works himself to death. When another son suggests that leaving the farm and working for steady wages is a good idea, Moisan explodes with anger. He reminds the lad what the Bishop had said: "[W]hen a man loves the land it's just like loving God ... [and] if you desert the land you're practically headed straight for hell." The boy is not convinced and leaves for New England, where he marries a girl who speaks no French.[90]

As the many children grow, marry, and have more children, the farm is put under severe strain. Moisan, clinging to traditional ways, refuses to put his savings in the bank and is ruined. He is forced to cede the farm to one of his sons, disinheriting the others. Finally, he is hustled off to New England to stay with his now English-speaking third son. There he becomes stranded, working as a night watchman, in a hostile alien environment among *les anglais*.

Thirty Acres caused a sensation in Quebec. The story begins near the end of the nineteenth century when the Catholic Church was "jealous of any call for loyalties" outside itself and was "confident that agriculture would remain the cornerstone of the economy."[91] It ends during the Depression when life on the farm is full of misery, and bare subsistence and widespread unemployment crippled much of North America.

Less than thirty years later, Marie Claire Blais's novel, *A Season in the Life of Emmanuel* (1965), tackles a similar theme. Written during the Quiet Revolution, it reverberates with anger and bitterness. Nicole Brossard claims that at the time of the novel's publication, she felt their generation's "wholesale revolt against the clergy," and saw the novel as a "merciless critique of Quebec society."[92] When the novel opens, Emmanuel is a newborn baby, the sixteenth child, who is cared for by his grandmother because his mother has gone back to working in the fields. The author imagines that Emmanuel is already familiar "with cold, with hunger, and perhaps even with despair."[93]

The grandmother nurses secret longings for a better life, and dotes on an older child, Jean-Le Maigre, who is sickly but "talented; Monsieur le Curé said so." The father insists that "school isn't necessary," because he knows what his children are "destined for." Jean-Le Maigre reads and writes compulsively, but must hide both books and his writing, which are destroyed if found by his father. Religion and church-run institutions are the only forces outside of the family. As Jean-Le Maigre and a younger brother, Number Seven, engage in drinking, smoking, stealing, and adolescent sex, they worry about the state of their souls, although Jean-Le Maigre claims that "all poets have a predilection *for debauchery*." After setting fire to the school, the boys are sent to the reformatory, an institution run by priests that resembles the lower reaches of Dante's *Inferno*. Finally, the grandmother arranges for Jean-Le Maigre to go to the Novitiate, where he is to be educated and ordained a priest. Ironically, it is there that he meets the devil in the form of Frère Théodule, a pedophile and necrophiliac, under whose care he dies. This novel is heavy with incest, child abuse, and masochism. The more the characters dwell on religion, the more likely they are to find ways to self-destruct. One sister, a fasting saint to the family, becomes a prostitute. Marie-Claire Blais has written a dark novel, one that seems to continue where Ringuet's *Thirty Acres* left off.[94]

Rudy Wiebe's *The Scorched-Wood People* (1977) is a fictionalized account of two Métis rebellions that took place in western Canada from 1869 to 1871 and in 1885. These French-English conflicts came to bloodshed and were the nearest thing to an "Indian war" in Canada's history. As in *Big Bear*, Wiebe uses no fictional characters and events are firmly grounded in history. The story is told from the Métis' perspective. Louis Riel, leader of the rebellions, sees himself chosen by God to lead his people and save them from the advance of civilization, which threatens the Métis' traditional way of life. The second rebellion is bloodier and more serious, because the plains Natives joined the Métis. Ontario and Quebec have very different views of the rebellions. In Quebec, Riel is a hero, protecting the French language and the Catholic religion from the English; in Ontario, he is a criminal who usurped the legitimate government and executed a Canadian citizen.

When the first moves are made to develop the western prairies, surveyors trampling their property alarm the Métis, who organize a provisional government, take over Fort Garry, repulse the new governor, and imprison a few Canadians. Their demands include the equality of the French language in all official matters, respect for property and customs, and for Manitoba to enter Canada as a province rather than a territory. All of these conditions are met, but, when one of the prisoners is executed, Ontario explodes with outrage. A price is put on Riel's head and, although he is repeatedly elected to the House of Commons, he is never able to take his seat.

The years between the rebellions are spent by Riel in hiding and exile. A letter from the Archbishop of Quebec saying that God "has given you a mission which you must fulfil," is a treasure on which Riel dwells. During a church service, he hears God speaking to him, saying: "Rise, Louis David Riel. You have a mission to complete for which all mankind will call you blessed." During a period of madness he is taken to a mental hospital in Quebec, where the Mother Superior is afraid to admit him: "If the Government — or Orangemen learn he is here." He is admitted, however, and a sympathetic doctor diagnoses Riel with "a clear case of megalomania, of messianic paranoia."[95]

Riel spends several years in the United States, then is called to lead a second rebellion in Saskatchewan. When he tells his military leader, Gabriel Dumont, that there is to be no bloodshed, Dumont merely laughs. A priest tells the people that it is a sin to rebel against the civil authorities, but Riel defies him, goes to the pulpit, and prays to God to "execute vengeance on the heathen, steel us in hatred, your divine and perfect hatred." The Mounted Police are repulsed, but Canadian troops are sent, and the rebellion is crushed. When Riel surrenders, lawyers are sent from Quebec to defend him, but the only defense is insanity, and Riel refuses to cooperate. "[Prime Minister] Macdonald has to hang me," he writes while in prison, "Then the people can make me a saint."[96]

Wiebe's novel invites comparison with *The Confessions of Nat Turner,* for both protagonists see themselves to be on a divinely sanctioned mission to save a people. While Turner takes his inspiration from the Bible, Riel has the backing of a church, a church with so much influence that his fate nearly tore the nation apart. The hanging of Nat Turner caused scarcely a ripple in the flow of American history.

4

Conclusion

GEORGE WOODCOCK SAYS THAT IN ALL of Rudy Wiebe's novels, "the moralist has been predominant over the historian." He objects to distortions of history in *The Scorched Wood People*, claiming that "a religious novel about the Christian spirit and a historical novel about the fate of a people are two different things," and that Wiebe has not done justice to either.[97] Woodcock's criticism is germane for our time. With a sharp decrease in the felt presence of God in contemporary life and literature, today's writer of historical fiction is likely to put the emphasis on morality. This is particularly true in American literature, where the past is widely seen as a series of evil events. A reader can sense Styron's outrage as he depicts the lawyer "defending" Nat Turner speaking to the court about "the basic weakness and inferiority, the moral deficiency of the Negro's character," who is "cousin" to the human races, but "far closer to the skulking baboon of that dark continent from which he springs."[98] The author's "meditation on history" is a bleak one indeed.

Americans cannot seem to stop inventing theologies that occur at both ends of the political spectrum, particularly in California, which has long replaced western New York as the breeding ground of new sects. Bloom claims that it is a vain enterprise to urge the "need for community" on religious Americans, because "the experiential encounter with Jesus or God is too overwhelming for memories of community to abide."[99]

American churches, like American citizens, have always been highly individualistic. The fact that slavery tore apart the principal Protestant sects in the United States shows how little influence the "head office" has had in American ecclesiastical history. Mark Schorer reports that when Sinclair Lewis was working on *Elmer Gantry,* he lived near a Methodist Episcopal Church,[100] a hybrid that would rarely be found in Canada. Bloom's 1992 comment about "five separate kinds of Baptists" was based on an imminent split in the Southern Baptist Convention. According to Bloom, the Baptists — the largest denomination in the United States — were particularly successful in the South because they led away from theological training for the ministry, stressed "mystical inwardness," and claimed that only "Jesus" could call someone to preach; it was not to be "hired, or taught."[101] Ironically, this sounds like Emerson.

The irony with which Canadian authors have depicted clergymen, with their exalted social positions is usually humorous but delicate, at least in English-Canadian fiction. An Elmer Gantry would be difficult to find in a Canadian novel. Members of the Canadian clergy were historically the best-educated and most knowledgeable people in town; they had met the standards set by respected and authoritative institutions. Leacock's high-stepping Anglican rector and stuffy old Presbyterian minister are figures of fun, but not so far from reality.

Quebec's Quiet Revolution ended the hegemony of the Catholic Church, an event both predicted and dramatized in the province's literature. Before the 1960s most Canadian provinces were not averse to public school religion classes taught by clergymen, and provincial support for Catholic schools was still in place in several provinces at the end of the twentieth century. Church control of education was only recently ended in Quebec and Newfoundland by changes to the federal constitution. However, churches have not bowed out of educational concerns. Even today, some provinces support religious education for elementary and high schools. Departments of religion thrive in Canadian universities, some of them now world famous. The relative strength of religious institutions in Canada compared with the United States has given some of the mainline denominations enough flexibility to adopt modern policies, such as the ordination of women and homosexuals. The official policy of the denomination is extremely important to individual churches, and those that have broken away have found it a wrenching experience.

Margaret Atwood's *The Handmaid's Tale* (1985) can stand as a satire of fundamentalist Christianity from a secular point of view in both Canada and the United States. This dystopia is set in the near future somewhere in New England, after a nuclear explosion and a group of religious fanatics have "shot the President and machine-gunned the Congress." The United States has been renamed Gilead. A society that parodies the New England Puritans is imposed, and the heroine and narrator is forced to dress like a nun — although her dress is red, suggesting a whore. Her only function is to bear a child for the distinguished man in whose household she is a prisoner. The birthrate has dropped dramatically, there is widespread infertility, and only one out of four births produces a normal child. When it is time for her to be subjected to sex with the master of the household, the act is treated like a religious ceremony, with prayers and Bible readings, although there is no love and no sense of worship. The heroine prays silently: *"Nolite te bastardes carborundorum.* I don't know what it means, but it sounds right, and it will have to do, because I don't know what else I can say to God."[102]

The final chapter, entitled "Historical Notes on *The Handmaid's Tale,"* describes a lecture given at a university in Canada's far north in the year 2195. The chairwoman is from the Department of Caucasian Anthropology; so presumably the praying and Bible readings were ineffective, and the Caucasian race has died out. *The Handmaid's Tale* is a recently discovered artifact that throws some light on the mysterious society of Gilead. Artificial insemination and fertility clinics were outlawed as "irreligious," but surrogate mothers were "considered to have biblical precedents; they thus replaced the serial polygamy common in the pre-Gilead period with the older form of simultaneous polygamy practised both in early Old Testament times and in the former State of Utah."[103] There is much sardonic humor in this novel, but it is devoid of religious sentiment.

Bloom wonders why the United States has "produced so few masterpieces of overtly religious literature." He claims that devotional literature "of any aesthetic eminence, or of any profound spirituality, hardly exists" in America.[104] The same can be said about Canada, yet the key word is "overt." Both nations have produced writers who are deeply religious — Flannery O'Connor and Robertson Davies are notable — yet their works are necessarily addressed to a secular audience. Perhaps overtly religious literature belongs to an earlier age.

At the end of the twentieth century, church attendance in Canada had dropped dramatically, far lower than in the United States. Religion does not stay down forever, as the Russians discovered, and the trend may be reversed. If it does, it seems likely that Canadians will rejuvenate their churches, while Americans will continue to invent new techniques for the individual to become one with a transcendent being.

Notes

1. Robert T. Handy, "Protestant Patterns in Canada and the United States: Similarities and Differences," *In the Great Tradition: In Honor of Winthrop S. Hudson, Essays on Pluralism, Volunteerism and Revivalism*, ed. J.D. Ban and Paul R. Dekar (Valley Forge, PA: Judson Press, 1982), 35–48. Handy lists ten points of difference, which for present purposes can be reduced to three categories.
2. P Miller, *Errand*, 110, 101.
3. Predestination, the cornerstone of Calvinism, was an important and contentious issue with all Christians in the seventeenth century.
4. Perry Miller, *Jonathan Edwards* (New York: Meridian Books, 1959), 30.
5. Berkovitch, *Origins*, 18–19.
6. In Connecticut, death was the penalty for "witchcraft, blasphemy, murder, bestiality, sodomy, adultery, rape, kidnapping, false witness with intent to deprive of life, and attempting ... 'rebellion against the Commonwealth'." In 1650 the list included those over sixteen who "curse or smite their parents, and stubborn and rebellious sons" (P Miller, *Errand*, 34–35).
7. P Miller, *Edwards*, 110.
8. *Ibid.*, 133, 148.
9. Franklin, *Autobiography*, 116.
10. Berkovitch, *Origins,* 108.
11. Perry Miller, *The Life of the Mind in America: From the Revolution to the Civil War* (New York: Harcourt, Brace and World, 1965), 37.
12. Harold Bloom, *The American Religion: The Emergence of the Post-Christian Nation* (New York: Simon and Schuster, 1992), 55.
13. *Ibid.*, 59.
14. De Tocqueville, II:159.
15. Nathan O. Hatch, *The Democratization of American Christianity* (New Haven: Yale University Press, 1989), 129.
16. Bloom, *Religion*, 71.
17. Richard Hofstadter, *America at 1750: A Social Portrait* (New York: Alfred A. Knopf, 1971), 205.
18. Careless, *Canada*, 169–70.
19. Richard Allen, "Providence to Progress: The Migration of an Idea in English Canadian Thought," *Canadian Issues/Themes Canadiens*, Vol VI, *Religion/Culture* (Association for Canadian Studies, 1985), 36.
20. Qtd by Handy, 47.
21. In 1961, over ninety percent of the Canadian population adhered to six denominational families. Handy, 41.
22. The Presbyterians, Methodists, and Baptists were nearly torn apart over slavery. In 1990, Bloom could distinguish "five separate kinds of Baptists" in the nation. Bloom, *Religion*, 191.
23. Kazin, *God*, 129.
24. *Ibid.*, 13.

25   David S. Reynolds, *Beneath the American Renaissance: The Subversive Imagination in the Age of Emerson and Melville* (New York: Alfred A. Knopf,1988), 61, 64, 430. No Catholic was able to be elected President of the United States until John F. Kennedy put the issue to rest in 1960.

26   Thorner, 138.

27   Clift, 50, 51.

28   Frye, *Ground*, 84.

29   Hatch, 226.

30   Sutherland claims that "the Jansenism of French Canada and the Calvinism of English Canada inculcated exactly the same attitudes regarding man's relationship to God and his role on earth." 72, 63.

31   Berkovitch, *Origins*, 86–89.

32   *Ibid.,* 87, 89.

33   Bloom, *Religion*, 16.

34   The term "Transcendental" is taken from Immanuel Kant. See Chapter II.

35   *Emerson*, 97, 100, 102.

36   *Ibid.*, 57, 135.

37   Kazin, *God*, 42.

38   Emerson, *Emerson*, 153, 158.

39   Emerson, *Works,* XII: 195.

40   Emerson, *Works*, XI: 515, 540.

41   Richard Ruland, Introduction, *Twentieth Century Interpretations of Walden* (Englewood Cliffs, NJ: Prentice Hall, 1968), 5.

42   Thoreau, *Walden*, 74.

43   Ruland, 5.

44   Thoreau, *Walden*, 165–66, 266–67.

45   Thoreau, *A Yankee in Canada, The Writings of Henry David Thoreau*, vol V, *Excursions and Poems* (Boston: Houghton Mifflin, 1906), 64–65.

46   *Ibid.*, 13–14.

47   Herman Melville, *Moby Dick* (New York: W.W. Norton, 1967), 144; Ch 36, 147; Ch 37.

48   Bloom, *How to Read*, 237.

49   Melville, *Moby Dick*, 139–40; Ch 35.

50   Herman Melville, *Billy Budd, Foretopman, The Shorter Novels of Herman Melville*, ed. Raymond Weaver (Greenwich, CT: A Fawcett Premier Book, 1967), 245–46; Ch 17 253; Ch 18, 258; Ch 19.

51   *Ibid.*, 260; Ch 20, 264; Ch 22.

52   Hatch, 125, 134.

53   Sinclair Lewis, *Elmer Gantry* (New York: Signet Classics, 1980), 53–54; Ch 3.

54   *Ibid.,* 72; Ch. 4, 100; Ch. 7.

55   *Ibid.*, 156–57; Ch. 11.

56   *Ibid.,* 316; Ch 23, 344; Ch 27.

57   *Ibid.*, 416; Ch 33.

58   Mark Shorer, Afterword, *Elmer Gantry*, 428.

59   William Styron, *The Confessions of Nat Turner* (New York: Signet Books, 1968), Author's Note.

60 Throughout the novel Nat Turner is referred to by his first name. This was the custom at the time as slaves normally did not have last names.

61 *Ibid.*, 239, 245; Pt. 2.

62 *Ibid.*, 62; Pt. 1.

63 *Ibid.*, 204–5, 228, 237; Pt. 2.

64 *Ibid.*, 265, 279; Pt. 3.

65 *Ibid.*, 303–4; Pt. 3, 92–3; Pt. 1.

66 Anne Tyler, *Saint Maybe* (Toronto: Penguin Books, 1992), 127, 128; Ch 3.

67 *Ibid.*, 136; Ch 3, 201; Ch 6, 275; Ch 8.

68 *Ibid.*, 153; Ch. 4, 241; Ch. 6, 263; Ch. 8.

69 Ibid., 268; Ch 8, 257; Ch 7.

70 Lipset, *American Exceptionalism*, 279.

71 Duffy, *Iceberg*, 11.

72 Connor, *Glengarry*, 28, 56.

73 The term "armenian" was used by the Puritans to designate a heretic.

74 Connor, *Glengarry*, 179, 137–38.

75 *Ibid.*, 212–13, 204.

76 J. Lee Johnson and John H. Johnson, "Ralph Connor and the Canadian Identity," *Queen's Quarterly* 79 (Summer 1972), 165.

77 Leacock called the Anglican Church Episcopal because of the need to sell his books in the United States.

78 Stephen Leacock, *Arcadian Adventures With the Idle Rich* (Toronto: McClelland & Stewart, 1989), 132, 133. The city is never named, presumably because it is meant to be an American city, but it is really a thinly disguised Montreal. It is unlikely that an American Presbyterian minister would be lecturing in philosophy at a nearby university.

79 *Ibid.*, 136, 155, 157.

80 *Ibid.*, 173, 168–69, 179.

81 Ralph L. Curry, Introduction to *Arcadian Adventures,* by Leacock (Toronto:McClelland & Stewart, 1969), viii.

82 Sinclair Ross, *As For Me and My House* (Toronto: McClelland & Stewart, 1989), 8.

83 *Ibid.*, 9, 58.

84 *Ibid.*, 3–7, 25, 23.

85 *Ibid.*, 69, 152.

86 Roy Daniells, Introduction, *As For Me and My House,* by Ross (Toronto: McClelland & Stewart, 1960), vii.

87 Antoine Sirois, Afterword, *Thirty Acres* by Ringuet, Trans. Felix and Dorothea Walters (Toronto: Macmillan, 1989), 301.

88 Ringuet, *Thirty Acres*, 39, 40.

89 *Ibid.*, 88–89.

90 *Ibid.*, 156, 131.

91 Clift, 53.

92 Nicole Brossard, Afterword, *A Season in the Life of Emmanuel*, by Marie-Claire Blais (Toronto: McClelland & Stewart, 1992), 135.

93 Blais, *Emmanuel*, 10.
94 *Ibid.*, 14, 12, 40.
95 Rudy Wiebe, *The Scorched Wood People* (Toronto: McClelland & Stewart, 1977), 139; Sec. 2:3, 155, 166; Sec. 2:5.
96 *Ibid.*, 226; Sec 3:1, 337; Sec 3:2.
97 George Woodcock, *Northern Spring: The Flowering of Canadian Literature* (Vancouver: Douglas & McIntyre, 1987), 100, 101–2.
98 Styron, 91, 100.
99 Bloom, *Religion*, 27.
100 Mark Schorer, Afterword, *Elmer Gantry*, 420.
101 Bloom, *Religion*, 191, 194–5.
102 Margaret Atwood, *The Handmaid's Tale* (Toronto: Seal Books, 1986), 162, 86.
103 *Ibid.*, 287.
104 Bloom, *Religion*, 257.

Chapter
Six

Gender, Ethnicity, and Class

1

Struggles for Equality in North America

EQUALITY — RACIAL, SEXUAL, RELIGIOUS, AND SOCIAL — is a fairly recent ideal in the western world, and is still far from being worldwide. A.O. Lovejoy's *The Great Chain of Being* explains how a hierarchy, with God at the top and gradations below, seemed logical before modern science began raising doubts about the activities, let alone the existence, of God. Thoughts of equality as a realizable ideal began with the Enlightenment in the eighteenth century. As Marlene LeGates says, references to "reason, nature, and equality began to replace reliance on Christian and classical authorities."[1] However, Jefferson's words, "all men are created equal" were revolutionary. The majority of people in 1776 did not believe that all men were created equal, since the world around them showed otherwise.

Jefferson expressed an Enlightenment ideal, but what did he mean by "men" and why did he substitute "the pursuit of happiness" for "property," the normal third item in this eighteenth-century holy trinity?[2] "Men" was then used as a generic term that might include women, modern feminism being a hundred years into the future. The more profound question is whether or not he included slaves, since slaves were seen by their owners as property, the term deleted from the Declaration. Most of the delegates to the Continental Congress from the southern colonies were slave owners, yet they all signed their names to the Declaration, with no intention of putting this ideal of human liberty and equality into practice. Jefferson claimed that he meant *all* men, but antebellum southern legislators chose to believe otherwise and blocked his attempts to mention slavery specifically. Jefferson's words still haunt Americans.

The Industrial Revolution tended to work against women's rights. In an agricultural society the work of men and women is almost on a par, since it is

177

difficult to determine the relative value that each contributes to the family welfare. In the early days of representative government the franchise was attached to property ownership. Women often voted on behalf of husbands who were absent or deceased, or if they themselves had the requisite property and status, for few of the North American colonies had a law excluding women. Gradually they were disenfranchised, as so-called "reform bills" specified who was eligible to vote.

The 1832 British Reform Bill broadened the franchise, but specifically barred women from voting. In both the United States and Canada, the property qualification was gradually removed for men, while women continued to be barred because of their gender. Louis Menand claims that the Second Great Awakening (1800–1840) spawned women's rights, spurred abolitionism, and spun off numerous religious sects in the United States. Agitation on behalf of women's rights essentially began in England with Mary Wollstonecraft's *A Vindication of the Rights of Woman* (1792). Arguing that virtue must be taught, she stressed education for women, saying: "it is a farce to call any being virtuous whose virtues do not result from the exercise of its own reason." [3] In antebellum United States, women's rights were overshadowed by abolitionism, even though such outspoken abolitionists as Wendell Philips and William Lloyd Garrison insisted on women being treated as equals — a position that caused much dissent among their followers.[4] Women's rights were not a serious issue in Pre-Confederation Canada, which was still largely in a pioneer state of development. However, upper-class women felt free to express and publish their views. Many such works are now prominent in the Canadian literary canon.

As machines replaced more human labor and men left the fields to enter the world of business and the professions, women were expected to become "ladies," to keep the home fires burning, and to busy themselves with good works. It was in England and New England — the most technologically advanced places in Western society — that ladies began attacks upon their political and legal restrictions. The myth of women's moral superiority was widely promoted, at least partly to deflect growing female demands. Opposition to women's education and entry into public life was widespread in the nineteenth century. Henry James, Sr. wrote in 1853 that woman is "by nature inferior to man ... she is, very properly, her husband's 'patient and repining drudge.'" He also argued against any serious education for women.[5] It was in the West — the poorer parts of both the United States and Canada — that women had the earliest civil rights. Their positions on the family farm and frequent need to run businesses made them involved citizens. The American state universities in the West could not afford to provide separate facilities for men and women, so they became co-ed. Charles W. Eliot, president of Harvard from 1869 to 1909, said that the only excuse for co-education was poverty. When the United States passed the Nineteenth Amendment that gave women the franchise, most of the western states had already done so, while the entire South and all of New England except Maine had given women no voting rights.

The breakthrough came with World War I, when women were needed to fill jobs normally restricted to men. The first wave of modern feminism — in the late nineteenth and early twentieth centuries — took place in Western Europe as well as in English-speaking North America and was driven by fairly privileged women. Canada's Parliament passed the Women's Franchise Act in 1918, slightly before the British Parliament and the American government, and the provinces that had not already done so quickly followed, except for Quebec. There, women were not given the vote until 1940. There were serious gaps across the nation. Native men and women were not included; neither were people of Asian descent, because they did not qualify as British subjects.

Abolitionism was another European movement that built up steam in the United States as part of the Second Great Awakening. Britain and the United States banned the slave trade in 1807 and 1808 respectively,[6] and at the Congress of Vienna in 1814 the British put pressure on other European nations to do the same. Any slaves still present in Canada were freed when Great Britain passed the Emancipation Act of 1833, liberating all slaves in the Empire. This put the United States into an explosive situation as the Scandinavian countries, France, and Holland followed the British example, hastening a broad ethical movement in the western world. The southern states had been fearful of emancipation for many years. In 1799, John Ball of South Carolina wrote to his son, a student at Harvard, pointing out that if a "general emancipation" should take place, "you are a ruined man and all your family connexions made beggars."[7] The southern states had a strong hold on the antebellum federal government, so as slavery spread to new states in the West and the courts enforced fugitive slave laws, outrage in the North grew and the Underground Railroad to Canada became increasingly active.

A regressive movement known as Social Darwinism infected the United States, Canada, and much of Europe in the late nineteenth and early twentieth centuries. Based upon supposedly scientific theories of eugenics, Social Darwinism generated a scale of what was perceived to be different levels of development among humans. Anglo-Saxons were regarded as most "evolved," and were trailed by, in descending order, Eastern Europeans, Jews, Native North Americans, Japanese and Chinese. Blacks were at the bottom. This racist and xenophobic concept became widely popular, was an adjunct to imperialism, and led to numerous restrictive laws. Canada instituted a head tax on immigrants considered undesirable, raised it dramatically, and then essentially stopped immigration from India and China in the early twentieth century. Nothing that was done in Canada, however, was as culturally harmful as two Supreme Court decisions made in the United States in the 1890s. In *Plessy* v. *Ferguson* (1896), "separate but equal" facilities sanctioned apartheid, and in *Williams* v. *Mississippi* (1898), the Court allowed southern states to disenfranchise their Black citizens. The Jim Crow era was to last almost sixty years. Menand claims that the years of World War I saw "possibly the most intense racial xenophobia in American history."[8]

Ironically, Social Darwinism was contemporary with the first wave of modern feminism. Many middle-class feminist leaders found it appealing, as they saw "ignorant" male immigrants, whom they considered beneath them, qualifying to vote while they were excluded. Harriet Peirce, wife of the American philosopher Charles Peirce, was an outspoken feminist who demanded that men pay their wives for housework. She loathed the Irish and was an opponent of immigration.[9] In Canada, Flora Denison, at an International Woman Suffrage Alliance in Copenhagen, spoke of Canada's male immigrants as "illiterate and often the scum of the earth."[10] She was voicing opinions that were current among "reformers."

In spite of several reform movements shared by the United States and Canada with Western Europe, there were distinct differences between the two nations in attitudes toward gender, ethnicity and class. Although America's founders omitted slaves and Natives when they talked of all men being created equal, they did believe that they had eliminated the British class structure and that all white men had equal chances to rise to the top socially and economically. Jefferson and Adams wrote extensively on the desirability of an aristocracy of talent — Jefferson was the more idealistic, Adams the more cynical.[11] The latter's cynicism was well placed, for the concept was revived in the late nineteenth century as a justification for Social Darwinism and notions of superior and inferior races.

The Loyalists expressed no noble sentiments about equality and openly tried to duplicate British class society. This attitude was sustained by impoverished upper-class British, who emigrated after the Napoleonic Wars, preferring to relocate in the Empire rather than move to the United States. When Catharine Parr Traill and her husband left England, they had to pay handsomely to travel on a brig, because the only passenger ship bound for Canada was "swarming with emigrants, chiefly of the lower class of Highlanders."[12] Englishwoman Anna Jameson visited Upper Canada in 1836 and found Toronto a "fifth-rate provincial town" with "a petty colonial oligarchy, a self-constituted aristocracy."[13] Quebec continued the feudal seigneurial system of New France until 1854, and in Prince Edward Island absentee landlords — most of them British aristocrats — kept generations of tenant farmers working the land. Canada was not as well endowed with fertile farmland as the United States, but there was enough of it to make ideas of a landed aristocracy unrealizable. The authority of the Catholic Church and language barriers kept most French farmers working as tenants (*habitants*), but English-speaking immigrants could usually get their own land.

A major difference between the future nations was in attitudes toward "miscegenation" and sexual relations between races. Samuel de Champlain (c. 1570–1635), a founder of New France, favored a founding race born of French men and Native women. For a brief period at the end of the seventeenth century, the French government offered a fifty-livre dowry to Native women who married French men and turned Catholic. However, instead of settling down to farming the men adopted the lifestyle of the Native peoples, so the government discontinued the policy and sent French women (*les filles du roi*) to the colony. Many French fur traders continued to take Native wives, resulting in the Métis population that has been such a significant force in Canadian history.

When the Hudson's Bay Company was founded in 1670, settlements were outlawed and white women and missionaries excluded. The result was that a large mixed race population grew up around each trading post. It was a hundred and fifty years before the Company relented and allowed a group of Scots to form the Red River Settlement in Manitoba. The immigrants and Métis soon clashed, leading eventually to the Riel and North-West Rebellions. There were numerous Natives among the Loyalists in Upper Canada and intermarriage was sufficiently acceptable that some Upper Canada officials took Native wives. In spite of this promising beginning and the fact that there were no Jim Crow laws or serious "Indian wars," Blacks and Natives have been treated only marginally better in Canada than in the United States.

Ethnic conflict in Canada has been mainly religious and linguistic. While today issues of race and racism have been brought more to the forefront, historically French-English differences received greater attention. French resentment of the English majority was kept barely below the boiling point for two centuries. There are a number of reasons for this hostility. First, the Seven Years' War has always been known in Quebec as The Conquest, a constant reminder of the oppression its people have felt. Second, the absence of the French government left the Catholic Church as the primary authority for the French people. The Church, which ran all educational and social institutions, minimized education, encouraged people to stay on the farm and have large families, and was openly hostile to business and industry. Known as "revenge of the cradle," this policy expanded the French-speaking population, but hampered the growth of a middle class and kept most of the people poor. The English, meanwhile, grew wealthy and built large homes and factories in the midst of French poverty. An English Canadian was usually the boss of these factories, and since the boss would not bother to learn French, any ambitious employees had to learn English. The third reason for French resentment was English Canadians' tenacious clinging to the British Empire. The French felt that they were the only genuine Canadians, resented the near-hysterical crowds greeting visiting British royalty, and were outraged at attempts to conscript their young men for both World Wars, which they regarded as Britain's wars. These reasons for resentment have largely disappeared since the Quiet Revolution of the nineteen sixties, but at the end of the twentieth century, many in Quebec still envision a North American counterpart to the European Union, in which they can take their place as an independent nation.

"Miscegenation" was not acceptable in the United States, at least on the surface. While early settlers of New France were making allies of various Native tribes and frequently intermarrying with them, the early residents of New England had no such inclinations. Winona Stevenson cites a decree from Charles I that gave the settlers "carte blanche" to "wage wars on the barbarians."[14] The Puritans came to the New World to farm and spread God's word, not to make money from furs. Richard Slotkin reports that to be taken captive by Natives was seen by the Puritans as a "spiritual and physical catastrophe." The captives either vanished into the wilderness, or "returned half-Indianized or Romanized, or converted to Catholicism and stayed in Canada, or married some 'Canadian half-breed' or 'Indian slut,' or went totally savage."[15]

In spite of the marriage of the Native princess, Pocahontas, to John Rolphe in Virginia in 1614, marriage between whites and Natives was rare in pre-Revolutionary America. Marriage between whites and Blacks was unthinkable. American politician Henry Clay — a slaveholder who, like Jefferson and Madison, opposed slavery in theory — attacked the abolitionists in a speech given to the Senate in 1839: "They promote intermarriage and amalgamation, an unnatural and revolting admixture alike offensive to God and man."[16] Although clandestine sexual relations between white men and Black women (free or slave) went on from the earliest days of slavery in North America, a white woman with a Black man rapidly became a capital offence, an excuse for lynchings. We saw an example in Faulkner's *Light in August*, in which the town vigilante castrates the dying protagonist with the words, "[n]ow you'll let white women alone, even in hell."[17] Southern white women were glorified as icons of beauty, purity and saintliness, thus turning them into "ladies" more effectively than any other women in North America. Mary Chestnut, wife of an American senator and a *"born rebel"* from South Carolina, was "unsettled" by watching the sale of an attractive slave girl for "a thing we can't name." Every "lady tells you who is the father of all the mulatto children in everybody's household, but those in her own."[18] As Alfred Kazin says, wives of planters could "say nothing" as they moved among their husband's "bastards." He adds: "No people in the officially democratic United States of America were so bossy, thrusting, and cocksure as a Southerner who thanked God every day he was not a 'nigger'."[19]

A previously mentioned feature of American society that lowered the status of women was the glorification of masculinity. This was in part a by-product of wanderlust and hostility to institutions, but also derived from the perception of English society as effeminate. Such attitudes did not exist in pre-Confederation Canada. There was no lack of women writers on both sides of the border, but in the United States they were more inclined to do what was expected of ladies; they wrote sentimental romances. Hawthorne's complaint to his publisher about that "damned mob of scribbling women," who were keeping him from success because the public taste was occupied with their "trash," would have included such women writers as Louisa May Alcott and Harriet Beecher Stowe.[20] Their novels are certainly sentimental. While *Uncle Tom's Cabin* was so popular that it influenced the course of the Civil War, Stowe's other writings are rarely read today. Alcott's work remains popular, but mainly with children. It would be many years before women writers began challenging men for a stronger role in American "literature." In contrast, Canadian women writers have always held their own with the nation's male writers.

Individual attitudes toward gender, ethnicity, or class differences tend to merge. Thus, the tolerant person will usually be happy in the company of others regardless of their religious, racial, gender, or social differences. In contrast, a class-conscious individual is inclined to be racially and sexually intolerant, to think of other humans in terms of a hierarchy. The examples used in this chapter, while stressing race, gender or class, illustrate attitudes that encompass all forms of bigotry.

2

The Rocky Road Toward
Civil Rights in the United States

JEFFERSON, IN FRANCE IN THE 1780s, planned to set an example for the South by freeing all of his hundred and eighty slaves, but when he returned to Virginia he found that his plan was "not practicable." He changed his mind because he had debts and his daughter needed a dowry.[21] This economic argument was the foundation of the intractable white southern resistance to the emancipation of slaves. As slave owner John Ball wrote to his son, it would turn them into "beggars."[22]

Harriet Beecher Stowe's *Uncle Tom's Cabin* (1852), published less than a decade before the Civil War, hit the public like a thunderbolt. It was translated into thirty-seven languages, compared favorably with some of the world's greatest writings, and it led President Lincoln to greet the author with the words: "This is the little lady who brought about the great big war." Stowe believed that women were the "more emotionally sensitive and generous half of the human race"; she showed "the slave as a human being in a family." [23] Southern critics argued that Stowe had never been south of Kentucky and that the incidents were highly exaggerated, but they could not explain away the fact that slaves were bought and sold like cattle and that there were no laws to protect them from a brutal master or from the consequences of one with a poor business head. The western world was stunned by the novel and turned against slavery with a passion that no amount of protest from the South could daunt.

The sufferings of Uncle Tom — first, when he is sold away from his family to cover a debt incurred by a "kind" but incompetent master; second, when he is again sold because another "kind" but irresponsible master is accidentally killed; and third, under the brutal treatment of Simon Legree — is one strand of a dual plotline. Tom moves south toward a sacrificial death, while Eliza and her child, who is also sold to cover the master's debt, move north toward Canada and freedom. Eliza's husband, George Harris, has a different owner, a cruel one, so he too runs away. When asked why his wife would leave a "kind" master, George replies: "Kind families get into debt, and the laws of *our* country allow them to sell the child out of its mother's bosom to pay its master's debts."[24]

Uncle Tom's Cabin is centered on family relationships. The most moving parts of the novel deal with children being sold away from their mothers. There are two such incidents at slave auctions, plus tales from female slaves of losing their children, and of their hopes — always shattered — to keep the youngest. As the "quadroon," Cassie, tells Tom, "you can do anything with a woman when you've got her children." When the trader, Haley, is negotiating with Shelby, Tom and Eliza's master, he explains that Negroes are not like "white folks, that's brought up in the way of 'spectin' to keep their children and wives." [25] When Eliza overhears the news, she takes her child and runs. Surprisingly, the greatest amount of sentimentality in the novel is reserved for the death of the white child, Eva, suggesting that Stowe was infected with the "fairness is virtue" literary tradition.[26] The only slaves who make it to Canada are light skinned enough to pass superficial inspection. They are also the most desirable to white masters.

This novel is hierarchical, even geographically. Tom moves south to increasing misery, while Eliza, George, and their child move north to freedom. Every plantation has its hierarchy of slaves. Shelby explains to his wife that he sold Tom and Eliza's child because he could get more money for them. The wife knew nothing of her husband's debts and when she suggests ways of making more money, he retorts that she doesn't "understand business; women never do, and never can." The first house to which Eliza runs after crossing the Ohio river is owned by a senator, who has just signed into law a bill forbidding residents of Ohio from aiding escaped slaves. His normally docile little wife says that it's a "shameful, wicked, abominable law, and I'll break it ... the first time I get a chance." The senator explains that "great public interests [are] involved," so "we must put aside our private feelings." When a bleeding and torn Eliza appears in their kitchen, clutching her little boy, the senator finds that his private feelings overcome the great public issue. He hastily takes Eliza to a safe house, where she begins her journey through the Underground Railroad.[27]

Tom's death is like a crucifixion, but he has such an unshakable religious faith that he morally triumphs over Simon Legree. This parallels Styron's Nat

Turner, another sacrificial Christ figure. Kazin asserts that *"Uncle Tom's Cabin* showed the power of religious sentiment as no other American work of literature had done," that it transformed public opinion so that many Americans "came to accept emancipation as 'righteous' and 'just'."[28]

The fervor of the abolition movement before the Civil War was a high point of moral outrage in American history. It was particularly strong in New England and with the Quakers of Pennsylvania. When the first wave of modern feminism gathered strength, it was seen by many as a falling off from the great days of abolitionism. At least that is how Henry James portrays it in his novel, *The Bostonians* (1886), a satirical view of early New England feminism. According to Irving Howe, all of the characters are "displaced persons, floating vaguely in the large social spaces of America."[29]

Set in the 1870s, *The Bostonians* tells of the battle for the heart and mind of Verena Tarrant — a beautiful American innocent, who has the gift of effective public speaking — between Olive Chancellor, a lesbian and proper Bostonian, and Basil Ransom, a handsome and learned southern reactionary. Both Olive and Basil love Verena, but both have socio-political reasons for wanting to hold her. For Olive, Verena is the most effective member of the women's movement, a young woman who can hold crowds spellbound and convince masses of people that women deserve equality with men. Ransom is determined to remove her from the limelight, as he does not approve of women in public life. He believes she is doing harm by contributing to "a feminine, a nervous, hysterical, chattering, canting age." He is completely candid with Verena, expressing opinions that she has never heard and which initially leave her feeling "cold, [and] slightly sick."[30] In imagining the character of Basil, James may have had his own father in mind.

Neither Olive nor Basil is a sympathetic character. Olive is "a spinster" as Shelley is "a lyric poet," who had found comfort in the fact that "she hated men as a class." Olive is a social snob, who idealizes the very poor. "She liked to think that Verena ... had known almost the extremity of poverty ... [it] added to her value for Olive." Olive finds Verena's father "quite inexpressibly low," her parents of "a class that ... discredited the cause of the new truths." Before meeting Verena, Olive had longed for a close friendship with a poor young woman, but had found all her candidates preoccupied with "Charlie." Meeting

Verena is the answer to her prayers and she manages to "buy" the girl from her parents, but is haunted by the fear of Verena getting married. Olive longs to be a martyr, like her brothers who were killed fighting for the Union in the Civil War. There are hints throughout the novel that she will get her wish in an unwished-for manner.[31]

Basil, a poor southerner from Mississippi who fought for the South in the Civil War, is an ambitious but unsuccessful lawyer living in New York. He is Olive's distant cousin, who responds to her invitation to call if he is in Boston. He stays for dinner, then accompanies her to a meeting on women's rights, where both see and hear Verena for the first time. Olive's world is everything that Basil detests and the two of them become almost instant enemies. Although Basil falls in love with the beautiful and talented Verena, he considers the content of her speeches to be "fluent, pretty, third-rate palaver." He too detests her parents, particularly the father, a "mesmeric healer," whom he sees as a "carpetbagger." Verena's father places his hands on her head, presumably to transfer mystical power to the girl, who innocently says of her triumphant talk, "It isn't *me*." This is a powerful ironic forecast, for as Basil courts Verena, he gains a psychological hold on her. In the final dramatic scene, when Verena is prepared to speak to a large audience in the Boston Music Hall, she finds that she cannot speak with him present. She fruitlessly begs him to go away. Basil "saw that he could do what he wanted" with Verena and the situation "challenged all his manhood." "You are mine, you are not theirs," he says to Verena, "not for millions, shall you give yourself to that roaring crowd." He leads her away and Olive has her martyrdom facing the roaring crowd. James ends his novel with the prediction that Verena will shed many tears in the marriage she is about to enter.[32]

Verena Tarrant is an excellent portrayal of an American innocent. When Basil hears her speak the first time, uttering such "inanities" as "the rights and wrongs of women, [and] the equality of the sexes," he quickly determines that "she didn't mean it, she didn't know what she meant, she had been stuffed with this trash by her father." When Verena moves in with Olive, her reformist education continues on a higher level. Basil's hold on her begins when he says: "You always want to please someone, and now you go lecturing about the country ... in order to please Miss Chancellor, just as you did it before to please your father and mother. It isn't *you*." Although she struggles against him, his words "had sunk into her soul and worked and fermented there. She had come at last to believe them."[33]

Prior to the Civil War, George Fitzhugh, an aristocratic southerner who wrote "polemics in defense of our Slave Society, the most stable and serene way of life yet contrived by man," added that nothing proved the "dissolution and demoralization" of the northern states more than "the emergence of women" who "bestirred themselves with cant about their 'rights'."[34] Howe writes that Basil is "trying, by the force of his will, to extricate himself from defeat."[35] When he tells Verena, "It isn't *you*," he urges her to stand "forth" in her "freedom," a southerner's late nineteenth-century concept of freedom.[36]

The Basil Ransoms of American society would get their wish for a he-man society at the end of the nineteenth century with the rise of imperialism and the presidency of Theodore Roosevelt. It would be accompanied by Social Darwinism, the Jim Crow era, and increasing xenophobia. Few American novels have depicted Jim Crow in America more effectively than Harper Lee's *To Kill a Mockingbird*, published in 1960, just as this sanctioned apartheid era was coming to a turbulent end.

To Kill a Mockingbird is set in a small town in Alabama in the 1930s. It is narrated by a little girl, Jean Louise Finch, known as Scout, who is almost six years old at the beginning and almost eleven at the end. Scout has an older brother, Jem; a lawyer father, Atticus; and a Black cook and substitute mother, Calpurnia. About halfway through the novel, Atticus's sister, Alexandra, comes to stay with them, wants to fire Calpurnia, and tries to teach Scout the feminine graces. She fits into their small town society "like a hand into a glove," but never fits well with the family. Trouble starts almost immediately, as "Aunty" discovers that the children have not been taught that they are "the product of several generations' gentle breeding." Atticus tries to oblige her, but will not indoctrinate his children with snobbish sentiments, nor will he fire Calpurnia. [37]

The novel centers on a trial, at which Atticus is defending a Black man, Tom Robinson, who has been accused of raping a white woman. Atticus intends to fully defend Tom, whom he knows to be innocent. Jem tells Scout that Aunty "almost said Atticus was disgracin' the family," and Scout overhears her father say to her aunt: "... in favor of Southern womanhood   as much as anybody, but not for preserving polite fiction at the expense of human life."[38]

The night before the trial Tom is moved to the local jail, where Atticus sits reading, prepared to stop a possible lynching. A worried Jem sneaks downtown and cannot prevent Scout from following him. The lynch mob arrives and is preparing to force Atticus out of the way when the children run to their father. Jem refuses to obey the order to go home and take his sister, when Scout recognizes one of the men and starts making polite conversation, as she has been taught. Mr. Cunningham's boy, Walter, is in her class, he is a good boy, and Scout brought him home for dinner one time. Cunningham is embarrassed and takes the mob away. After the trial Scout is told by her aunt that she may not play with Walter Cunningham. When Scout protests and asks why, her aunt says: "Because—he—is—trash, that's why you can't play with him." Earlier Scout had heard a definition of "trash" quite different from that of her aunt. Jem is greatly upset that the jury condemned Tom Robinson when Atticus had so clearly proved him innocent, so Atticus tries to explain southern society. Telling Jem that he would see "white men cheat black men" every day of his life, Atticus says Jem is never to forget that "whenever a white man does that to a black man, no matter ... or how fine a family he comes from, that white man is trash." Robert E. Lee Ewell, the white farmer who accuses Tom Robinson of raping his daughter, is trash by any definition. Although the jury pronounces Robinson guilty, the whole town knows what happened and Ewell is furious. He stops Atticus Finch on the street, spits in his face, and says he will "kill him." [39]

Harper Lee's technique of presenting her narrative through the eyes of an intelligent child shows the characters in this small-town southern world through different eyes: Jem; their family friend, Miss Maudie, who says that the townspeople are rarely called upon to be Christians, but when they are they have "men like Atticus to go for us"; Reverend Sykes, the Black minister, who takes the children onto the "Negro" balcony to watch the trial; and, of course, "Aunty," who tries unsuccessfully to inculcate ideals of southern womanhood. When Jem asks why people like Miss Maudie never sit on juries, Atticus says that women are not allowed on juries. Scout is "indignant." "You mean women in Alabama can't—?" Left unsaid is that Black men in Alabama were not allowed to sit on juries either.[40]

To Kill A Mockingbird did not have quite the impact on American society as Uncle Tom's Cabin, but it came close, was widely translated, and won the 1961 Pulitzer Prize. Malcolm Bradbury lists Harper Lee as a major female writer of post-World War II American fiction and links her to the rise of the women's movement.[41] Lee never published another novel and became something of a recluse, which may account for the fact that Mockingbird is now widely seen as more notable historically than as an outstanding work of literature. In this respect it joins Uncle Tom's Cabin as a landmark commentary on American race relations — the two books published just over a century apart. Numerous works on American race relations have been published since, none more significant than the novels of Toni Morrison.

Morrison says that she does not mind being classified as a woman writer, or even as a Black woman writer. More accurately, she is an American Black woman writer, one who has "access" to a "range of emotions and perceptions" greater than most other Americans.[42] This is particularly apparent in her 1987 novel, Beloved, based loosely on the story of Margaret Garner, a Kentucky slave who escaped with her four children, then attempted to kill them when she was about to be captured. She succeeded with one child. Morrison did not delve further into Margaret's story, but did intensive research into the situation in Kentucky and southern Ohio before and after the Civil War. She is able to convey the "feelings" engendered by the unholy combination of motherhood and slavery in a way that Harriet Beecher Stowe was not. Beloved is a complex and sophisticated novel that earned its author the 1993 Nobel Prize in literature.

All of the characters in the novel believe in ghosts, so, in true "magic realism" form, the dead child returns; first as a ghost, later as a living young woman. Beloved opens about two-thirds of the way through the chronological story, and contains multiple flashbacks as it proceeds. The Civil War is over and the protagonist, Sethe, is living in the outskirts of Cincinnati with her youngest child, Denver. Her mother-in-law, Baby Suggs, has died and her boys have run away.

Sethe and Paul D are the only adult survivors among the former slaves at Sweet Home, a Kentucky plantation owned by a couple named Garner. The kindly Garners treat their slaves with relative dignity, but when Mr. Garner dies suddenly, his sick wife calls in her brother-in-law, who comes with two sadistic nephews to turn Sweet Home into a hellhole. The slaves plan an escape, which is foiled, although Sethe is able to send away her three children. Pregnant with Denver, she remains to try and find her husband, Halle; instead she is caught by the nephews, who beat her with rawhide and have the milk sucked from her breasts. She runs away, giving birth en route, and arrives with the baby at her mother-in-law's house. Paul D is sent to a Georgia chain gang and the only thing known about Halle is that he went insane.

Most of the action in this novel is propelled by two characters who are nameless: the brutal brother-in-law, known only as "schoolteacher," and the murdered baby girl called Beloved. Both are devil figures. Schoolteacher, who ends the cooperative congenial life at Sweet Home, loses all of his male slaves, then comes after Sethe and her children. The result is two wounded boys and a dead ten-month-old girl. The downward pull of these two characters is slowly offset by Paul D and Denver, both of whom manage to overcome the past and seek a hopeful tomorrow.

Critics have had mixed reactions to the ending of the novel, which can only be called happy, seemingly impossible in a work so filled with human wretchedness. Denver, who is earning money and getting educated, urges Paul D to try and save her mother. Morrison's handling of the ending is a triumph.

It is the voices in *Beloved* that convey to the reader those emotions and perceptions to which Morrison, as an American Black woman novelist, has access. The principal voice is that of Sethe, but Baby Suggs, Denver, Paul D, and even some white characters contribute. When Sethe decides that she has her daughter back and that her only happiness is in one room with Beloved, she locks the door, not hearing "the voices" that ringed the house like a "noose." At first, Denver is protective of her sister, helping her drive Paul D away and intent on saving her from Sethe, for "the thing that makes it alright to kill her children" might happen again. Although she is inside that noose, Denver is able to learn. When food runs short and all they have is given to Beloved, she musters the courage to look for work, then recognizes that Sethe needs protection from Beloved, not the other way around.[43]

Paul D finds Sethe — now delivered from Beloved — lying on Baby Suggs' bed, frail and ready to die. The first sign that she might live is in her comment, "He couldn't have done it if I hadn't made the ink,"[44] a cryptic and tortured memory that refers to "schoolteacher" telling his pupils to write a comparison of the human and animal characteristics of slaves. White southerners often made the argument that slaves were more like animals than like humans. An example was discussed in Chapter Five, where the defense lawyer for Nat Turner says that the "Negro" character is closer to "the skulking baboon" than to the human race.[45] When schoolteacher sees the carnage wrought by Sethe, he is angry with his nephew for having "overbeat" her, asking what a horse would do if it was beaten "beyond the point of education." The stupid nephew can only babble: "What she go and do that for?"[46]

Sethe explains to Paul D why she tried to kill her children. He understands that when she arrived in Ohio she could "love" big, for as a slave, "you protected yourself and loved small." When she saw schoolteacher coming she collected her children and took them "where they would be safe." Paul D cannot accept that the only place she could think of was the next world: "You got two feet, Sethe, not four," he says. Sethe has been ostracized from the Black community and when Paul D compares her to an animal, she thinks he is like all of the others, unable to understand the intensity of her love for her children. When her dead daughter returns, she has all she needs to be happy.[47]

Toni Morrison has said that one of the "nice" things women do is "nurture and love something other than themselves," an emotion so strong that it is "also a killer." The return of Beloved is Sethe's "second chance, a chance to do it right." Of course, says Morrison, she does it "wrong again."[48] Beloved returns to reclaim her life, a life she can have only by taking it from her mother. When the neighbor women gather to rescue Sethe, they see her standing in the doorway holding hands with the "devil-child," who has "taken the shape of a pregnant woman." Sethe "looked like a little girl" beside her.[49]

Margaret Atwood claims that Beloved allows the reader to "experience American slavery ... as one of the most viciously antifamily institutions human beings have ever devised."[50] Baby Suggs recalls that when her last child, Halle, was born she barely looked at him, for it was not worth bothering to "learn features you would never see change into adulthood." She had "held a little foot" and examined "fat fingertips" seven times, but had never known "what their permanent teeth looked like." The only substitute for the lost family in *Beloved* is the Black community. When Baby Suggs turned two pails of blackberries into a feast for all the neighbors, she went too far. "Loaves and fishes were His powers," thought the neighbors, who then failed to warn her that strange white men have been seen and are riding toward her house. Baby Suggs is clairvoyant, feels the resentment, but approaching danger is obscured by the image of "high-topped shoes." As the sheriff departs with Sethe and her infant, two white children arrive with high-topped shoes, ordering her to have them repaired by Wednesday. The bitterness of such ironic juxtapositions makes Morrison's skill at ending the novel with something approaching happiness all the more stunning.[51]

Barbara Kingsolver's 1993 novel, *Pigs in Heaven*, opens with the statement: "Women on their own run in Alice's family," an assertion that implies unhappy marriages. Taylor Greer — Alice's daughter and the novel's protagonist — is an unmarried mother. Her adopted daughter, a Cherokee Indian named Turtle, was handed to Taylor in a parking lot as an abused three-year-old. An intense love has developed between Taylor and Turtle, so when a Cherokee lawyer, Annawake Fourkiller, discovers Turtle and coolly informs Taylor that her adoption of the child is not legal, Taylor flees with her child, maternal instinct topping rational thought. When Alice joins Taylor and Turtle in their flight she recognizes that Taylor is "genuinely a mother." [52]

This novel circles around two dilemmas: Turtle's devotion to Taylor versus her need for Cherokee culture, and Taylor's challenged belief in her own ability to be a good mother and earn enough to support them. Alice had worked as a cleaning woman and raised her daughter alone, so Taylor sees no reason why she cannot do something similar. Both dilemmas boil down to individualism versus institutional needs. Turtle's best interest is the reigning debate. Before their flight, Taylor and Turtle had been living with Jax, a jazz musician who loves Taylor, wants to marry her, and is devoted to Turtle. They had lived as a family and, although poor, had been able to manage comfortably. Taylor's upbringing had left her cool to the very idea of marriage. Jax explains Taylor to Annawake, who returns to find him alone: "Me, the great Jax, she *enjoys*, but Turtle she loves. She didn't exactly have to meditate before she walked out of here. It was no contest." Annawake tries to explain the importance to both Turtle and the Cherokee nation of the child's tribal identity, and says that she "is trying to see both sides," but Jax insists that neither she nor Taylor can see both sides. "It's impossible. Your definitions of 'good' are not in the same dictionary." Gradually the institutional argument gains strength, as Jax, then Alice, are persuaded that the Cherokees have a case and that a compromise is necessary. Taylor's dilemma is resolved when she is forced to admit that she cannot support the two of them and be a good mother at the same time. The novel winds up a bit too neatly, with Alice marrying Turtle's Cherokee grandfather, and Taylor returning with Turtle to marry Jax, but committed to sending the child to her grandparents for three months every summer.[53]

The history of the Cherokee, from the Trail of Tears to the present, is told piecemeal by Annawake as she presses her case for Turtle to be returned to her people. Kingsolver does not avoid the problems of alcoholism and suicide on Native reserves, but stresses the importance of the tribe as an extended family. A child who has lost its parents can be raised by any number of other relatives.

The title, *Pigs in Heaven*, refers to the Cherokee myth of six boys who were taken into heaven to form a constellation — the one generally known as the Pleiades. The meaning of the myth is ambiguous. Annawake explains to Jax that it means, do "right by your people or you'll be a pig in heaven." Later the reader is told that the constellation is meant to "remind parents always to love their kids." Annawake admits that all of the Cherokee myths say in essence, "[d]o right by your people." Reinforcing this concept are stories of the unhappy results of Native children who have been adopted by whites. Annawake's twin brother was adopted by a white family, got into trouble as a teenager, and is now in Leavenworth prison. She feels certain that it would not have happened if he had remained with the tribe; that brown skin on a teenager inevitably results in prejudice and exclusion from adolescent society.[54]

Taylor's failed attempt to live as a family of two, without financial assistance, is a contrast to the sheltering, community-based aspects of Cherokee culture. The shattering of her self-confidence is the most devastating aspect of her frustrating flight with Turtle. Tearfully she tells Jax: "I always knew I could count on myself," now she sees a "screwup." Later she admits that the two of them are not "enough. We're not a whole family."[55]

The ironic detachment of Henry James's *The Bostonians* stands in sharp contrast to the four novels written by women, all of which delve deeply into human emotions. James' novel is valuable in the present context chiefly as an illustration of the obstacles faced by nineteenth-century women as they strove to remove the many restrictions that barred them from public life.

3

Religious and Class
Differences in Canada

ANNA BROWNELL JAMESON WAS THE WIFE of an Upper Canada Vice-Chancellor — the colony's highest legal position. She was known as the "Chancellor's Lady," although the marriage was unhappy and she spent only nine months in the colony (December 1836 to September 1837). She was a published author — particularly known for *Characteristics of Women* (1833) — and an independent soul; her husband had been in Canada since 1833. According to Clara Thomas, the " 'woman question' was one of the preoccupations of all of her writing."[56] During her short stay in Canada, she traveled extensively and wrote of her experiences in *Winter Studies and Summer Rambles in Canada*, published in 1838 in three volumes. This was her third work using the travel-diary format, with herself as protagonist. It shows what an upper-class woman could get away with at a time when restrictions on women were rapidly tightening.

Jameson found society in Upper Canada a concentration of "our old and most artificial social system," framed out of "repugnance and contempt for the new institutions of the United States"; it is "conventionalism in its most oppressive and ridiculous forms." She seems to have spent as little time as possible in Toronto, traveling outside it both winter and summer. The Native peoples, particularly the women, were of great interest to her. Stopping in a village on her way to Niagara Falls, she is introduced to a Mr. Kerr, a gentleman who has "Indian blood" and is "the possessor of large estates" nearby, "partly inherited from his father-in-law, Brandt, the famous chief of the Six Nations." Kerr's wife is a woman of "unmixed Indian blood" and their ten-year-old son the "present acknowledged chief," as the "hereditary chieftainship" is "transmitted *through* the female, though passing *over* her."[57]

Jameson's "Summer Rambles" recount an astounding journey undertaken by an unaccompanied woman into parts of Upper Canada accessible only by water. Her new friends in Toronto are full of advice and "solicitude," the "chief justice" sending her "a whole sheet of instructions, and several letters of introduction." As she is about to depart by steamboat, she is called back to meet the missionary from Sault Sainte Marie and his Native wife. Jameson is charmed by "Mrs. MacMurray, otherwise O-ge-ne-bu-go-quay, (i.e. *the wild rose*)." Mrs. MacMurray explains that her sister is married to the "Indian agent" at Michillimackinac, "a man celebrated in the United States for his scientific researchs." Jameson is warmly invited to visit both families if she is able to reach their remote homes.[58]

En route, Jameson is asked by a young man for assistance in finding a wife, one with "the fashionable education of the old country." She demurs, for "a woman who cannot perform for herself and others all household offices, has no business here." She then delivers a tirade against women brought up with "a want of cheerful self-dependence, [and] a cherished physical delicacy." Speaking of such "nonsensical affectations" in her "own sex," she can only "pity the mistakes and deficiencies of those who are sagely brought up with the one end and aim—to get married."[59]

From Detroit, Jameson secures passage on a ship for Chicago, which will take her to Machinaw. While visiting the Schoolcrafts, she is invited to attend meetings with representatives of the various local Native tribes. With little warning, she is offered accommodation to Sault Sainte Marie on a small bateau rowed by five voyageurs. After a two-day trip, camping at night, she and Mrs. Schoolcraft arrive. They are greeted by the MacMurrays and Mrs. Johnston, the mother of Jameson's two friends and a "woman of pure Indian blood." Her sons-in-law, "Mr. MacMurray and Mr. Schoolcraft, both educated in good society ... looked up to this remarkable woman." Jameson becomes the first white female to "shoot the rapids," and her daring leads to her adoption by the Chippewas, who give her the name, "Wah,sah,ge,wah,no,qua, ... *the woman of the bright foam*."[60]

On her way back to Toronto, Jameson and the MacMurrays stop at Manitoulin Island for the annual presentation of gifts to the Natives. From there she continues by canoe, "the only woman" in a group with twenty-one men.[61] Few women at any time in history would have undertaken such a journey, but in 1837 this was particularly remarkable.

Martha Ostenso's novel *Wild Geese* caused a sensation when it was published in 1925. One of three important prairie novels that introduced realism to Canadian readers, Ostenso's novel has had less critical attention than Grove's

Settlers of the Marsh and Stead's *Grain*.[62] Winner of the important Dodd Mead award, *Wild Geese* is told from a woman's point of view. The novel is set in northern Manitoba among immigrant settlers — most of whom are Icelandic — and is seen mainly through the eyes of Lind Archer, the teacher who comes in early spring and departs late autumn, the winter being too severe to keep the one-room log schoolhouse open. Lind boards with the Gares.

Caleb Gare is head of the school board and one of the most diabolical characters in Canadian literature; a man who terrorizes his family and has earned the enmity of the community. Caleb's specialty is blackmail, used most effectively on his wife, but also on neighbors, whose minor misdeeds are discovered and used to add to Caleb's landholdings. His chief weapon is his wife Amelia's secret of having borne a child out of wedlock, known only to the two of them and to one other man. Their four children are nearly grown and could overcome Caleb physically, but obey him out of habit and concern for their mother. He is determined to keep all of them on the farm as cheap labor, so thwarts their desires to marry or in any way ease their lives of continuous drudgery. Three of them are thoroughly cowed, but his younger daughter, Judith, is high-spirited and rebellious. When her boyfriend, Sven Sandbo, returns home in city clothes, flaunting a silver cigarette case and offering Judith a gold-plated vanity case, she rears her horse and rides off, leaping the fence "like a slender boat rising on a wave." Such "showing off" is not for her.[63] Critic Carlyle King calls her "as wild as a bronco and as vivid as a tigress."[64]

Amelia's illegitimate son, Mark, was fathered by a man she loved, who was gored by a bull before they could marry. Caleb knew this when he married her, realizes that she has never loved him, and feels that he is the aggrieved party. Mark Jordan is now a handsome young architect who was raised by priests in the belief that his parents were upper-class British. He is spending the summer on a neighboring farm and romancing the teacher. Amelia believes that knowing he is illegitimate would ruin him. Since he is the offspring of the man she loved, Amelia is prepared to sacrifice the four children she has had by a man she hates. Mark "must never know. She would break under Caleb" first, and his "offspring" would be the "sacrifice." Mark had "grown to manhood in the belief that he was well-born." The novel ends happily with Amelia's secret secure. Caleb is sucked into the muskeg while trying to save his field of flax from an approaching fire, Judith and Sven have escaped; and finally Mark and Lind depart for a happy life together, unaware of his parentage. [65]

This novel is class driven. Judith and Sven, as children of farmers, are in the same class. No matter how much the four fraternize, Mark and Lind are of a higher class. At the other extreme, Malcolm, a former hired man who is part Native, is in love with Ellen. He returns to ask her to marry him, but she is afraid to defy her father. Caleb shows Malcolm around, lying about the fine house he plans to build for his daughters to entertain their "beaux," young men with "farms of their own." Ellen is embarrassed but tries to tell herself that Malcolm "should be shown his place." Malcolm leaves, convinced he is not good enough for Ellen.

The suffering of women is central to *Wild Geese*. Amelia can think of no solution to her problem except to submit to Caleb's torments and to back him in his determination to keep all of their children laboring on the farm. When she learns that Judith is pregnant and so must escape with Sven, she contemplates killing Caleb, for what does "life mean, anyway, for her." She finds an old letter with the news that the man who knows her secret is dead. Caleb discovers that Judith has escaped, and takes a rawhide to Amelia to try and force her to go to Mark with the news of his parentage. She is prepared to die rather than comply.[66]

Wild Geese gives a vivid picture of the hardships of settlers on the northern prairies. The characters are well developed, except for Gare, whom Dick Harrison calls "a creature of romance." The author certainly had the Old Testament Caleb in mind (Numbers 14:30), but as the archetypal "prairie patriarch," he is carried to extremes.[67] Caleb is meant to be a symbol of the harshness of the land — "as tyrannical as the very soil from which he drew his existence" — and clearly it is his only love. Contemplating his field of flax, he runs his hand over it in a "caress — more intimate than any he had ever given to a woman."[68] The plot is manipulated in order to bring Mark Jordan near and to intensify Amelia's suffering, and Caleb's sudden death — he is literally consumed by the land — is a bit too convenient. Had the author arranged for Mark to fall in love with Judith, the plot would have hinged on a different dilemma. Illegitimacy, abetted by class differences, was enough in the 1920s, without any hint of incest.

Hugh MacLennan had as deep an understanding of French/English ethnic differences as any Canadian writer. His novel, *Two Solitudes* (1945), made such an impression that the book's title has become a Canadian platitude. The novel covers two generations in Quebec, from late in World War I to the opening of World War II, and has villains and heroes on both sides of the religious and linguistic divide. The protagonists, Athanese Tallard and his son Paul, are caught in the middle and Tallard is crushed. Descendant of the parish seigneurs, the largest landowner, and a Member of Parliament, he dies a ruined and penniless man. Paul is half-English, perfectly bilingual and bicultural, and rejected by both English and French. He reaches adulthood in the pit of the depression, but as he leaves for World War II, he appears to be a survivor.

The extreme French position is voiced by Father Emile Beaubien, priest in the fictional Quebec parish of Saint-Marc-des-Érables, who "literally ... believed that God held him accountable for every soul in the place." Father Beaubien is angry when Tallard sells land to an Englishman and outraged when he makes plans to open a factory. It is 1917, World War I rages and the Canadian government has recently imposed conscription on the nation's young men. Father Beaubien "thought of the war and the English with the same bitterness. How could French-Canadians — the only real Canadians — feel loyalty to a people who had conquered and humiliated them, and were Protestant anyway?" A speech Tallard gave in the House of Commons is denounced by both sides; the editor of the French paper writes: "You can be with us, or you can be against us. You cannot stand in the middle." The English paper says that the speech "is a pitiful example of the kind of hedging which the eternal Quebec pressure forces even on its better members of Parliament." Tallard's embittered son by his first wife, Marius, is hiding from the military police and supplies Father Beaubien with the family secret that allows him to triumph over Tallard.[69]

The extreme English position is expressed by Janet Methuen, daughter of John Yardley, the kindly old sea captain who buys land from Tallard. Janet, whose maternal grandfather had "upheld the white man's burden," has married into an upper-class Montreal family that considered itself "an extension of the British Isles." They live so properly that "no one could possibly mistake them for Americans." Janet "worked on every war committee in Montreal," and allotted herself "the same rations allowed people in Britain. To make herself feel worthy of the British she was prepared to go hungry." Janet tells the military police where Marius is hiding and informs her distressed father that it's time these French Canadians "were brought to heel." When her husband is killed in the war, Janet turns herself into a martyr, remains with her in-laws, and raises her daughters according to the strictest upper-class rules.[70]

Tallard's showdown with Father Beaubien occurs in stages. At the first meeting the priest, who is incensed because all "the other men in the parish ... knew that the cloth he wore had raised him above ordinary mortals," demands to know why Tallard does not "attend Mass and confess" and what he intends to do about Marius. If Marius goes into the army he will have to live with an unbeliever "in the next cot." Their second meeting is about the proposed factory. Father Beaubien will not allow Tallard "to spoil this parish" by bringing in the English, who "are not Catholics," to use the people as "cheap labour." He challenges Tallard: "You are a good Catholic or you are not. You cannot defy the church and God's own priest and feel no effect." Finally the priest confronts him in front of the villagers and says he will tell the people "that you are no longer a good Catholic," so they "will know that God will not bless them if they elect a man like you."[71]

Tallard is so angry that he impulsively moves to Montreal and becomes a Presbyterian, a disastrous move. Now his English business partner, Huntly McQueen, makes a deal with the Bishop to build the factory, but only if Tallard is not involved. Tallard, certain that he has been double-crossed, accuses McQueen: "It's the old story. You play us off, one against the other." McQueen tries to be conciliatory, but reminds him: "we must keep personalities out of business." Tallard remains in Montreal — now ostracized by both sides — and sends Paul to an English boy's school, where he is taught that his country is "not Canada but the British Empire." Tallard dies leaving his wife and Paul nearly destitute.[72]

Several times in the novel French and English Canadians are spoken of as different races. Marius dislikes Paul because he is "half-English ... The pure race is everything to him." Janet's rebellious daughter, Heather, who marries Paul, is "terribly conscious of their different races and language." Heather is also a feminist and resents the limited professions available to women, especially women of her class. If "you were a girl in their man's world you were struck out before you reached the plate unless you were a bitch." When Paul tells her that every French-Canadian is born in a "strait-jacket," Heather reminds him that every "girl's born in one." Janet tries every manipulative technique in her arsenal to prevent Heather from marrying Paul. Her failure gives the novel its hopeful ending.[73]

Canadian critics generally agree that MacLennan was more a "social novelist" than a literary artist. George Woodcock notes that he is "unashamedly didactic," but is a "Canadian mythmaker" whose work marked "a turning point in the development of a distinctly national literature."[74] John Moss says that the novel provides "fine insights into the medieval Catholicism that dominated Quebec."[75] It also offers a vivid picture of the upper-class English of Montreal, who dominated the business and industrial world until the Quiet Revolution of the 1960s. English Canada's devotion to British culture as the ultimate in social correctness comes through clearly, a compulsion due partly to the need to show that they were not Americans. It also set them firmly apart from French Canadians.

Margaret Laurence's novel, *The Diviners* (1970), is the story of Morag Gunn, orphaned at the age of five, who is raised by Prin and Christie Logan on the wrong side of the tracks in the small Manitoba town of Manawaka. Christie is the town garbage collector, who tells Morag tales of her Scottish ancestors, in particular of Piper Gunn, who played his bagpipes and led the destitute Scots on board ship and then from the shores of Hudson's Bay to the Red River Settlement in Manitoba. The Logans are kind and devoted to Morag, but she does not return the love. She is ashamed of them, yearns to leave Manawaka and hopes never to return.

Morag's first boyfriend is Jules Tonnerre, a Métis who lives in a shack with an alcoholic family. He is also raised on tales of his ancestors, particularly the Riel Rebellion, when the Métis clashed with the Red River settlers and later with Canadian troops. Morag and Jules are ambiguous about the legends of their past. As outcasts from town society the tales are a source of pride, but they also believe that what happened in the past is no help to their present situations. "What does it matter, Christie?" Morag says, "It was all so long ago." "It matters to me," Christie rants. Telling Morag that he is a "disgrace" to his "ancestors," he urges her to "get the hell out of here ... and make something of yourself." She needs no urging and leaves for Winnipeg and university as soon as she has saved enough money.[76]

Before leaving Manawaka, Morag encounters Jules, just returned from World War II. When she tells him that she is going to "college. And I'm never coming back," he responds: "Go to college and marry a rich professor, how about that." He becomes vaguely hostile, for "she is now on the other side of the fence." She does marry a professor, and is too besotted to recognize his ominous comment: "I can afford to keep a wife."[77]

Professor Brooke Skelton is English, son of a schoolmaster in India, who was regularly caned and sent to an English boarding school at the age of six. He has nightmares and calls out for his *ayah*, who was fired for fondling him. He insists that Morag is innocent, calls her "child" and "little one," and keeps putting off having children. As tensions build, she becomes deceitful, determined never to let him see "*the Black Celt in me*." Morag is called back to Manawaka when Prin is dying and gets her first stirrings of guilt for neglecting the Logans. The next time Brooke calls her "little one," she explodes and begins to swear like Christie. Brooke reminds her that when they first met she said she "had no past. I liked that," he says.[78]

The break comes after she encounters Jules in Toronto. He is now a singer and songwriter who moves restlessly around the country. She takes him home and the two are in the kitchen drinking scotch when Brooke returns. Calling Morag into another room, Brooke tells her to get rid of Jules, sneering that her "past certainly *is* catching up" with her, and that he thought it was "illegal to give liquor to Indians." Jules overhears and leaves, so Morag follows him. The next day she takes the money from a novel she has published and moves to Vancouver. There she bears Jules' child. The baby girl looks like her father and is given the name Piquette Tonnerre Gunn, after Jules' sister who died in a fire. Morag is pleased that the baby looks like her father, but the landlady asks: "Did you get yerself mixed up with a Chinee or a Jap, dear?" Jules visits occasionally and Pique, in effect, takes on the burden of the past from both parents. She too becomes a singer and songwriter and goes to Manawaka, finding the Logans' graves and the remains of Jules' family. Morag's anxiety over her hitchhiking daughter highlights her inability to love and care for the Logans.[79]

Morag is haunted by her hometown. "She wouldn't go back to Manawaka for all the tea in China ... And yet the town inhabits her."[80] W.J. Keith claims that there is "a lack of cohesiveness" when the action takes place outside of Manawaka.[81] The place also appears to haunt Jules, for he writes a song about his grandfather who fought with Louis Riel. Pique also writes a song — "The Mountain and the Valley Hold My Name"[82] — that she sings to Morag as her explanation for going west again. Morag shows the song to Jules on his deathbed.

Keith has noted problems with the novel's male characters. While Christie is a "triumph, one of the most original and memorable characters in Canadian Literature," Jules and Brooke are far too symbolic. With Morag's desire to be socially accepted in Manawaka, her friendship with the uncouth Jules seems to be "forcing a political point," while Brooke is a "[t]op-heavy" symbol of "English authoritarianism."[83] Morag becomes a woman who is fully herself only after she leaves Brooke and bears Pique. Her wanderings after that seem pointless. Although she never loses her inner ghosts, she finally realizes that Pique must return to the place from which her parents never fully escaped.

Margaret Laurence's comment about Native Canadians as "other people's ancestors who become mine,"[84] is a profound insight on Canadian cultural history. The image of the Métis, or people of racially mixed ancestry, can be seen as the story of Canada itself: Native and European, English and French, American and British. Although Quebec is never mentioned in *The Diviners*, the Métis are half-French and Roman Catholic. Neither the reader nor Morag is surprised when Pique says she has been called "a dirty half-breed" at school.[85] Pique has already decided that she must go home, and the prejudices of her schoolmates now seem almost irrelevant.

A very different story of a woman's struggles is told in Gabrielle Roy's novel, *Windflower* (in French, *La rivière sans repos*). Although it was published and translated in 1970, it only slowly became widely read in English. Roy was born in Manitoba, her parents part of a large emigration from Quebec in the late nineteenth century. Her first novel, *The Tin Flute* (in French, *Bonheur d'occasion*, 1945) made her famous in both English and French Canada. As the story of a poor family with many children, it recalls *Thirty Acres* and *A Season in the Life of Emmanuel*. *Windflower,* Roy's last novel, has a similar theme to *Pigs in Heaven*, for it tells of a mother's struggles to keep a mixed-race child.

Windflower is set on the tundra in northern Quebec, at about the time of the Korean War. Fort Chimo has a Hudson's Bay store, an RCMP station, and an American Army post. It also has a movie theater, "where Father Eugene provided two shows a week: one for the whites, one for the Eskimos — best not to mix the groups." Four Inuit girls are returning from a movie, laughing about how ugly Clark Gable is and the strange habit of kissing. After they go their separate ways, one girl, Elsa Kumachuk, is accosted and raped by an American soldier. She does not resist and might have put the incident behind her except that she is pregnant. Her parents laugh about it, but the Anglican pastor is outraged: "Who did this to you, Elsa?" he demands. She is vague, does not know his name, but thinks he had blue eyes and blond hair. The GIs are forbidden to mix with the Inuit girls, but there are already some mixed-race children around. Nothing more would have happened, except that Elsa delivers a blond, blue-eyed baby boy with soft wavy hair.[86]

With her first look at the baby, Elsa "felt herself sink into bottomless depths of love." At six months, in "his full splendour of dimpled pink babyhood," he becomes the darling of the community. The women beg to hold him and a large group watches his bath, which Elsa ends triumphantly by curling his hair around her finger. "Jimmy so conquered the hearts of the Eskimo people that afterwards he could always do with them whatever he wanted." Jimmy's mother refuses to marry, can deny him nothing, and will take advice only from white people. Mademoiselle Bourgoin, the head nurse, insists on regular habits, unaware that she had obliged "a whole population to arrange its life to suit a baby." Elsa now insists on cleanliness and privacy in the cluttered family cabin.[87]

In order to buy the things she wants for Jimmy, Elsa goes to work for Madame Beaulieu, the wife of an RCMP officer. Mme. Beaulieu will not allow her to bring Jimmy to work, for it would be one more crying baby in "such a small house." To Elsa it looks like a palace, with its "four rooms, each possessing doors and windows." Problems quickly arise, as Elsa's wages are spent the day she receives them, and Jimmy grows attached to his grandmother, no longer fussing when Elsa leaves. Elsa and her mother, Winnie, have regular arguments about "progress," Winnie always having "been satisfied with what she had" and never trying to "improve herself." Elsa begins cleaning at home, but repeatedly returns to find Jimmy playing in unsanitary conditions. She buys him everything that Mme. Beaulieu's children have, but Jimmy has taken to tantrums. Winnie begins to feed him sweets, there being "no deceit or trickery to which she would not stoop" to get him to "tell her he loved her better than his mother."[88]

The pastor asks Elsa why she buys her child such expensive things. "Why, because he's Jimmy" is the astonished reply. The pastor warns that the day may come when Jimmy will "be ashamed of you and Winnie and Thaddeus," but Elsa has only a vague concept of the future. Gradually the pastor's message penetrates and she realizes that "the white men would be quite capable" of taking Jimmy "away from her." Like Taylor in *Pigs in Heaven*, she takes her child and leaves. This means crossing the river to live with her Uncle Ian and learn "the old ways." It works surprisingly well and Jimmy becomes a more relaxed child. One day the policeman pays Elsa a visit and informs her that the law requires that Jimmy go to school. Ian, Elsa and Jimmy leave in a blizzard, fleeing to Baffin Island where Ian says the law will not find them. Predictably, Jimmy becomes ill. As his temperature mounts, Elsa remembers the old graveyard, full of the graves of children and young people. Ian reluctantly agrees to return and they race for the settlement, where Jimmy is saved with a shot of penicillin. Ian is confused. He "thought of the death of his first wife in her twenties," and of the many "children he had not managed to save." "Penicillin — that was what 'they' had now, besides everything else, to trap free men." Elsa has had her fling with the old ways and is now back to striving for progress.[89]

Elsa now spends her days making Inuit souvenirs, but is always short of money through trying to meet Jimmy's demands. She buys him a bicycle and baseball equipment, cooks hamburgers, and supplies money for Cokes, chewing gum, and comic books. He plays only with the white children, so when they are sent away to school he is lost and disdainful toward the Inuit children. Jimmy begins asking where he came from and who his father was. Elsa invents a romance, but is unable to tell Jimmy his father's name. When Jimmy disappears — having stowed away on a cargo plane — the police find him at a nearby town. Elsa asks timidly if Jimmy "wants to come back." The policeman is outraged — Jimmy is fifteen — and asks Elsa if she has ever "refused him anything." When a surly Jimmy is returned, Elsa "knew then that he was lost to her." In order to get him to talk to her, she schemes with him to make his second and successful escape.[90]

Elsa slips by stages "into endless daydreaming." Looking around her empty cabin, she realizes that her life had been spent "creating a home that in an instant" was unmade. She sells her things and moves into a shack in the Inuit village.[91] Years later, Jimmy flies a plane over the village and talks to the priest. The villagers hear him on their radios, but Elsa's radio is broken. Jimmy is a legend in the village, but his mother is an old woman at forty, a humped figure moving slowly along the shore of the river.

Unlike the other examples in this chapter, *Windflower* ends without hope. Elsa is a woman destroyed by the white man's civilization. It is all the more poignant as no one is ever unkind to her and the white people at Fort Chimo make many attempts to help her. Phyllis Webb notes that "how to live" in this novel is more important than "how to survive," a point demonstrated when a sick and delirious Jimmy begs his mother to listen to Uncle Ian and run for Baffin Island.[92] There he would have lost his life, but died like an Inuit. The sense of despair and hopelessness in this novel is all too common in French-Canadian literature. We saw it in *Thirty Acres* and in *A Season in the Life of Emmanuel*. Since The Quiet Revolution, life has improved for most of Canada's French, but their writers sometimes look back with a deep sense of despair.

4

Conclusion

AT THE BEGINNING OF THE TWENTY-FIRST CENTURY, Canada and the United States are both multicultural societies with laws against gender and ethnic discrimination. As with most massive changes in cultural attitudes, unforeseen problems have arisen, especially connected with compensating various groups for past wrongs inflicted upon them. Thinking in group terms is a challenge in itself, for the history of both nations shows a striving toward treating people more as individuals than as members of groups.

The examples used in this chapter show that types of discrimination tend to overlap. Men who treat women as inferiors are very apt to think the same way about different races and classes. Women who are class conscious usually strive to be "ladies" and look down on members of other races or nationalities. The fact that hierarchical thinking was accepted during most of history and is still prevalent in much of the world suggests that total equality is an elusive goal.

Gender discrimination is somewhat different from any other type. Women are not a minority and politically they are capable of being every bit as formidable as men. Still, women, who make up fifty-two percent of the population, only comprise twenty percent of those in politics, and make up a tiny minority of the CEOs of major companies. The fact that enriched classes in schools are normally two-thirds girls and that more girls finish high school and attend university than boys has put to rest any previous notions of women's intellectual inferiority. Canada still has a higher percentage of outstanding women among its writers than the United States, but any other gender differences between the two countries are now insignificant.

Ethnic problems remain distinct in the two nations. Frye's 1977 comment, "Canada does not have quite so heavy a burden of guilt toward red and black people as the United States,"[93] is still valid, although Canada seems to have more problems settling Native claims than the United States. Treaties made by the British in colonial days are still on the statute books and often conflict with present reality. Canada has had more success with the Inuit, as the recently created territory of Nunavut gives many of the northern people a large degree of self-government.

The heritage of slavery and Jim Crow still plagues the United States and undoubtedly will for some years. American writers of all races are treating the subject. We saw an example in Toni Morrison's *Paradise*. Another relevant work is Philip Roth's *The Human Stain* (2000), which tells the story of a classics professor with a mixed-race background who had passed himself off as Jewish during the Jim Crow era. He is drummed out of the university for a supposed racial slur, yet cannot reveal his secret, which has been kept even from his family. As was said at the beginning of this chapter, Jefferson's words still haunt the Americans. In spite of the tone of despair expressed by many of Canada's French writers, there is nothing in Canadian literature with a Canadian setting that exudes such bitter irony as is found in Morrison's and Roth's novels.

Looked at historically, legitimized class distinctions are largely a thing of the past in North America. As more schools and businesses adopt a merit-only policy, class as an inherited position will become increasingly meaningless. Sadly, gender and ethnic distinctions are not as easily eliminated as those of class. Women, Natives and Blacks suffer from "high visibility" and formerly all-white male establishments suddenly found it necessary to hire tokens to prove their broad mindedness. Fortunately the tokens have rarely turned out to be a liability, so innumerable doors of opportunity have opened that were closed since the beginning of North American settlement. But the problems are far from over. The aristocracy of talent that Adams and Jefferson hoped for may be an imperfect blessing, but it appears to have arrived.

Notes

1   Marlene Le Gates, *In Their Time: A History of Feminism in Western Society* (New York: Routledge, 2001), 148.
2   The Declaration and Resolves of the First Continental Congress, 14 October 1774, state that "The inhabitants of the English Colonies in North America … are entitled to life, liberty, and property." Morison, 119.
3   Mary Wollstonecraft, "From *A Vindication of the Rights of Woman*," *Woman in Western Thought*, ed. Martha Lee Osborne (New York: Random House, 1979), 132.
4   When Garrison proposed that women be given an equal voice in his abolitionist society, three hundred members walked out and formed their own society.

Garrison refused to back down on "the woman question." Stephen B. Oates, *The Approaching Fury: Voices of the Storm, 1820–1861* (New York: Harper Collins, 1997), 41–2.

5 Qtd by Louis Menand, *The Metaphysical Club* (New York: Farrar, Straus and Giroux, 2002), 86.

6 Thomas Jefferson was president in 1808.

7 Qtd by Edward Ball, *Slaves in the Family* (New York: Ballantine Books, 1999), 259.

8 Menand, 374, 387.

9 Ibid., 162.

10 Alison Prentice, Paula Bourne, Gail Cuthbert Brandt, Beth Light, Wendy Mitchinson, and Naomi Black, *Canadian Women: A History* (Toronto: Harcourt Canada, 1996), 217.

11 Lester J. Cappon, The Adams-Jefferson Letters, Vol. II (Chapel Hill: University of North Carolina Press, 1959), 365–66, 371, 389.

12 Traill, 16.

13 Anna Brownell Jameson, *Winter Studies and Summer Rambles in Canada* (Toronto: McClelland & Stewart, 1965), 49.

14 Winona Stevenson, "Colonialism and First Nations Women in Canada," *Scratching the Surface: Canadian Anti-Racist Feminist Thought*, ed. Enakshi Dua and Angela Robertson (Toronto: Women's Press, 1999), 53.

15 Slotkin, *Regeneration,* 98.

16 Oates, 52.

17 Faulkner, *Light in August*, 439; Ch 19.

18 Oates, 382, 385–86.

19 Kazin, *God*, 240–41.

20 Letters of Hawthorne to Wm. D. Ticknor, 1851–1864, Vol. I (Newark, NJ: The Carteret Book Club, 1910), 75.

21 Oates, 4.

22 E. Ball, *Slaves*, 259

23 Kazin, *God*, 76, 78, 75.

24 Harriet Beecher Stowe, *Uncle Tom's Cabin* (London: J.M. Dent & Sons, Ltd., 1976), 118; Ch. 11.

25 *Ibid.*, 363; Ch. 34, 15; Ch. 1.

26 See Chapter II.

27 Stowe, 256; Ch. 21, 85: Ch. 9.

28 Kazin, *God*, 80.

29 Irving Howe, Introduction, *The Bostonians*, by Henry James (New York: The Modern Library, 1956), vi.

30 James, *The Bostonians*, 343; Ch. 34.

31 *Ibid.*, 18, 22; Ch. 3, 111–12; Ch. 14, 35; Ch. 5.

32 *Ibid.*, 328; Ch. 33, 32; Ch. 4, 58; Ch. 8, 55; Ch. 7, 455; Ch. 42.

33 *Ibid.*, 62; Ch. 8, 346; Ch. 34, 396; Ch. 38.

34 Oates, 130, 129.

35 Howe, xxv.

36 James, *The Bostonians*, 346; Ch. 34.

37 Harper Lee, *To Kill a Mockingbird* (Toronto: Popular Library, 1962), 134, 135;

Ch. 13.
38 *Ibid.*, 149; Ch. 15.
39 *Ibid.*, 227, 223, 220; Ch. 23.
40 *Ibid.*, 218; Ch. 22, 224; Ch. 23.
41 Malcolm Bradbury, *The Modern American Novel* (New York: Oxford University Press, 1992), 273.
42 Mervin Rothstein, Byline, *The New York Times*, August 26, 1987, final ed.: C-17. Online.
43 Toni Morrison, *Beloved* (New York: New American Library, 1988), 183, 206.
44 *Ibid.*, 271.
45 Styron, 100.
46 Morrison, *Beloved*, 149–50.
47 *Ibid.*, 162–65.
48 Rothstein, Byline.
49 Morrison, *Beloved*, 261, 265.
50 Margaret Atwood, "Haunted By Their Nightmares," The New York Times, September 13, 1987, final ed.: 7–1. Online.
51 Morrison, *Beloved*, 139, 137, 138.
52 Barbara Kingsolver, *Pigs in Heaven* (New York: Harper Perennial, 1994), 3; Ch. 1, 138; Ch. 13.
53 *Ibid.*, 86, 89; Ch. 9.
54 *Ibid.*, 88; Ch. 9, 314; Ch. 30.
55 *Ibid.*, 247; Ch. 24, 291; Ch. 28.
56 Clara Thomas, Introduction, *Winter Studies and Summer Rambles in Canada*, by Jameson, xiii.
57 Jameson, 49, 50, 52, 37.
58 *Ibid.*, 75, 76.
59 *Ibid.*, 87.
60 *Ibid.*, 127–128, 135.
61 *Ibid.*, 155.
62 See Chapter IV.
63 Martha Ostenso, *Wild Geese* (Toronto: McClelland & Stewart, 1971), 74; Ch. 5.
64 Carlyle King, Introduction, *Wild Geese*, by Ostenso, v.
65 Ostenso, 88; Ch. 6, 224; Ch. 22, 134–35; Ch. 12.
66 *Ibid.*, 224; Ch. 22.
67 Dick Harrison, *Unnamed Country: The Struggle for a Canadian Prairie Fiction* (Edmonton: The University of Alberta Press, 1977), 108, 111.
68 Ostenso, 33; Ch. 2, 119; Ch. 10.
69 Hugh MacLennan, *Two Solitudes* (Toronto: MacMillan of Canada, 1967), 3, 6; Ch. 2, 70; Ch. 8.
70 *Ibid.*, 148–49; Ch. 15, 112; Ch. 11, 187; Ch. 24.
71 *Ibid.*, 140–42; Ch. 14, 167–68; Ch. 20, 184; Ch. 23.
72 *Ibid.*, 216; Ch. 27, 232; Ch. 28.
73 *Ibid.*, 362; Ch. 43, 355; Ch. 42, 288; Ch. 35, 31; Ch. 4, 3; Ch. 2, 323; Ch. 38.
74 Woodcock, *Canadian Fiction*, 74–75.
75 John Moss, *Canadian Novel*, 179.

76 Margaret Laurence, *The Diviners* (Toronto: Bantam Books, 1975), 162; Ch. 4.

77 *Ibid.*, 165; Ch. 4, 202; Ch. 5.

78 *Ibid.*, 227, 224, 227; Ch. 6, 256–57; Ch. 7.

79 *Ibid.*, 269; Ch. 7, 306; Ch. 8.

80 *Ibid.*, 227; Ch. 6.

81 W.J. Keith, *An Independent Stance: Essays on English-Canadian Criticism and Fiction* (Erin ON: The Porcupine's Quill, 1991), 215.

82 M. Laurence, *Diviners*, 440–41; Ch. 11.

83 Keith, *Stance*, 215.

84 See Chapter II.

85 M. Laurence, *Diviners*, 421; Ch. 10.

86 Gabrielle Roy, *Windflower*, trans. Joyce Marshall (Toronto: McClelland & Stewart, 1991), 3; Ch 1.

87 *Ibid.*, 17, 18, 21; Ch. 3.

88 *Ibid.*, 26, 30, 29; Ch. 4, 56; Ch. 7.

89 *Ibid.*, 47, 48; Ch. 6, 50; Ch. 7. 70, Ch. 9.

90 *Ibid.*, 131, 132; Ch. 16.

91 *Ibid.*, 134–35; Ch. 17.

92 Phyllis Webb, Afterword to *Windflower* 155.

93 See Chapter II.

Chapter
Seven

Violence

1
Rights, Human Perfectibility,
and the Rule of Law

NOTHING IS MORE APPARENT to the most casual observer of the North American scene than the excessive amount of violence in the United States and its comparative absence in Canada. Statistics on crime rates in various cities consistently indicate that Canada experiences about one-third of the violent acts committed in the United States.[1] The statistics do not indicate how entrenched in the two cultures is the American propensity for and Canadian aversion to violent acts.

These cultural differences have roots in the debate preceding the American Revolution. Max Beloff notes that in Thomas Paine's *Common Sense,* "the idea of natural rights and a radical suspicion of all government ... are brought together to form a justification of American independence."[2] Of course, the Revolution was a success and, as Frye says, a "revolutionary tradition" is inclined to lead to "an impatience with law."[3] However, Paine's argument did more than lead to revolution; it left in place a belief that the individual is capable of making moral decisions unaided, and that institutionalized authority is a natural enemy. Paine did not anticipate violence; in the same pamphlet he says that in America "there is nothing to engender riots and tumults."[4]

That early dispute between Britain and the American colonies was critical to the development of American attitudes toward violence. Locke's theory was interpreted in Britain to support the supremacy of Parliament and the right of the people's elected representatives to be the final authority. In America, Locke's theory came to mean the fundamental goodness of the individual, so long as he or she was not oppressed by institutionalized authorities. Beloff says

215

that the Declaration of Independence, which uses language less utilitarian than Paine's, expresses "the same attitude to natural rights and the liberties springing from them." The Declaration "set out the completed doctrinal basis for American nationhood," where the "pursuit of happiness had replaced property among man's unalienable rights." Beloff concludes, "with this momentous declaration, the history of American political thought finally separates from the parent stem."[5] Neither the Loyalists nor the French ever accepted Jefferson's and Paine's arguments, and this fundamental philosophical difference still divides Canada and the United States.

Until the middle of the nineteenth century, Canada had almost as violent a past as the United States. The many wars between France and England had their bloodiest North American encounters on what is now Canadian territory. Early New France faced possible extinction by the Iroquois, and in Newfoundland the Beothuk Indians were hunted "down like animals," the last one dying in 1829.[6] The early years of the British North American colonies were far from peaceful, with riots breaking out in both Upper and Lower Canada in the 1830s. Later in the century, Canada was able to settle the West with minimal violence, but that process was made significantly easier by the American slaughter of the buffalo.

Both nations started with seeds of potential violence in the ground: in the United States, slavery, faith in individual virtue, and an ingrained suspicion of government; in the British colonies, French-English differences and the stresses of colonial government. The American seeds blossomed like dandelions, while the Canadian ones generally died in the ground. A number of forces caused such a dramatic difference between peoples who were very much alike and who lived under similar conditions.

Early Puritans had untiringly sought manifestations of the devil and looked on religious tolerance as a means for the devil to gain a foothold in the New World. They whipped, tortured, and hanged those deemed to be sinners, their fervor reaching its peak with the Salem witch trials of 1692. Gradually the devil became secularized, but his pursuit continued unabated — and not just in New England. Early in the nation's history the general public saw the obstructive Native as the principal incarnation of the evil one.

Richard Slotkin — who calls the Puritans "the archetypal colonizers" — points out how the attitude of the Puritans toward Native Americans set the tone for early American hostility: "The pressure of demographic expansion, coupled with the psychological fear of acculturation, moved the Puritans toward a policy of exterminating the Indians."[7] Secure in their faith and viewing themselves as God's Elect, Puritans came to the New World to teach, not to learn from those they considered savages or incarnations of the devil.

Hostility to government, a product of the Revolution, continued to gain strength after independence, as arguments between the Federalists and the Republicans grew heated. Jefferson had so much faith in human goodness that he had no doubt that "men may be trusted to govern themselves without a master."[8] He also thought that violence was necessary to defend human liberty. In 1787, his response to Shays' Rebellion[9] was that "a little rebellion now and then is a good thing."[10] In a letter to John Adams's son-in-law, he continued the argument: "God forbid we should be 20 years without such a rebellion ... What country can preserve its liberties if its rulers are not warned from time to time that this people preserve the spirit of resistance? Let them take arms ... What signify a few lives lost in a century or two? The tree of liberty must be refreshed from time to time with the blood of patriots and tyrants. It is its natural manure."[11] Jefferson's faith remained intact after the Terror of the French Revolution. The "deaths seemed to him necessary and, in some cases, salutary." He claimed that rather than see the Revolution "failed, I would have seen half the earth devastated."[12]

Frontier violence did not generally break any American laws, but aiding escaped slaves did. As the abolition movement grew, contempt for federal laws increased. Individuals and organizations assisting the Underground Railroad actively sought to circumvent both federal and many state laws. Ironically, a parallel situation developed in the South, where slave states promoted States' Rights, arguing that the federal government had no authority to interfere with state laws.

The American combination of legalized slavery, a stark and unambiguous view of good and evil, and an unrealistic approach to human judgment was explosive enough, but other factors supported this unholy mixture. The constitutionally guaranteed right to bear arms was part of a package that established a government virtually unable to maintain order and protect minorities. Also, the Catholic ability to deal with fallible human nature and to put a damper on "Garden of Eden" and "redeemer nation" ideas was effectively absent in the young country.

The forces that constrained violence in Canada included British insistence on law and order, the strength of the churches (particularly the Catholic Church), and the Loyalists' disdain for the unruly behavior they had experienced in revolutionary America. Disorder is common in a new situation undergoing rapid development, but Michael Cross notes that it was constrained by "the leadership of small semi-aristocratic groups who filled the vacuum left by the absence of established institutions."[13] These groups were largely composed of Loyalists who had been so repelled by the vigilante rule they had left behind that they adopted a powerful anti-revolutionary stance. Finally, violence was discouraged by the sense of defeat felt by French and English alike. They saw themselves as losers, small in numbers, and struggling to survive in a vast northern wilderness. Any aggression would lead to defeat, and infighting would seriously weaken their chances for survival. When the colonies finally joined into a nation, the federal government was given "a general authority over all matters affecting 'peace, order and good government.'"[14] Those words were clearly meant to be a contrast to "life, liberty and the pursuit of happiness."

Jefferson's comments, suggesting that lawless behavior can have moral justification, plus the pursuit of happiness as a fundamental right, put a high priority on success and minimized the means used to achieve it. As Lipset notes, "Americans are much more likely to be concerned with the achievement of approved *ends* ... than with the use of appropriate *means*."[15] There are legions of violent acts in American literature, many of them undertaken for virtuous reasons. Literary themes that encompass violence cover a wide spectrum. There are many criminals — earthly manifestations of the devil — who, like Milton's Satan, can be very attractive. Numerous heroes — all brave and most of them virtuous — either operate where there is no functioning government or consider themselves above such slow-motion law enforcement. Group conflicts, which may or may not be racially motivated, appear primarily as frontier violence in the nineteenth century and as mob conflicts in the twentieth century.

In Canadian literature, the horrors of war and "nature as destroyer" are the most common violence themes. In non-war settings, human violence is suppressed and discredited, with a protagonist who often struggles to find peaceful solutions to potentially explosive situations. Fictional heroes never achieve glory by killing; rather, it is the avoidance of violence that makes them outstanding. Those who do succumb are usually depicted as weaklings, whose dangerous behavior discredits the community. W.H. New writes, "Canadian pop culture relies ... on avoiding violence, for while violence is acknowledged as a fact of life, it is generally represented as an act requiring therapeutic resolution."[16]

It is hardly surprising that early writing in Canada shows considerable preoccupation with war, for wars had shaped the colonies and forced sudden and dramatic changes in government, law, and culture. The bloody battles between the English and French at Louisbourg in 1745 and 1758; the Battle of the Plains of Abraham, which left New France in the hands of the British in 1759; Pontiac's uprising against the British from 1763 to 1765; the American invasion of Quebec in 1775; the American Revolution from 1775 to 1783; the American invasions of Upper and Lower Canada in 1812; and the Fenian Raids of 1866 are the most notable violent events that preceded the unification of the British North American colonies into the nation of Canada. In John A. Macdonald's 1867 letter to a friend in India, he refers to "those wretched Yankees" who are "sure to invade," and he facetiously suggests sending an army from India to hold San Francisco "as security for Montreal and Canada."[17]

Although order was not always maintained in the pre-Confederation period, the citizenry was overwhelmingly opposed to violence. The most severe challenge to the maintenance of a violence-free society came shortly after Confederation, when Canada set out to link Ontario with British Columbia and to settle the prairies. The Americans' rapid movement westward following the Civil War began to encroach on what are now the Canadian prairies, and the colony of British Columbia was facing annexation. Most of that vast western landscape, known as Rupert's Land, belonged to the Hudson's Bay Company. In 1870, it was transferred to Canada, an area of approximately 300,000 square miles.

Wallace Stegner (1909–1994), an American writer who spent part of his boyhood in the Cyprus Hills of southern Saskatchewan, wrote about the development of western Canada in *Wolf Willow: A History, a Story and a Memory of the Last Plains Frontier* (1955). Stegner gives a vivid portrayal of the Canadian prairies at three periods of their history and of the national determination and relative success at maintaining peace. "Memory" recalls his family's homestead between 1914 and 1920; "Story" is set in Alberta during 1906 and 1907, one of the most terrible winters in living memory; and "History" goes back to the fur trade but concentrates on the 1870s and 1880s, when Canadians frantically built a transcontinental railroad to hold British Columbia and keep back the encroaching Americans. In "History," two men were sent west on separate reconnaissance missions and both recommended that troops be sent wearing red uniforms. "Since the middle of the 18th century the red coat of the British dragoons had meant, to Indian minds, a force that was non and sometimes anti-American."[18]

"Memory" includes Stegner's first impression of Canada. He was five years old, sitting in a dingy waiting room with his mother and staring at some portraits on the wall. The "resolute, disciplined faces and the red coats glimmering in the shabby room" filled him with awe. If he had known the entire history of Canada and the United States, he says, he could not have picked out "a more fitting symbol of what made the Canadian West a different West from the American." "History" describes the first troop of 275 Mounties, resplendent in "scarlet tunics ... gleaming metal [and] polished leather," who rode west in 1874 to establish and maintain law and order and to convince the Natives that the international boundary was "a color line: blue below, red above, blue for treachery and unkept promises, red for protection and the straight tongue."[19]

Stegner tells the story of Commissioner Macleod, following his arrival at Fort Whoop-Up in what is now southern Alberta, and his encounter with the whiskey traders. "He threw out patrols which very soon caught a whiskey trading party coming up the Whoop-Up Trail; Macleod confiscated the whiskey and threw the traders in his new log jail. Within weeks he held a conference with the Blackfoot ... [which] resulted in a lasting pact of friendship with Crowfoot, greatest of the Blackfoot chiefs." Stegner makes it clear what was at stake: "Left to run its course," the whiskey trade "could hardly have avoided stirring up in the Alberta country a racial war as vengeful as the Minnesota Massacres of 1861–62, and it would as certainly have brought defeat and tribal collapse to the Blackfoot. The pattern had been repeated many times south of the Line." The Native was not the only one in danger, for "the Blackfoot might choose at any time to take the risk and wipe the little force of a hundred and fifty Mounties out. If the police had worn blue coats instead of red, the Blackfoot might well have tried."[20]

The famous story of Superintendent Walsh meeting the Sioux, who had moved north across the border after the Battle of Little Big Horn (1876), is also part of Stegner's "History." Little Big Horn was "a bloodletting of white soldiers unmatched since Braddock's defeat" a hundred years earlier. With twelve men, Walsh rode to the Native encampment of three thousand, where "American scalps still hung drying in the smoke." He met with the chiefs and told them "how they would behave if they wanted to stay in the Great Mother's country … They would do no injury to man, woman, or child; they would steal nothing, not so much as a horse; they would not fight, either among themselves or with the Canadian Indians"; and they would not smuggle ammunition to their friends in the United States. Walsh and his men were outnumbered thirty or forty to one that day, but he "told them the rules and they said they would obey."[21] The new nation of Canada was serious when it set forth the motto: Peace, Order, and Good Government.

2

High Hopes and Hidden Devils in the United States

PROJECTING THE DEVIL ONTO THE FACE of the Native peoples began very early, but got a distinct boost immediately after the Revolution, when, freed of the Quebec Act, Americans rushed to take over the fertile Ohio valley and the long north-south frontier began its steady movement westward. Slotkin claims that violence "is central to both the historical development of the Frontier and its mythic representation," and thus "the 'savage war' became a characteristic episode of each phase of westward expansion." Of greater significance is his claim that the "compleat 'American' of the Myth was one who had defeated and freed himself from both the 'savage' of the western wilderness and the metropolitan regime of authoritarian politics."[22] Thus, the approach of the law "behind" the frontiersman was in some respects as great a threat as the Native tribes he was facing.

In Cooper's novel *The Pioneers,* Natty Bumppo, or Leatherstocking, fled civilization for the sanctity and security of the wilderness. There he could live according to nature's law; the law of man was intolerable to him. Five novels later, in *The Deerslayer* (1841), Leatherstocking is in his early twenties just as the Seven Years' War is beginning.[23] In this novel, the last of the series to be published but the first chronologically, Leatherstocking readies himself for his passage into manhood by killing his first Native. He has already received the sobriquet "Deerslayer" for his fine marksmanship, but has not yet aimed his gun at a human being. Early in the novel he is asked by a traveling companion, known as Hurry Harry, if he has ever shot "anything human or intelligible?" Deerslayer, somewhat embarrassed, admits that he has not, "seeing that a fitting occasion never offered." Hurry is surprised that Natty has never had reason to "do the law" on anyone, "by way of saving the magistrates trouble." He considers "game, a red skin, and a Frenchman as pretty much the same thing."[24]

The "fitting occasion" soon arises. Natty shoots his first "Indian," but declines the customary aftermath of scalping, although at the time, both the

British and French governments offered bounties for Native scalps. The shooting was in self-defense and so skillfully done that the dying Native renames him "Hawkeye." He is such an honorable frontiersman that when he is captured by Iroquois and is given a furlough to negotiate, he returns to face torture at the exact time promised. When fighting breaks out, Hawkeye kills two Natives with one bullet. At the end of the novel, he sidesteps the amorous approaches of a young woman by telling her that he is going to war. "And do you so delight in violence and bloodshed?" she asks. He admits, "I've feelin's for the callin', which is both manful and honorable."[25]

Cooper had spent some years in Europe between the beginning and end of the Leatherstocking series, and was preoccupied with regaining his property rights. Consequently, he has Hawkeye spend a great deal of time talking, explaining right from wrong, the "gifts" of different races, and the meaning of honorable actions, which do not include envy of other peoples' property. Above all, he explains what is and is not lawful. "God," he says, "gave each race its gifts. A white man's gifts are christianized, while a red skin's are more for the wilderness. Thus it would be a great offence for a white man to scalp the dead, whereas its a signal vartue in an Indian. Then, ag'in, a white man cannot amboosh women and children in war, while a red skin may ... [F]or them it's *lawful* work." Hurry Harry responds, "As for scalping, or even skinning a savage, I look upon them, pretty much the same as cutting off the ears of wolves for the bounty." Hawkeye insists that white men must obey their laws, then echoes America's founders and anticipates Thoreau: "When the colony's laws, or even the king's laws, run ag'in the laws of God, they get to be onlawful, and ought not to be obeyed."[26]

Cooper, the most important antebellum novelist to fictionalize conditions on the American frontier, set a standard for the hundreds of western novels that were such popular fare in the succeeding century. Leatherstocking is a honorable man, but Henry Nash Smith notes that the hero of the western novel changed significantly as the genre developed. By the late nineteenth century, the western hero had become "a self-reliant two-gun man who behaved in almost exactly the same fashion whether he were outlaw or peace officer." This was an important change from the "code of gentility that had commanded Cooper's unswerving loyalty."[27] To readers of the day, the vigilante, the roving frontiersman with his six-shooter, who cleared the land of evil in preparation for the fulfillment of the American Dream, was a virtuous man. But Smith is able to recognize that among literary figures, the "good" and the "bad" became indistinguishable.

Thoreau's essay "Civil Disobedience" appeared in 1849, sixty-two years after Jefferson's startling comments on Shays' Rebellion. Thoreau expresses the same faith in human perfectibility as Jefferson. Not only does he accept the motto, "That government is best which governs least," he prefers a government that "governs not at all," and predicts such a condition "when men are prepared for it." His plan for no government would allow each individual to do what he or she believes to be right: "It is not desirable to cultivate a respect for the law, so much as for the right." "Action from principle," he says, "is essentially revolutionary," for it divides states, churches, families, and even "the *individual*, separating the diabolical in him from the divine."[28] This sounds much like Emerson's praise for the "cannon" that is "aimed by ideas" and men who "die for what they live for,"[29] except that Emerson was talking about the American Revolution and Thoreau about an American government that protected slavery. Speaking of this government, Thoreau wrote that if it "requires you to be the agent of injustice to another, then, I say, break the law."[30] Considering the times in which he lived, it is difficult to disagree with Thoreau, but he was solidifying a tradition that was to have prolonged and unintended consequences.

Jefferson, Emerson, and Thoreau refused to consider the possibility that their ideal society might be unrealizable, or that the human conscience might give bad advice. Their comments seem to be the educated counterpart of the unschooled preacher insisting that the truth is self-evident. Emerson developed the dialectics of what Quentin Anderson calls the "imperial" self, for he judged society to be "irrelevant to human purposes" and located any god within the self.[31] Such reasoning made it not only acceptable, but positively virtuous for each individual to make his or her own moral decisions and thus to defy the laws of society if they were believed to be wrong.

America's fascination with manifestations of the devil began early and has never weakened. David Reynolds speaks of the *"likable criminal or justified pariah"* becoming a popular stereotype. Crime reports were "in the main, gloating records of unthinkable atrocities" that "emphasized man's depravity without mentioning redemption." He adds that America had a "neurotic obsession with puritanical virtue," but that nagging doubts about religion drove reformers to "new extremes to find rhetorical and imaginative replacements for bygone religious certainties." Hence, writers became adept at using "horrific Calvinist images."[32] Almost all major American writers of fiction in the antebellum period created diabolical characters. Hawthorne's are often scientists, who destroy those closest to them in pursuit of their mad passions. In "The Birthmark" Aylmer kills his beautiful wife attempting to remove a birthmark from her cheek, in "Rappaccini's Daughter" Dr. Rappaccini raises his daughter on poisons, and in *The Scarlet Letter* Chillingworth turns into a devil figure as he works at damning the minister. Melville's diabolical characters tend to be oxymoronic. In *Moby Dick* Captain Ahab is a devil with god-like qualities, while the evil protagonist of *The Confidence Man* (1857) resembles a Christ figure. Three of Poe's best known tales, "The Tell-Tale Heart," "The Black Cat," and "The Cask of Amontillado" — all published in the 1840s — have narrators who are murderers, obsessed with their cleverness in carrying out their crimes or concealing their victims' bodies. In "The Black Cat," the narrator, maddened by the presence of a pet cat, expresses his outrage that "*a brute beast*" could cause him, "a man, fashioned in the image of the High God — so much of insufferable wo!" He then kills his wife with an axe when she tries to protect the hated cat and boasts of his skill in concealing her body.[33] In such a zeitgeist it is hardly surprising that women writers failed to find a niche for themselves.

Violence in American literature continued unabated after the Civil War. The rage and despair Mark Twain experienced late in life can be traced to his belief that American ideals had failed. In this he resembles Henry Adams. Tony Tanner says that theirs was "not a despair of personal bereavement but of country — ultimately of man."[34] In his early years, Twain had accepted the glowing ideals of mankind and the United States espoused by Jefferson, Emerson, and Thoreau, but the bitterness of Twain's disillusionment becomes more apparent with each succeeding novel.[35] Henry Adams was raised with eighteenth-century ideals to believe that "God was a father and nature a mother, and all was for the best in a scientific universe." The relationship between Adams' destroyed ideals and the apocalyptic violence he visualized as a resolution is less direct than it was with Twain, who simply reversed his earlier opinion of human nature and fantasized scenes of massive destruction. Adams took up science and convinced himself that mankind was about to blow itself up. He found himself in a land "where order was an accidental relation obnoxious to nature." He speaks of "the persistently fiendish treatment of man by man; the perpetual effort of society to establish law, and the perpetual revolt of society against the law it had established; the perpetual building up of authority by force, and the perpetual appeal to force to overthrow it." Adams sometimes sounds like Twain: "Every day Nature violently revolted, causing so-called accidents with enormous destruction of property and life, while plainly laughing at man, who helplessly groaned and shrieked and shuddered, but never for a single instant could stop."[36] Tanner sums up the process through which both Twain and Adams seem to have passed. The "initial philanthrope gradually becomes misanthropic; the idealistic democrat shades into a scornful tyrant; hoping to bring light he ends by concentrating on destruction ... As the faith in man falls, so a savage authorial anger intrudes itself."[37]

Twain and Adams represent a minority view of the times. The American people of the late nineteenth century were dreaming of a glorious expansion of the nation and hatred of the Native peoples reached its peak. Cooper's "romantic view of the noble red man [was] violently denounced by Theodore Roosevelt in *The Winning of the West*."[38] This was the age of Social Darwinism, the he-man era when people spoke of inferior races. Roosevelt's view of the nation is best expressed in Owen Wister's *The Virginian* (1902), dedicated to Roosevelt, and one of the most popular novels in American literary history.

The Virginian is set mainly in Wyoming territory between 1874 and 1890. There is an unnamed narrator, a man from the east who becomes friends with the cowboy hero, known only as the Virginian. The hero is lowly but honorable, and through his own efforts rises to the status of landowner and gentleman. His Virginia origins imply an aristocratic heritage and Jefferson's natural aristocracy of talent, a view embraced by Roosevelt. The Virginian falls in love with a schoolteacher, Molly Stark Wood of Vermont, who has famous Revolutionary ancestors but a dearth of money, which leads her to reject an unloved suitor and travel west to earn her living. The Virginian decides to improve himself in order to be worthy of her. At this point, the author speaks directly to the reader, declaring that "through the Declaration of Independence ... Americans acknowledged the *eternal inequality* of man ... Let the best man win ... That is true democracy. And true democracy and true aristocracy are one and the same thing."[39]

Reading and improving his spelling and grammar are not sufficient to make the Virginian worthy of Molly; he must also convince her that the violence and lawlessness of frontier society is morally justified. The mores of the society are established early in the novel, when the Virginian plays poker with his pistol on the table, forcing the villain to "back-down." This begins an enmity that is not terminated until the end of the novel when hero and villain face each other with drawn pistols on the deserted streets of a town. The villain, Trampas, is suspected of cattle rustling, and the Virginian has had both opportunities and motives for killing him, but resists, although killing a man is "nothing to bother yu'—when he'd ought to have been killed." He encounters Trampas in town the day before he and Molly are to be married, and Trampas drunkenly threatens to kill him if he is not out of town by sunset. Friends offer to run Trampas out of town or lock him up until after the wedding, the Bishop advises him to flee, and Molly threatens to leave him if he stays to meet the challenge. It cannot be: "It had come to that point where there was no way out, save only the ancient, eternal way between man and man. It is only the great mediocrity that goes to law in these personal matters."[40]

There is a degree of law enforcement in Wyoming. The man who offers to lock up Trampas is acting mayor of the town, and the ranch owner for whom the Virginian works is a judge. When the ranch hands, led by the Virginian, trail some cattle rustlers into the Grand Tetons and capture two of them, they hang the men rather than take them back to be put on trial. The Virginian has no regrets, although one of the rustlers was an old friend of his. "I would do it all over again," he says, for "the thieves have got hold of the juries," and a regular jury "would have let him off." When Molly hears what happened, she is inconsolable, so her friends ask the judge to talk to her. The judge does not relish his task because he "had been a staunch servant of the law," and Molly promptly asks if he had come to tell her that he thinks well of "lynching." The judge distinguishes the lynching of Blacks in the South from the hanging of cattle thieves in the West, but Molly can see no difference in principle. The judge finally wins the argument by assuring her that juries in the West are corrupt and will always release a cattle thief. "[W]hen your ordinary citizen sees ... that he has placed justice in a dead hand, he must take justice back into his own hands."[41] In such a cultural climate, women writers had little hope of making themselves heard.

Clearly, Owen Wister and Theodore Roosevelt embraced Turner's frontier thesis, but added some of their own ideas of innate superiority. Slotkin points out that Wister was a wealthy and well-educated easterner who went west to escape the racially polyglot metropolis and to live the strenuous life. He "hoped the nascent aristocracy of the great cattle ranches might provide the 'permanent pattern' for a new American racial type." Slotkin claims that there were some thieves among the opponents of the Wyoming Stock-Growers Association (WSGA), but that most of them were small working ranchers. The point of view of the WSGA, he argues, "was written into the canon of American literary mythology by Owen Wister in *The Virginian*." Vigilantism was common in settler communities in America at that time, but "was transformed [by the WSGA] from an assertion of a natural and democratic right-to-violence to an assertion of class and racial privilege."[42] The cattle wars of the American West were more often class wars than — as the judge persuades Molly — steps toward a virtuous civil society through summarily disposing of the lawbreakers.

The amount of violence in American literature remained high after World War I, despite the diminishing popularity of frontier fighting as a subject. There is no shortage of violence in the works of Faulkner, Hemingway, and other American writers of the 1920s and 1930s. More in keeping with the outraged attitudes of Twain and Adams, a novel that stresses a peculiarly American form of violence is Nathanael West's *The Day of the Locust* (1939). The novel is set in Hollywood, the artificial world that appears in many succeeding American novels. It is told from the point of view of Tod Hackett, a young man from the Yale School of Fine Arts who is working in set and costume design. The story is episodic and pictorial; the emphasis is not on movie stars, but on failures, the disappointed. West was a Hollywood screenwriter in the 1930s, who witnessed the "lonely crowd of the depression." Kazin points out that "West's keenest insights" show that the "Hollywood crowd" really wanted to "kill its idols." The original title for the novel was *The Cheated*.[43]

There is no lack of physical violence in *The Day of the Locust* — scenery collapses during a filming of the Battle of Waterloo, killing many extras; there is a gruesome cock fight; a party turns into a brawl; and a large gathering of people becomes a destructive mob — but psychological violence predominates. Tod is struck by the number of people who have come to California to die, who worked for years at tedious jobs and saved their pennies in order to retire to the paradise of southern California. He senses that their resulting disappointment and boredom can only lead to violence. As he sketches people who have joined bizarre religious sects, he decides that he will not satirize or pity them, he will "paint their fury with respect, appreciating its awful, anarchic power and aware that they had it in them to destroy civilization." The mob scene at the end of the novel is almost pointless, for the people have gathered only to watch the opening of a new movie. Tod says, "the crowd would turn demoniac" when the stars begin to arrive, so that the "police force would have to be doubled" and nothing but "machine guns" would stop it. He insists that they are not "harmless curiosity seekers," but people who are fed daily on "lynchings, murder, sex crimes" — a diet that has made "sophisticates of them."[44]

The scapegoat in the novel, a man named Homer Simpson, is a painfully timid bookkeeper from a small town in Iowa. Tod sees him as "an exact model for the kind of person who comes to California to die." Homer falls for a superficial girl, an aspiring movie star, who uses him outrageously and then leaves him a destroyed man. The more he buys for her and waits on her, the more bored and abusive she becomes, so he increases "his servility and his generosity." He is like "a cringing, clumsy dog, who is always anticipating a blow." The reader never knows if Homer survives physically, but by the end he has clearly gone insane.[45]

This novel shows the American Dream as a scene from hell. As Tod wanders through movie sets, he passes through a saloon door to a Paris street, then to a Romanesque courtyard. He sees people eating cardboard food in front of a cellophane waterfall, just before the hill collapses during the filming of the

Battle of Waterloo. A tall handsome dolt, dressed as a cowboy, has a "two-dimensional face." An aging actor has "very little back or top to his head"; it is "almost all face, like a mask, with deep furrows ... plowed there by years of broad grinning and heavy frowning. Because of them he could never express anything subtly or exactly."[46]

West was killed in an accident at the age of thirty-seven, but he left two major novels, *The Day of the Locust* and *Miss Lonelyhearts*. Harold Bloom says that West "was not a satirist, secretly hoping to improve us, but a demonic parodist, providing some music to celebrate our march down into hell."[47] For Twain, Adams, and West, the American Dream is an illusion with no resolution except a cataclysm, an apocalyptic end.

Black-white racial violence in American literature is primarily a twentieth-century phenomenon. Ralph Ellison was an early Black writer interpreting the bitter heritage, particularly emphasizing psychological violence. As was illustrated in *Huckleberry Finn* and *The Confessions of Nat Turner*, the degrading humiliations to which Black Americans have been subjected are as pronounced as the beatings and killings. Toni Morrison commented ironically that *Uncle Tom's Cabin* was not "written for Uncle Tom to read."[48]

The unnamed narrator of Ralph Ellison's *Invisible Man* (1952) is living comfortably and secretly in the basement of a whites-only New York apartment building. *Invisible Man* ends on a hopeful note, a suggestion that the narrator will soon emerge from his underground isolation and normalize his life. Wondering if he has stayed underground too long, he considers, "[p]erhaps that's my greatest social crime, I've overstayed my hibernation, since there's a possibility that even an invisible man has a socially responsible role to play."[49] Like in Morrison's *Paradise* and *Beloved*, there is a hint at the end of the novel that the United States is not, after all, going to hell.

Ellison received so much criticism for the hopeful ending to his novel that in 1981 he wrote a detailed introduction to a new edition, explaining what he meant by calling a Black man invisible. Recalling a "sociological concept which held that most Afro-American difficulties sprang from our 'high visibility,'" Ellison says that high visibility actually rendered one "*un*-visible"; that the "trappings of racial stereotypes" make it impossible for most people to see the person under the skin. This is not a difficult concept, but Ellison goes further. He recounts the story of a captured Black American pilot in World War II who found himself the senior officer in a group of white American prisoners, where the resulting "dramatic conflict" was exploited by the German camp commander for his own amusement. Later, the pilot was forced to crash-land on a southern plantation, where he was assisted by a Black tenant farmer "whose outlook and folkways were a painful reminder of his own tenuous military status and their common origins in slavery. A man of two worlds, my pilot felt himself to be misperceived in both and thus at ease in neither." In other words, he had trouble seeing himself. Ellison claims that he developed his protagonist over a period of years, immediately after World War II and before the Civil Rights movement. He strove for a Jamesian-type character with the "virtues of conscience and consciousness," and to avoid "another novel of racial protest." His narrator was to be "forged in the underground of American experience" and to "emerge less angry than ironic." He would be a "blues-toned laugher-at-wounds who included himself in his indictment of the human condition." This was not an easy task that Ellison set himself, and the resulting novel was certain to invite misunderstanding.[50]

The ambiguity of the protagonist's attitude toward the Jim Crow world of his day is triggered by his grandfather's strange dying words: "our life is a war ... Live with your head in the lion's mouth. I want you to overcome 'em with yeses, undermine 'em with grins, agree 'em to death and destruction, let 'em swoller you till they vomit or bust wide open."[51] The family thought the old man had gone out of his mind, but the narrator puzzles over those words, sensing an important message that he cannot understand.

There is a great deal of physical violence in *Invisible Man*. The narrator gives a prize-winning speech at his high school graduation and is invited to repeat it to a group of white men. He finds himself part of a group of Black boys hired to amuse the town's leading citizens by being blindfolded, herded into a boxing ring, and ordered to fight. Cries such as, "Let me at that big nigger" are mixed with kicks and blows. When he falls and pretends to be knocked out, he is yanked to his feet and told to get "going, black boy." The exhausted and bloodied boys are paid with money scattered on an electrified carpet. The white men roar with laughter, pushing and kicking the boys onto the carpet. Finally, the narrator is told to give his speech, which he does swallowing blood and saliva. To his amazement, he is given a leather briefcase and a scholarship to the local "Negro" college.[52]

This novel is the story of one young man's education — an education in physical and psychological violence. He strives to avoid violence, but fights back when attacked. As a model third-year student at the college, he is allowed to drive a white trustee and founder. He obediently takes the man to the old slave quarters, where the trustee encounters more of life in the raw than he had ever seen. Dr. Bledsoe, the principal of the college, is so angry that he expels the young man, telling him that he has done "incalculable damage" to the school and that "the dumbest black bastard in the cotton patch knows that the only way to please a white man is to tell him a lie." Bledsoe agrees to give him letters to white trustees in New York, where he can work and save money. As our narrator leaves for New York, he senses his grandfather "grinning triumphantly."[53]

Among the horrors the narrator remembers from his time in New York City are incidents involving other Blacks, all of whom are trying in distorted ways to adapt to a Jim Crow world. He discovers that Bledsoe's letters tell the trustees that the young man has harmed the college and will never be readmitted. An old Black man at a paint company, flaunting his own knowledge, causes an explosion. The narrator is injured, given shock treatment, and forced to sign an affidavit releasing the company from responsibility in order to receive compensation while he recovers. One day, he gives an impromptu talk to a mob in Harlem, defusing a near-violent encounter with the police. His performance is seen by some members of The Brotherhood, a euphemism for the Communist Party, and he is hired to give speeches. He does excellent work in Harlem, then is suddenly reassigned, and then called back to Harlem where the shooting of an unarmed Black man by the police has the people ready to riot. He is told by the Brotherhood that the time is not right for an uprising and that he is to prevent it. He angrily suggests that they are "sacrificing the weak," but is reminded that he must have "confidence in those who lead you — in the collective wisdom of Brotherhood." It is too late, and a massive urban race riot results. As the riot winds down, the narrator recognizes his own invisibility; he had been accepted by the Brotherhood because to them "color made no difference, when in reality it made no difference because they didn't see either color or men." Finally, he recognizes the "beautiful absurdity" of the "American identity" and the meaning of his grandfather's words: to "affirm the principle on which the country was built" and not succumb to the men who "did the violence."[54]

Invisible Man is a very American novel. It elevates the individual over the collective, and expresses faith in the founding ideals of the nation, no matter how much those ideals have been violated. Bloom argues that "Invisible Man's personality renders any name redundant. We hear his voice incessantly: ironic, eloquent, jazz-influenced, sometimes furious with outrage, yet always open to a vision ... [of] humane sensibility." Bloom calls the novel "a demonic or tragic parody."[55]

The criminal or psychopath has remained a prominent character in American fiction. Poe is both the popularizer of the Gothic tradition in the American South and the inventor of the detective story. Southern Gothic writers like Faulkner and Flannery O'Connor followed in his footsteps and created dozens of characters of doubtful sanity who are particularly known for their brutalities.

The urban criminal, prominent in American crime fiction, has remained a figure of fascination. Whether the protagonist is a criminal or a detective, however, he or she behaves in almost exactly the same way, following the pattern noted by Smith in the western novel. Although many nations show a broad popular taste for the detective novel, American fictional detectives — such as Dashiell Hammett's Sam Spade and Raymond Chandler's Philip Marlowe — struggle with violence that is greater and more sustained than that found in any other western country.[56] The criminal is not limited to detective or crime fiction, however. Mario Puzo's *The Godfather* (1969) introduced a family of criminals to the American literary scene that has remained wildly popular. E.L. Doctorow's *Billy Bathgate* (1989), the story of the notorious Dutch Schultz gang that operated in New York in the 1930s, is another example. These criminals almost require an American setting, for their wealth, freedom to operate, and frequent overt violence would be almost unimaginable in any other western nation.

A novel that harks back to Thoreau and the American western tradition of taking the law into ones' own hands is Russell Banks' *Cloudsplitter* (1998). A fictionalized story of John Brown, the fire-breathing abolitionist who raided the federal arsenal at Harper's Ferry, Virginia before the Civil War, *Cloudsplitter* is narrated by Brown's third son, Owen. This family saga places the reader in parts of antebellum America and provides a vivid picture of the intense passions of the anti-slavery movement. John Brown is like an Old Testament patriarch who is repeatedly compared to Abraham; Owen is his Isaac, the son who never married, could not pull away from his father, and survived Harper's Ferry convinced that he had betrayed Father Abraham and his "little army of the Lord."[57]

Religion is the force that drives John Brown. He has the fervor of a Cotton Mather, never questions the righteousness of his cause, and welds his family together with horrifying stories of slavery. He reads newspaper ads for runaway slaves, who are identified by their wounds. To add emphasis, he passes the paper to a young Owen, telling him to read "these words, so that we may better hear in thy innocent voice their terrible, indicting evil." Owen reads notices for the return of slaves with whip and brand marks, gunshot wounds, and missing toes or eyes, a litany of horrors that make the Brown family "blood ties mystical and transcendent." Owen and his two older brothers become free thinkers and cannot accept their father's religious views, so they are "stuck with Father himself for a God." A natural corollary to such an attitude is that the laws of man are at best secondary, and the lawlessness of the Browns gradually increases as the situation in the nation deteriorates. Early in the novel, the family goes bankrupt, and the older boys take up armed positions to defend the property when the sheriff comes to evict them. To Owen's disappointment, his father gives way: "We must obey the law, children." After the passage of the Fugitive Slave Act and demonstrations in Boston, New York, and Philadelphia, the Browns begin openly preaching violence. With the Kansas-Nebraska Act, which "split the country" and set North and South competing for Kansas "like France and England at war over Canada a century earlier," the Browns become guerrillas, and then terrorists. They take "special pleasure" in breaking local "black laws" passed by Southern sympathizers in Kansas. The pro-slavery and anti-slavery groups hurl violent epithets at each other. Owen explains that they "shrieked at us from Satan's camp, and we trumpeted back from the Lord's." Repeatedly, John

Brown explains to his followers that it is a "soul-damning sin ... to submit to laws and institutions condemned by our conscience and reason."[58]

Simultaneous with the growth of their religious fervor and opposition to the law is the Browns' increasing willingness to kill. The family moves to northwestern New York to establish a new branch of the Underground Railroad, and there they encounter danger from bounty hunters. When the Browns bring an escaped slave couple to a Quaker captain who will take them across Lake Champlain to Canada, Billingsly, a slave-catcher, confronts them with a gun. John Brown captures Billingsly and prepares to shoot him. The Quaker captain objects, and Owen suggests putting manacles on the man and leaving him in the woods. Later, Brown thanks Owen for saving his soul, saying he is "not ready to kill a man." Brown explains his problem: "My killing him would have been murder, pure and simple. I have no cold blood, Owen. Not a drop. I must acquire it." Shootouts become more frequent, not just with slave-catchers, but with lawmen armed with warrants. By the time the Browns have moved to Kansas, they have become seasoned killers. Owen in particular blames himself for the accidental death of his Black friend Lyman Epps, and is prepared to go with his "father and brothers and haul five men who claimed to love slavery and hate Negroes out of their cabins and butcher them for the sheer, murderous pleasure of it." The raid on Harper's Ferry is almost suicidal. Owen is ordered to stay behind and guard the arms and papers, so he watches from a tree as the Virginia militia and the Jefferson Guards (formed after the Turner rebellion) arrive, kill his friends and brothers, and capture John Brown, who will be hanged. The two men with Owen suggest a rescue attempt, but Owen knows it is hopeless and says: "My father does not want me to save him." Owen sees "Father Abraham, making his terrible, final sacrifice to his God."[59]

Walter Kirn claims that *Cloudsplitter* is "a domestic drama at heart, not a historical saga," and that "its fundamental issue isn't slavery but the challenge of living with a fanatic."[60] This is partly true, but the historical aspects of the novel are powerful, and *Cloudsplitter* may become an important work in the American literary canon. Slotkin facetiously calls John Brown "Hawkeye as Revolutionary" and identifies him with frontier mythology, although "Brown departs from the western stereotype in his identification of his own cause with that of the Negro, and in his ultimate 'conversion' to the pursuit of the 'Cause' as a substitute for the pursuit of his own interests."[61] Like a classical hero, John Brown had a people to save.

It is disturbing how much the American propensity for violence has been associated with race. The Native Americans, who tried to hinder the westward movement of the American frontier, were so hated that they became the subject of the cliché, "the only good Injun is a dead Injun." Slavery nearly tore the United States apart. After the Civil War, the North was so exhausted and the South so unprepared for emancipation that enactment of Jim Crow laws, added to the bitterness of reconstruction, caused racial disharmony to continue for another century. At the end of the twentieth century, guilt over past actions and attitudes is contributing to more violence. It sometimes seems as though the American people have forgotten that there are ways other than violence to solve a nation's problems.

3

Law and Order as a
Survival Technique in Canada

THE THREE WARS, WHICH DID SO MUCH TO SHAPE present day Canada, loomed large in the minds of Canadians in the nineteenth century. These wars provide the setting for much of the century's writings, the favorite being Quebec before and during the Seven Years' War. Among English Canadians, a felt need to justify the conquest of French Canada and see the nation as a peaceful whole is clearly an objective of Kirby's *The Golden Dog* and Parker's *The Seats of the Mighty*. Both are loosely based on actual events from the Seven Years' War.

"Nature as destroyer" appears in most nineteenth-century Canadian narrative poems, where characters succumb to or narrowly escape blizzards, falling trees, and other natural calamities, but rarely inflict violence on each other. The animal stories of Roberts and Seton made the first serious cases for non-violent treatment of wild animals — not neglected or abused pets or domestic animals, but creatures in their natural habitat. John Polk argues that these animal stories are "more closely allied with the mainstream of our literature" than most Canadians realize.[62] The tragic or elegiac endings, where the protagonist is the hunted rather than the hunter, have sometimes been interpreted as "expressions of national self-pity."[63] Atwood claims that "Canadians themselves feel threatened ... [so] their identification with animals is the expression of a deep-seated cultural fear."[64] However, Canadian responses to animal stories, including those of Bodsworth and Mowat, can also be seen as an affirmation that both morally and strategically non-violence is the better policy. This is not to belittle the poignancy of these stories, but to recall that both Roberts and Seton insisted on scientific accuracy in their stories. Roberts speaks of "a psychological romance constructed on a framework of natural science,"[65] and both writers sought to influence policy and not just pull heartstrings.

Polk notes the different approach in the United States, where attitudes to wild creatures remain "firmly anthropocentric ... Nature exists to challenge man, to jolt him into self-discovery, [or] to reveal the truths of a transcendental universe."[66] From Natty Bumppo's sharp shooting and the pursuit of Moby Dick to Faulkner's Old Ben and the giant fish in Hemingway's *The Old Man and the Sea,* American stories are told from the hunter's point of view, no matter how much the protagonists struggle to identify with the hunted creatures.

Homicides and group violence are as rare in Canadian fiction as they are in Canadian life, and the examples that can be found illustrate an intense desire to maintain a lifestyle free of such incidents. Ralph Connor's first novel, *Black Rock, A Tale of the Selkirks* (1898), is set in British Columbia in the 1880s, when both frontier violence and the cowboy novel were peaking in the United States. *Black Rock* makes an excellent contrast to Wister's *The Virginian,* written about the same time and almost as popular in its day. Conditions in *Black Rock* are similar to the American West; society is poorly organized, there is minimal government, and moral leadership is needed. However, in the Canadian novel there are no fights with criminals or Natives, and there is a small but effective police force. Moral leadership is provided by the clergy and, instead of a vigilante with a gun, the hero is Craig, a young Presbyterian minister, who skillfully works with tough lumbermen and miners. Craig is assisted by a young woman, Mrs. Mavor, the widow of a miner, whose beautiful singing and moral courage provide much-needed inspiration to the men. Several of the men are in love with her, but Craig discourages them, knowing that she still mourns for her dead husband. Craig personifies the sentimental religiosity that has made Connor's novels less popular with later generations, but forecasts the importance of the church in Canadian society. Craig claims that the "Church must be in with the railway ... [and] have a hand in the shaping of the country." He proposes organizing "a little congregation here in Black Rock." When told that it is a hopeless business, he retorts: "Hopeless! hopeless! ... there were only twelve of us at first to follow Him, and rather a poor lot they were." Of course, Craig succeeds, and eventually he and the lovely widow are married and settle in the West.[67]

The saloon in the small town of Black Rock is a place of evil and a setting for potential violence. Craig considers drinking to be the work of the devil, and strives to find other amusements for the men. Two brawls occur at the saloon, but both times death is narrowly averted. The Irish saloonkeeper, Slavin, is a devoted husband and father. When his infant son falls ill, Slavin sobers up the drunken doctor, who gives the baby a drug overdose. The priest is too far away to baptize the dying baby, so the baby is "baptized by the Presbyterian minister with holy water and with the sign of the cross." Father Goulet eventually arrives, assures the mother that her "little one is safe," and stops Slavin from strangling the doctor. The priest asks, "who gave him drink? ... [who] wrecked his life?" and says sternly, "Repent of your sin and add not another."[68]

The principal villain in this novel is an American gambler named Idaho Jack, who is accustomed to keeping his gun on the table during a card game. This is a contrast to *The Virginian*, where the hero justifiably puts his gun on the table when playing cards. In *Black Rock*, Policeman Jackson, "Her Majesty's sole representative in the Black Rock district," walks in on a game, gently taps the pistol, and says: "Now, the boys know I don't interfere with an innocent little game, but there is a regulation against playing it with guns ... I'll just take charge of this," he says, picking up the revolver, "it might go off." Idaho's rage "was quite swallowed up in his amazed disgust at the state of society that would permit such an outrage upon personal liberty."[69]

No greater contrast can be found between the literature of the two countries than in their Western fiction. In the United States, shoot-outs are the norm while the hardships of settlers are rarely mentioned. The lives of the settlers are central to Canadian Western fiction, and what grim lives they generally are. John Moss claims that novels "of the family farm are the Canadian version of Greek tragedy."[70] There is much suffering and some brutality, and accidental deaths are fairly common, but there are no violent encounters with Native peoples and virtually no outlaws.

Frederick P. Grove's *Settlers of the Marsh* (1925) differs from other prairie novels in the Canadian canon because it tells of a murder — an unusual feature. Young Niels Lindstedt is a Swedish immigrant, has been in Canada only three months, and is hired with his friend Nelson to dig a well for farmer Amundsen. The two of them nearly perish in a November blizzard while hunting for the farmhouse. Niels is attracted to the daughter, Ellen, who is reserved and "works like a man." Amundsen has a dying wife and refuses to call a doctor, although he brags about owing no one. Niels finds him "repulsive" in his "self-sufficiency."[71]

Niels saves his money, stakes a claim, works hard and long, then builds a four-room house, the largest in the district. He hears that Amundsen was killed in an accident, but when he attempts to propose to Ellen, she stops him. Later he insists, telling her how much he has dreamed of her as his wife, and that he had sworn to himself that no wife of his would ever have to work as hard as his mother had to feed her children. Ellen asks him to turn away while she tells her story. She describes watching her mother worked to death, deliberately bringing on miscarriages whenever she got pregnant, yet unable to avoid her husband's demands for sex. One night she hears her mother beg: "John, it means a child again. You know how often I have been a murderess already. John, Please! Please!" The next pregnancy kills both her and the baby, but just before her death, she begs Ellen to "never let a man come near" her. Ellen swears to her mother that she will not.[72] Puritanical Canadian critics called the novel obscene.

Despite his basic intelligence, Niels is naive. Critic Kristjana Gunnars points out that he almost has a "desire for ignorance." [73] He has met another woman in town, Clara Vogel, who tells him, "You are a conqueror, Niels; but you do not know it. With women you are a child … [I]f you are ever to marry, the woman will have to take you." Clara marries him, but she makes no attempt to function as a farm wife, and begins spending more and more time in the city. He had wondered why none of his friends had come to call. Clara has to explain to him that he has married the district whore: "You married me because you were such an innocence, such a milk-sop that you could not bear the thought of having gone to bed with a woman who was not your wife." She begins operating as a prostitute in their house, and Niels is driven nearly to madness. As he approaches the house with a rifle that has never been used, two men leap out of the window. He shoots her.[74]

The next day he signs over his farm to his farm hand, who hysterically begs Niels to hide. Niels calmly replies, "Hide? No. I am going to town." He walks out of the door mumbling, "Hanged by the neck until dead." Niels turns himself in and is imprisoned for ten years. The prison warden befriends him, Niels improves his education, and his sentence is reduced. When he is released, Ellen is waiting for him.[75]

English-French relations have probably been the greatest challenge to the Canadian determination to maintain a violence-free society. For decades,

Protestant-Catholic antagonism was kept barely below the boiling point by Orangemen from Northern Ireland and Irish-Catholic extremists, known as Fenians, who precipitated Confederation and were responsible for Canada's only nineteenth-century political murder, the shooting of Darcy McGee in 1868.

We saw in Hugh MacLennan's novel *Two Solitudes* how English and French worked against each other in World War I. World War II brought a similar but less intense dispute over conscription. These disagreements did not lead to violence, and French-English relations generally remained calm until Quebec's Quiet Revolution of the 1960s, when social and educational reforms were accompanied by demands for special status and the first movements toward separatism. Bombs were planted in mailboxes in the early 1960s and one man was killed. After the Centennial celebrations of 1967, the separatists became active again, exploding several bombs in Montreal and kidnapping two men, one of them becoming Canada's second political murder.

MacLennan's novel *Return of the Sphinx* (1967) was written in the early sixties before the worst violence occurred. In this novel, Alan Ainslie, a child in MacLennan's earlier novel, *Each Man's Son* (1951), is now an aging man, Minister of Cultural Affairs in the federal government, and father of two grown children. His wife came from a prominent and cultivated French-Canadian family and their children are bilingual and bicultural. The youngest, Daniel, becomes involved with a group of separatists who have recently staged a riot. Ainslie, unaware that Daniel is involved, invites the leaders of the riot into his office for an interview. Ironically, the young rioters are all wearing peace buttons.

Relatives and friends try to talk sense into Daniel, mainly with stories about the violence they experienced in World War II. Alan was a pilot whose plane was shot down. He saved the lives of his crew by holding the burning plane on course until all had bailed out. Alan survived but has a skin graft, a glass eye, and walks with a limp. His navigator and best friend has a childhood memory of his once handsome father returning from World War I "a mangled, wheezing wreck." The mother of Daniel's girlfriend, a child in Morocco during the war, saw her father's ship blown up; later she sold herself to an American soldier for "two dozen tins of Spam and half a dozen cartons of cigarettes" which she sold for more food. Her lover was killed and her baby born just after her sixteenth birthday.[76]

None of these stories can sway Daniel. When an unexploded bomb is found in his car, he is arrested by the RCMP. As with most Canadian fiction, violence is reported later or narrowly averted. Daniel, as a young ideologue who would resort to violence for what he believes is a just cause, threatens to bring down the entire social structure that French and English Canadians have so patiently built up. Unlike in the United States, violence can threaten the very existence of the nation.

One of the most effective yet often hilarious treatments of the different French-English attitudes toward World War II can be found in Roch Carrier's novel *La Guerre, Yes Sir!* (1968; English translation 1970). Set in a small Quebec town, it deals with a bizarre situation: the return of a dead villager, a war casualty, by English soldiers. For any of their sons to be forced to go overseas and risk death was a great outrage to the French, seen as violence that the English had inflicted upon them. The protagonist in this novel is the community, for "life in the village" is "lived in common."[77]

The shocking opening of *La Guerre, Yes Sir* shows Joseph, a villager, chopping off his own left hand, because "[t]hey've already made jam out of Corriveau with their goddam war ... They won't get me." Later, Joseph's wife finds a group of children using the frozen hand as a hockey puck. Corriveau, the dead soldier, is returned by English soldiers who speak no French, and the villagers speak no English. The necessary translating is tackled by Bérubé, a soldier on leave who has been "looking after the toilets in G wing of B building at the air force base in Gander, Newfoundland," and by his new wife, Molly, a former prostitute. Not much translating is done, for the soldiers and the villagers have nothing to say to each other, merely harboring unflattering thoughts. The English are referred to as *maudits Anglais*, while the English think of "these French Canadians" as "savages."[78]

The wake for Corriveau is the central event in the novel. All of the villagers come to pay their respects and pray for the soul of the dead soldier, but as they eat *tourtières* made from a freshly killed pig and drink hard cider, the wake turns into a brawl. The English soldiers stand at attention, radiating disapproval. Fighting breaks out when Bérubé beats up a man to demonstrate the terrible life of a soldier. When the English soldiers attempt to disperse the villagers by throwing their winter attire in the snow, the villagers return, ready to fight. That the *Anglais* would chase them out of Corriveau's house, "a house that had come down through five generations of Corriveaus, all living in the village and in the same house on the same bit of land for more than a hundred years," was not to be tolerated.[79]

The violence in this novel, as with most violence in Canadian literature, is contained within social parameters. The considerable amount of dark ironic humor highlights the incompatibility of these two groups who are unable to understand each other's language or culture, but are trying to do the right thing for a dead soldier. The funeral the next morning puts an end to this ludicrous situation.

Margaret Atwood's novel *Alias Grace* (1996) tells the story of two murders that took place in Canada West[80] in 1843. This was a notorious case that Susanna Moodie wrote about in *Life in the Clearings*. Moodie took great interest in Canada's prisons and prisoners. She proudly claimed that executions are rare in Canada, and that there are men and women in the prisons "who could not possibly have escaped the gallows in England." She tells the story of Grace Marks as recounted by her lawyer, who heard it from Grace's partner in crime, James McDermott, the night before he was hanged. Because of the lawyer's pleading, Grace was spared the gallows and sentenced to life in prison, where she told the lawyer that she wished she too had died, for she could not rid herself of the vision of the woman she helped to murder: "her terrible face and those horrible bloodshot eyes have never left me for a moment." Moodie wrote a poem about Grace Marks, and later reported that she had succumbed to insanity. Moodie visited Grace in the asylum in Toronto.[81]

In an afterword to her novel, Atwood explains that Moodie's account was third-hand — Grace was returned to the penitentiary shortly after Moodie saw her in the asylum and was pardoned in 1872. Grace went to New York State where the record ends, although it was rumored that she married there. Atwood stays close to the known facts of the grisly double murder. James McDermott, stableman for Thomas Kinnear, struck Kinnear's housekeeper and mistress, Nancy Montgomery, with an axe and threw her into the cellar. She was not dead, so, according to McDermott's testimony, he and Grace strangled her with Grace's scarf. When Kinnear returned home, McDermott shot him, and he and Grace took money and valuables and fled. They were captured in Lewiston, NY, and returned to stand trial. Both were convicted and sentenced to hang, but their lawyer, arguing that Grace's part in Nancy's murder was questionable and that she was barely sixteen years old, got her sentence reduced. McDermott was hanged before a large crowd in November 1843. Nancy was found to have had an illegitimate child and was pregnant at the time of her murder. McDermott claimed that Grace had lured him into doing the murders with sexual favors, while Grace claimed that she feared McDermott and was forced to assist him. This was one of the most notorious cases in mid-nineteenth-century Canada. Atwood argues that the "combination of sex, violence, and the deplorable insubordination of the lower classes was most attractive to the journalists of the day."[82]

As with so much Canadian fiction, the actual violence in this novel is muted, and events are recounted or remembered later. Grace tells her story to a young Dr. Simon Jordan, who is interested in the human mind and hopes to open a modern, humane mental hospital and to raise the money with his report on Grace Marks. Grace claims to have had periods of amnesia and to have no memory of the actual murder of Nancy. The focus of the novel is on nineteenth-century attitudes toward mental illness rather than on violence. Phrenology and spiritualism were widespread beliefs at the time, although Dr. Jordan will have none of it. When Grace is hypnotized by a Dr. Jerome DuPont — a trained "Neuro-hypnotist" whom she had previously known as Jeremiah the peddler — Grace's voice and personality change. She says her name is Mary Whitney and that it was she who lured McDermott and helped to murder Nancy. Several people watch the hypnotic session and talk to the transformed Grace Marks. Jordan asks if she helped to strangle Nancy and the voice answers, "It was my kerchief that strangled her ... Such a pretty pattern it had on it." Others join the questioning: "'You killed her,' breathes Lydia ... 'Oh Grace,' moans the Governor's wife. 'I thought better of you! All these years you have deceived us!' The voice is gleeful. 'Stop talking rubbish,' she says. 'You've deceived yourselves! I am not Grace! Grace knew nothing about it!'" The group is so shocked that efforts to get Grace pardoned are halted; no lawyer or public official would credit what they had seen.[83]

Grace is no stranger to violence. An immigrant from Northern Ireland with a drunken and abusive father and a constantly pregnant mother who dies on the voyage, Grace is forced to care for her younger siblings until, at the age of twelve, her father forces her to lie about her age and go to work. She admits to having had thoughts of killing her father. She works for a wealthy family in Toronto, where a slightly older servant, Mary Whitney, becomes her first and only friend. Mary explains what is happening when a frightened Grace experiences her first menstrual period, and warns her to beware of men. Mary is pregnant, deserted by her lover, and has a botched abortion from which she bleeds to death. Grace is sleeping on the floor next to the bed when Mary dies. The shock sends Grace into prolonged unconsciousness from which she briefly awakes, claiming that she is Mary and asking about Grace. Later, Grace is told what happened but has no memory of it. She had been told to open a window when someone dies to enable the soul to escape, but had forgotten. The voice of Mary, coming from the hypnotized Grace, says that she only inhabited Grace's "earthly shell. Her fleshly garment. She forgot to open the window, and so I couldn't get out! But I wouldn't want to hurt her. You mustn't tell her!"[84]

When Grace and McDermott are arrested in Lewiston, they are hustled out of town in a hurry for fear a mob might try to rescue them, "as they might have done if McDermott had thought to shout out that he was a revolutionary, or a republican, or some such, and he had his rights, and down with the British."[85] This is the closest to a mob scene mentioned in the novel.

The foregoing literary examples, containing incidents of violence, demonstrate the traditional Canadian aversion to using such means to solve problems or even to achieve worthy objectives. Somehow, someway, peaceful ways are usually found.

4

Conclusion

JOHN MOSS'S 1977 CRITICAL STUDY *Sex and Violence in the Canadian Novel* has received much adverse attention, especially his statement that "[t]here almost certainly is a higher incidence of sex and violence in the Canadian novel than elsewhere."[86] Bruce Powe wonders how seriously such a book should be taken, and notes that those "who know a lot about literature will be impatient with this sort of statement and those who do not will be misled."[87] Moss could not have had the United States in mind when he mentions "elsewhere," for Canadian writers cannot begin to compete with their counterparts south of the border in lurid depictions of sex and violence.

Explicit sex may well be as much the prerogative of men as tales of life on the road, but even Canada's male writers seem unwilling to depict sexual activity with the enthusiasm and aplomb of John Updike. On violence Moss is clearly wrong. He uses examples from the writings of Alice Munro, Margaret Laurence, Robertson Davies, Margaret Atwood, and Mordecai Richler, none of whose works can match the violence in novels by Twain, Faulkner, Hemingway, West, Pynchon, and Doctorow, to mention only a few.

A 1996 article in Toronto's *Globe and Mail* recounts the frustrations of two American journalists working in Canada. The trial of Paul Bernardo, defendant in a grisly Canadian kidnap-rape-murder case, ran contemporaneously with the O.J. Simpson trial in the United States. There was a media ban on the Bernardo case, while Simpson's was probably the most publicized murder trial in history. The author of the article, Charles Trueheart, could not understand why his Canadian colleagues respected this ban. Where "was the full-speed-ahead, read-all-about-it spirit that I assumed was in every journalist's soul?" He found himself asking editors, "why don't you just damn the torpedoes and publish the material?" Finally, one editor replied, "with a gentle rebuke ... 'In Canada, even editors obey the law.'"[88]

The pacifist tendencies that characterize Canadian culture have been viewed by some Americans as a sign of weakness, a failure to keep up with the times and a refusal to demand individual rights. During the Vietnam

War, many young Americans moved to Canada to escape the draft or otherwise protest against the war. Two of them, Edgar Z. Friedenberg and Stanley Fogel, have written books claiming that Canadians are overly timid, and that this timidity has seriously weakened the arts. They recommend more aggression.

Friedenberg, a professor of law, claims that Canadians lack civil liberties. He argues that "[w]hat is clearly absent from Canadian political consciousness, though salient in the American, is the conviction that the state and its apparatus are the natural enemies of freedom." He finds much more "openness" and a "freer play of expression" in the United States, which, he says, is of "redeeming social value." He concludes, "the enjoyment of conflict is not a part of the Canadian tradition as it is of the American." The 1977 Canadian film *Why Shoot the Teacher?* is his example of the arts in Canada being "curiously self-defeating." The protagonist, he claims, is "a patsy," while the conclusion shows that in Canada "rebellion cannot, must not, solve anything."[89] It is difficult to understand how rebellion could solve anything in a story about a teacher in rural Saskatchewan in the pit of the depression, but the western setting probably implies violence to the seasoned American.

Fogel praises those authors who "attempt to lacerate inflated, revered historical images" and approvingly quotes William Gass, who insists that the artist is naturally "an enemy of the state." He finds Gass's wise sentiments a contrast to the strong adherence to "the Canadian identity" by Canadian writers, which he does *not* see leading to sex and violence. Fogel is particularly outraged by the writings of Robertson Davies, "a gentleman first and a writer second."[90] R.P. Kerans explains that "Canadians do not greatly partake in the American mistrust of authority ... and, to an American, [are] almost maddeningly complacent."[91]

These books by Friedenberg and Fogel demonstrate the disillusionment that outraged Americans are likely to experience when they take refuge in Canada. Their underlying cultural assumption that conflict is needed in order to give meaning to both life and the arts has infected a number of Canadian critics with unfortunate results. Frye notes that "Canadian criticism has been plagued a good deal by the foolish notion that imagination is a by-product of extremes, specifically emotional extremes. We can't have a great literature in Canada because we're too safe, sane, dull, humdrum — not enough lynchings, one critic suggested."[92]

Non-violence should not be confused with timidity or stunted imaginations. Canadians have eschewed violence for perfectly valid reasons. In a thinly populated northern country, divided along religious and linguistic lines long before multiculturalism entered the public consciousness, civility and compromise were the only foundations upon which it was possible to thrive. Canada's artists have instinctively recognized the necessity. American critics who find the results dull or unimaginative may be making judgments on the basis of their own preconceptions rather than on strictly artistic grounds.

Lipset cites many observers who have stressed that the United States is "distinguished by an emphasis on adversarial relations among groups," while Canada has had the greatest need and the strongest determination to avoid conflict. Americans also feel compelled to define their conflicts in moral terms; as Lipset adds, they must be on "God's side against Satan." Conflicts so defined "are more intense, as in America, than those which are seen primarily as reflecting interests, as in Europe."[93] Canada is more like Europe; opposing groups are seen to have different interests, but neither appears to be henchmen for the devil.

Whether the conflict is between groups or individuals, the American propensity to resort to violence appears to be endemic, like a collective memory of Jefferson's words that "a little rebellion now and then is a good thing."[94] Ultimately, almost all the violence depicted by American authors seems to hark back to those early, inflated hopes and dreams teetering on the brink of a Calvinist hell.

Notes

1 Lipset cites a 1985 study that shows all categories of crime in the United States to be three times higher than in any other developed nation, with an incarceration rate four times that of Canada. The lead is much greater for violent crimes. Lipset, *Exceptionalism*, 46–47.

2 Beloff, 37.

3 Frye, *Garden*, 248.

4 Qtd by Bercovitch, "Rites," 18.

5 Beloff, 38.

6 Cross, 159.

7 Slotkin, *Regeneration*, 42.

8 Padover, 71.

9 Daniel Shays led an armed insurrection of New England farmers, protesting high taxes, foreclosures, and high salaries of government officials. Troops were sent, but later the rebels' grievances were addressed.

10 Peterson, 417.

11 Padover, 72.

12 J. Miller, 127.

13 Cross, 161.

14 Careless, *Canada*, 255.

15 Lipset, *Exceptionalism*, 47.

16 New, *Borderlands*, 53.

17 Macdonald, Unpublished Letter. See Chapter 1.

18 Wallace Stegner, *Wolf Willow: A History, a Story, and a Memory of the Last Plains Frontier* (New York: Viking, 1963), 101.

19 *Ibid.*, 100, 105, 101.

20 *Ibid.*, 109.

21 *Ibid.*, 115.

22 Slotkin, *Nation*, 11.

23 D.H. Lawrence says that the "Leatherstocking novels ... go backwards, from old age to golden youth. That is the true myth of America." *Studies*, 54.

24 James Fenimore Cooper, *The Deerslayer* (New York: Penguin Books, 1987), 22; Ch 1, 44; Ch 2.

25 *Ibid.*,124; Ch 7, 539–40; Ch 32.

26 *Ibid.*, 50–51; Ch 3.

27 H.N. Smith, *Virgin Land*, 119.

28 Thoreau, *Walden*, 667, 669, 676.

29 Emerson, *Works*, XI: 515.

30 Thoreau, *Walden*, 677.

31 Quentin Anderson, *The Imperial Self: An Essay in American Literary and Cultural History* (New York: Vintage Books, 1972), viii, 5, 21.

32 Reynolds, 178, 161, 89.

33 Edgar Allan Poe, *Selected Writings of Edgar Allan Poe*, ed. Edward H. Davidson (Boston: Houghton Mifflin, 1956), 205.

34 Tony Tanner, "The Lost America – The Despair of Henry Adams and Mark Twain," *Mark Twain: A Collection of Critical Essays* (Englewood Cliffs, N.J.: Prentice-Hall, 1963), 159.

35 Twain's scenes of massive destruction began with the ending of *A Connecticut Yankee*, but are most extreme in his last novel, *The Mysterious Stranger* (1916).

36 Adams, *Education*, 457–58, 495.

37 Tanner, "America," 161–62.

38 Allan Nevins, Afterword, *The Deerslayer*, by Cooper (New York: Signet Classics, 1963), 540.

39   Owen Wister, *The Virginian* (New York: A Tom Doherty Associates Book, 1998), 117; Ch 13.
40   *Ibid.*, 23; Ch 2, 214; Ch 23, 372–73; Ch 35.
41   *Ibid.*, 330–31; Ch 32, 346, 348, 351; Ch 33.
42   Slotkin, *Nation*, 169–70, 175, 174.
43   Alfred Kazin, Introduction, *The Day of the Locust*, by Nathanael West (New York: Penguin, 1983), xii, xv.
44   West, *The Day of the Locust*, 141; Ch 19, 190, 192; Ch 27.
45   *Ibid.*, 50; Ch 6, 143; Ch 20.
46   *Ibid.*, 95; Ch 14, 109; Ch 15.
47   Bloom, *How to Read*, 249.
48   Toni Morrison, *Playing in the Dark: Whiteness and the Literary Imagination* (Cambridge: Harvard UP, 1992), 16–17.
49   Ralph Ellison, *Invisible Man* (New York: Vintage Books, 1990), 581, Epilogue.
50   Ellison, Introduction to *Invisible Man*, xv, xvi, xi, xiv, xix, xviii.
51   Ellison, *Invisible Man*, 16; Ch 1.
52   *Ibid.*, 21–2; Ch 1.
53   *Ibid.*, 139–40, 147; Ch 6.
54   *Ibid.*, 505, 508; Ch 23, 559; Ch 25, 574; Epilogue.
55   Bloom, *How to Read*, 267, 265.
56   Dashiell Hammett (1894–1961) began Sam Spade's adventures in *The Maltese Falcon* (1930), and Raymond Chandler (1888–1959) introduced Philip Marlowe in *The Big Sleep* (1939).
57   Russell Banks, *Cloudsplitter* (Toronto: Vintage Canada, 1998), 639, 570.
58   *Ibid.*, 70–73, 105, 97, 536, 564, 567, 642.
59   *Ibid.*, 240, 606, 744, 753.
60   Walter Kirn, "The Wages of Righteousness," *The New York Times Book Review,* 22 February 1998: p. 9.
61   Slotkin, *Fatal Environment*, 262, 265.
62   James Polk, "Lives of the Hunted," *Confederation Literature,* ed. McMullen, 109.
63   Alec Lucas, Introduction, *Wild Animals*, by Seton, ix.
64   Atwood, *Survival*, 79.
65   Charles G.D. Roberts, *The Kindred of the Wild: A Book of Animal Life* (Toronto: Copp Clark, 1902), 24.
66   Polk, 103.
67   Ralph Connor, *Black Rock: A Tale of the Selkirks* (Chicago: M.A. Donahue, n.d.), 99; Ch 6.
68   *Ibid.*, 158, 161; Ch 10.
69   *Ibid.*, 117–18; Ch 8.
70   John Moss, *A Reader's Guide to the Canadian Novel* (Toronto: McClelland & Stewart, 1981), 111.
71   Frederick Philip Grove, *Settlers of the Marsh* (Toronto: McClelland & Stewart, 1989), 18, Ch 1.
72   *Ibid.*, 130–31; Ch 3.
73   Kristjana Gunnars, Afterword, *Settlers of the Marsh*, 271.
74   Grove, *Settlers*, 100; Ch 3, 183; Ch 4.

75 *Ibid.*, 230–31; Ch 5.
76 Hugh MacLennan, *Return of the Sphinx* (Toronto: Macmillan, 1967), 174–75, 154.
77 Roch Carrier, *La Guerre, Yes Sir!* Trans Sheila Fischman (Toronto: Anansi, 1972), 83.
78 *Ibid.*, 5, 26, 30, 22, 59.
79 *Ibid.*, 89.
80 Previously called Upper Canada and later Ontario.
81 Moodie, *Clearings*, 155, 169.
82 Margaret Atwood, Afterword, *Alias Grace* (Toronto: Seal Books, 1997), 555.
83 Atwood, *Alias Grace*, 94; Ch 11, 480–81; Ch 48.
84 *Ibid.*, 483; Ch 48.
85 *Ibid.*, 424–25; Ch 43.
86 John Moss, *Sex and Violence in the Canadian Novel: The Ancestral Presence* (Toronto: McClelland & Stewart, 1977), 29.
87 Bruce Powe, *A Climate Charged* (Oakville, ON: Mosaic, 1984), 85.
88 Charles Trueheart, "Strangers in a not-so-strange land." *The Globe and Mail* October 5, 1996, D3.
89 Edgar Z. Friedenberg, *Deference to Authority: The Case of Canada* (White Plains, NY: M.E. Sharpe, 1980), 17, 19, 30–31.
90 Stanley Fogel, *A Tale of Two Countries: Contemporary Fiction in Canada and the United States* (Toronto: ECW Press, 1984), 13, 30, 53, 126.
91 Kerans, 220–221.
92 Frye, *Ground*, 87.
93 Lipset, *Exceptionalism*, 26, 20, 26.
94 Peterson, 417.

Chapter
Eight

Humor

1
The Development of
Two Humorous Traditions

THE NATIONAL CHARACTERISTICS that have been discussed so far come into particularly sharp focus in each nation's humorous writings. Humor, the generic term that includes wit, satire, and comedy, is so sensitive to contemporary national conditions that humor from another time or place often seems flat, incongruous, or even cruel. Nevertheless, the perceptive humorist strikes a chord with the national psyche and therefore the antics of Sam Slick or Davy Crockett, which evoked laughter from millions of people in the early nineteenth century but leave readers bored or repelled today, must still be treated as humor.

English and French Canadians did not find life in the nineteenth century very amusing, so there was little sense of a comic tradition in early Canada. The early humorous writings from Nova Scotia were largely aimed at a British or American audience and were not appreciated as part of a tradition until the second half of the twentieth century. The United States, on the other hand, quickly established a robust comic tradition, for the explosive sense of freedom that swept the nation at the conclusion of the American Revolution spawned much ribald humor. Free of a codified society, the people saw themselves characterized by a rough sincerity in contrast to the airs and graces of British aristocracy.[1] Burlesque and caricatures of their former rulers quickly became popular forms of entertainment.

A comic image of the nation is important to any humorous tradition. The best and most lasting in the United States is the "Yankee." Its origins are obscure, but the term was in use during the Revolution. The song "Yankee Doodle Dandy," with a variety of lyrics, was so popular that it was like a rallying cry. A Yankee was originally a New Englander. On the stage, he evolved into Uncle Sam, a tall, lean figure dressed in red, white, and blue, who was more acceptable to Southerners.[2] "Yankee" spearheaded a strong and distinctive American comic tradition that remains vital today.

Canada has always labored under two dichotomies — French-English populations and British-American influences — which means that no single character could represent the nation. Both Haliburton and Leacock were staunchly loyal to the British Empire although fascinated with American humor, to which their writings are thematically linked. Their works were very popular in the United States, and both edited anthologies of American humor.[3] The perspective that their British colonial status gave them on the American scene was the source of much of their comic effectiveness. This outsider's view, which developed into skilled parody, underlay much of Canada's popular humor at the end of the twentieth century.[4]

Finding a comic image of a Canadian has been a difficult process. References to Canadians as Canucks have appeared in the literature since 1849, but the sobriquet has referred sometimes to an English Canadian and sometimes to a French Canadian, and has never had a visual representation like John Bull or Uncle Sam. Johnny Canuck, a comic book character during World War II, never caught the public's imagination, yet the term has persisted and is now recognized worldwide. Robertson Davies has suggested some hilarious images for the nation, one of them being a "large-eyed pitiful girl" in a shotgun marriage to an "evil-visaged Scotch banker."[5] French Canada might accept this image, but English Canada thinks better of itself.

The French-English division in Canada, which has effectively blocked any comic character for the nation, has had widespread consequences, some of which are not appreciated. Considering that the Quebec flag is the fleur de lys — the flag of pre-revolutionary France — and the Canadian Maple Leaf is rarely seen in the province, that there are two sets of words for the national anthem, and that Quebec license plates sport the motto, *"Je me souviens"* (I remember),[6] it is difficult for Canadians to express the kind of robust humor that depends on firm national symbols. W.H. New notes that while Americans "ritualize their relationship with national symbols (identifying flag, anthem, and eagle as *moral* absolutes), Canadians tend ... to view ironically any expressions of an exclusive nationalism." New describes a cartoon in which a Canadian beaver sets up a roadblock with a single sapling in front of a gigantic truck driven by a huge and determined American eagle.[7] The cartoon is, of course, political, implying Canadian fear of an American cultural takeover and the futility of resistance. The beaver is widely used to represent Canada in political cartoons, but is often paired with a frog, a pejorative image of a French Canadian. In such cartoons, the beaver represents either English Canada or the federal government in opposition to Quebec separatists.[8]

In a very real sense, Frye was wrong to suggest that "Who am I?" has been less perplexing to Canadians than "Where is here?"[9] In *Mondo Canuck: A Canadian Pop Culture Odyssey* (1996), Geoff Pevere and Greig Dymond claim that Canadians are "in a state of constant becoming," and that there may be no other country in which "the process of self-definition [is] such an industrious national pastime." This, of course, is nothing new. It harks back to the early nineteenth century when English Canadians, insisting that they were British, assumed a negative identity: they were *not Americans*. Pevere and Dymond see this tradition "rooted in a conviction that somehow, in some way, Canadians are different."[10] They argue that Canadians' outsiders' view — that is, living in close proximity to the ubiquitous Yankee, abetted by a cold climate encouraging too much television, has led to Canada becoming a world leader in "the art of parody."[11]

Antebellum humor in the United States reflected national dreams of grandeur and the underlying sensitivities of a people with a discarded past who were inwardly cringing under harsh criticisms from Europe. Proceeding under the belief that the best defense is an offense, they embraced and inflated the criticisms. This led to an early inclination to shock genteel sensibilities, a trait that is still present in American humor. Exaggerated accounts of travels in the New World were the forerunners of the American tall tale, which, combined with opposition to perceived feminine graces, led to an extreme masculinity. The life necessarily led by women simply did not fit the American mood of the day and for many years after. The American tall tale — usually a monologue by an unattached male — generally recounts superhuman exploits and ridicules anything that hints of the class society and established institutions of Great Britain. Typically, the protagonist disdains "larnin," sneers at the past, and is "out in the world ... a doin."[12] This character became known as a crackerbox philosopher, an American caricature that has never completely died.[13]

The Yankee emerged from the Revolution, while the War of 1812, which was fought largely in the West, produced the backwoodsman. This character, obsessed with his strength, is illiterate and incredibly cruel, gouging being his favorite form of attack. The Yankee functions in opposition to the parent civilization, the backwoodsman to any civilization.[14] By the 1830s, these two characters were merging into the vernacular character immortalized by Mark Twain. He is almost invariably a lone wanderer and there is a marked absence of women, except for the odd tough counterpart who has little to do with domesticity.

Haliburton's Sam Slick, a Yankee peddler and clock maker, first appeared in Joseph Howe's newspaper, *The Novascotian,* in 1835 and was such an instant success that the series was published in book form the following year as *The Clockmaker.* The book was popular in both Europe and the United States, but for different reasons. The Europeans saw Slick as a burlesque of an American, while the Americans saw him as a genuine fast-talking and swift-dealing Yankee, so effective that he pushed other comic Yankees out of the limelight. Haliburton became widely spoken of as the father of American humor, although modern American scholars dismiss him as a foreign writer who lacked a sound ear for Yankee vernacular.

As we have seen, the Civil War and its aftermath forced a dawning realization that America was not becoming a Garden of Eden and that Americans could be failures. The previous underlying anger at anyone who doubted and belittled the national dreams often turned into rage at this evidence of failure. A new comic image of an American arose — almost the polar opposite of the backwoodsman — the timid "little man" of the twentieth century. The American little man became popular in the post-World War I period. Among the many humorists who developed this character, Ring Lardner (1885–1961), Robert Benchley (1889–1945), and James Thurber (1894–1961) are particularly notable. The "little man" is often married and entangled in a society that he finds intimidating, so he dreams of becoming a superman hero. True to the American tradition, the little man normally hates society, admires the unattached heroic male, has little sense of the past, and can turn violent or dishonest when frustrated. Norris W. Yates notes that the crackerbox philosopher usually knows who he is, while the little man often does not.[15]

Leacock's first book of humor, *Literary Lapses* (1910), appeared just as the little man was becoming popular in the United States. The first sketch, "My Financial Career," concerns a timid little man trying to open a bank account. The institution so frightens him that he does everything wrong, then flees the terrifying place and keeps his savings in a sock. Leacock's frequent use of American settings, lack of notable women characters, and sense of individualism were enough to endear him to Americans. Critics variously described him as a member of the "local color" school and as a writer who defended the individual and attacked institutions. Early advertisements for his books called him the "Canadian Mark Twain,"[16] a designation that has been no more lasting than Haliburton's reputation as the father of American humor.

The founding of *The New Yorker* in 1925 caused a split in the American humorous tradition. This highbrow magazine, written for urban sophisticates, shunned the folksy language of the crackerbox tradition. The split was largely a matter of style, however, for American humor continued to stress the lone male's dreams of grandeur and to focus on the failure, particularly the moral failure, of the American Dream. It was in the pages of *The New Yorker* that Thurber brought the little man to his peak of fame.

The Canadian humorous tradition is not so much split as two-pronged. Frye's claim that Thomas McCulloch's collection *The Stepsure Letters* (1862) is the origin of "genuine Canadian humour," based on "a vision of society," not on a "series of wisecracks" like the Sam Slick books, is not entirely accurate.[17] Certainly, the Canadian tradition took permanent root with Leacock's third book, *Sunshine Sketches of a Little Town,* in which the little town is the true hero, but Sam Slick never died. The Canadian determination to be "not American" had blossomed into a thriving parodic industry.

258 CANADIANS ARE NOT AMERICANS

2

Tall Tales and Biting Satire in the United States

WASHINGTON IRVING (1783–1859) IS CONSIDERED the first post-Revolutionary American man of letters. His *History of New York: From the Beginning of the World to the End of the Dutch Dynasty* (1809), written under the pseudonym of Diedrich Knickerbocker, is the first piece of sustained comic writing in American literature. As comic mythology rather than history, it contributed to the budding American trend of ridiculing any attempts to preserve the past. With the publication of *The Sketch Book of Geoffrey Crayon, Gent.* (1820), Irving was "duly hailed as the father of American literature," but much of this acclaim came from Britain, where he had lived for some years. Many Americans were suspicious of a writer who had left the new country. Emerson, for example, dismissed Irving's work as merely "picturesque." Malcolm Bradbury notes that Irving's reputation has fluctuated and that many Americans considered him "the source of the American 'genteel tradition,' ... which generations of feisty 'redskin' American authors have wanted to upturn."[18] A genteel tradition hardly suited early American aspirations, yet Irving introduced three of the most notable and lasting of American comic figures.

Irving's best-known stories, "Rip Van Winkle" and "The Legend of Sleepy Hollow," are the only stories in *The Sketch Book* set in America. Rip Van Winkle is a shiftless male or, as Bradbury says, "the rogueish boy-man in flight from shrewish women and work" so popular in later American literature.[19] Rip falls asleep before the Revolution and awakens to a new nation. George Washington has replaced King George as the national hero and Rip's unthinking words of loyalty to the former ruler turn the curious bystanders into a threatening mob: "A tory! a tory! a spy! a refugee! hustle him! away with him!"[20] Rip, a grown-up child, exaggerates his strange experience and turns it into a tall tale.

Ichabod Crane, in "The Legend of Sleepy Hollow," is Irving's satiric portrait of a New England Puritan, a comic Yankee who resembles Uncle Sam. When he goes courting, "his sharp elbows stuck out like grasshoppers ... [and]

the motion of his arms was not unlike the flapping of a pair of wings." Crane
is a learned man — "he had read several books quite through" — but is
superstitious, "a perfect master of Cotton Mather's *History of New England
Witchcraft.*" Crane's rival for the lovely Katrina is a man nicknamed Brom
Bones because of his Herculean frame. Bones is sure to be behind any
"madcap prank or rustic brawl" in the vicinity, and is an early example of the
comic backwoodsman. He imitates the headless horseman and throws a
pumpkinhead at Crane, effectively disposing of his rival in love.[21] The many
instances of rough, lowbrow humor that sprouted in all parts of the young
nation fall into three separate eccentric styles, two of which Irving recognized.
The first is the Yankee, best characterized in a series of newspaper sketches by
Seba Smith, later collected in book form as *The Life and Writings of Major
Jack Downing, of Downingville, Away Down East in the State of Maine* (1833).
Downing, using understated Yankee humor, writes in a folksy manner about
the current political scene and tells of his experiences with his friend President
Andrew Jackson: "This traveling with the President is capital fun after all, if it
wasn't so plaguy tiresome. We come into Baltimore on a Rail Road, and we
flew over the ground like a harrycane."[22] Downing was so popular that he
became the inspiration for other comic characters, such as Haliburton's Sam
Slick and James Russell Lowell's Hosea Biglow. The Yankee was an early
incarnation of the evolving crackerbox philosopher.

The second popular comic style, backwoods humor, is best seen in A.B.
Longstreet's *Georgia Scenes* (1835). This book, like Smith's, is a collection of
short pieces originally published in a newspaper. But unlike Smith's, the
stories are marked by violence and cruelty. Longstreet employs a distancing
technique — a learned and moral narrator observing the antics of rough-hewn
characters who would be called rednecks today. Richard Slotkin says these
narrators "stand between the rough characters of the backwash region and their
genteel readership" of the Northeast, which is "linked to a folkloric tendency
to hyperbole that converted aggression to humor."[23] One story, "The Horse
Swap," tells of two men trying to cheat one another in a horse trade. After
much dickering, the trade is completed and one buyer finds himself with a
horse that is blind and deaf and the other with a horse that has an enormous
sore on its back. The horse with the sore had been ridden all day and the

blanket is stuck to its back. The narrator is sickened at the sight and feels that "the brute who had been riding him in that situation deserved the halter," yet the reaction of the crowd is "mirth."[24]

Longstreet's distancing technique was used by other writers of backwoods humor, for it allowed both author and reader to laugh at cruelty, deformities, and gross dishonesty without being personally involved. Increasingly, these backwoods characters take pride in being accomplished liars and are casually unconcerned about the fate of others, particularly Blacks and Natives.

The third popular comic style of the antebellum period is blackface minstrelsy. Constance Rourke notes that to "the primitive comic sense, to be black is to be funny." The first known case of a white man blackening his face and collecting amusing song and dance numbers from the slaves occurred in the 1820s. Edwin Forrest was so successful that others quickly followed, the best known being Jim Crow Rice and Dan Emmet. Emmet claimed that he wrote the song "Ole Dan Tucker" when he was a teenager, but Rourke doubts his authorship and other such claims made by white minstrels, for these songs bear a marked resemblance to traditional comic airs found among the slaves. Emmet did write the song "Dixie," which in its first version reveals the Edenism prevalent in the early years of the nation:

> Dis worl' was made in jes six days
> An' finished up in various ways —
> Look away! look away! look away! Dixie land!
> Dey den made Dixie trim and nice
> But Adam called it Paradise — [25]

These three categories of popular comedy characters — the Yankee, the backwoodsman, and the blackface minstrel — had much in common and tended to blend into a composite. All were rural and projected a calculated illiteracy, all were male, and most were lone wanderers who seemed only remotely involved in society. In addition, most appeared on the stage, because comedy in the early days of the United States was highly theatrical. On the stage, the characters looked inhuman and, in the eerie half-light of primitive theatres, their antics reminded the audiences of the devil, with his ability to change shape and seduce the unwary. Not only were these rough comic characters popular in the theaters of the major cities, wandering troupes of actors also entertained in frontier communities. Rourke notes their similarity to the traveling evangelists who held religious camp meetings and "belonged to the theatre" in a "fundamental" sense.[26]

The tall tale is primarily identified with backwoods humor. It achieved a level of popularity that gives further evidence of the American penchant for violence, plus the extreme masculinity so pronounced through much of the nation's literary history. Backwoods comic characters were known as "screamers" or "ring-tailed roarers"; their monologues were marked by "[l]oquacity and exaggeration," their dialogues by "taciturnity and evasion," and they "sedulously avoided the truth."[27] Camp meetings were a common subject for humor.

G.W. Harris's *Sut Lovingood: Yarns Spun by a Nat'ral Born Durned Fool* (1867) is one of the best examples of the tall tale as backwoods humor. Lovingood attends a camp meeting because he has a grudge against a preacher. The preacher is holding forth about what the serpents in hell will do to the people: "He tole 'em how the ole Hell-sarpints wud sarve 'em if they didn't repent; how cold they'd crawl over thar nakid bodys, an how like untu pitch they'd stick to 'em es they crawled." Just as the people reach a pitch of screaming and moaning, Lovingood releases a bag of lizards up the preacher's pant legs. The preacher, thinking he is being attacked by the "Hell-sarpints," tears off his clothes and runs screaming into the hysterical crowd. Later he posts notices around town: "Ait ($8) Dullars reward ... [for] Sut Lovingood, dead ur alive."[28]

The peak of the antebellum tall tale came with inflated stories of the real-life adventures of Davy Crockett, a Tennessee frontiersman whose brutalized boyhood might have inspired the character of Huckleberry Finn. Crockett fought with Andrew Jackson in the Creek War, served in Congress, was touted as a possible candidate for President, then died heroically at the Alamo in 1836. He left an autobiography that was probably ghost written, and is full of exaggerations. By the mid-1850s, more than fifty Crockett Almanacs had appeared; his exploits made him the Superman of the day. The favorite story for anthologists is "Crockett's Morning Hunt," in which Crockett discovers on a cold morning that the "airth had actually friz fast in her axis." He thaws it with "hot ile" from a freshly killed bear.[29]

Crockett's cruelty runs throughout the series. In "Hands of Celebrated Gougers," for example, he describes what one of the hands, "that ar paw," would do to "that nasty scaly crawling race of mortal critters." It would "gouge thar eyes an' tongues out first, an' then punch thar bodies out of thar shells as handsome as a kernel out of a nut." Another famous hand "could take an injun's scalp," and then "make a mark in the critter's skull with that ar thumb nale, and the whole skin would peel off clar to the bone."[30] Slotkin claims that Jacksonian Democracy was characterized by "men like Davy Crockett" who became "heroes by defining national aspirations in terms of so many bears destroyed, so much land preempted, so many trees hacked down, so many Indians and Mexicans dead in the dust."[31] Today, it is difficult to believe that an American audience could ever have found this kind of thing amusing.

During the 1840s and 1850s, the first popular urban character arose — a lower class but street-wise, brash, and arrogant young man known as the "b'hoy." Unlike the rural characters, he is smart. The b'hoy appeared on the stage and in numerous stories, and is considered the inspiration for Melville's Ishmael and Whitman's narrator. Whitman, who grew up on the streets of Brooklyn, humorously describes himself as the b'hoy in one of his most famous poems, "Crossing Brooklyn Ferry":

> I am he who knew what it was to be evil,
> I too knitted the old knot of contrariety,
> Blabb'd, blush'd, resented, lied, stole, grudg'd.[32]

Whitman was not the only major writer who took popular comedy seriously, for they were all seeking an American art form that would free the nation from dependence on British cultural history, and many thought they had found it in vernacular humor. President Andrew Jackson horrified the learned citizens of the eastern seaboard with his crude manners and loose morals, but, as Emerson noted in his journal in 1834, Jackson's "rank rabble party … may root out all the hollow dilettantism" of our culture, providing "the kind of 'nerve' and 'dagger' necessary for energizing American literature."[33] Emerson's famous reference to himself as "a transparent eye-ball,"[34] made use of that popular frontier symbol, the gouging out of eyes. His readers recognized the reference, and numerous cartoons and comic references were inspired by it.

The general approach was dramatic: America's politicians and preachers went in for oratory — the declamatory style — and their vigorous stances were widely parodied on the nation's stages. Reynolds speaks of "a culture that produced showmanlike preachers, immoral reformers, and reverend rakes."[35]

The literati recognized that there was much myth making in American comedy and much that was poetically imaginative. Examples of popular humor abound in the works of the major writers. Frontier screamers appear in three of Hawthorne's stories; "My Kinsman, Major Molineux," "Young Goodman Brown," and "Ethan Brand," are all set gingerly in the Puritan past when the frontier was still in New England. Poe, who gave high praise to Longstreet's *Georgia Scenes*, put even more stress on scenes of brutality. Reynolds notes that the cruelty in Poe's writings puts him "at the tip of a huge cultural iceberg." Above all, Melville's Ahab embodies American popular stereotypes; he is a "towering immoral reformer," an "ungodly, godlike oxymoronic oppressor," a "justified criminal taking revenge," and an "attractively devilish sea captain." Reynolds claims that one of the reasons for the increasing complexity of Melville's narrative voice is his "openness to humorous idioms that exploded onto the literary scene in the late 1840s."[36]

The tall tale was beginning to get stale as the Civil War approached. At its end, Twain's writing career began, and almost everything about his personal experiences and the condition of the nation served to push the sensitive and imaginative young man toward the role of satirist. He was the first important American writer to have been born and raised on the frontier and, like Whitman, he grew up in poverty and experienced the roughness of low life. Also, like Whitman, he had taken the rhetoric of Manifest Destiny very seriously.

Twain and Artemus Ward (1834–1867) are credited with fusing urban and frontier vernacular into a truly indigenous American humor.[37] Twain's first nationally acclaimed story, "The Celebrated Jumping Frog of Calaverous County" (1865), is in the tradition of the tall tale, but with an unusual twist: the genteel narrator is the butt of the joke. He is cornered by a garrulous old westerner, who tells him a silly story about a betting friend with a high-jumping frog who loses a bet when his opponent fills the frog with quail shot. The narrator manages to escape just as the old man is about to launch into another tale about "a yaller one-eyed cow that didn't have no tail."[38]

Twain's most notable burlesque of frontier bragging is a sketch known as the "Child of Calamity," which was originally part of *Huckleberry Finn* but was unaccountably shifted to *Life on the Mississippi* (1883). Huck is listening to a group of men, "a mighty rough-looking lot," when a dispute breaks out. In preparation for the expected fight, each man flouts his qualifications. The first one roars that he is "the old original iron-jawed, brass-mounted, copper-bellied corpse-maker from the wilds of Arkansas," who was sired "by a hurricane" and "dam'd by an earthquake." The other responds by telling the men not to look at him with "the naked eye," for he puts his "hand on the sun's face" and makes it "night in the earth," he bites "a piece out of the moon" in order to "hurry the seasons," and when he shakes himself he "crumble[s] the mountains!" A "little black-whiskered chap" thrashes both of the braggarts, so the men settle down to a tall tale about the superiority of the muddy Mississippi over the clear water of the Ohio. "A Cincinnati corpse don't richen a soil any," says one of the men, but in "a Sent Louis graveyard" the trees grow "upwards of eight hundred foot high."[39] Twain kept the tradition of frontier humor alive into the twentieth century. The change in tone from comic bragging to satire made him a principal initiator of what Rourke calls the "American quarrel with America."[40]

As this bitterness of failed ideals developed, parody and satire became the principal tools of the humorist. The best-known parodist of the late nineteenth century was Bret Harte. One of his attacks was against the romanticism of Cooper's Leatherstocking series. In his story, "Muck A Muck, An Indian Novel, after Cooper," Harte has Natty Bumppo killing five wild animals with one bullet, and a ridiculously attired Native chief pretends to accede to the superior ways of the white man while deftly stealing the family silver.[41] Twain's "undeservedly" famous essay "Fenimore Cooper's Literary Offenses" accuses Cooper of being unrealistic. However, this was a cover-up; Leslie Fiedler and others have noted that Twain disliked "Cooper's Indians." Twain was "by instinct and conviction, an absolute Indian hater."[42]

Irish humor, from which the b'hoy character originated, became much more sophisticated when Finley Peter Dunne (1867–1936) began his weekly "Mr. Dooley" series in a Chicago newspaper. Dunne had as good an ear for dialect as Twain, and the popular series was collected in a number of books that appeared between 1898 and 1919. Mr. Dooley, a Chicago bartender, comments on the current political scene in the tradition of the crackerbox philosopher. Imperialism was in fashion, the Spanish-American War was expanding American hegemony on the world stage, and belief in the superiority of the Anglo-Saxon was widespread. Dunne's cutting satire exposes the sufferings endured by Irish immigrants at the hands of American xenophobes. On one occasion Mr. Dooley, as a sincere American, comments on the recently captured Filipinos: "we'll threat ye th' way a father shud threat his childer if we have to break ivry bone in ye'er bodies." On another, he recommends a book by Theodore Roosevelt, which he calls an "Accoount iv th' Desthruction iv Spanish Power in th' Ant Hills." Roosevelt attacked Cuba with a brigade known as the Rough Riders, and Dooley quotes him on his relations with his men: "I wud stand beside wan iv these r-rough men threatin' him as a akel, which he was in ivrything but birth, education, rank, an' courage." The Rough Riders would look up at the stars and "quote th' bible fr'm Walt Whitman."[43] Dunne's humor is a wonderful commentary on the class and racial sentiments expressed in Wister's *The Virginian*.

American humor, as it developed in the twentieth century, shifted its focus from the superman hero to the victimized or subtly criminal little man. Yates speaks of the "bitterness of blasted innocence" as typical of American humorists.[44] Exaggeration remained a hallmark, and the tribulations of the lone male, largely detached from society, continued to hold sway. The principal developers of the little man — Lardner, Benchley, and Thurber — tended to move away from the vernacular toward a more standard urban speech, but the fundamental traditions of American humor were retained. E.B. White and Katherine S. White note that the tall tale is commonly seen as the "rockbed" of American humor and that verbosity is "an occupational disease."[45] Thurber, the best known of the early writers for *The New Yorker,* had his greatest success with the little man character. His famous story, "The Secret Life of Walter Mitty," presents a henpecked little man who is unable to cope with even simple modern technology, and who dreams of himself in various heroic roles. These daydreams are unwitting parodies of stock characters and situations from movies and pulp fiction. Thurber's timid males often have domineering but equally simple-minded wives, and in the breakup of unsuccessful marriages the men sometimes resort to violence.

Sinclair Lewis put the little man into the nation's literary canon with *Babbitt* (1922). The American Adam is inverted in this novel. Lewis's satire, like much of Twain's, ridicules the idea of human perfectibility. George F. Babbitt, successful real estate salesman and Mr. Average American, is crass, self-deceiving, corruptible, and morally and emotionally shallow. How things look, getting to know the *right* people, and what it takes to get ahead are the forces that drive the Babbitts. Their bedroom is "right out of Cheerful Modern Houses," and every "second house in Floral Heights had a bedroom precisely like this." They live in the town of Zenith, which is big, "and Babbitt respected bigness in anything; in mountains, jewels, muscles, wealth, or words."[46] John Wickersham speaks of Lewis' "scathing literary tongue," but with the addition of "a healthy dose of comic irony."[47]

Babbitt is culturally unsophisticated, and proud of it. He gives a speech describing "Our Ideal Citizen": someone who "is busier than a bird-dog," reads a "good lively Western novel if he has a taste for literature," and contributes to "the prosperity of the city and his own bank account." The comic strips are Babbitt's "favorite literature and art," but his car is "poetry and tragedy, love and heroism" for him. A "family's motor indicated its social rank as precisely as the grades of the peerage determined the rank of an English family." When his son suggests that taking correspondence courses might be better than going to a university, Babbitt hesitates: "smater of fact, there's a whole lot of valuable time lost even at the U., studying poetry and French and subjects that never brought in anybody a cent." The determining factor, however, is that "its a mighty nice thing to be able to say you're a B.A."[48]

Babbitt's aesthetic ignorance is minor compared to his moral failure, and Lewis' satire cuts deepest as it reveals how American society offers him repeated opportunities for thievery and corruption. Babbitt is a Republican who repeatedly declares that what the country needs is "a good sound business administration," and he is fiercely opposed to labor unions: "there oughtn't to be any unions allowed at all; and as it's the best way of fighting the unions, every business man ought to belong to an employers'-association and to the Chamber of Commerce ... So any selfish hog who doesn't join the Chamber of Commerce ought to be forced to." Babbitt is involved in a number of crooked real estate deals. On one occasion, he learns that a grocer wants to expand by opening a butcher shop but does not own the vacant lot next door. He advises a speculator to buy the lot and then, using slick salesmanship, persuades the grocer that he has no choice except to pay a ludicrous price for the lot and go into debt. Babbitt discovers a talent for public speaking, becomes a kind of cheerleader for the town, and gives political talks for his preferred candidates. When he helps to elect a new mayor, he is offered some minor appointments, but prefers "advance information about the extension of paved highways, and this a grateful administration gave to him."[49]

Babbitt is, of course, out of his depth. When he finds that fawning and glad-handing do not raise his social position and several things go wrong with family and business, he becomes depressed. On a train ride, he can find no one to talk to except a former friend and politician who has turned liberal. Babbitt decides that he too should be idealistic and begins to assert some individualism. As a result, he is in danger of losing what business and social advantages he had; he quickly retreats to the old Babbitt. Lewis's satire is unrelenting. Only at the end of the novel does he allow his little man a degree of dignity. Babbitt stands up for his son against his outraged family after the boy has eloped and decided to quit university and become a mechanic. The name Babbitt suggests a rabbit. And, in many respects, Lewis's protagonist is a literary precursor to Updike's Rabbit Angstrom.

America's quarrel with America reached its peak as the 1960s approached. The satiric fictions of Joseph Heller, John Barth, and Thomas Pynchon depict American culture as a jungle: crass, brutal, and lacking human values. Heller's *Catch-22* (1955) is the best known of their works. The setting is an American Air Force base in World War II, where the protagonist, Yossarian, a bombardier on active service and an emotional wreck in need of retirement, is kept on active service by the colonel in charge. The incompetent colonel can think of no other way to win acclaim than by "forcing his men to fly more missions than everyone else."[50] Yossarian, despite being a captain and the most intelligent person in the novel, is a little man trapped in the clutches of an evil society. He is little man as victim; the author's satire is directed at society, not at him.

Catch-22 is like many comic novels with a serious message to impart; the laughable parts tend to be concentrated near the beginning of the novel, but the novel turns serious as the author brings his message into focus. This is also true of *Babbitt*; the protagonist appears to be something of a buffoon at first, but later becomes an object of disgust as the plot develops. The reader laughs when Yossarian calls an Anabaptist chaplain "Father," when the colonel longs to be written up in *The Saturday Evening Post*, and when the doctor does not want to "make sacrifices" he wants to "make dough." The laughter steadily diminishes, as the author's outrage becomes more apparent.[51]

Heller was himself a bombardier in World War II and flew more than sixty missions. The sense of personal outrage is probably the reason that *Catch-22* was far more successful than any of the author's other novels. The satire is directed at capitalism, a market system that in this novel catapults the most incompetent and selfish individuals into senior military ranks and values profit ahead of human lives. In the hierarchy of officers, the higher an officer's rank, the more stupid, insensitive, and self-serving he is, so that the desperate overextended men in the flight crews have no way around the colonel. The other side of the evil society arises from the antics of Milo Minderbinder, the chief mess officer, who is a modern-day robber baron. Milo promises the simple-minded senior officers their favorite dishes if they provide him with airplanes and compliant pilots so he can buy, sell, and transport huge quantities of produce and make an enormous profit. Milo keeps extending his activities until he is making deals with the belligerents to fight each other. When Milo's planes bomb their own base because it's "in the contract," even the stupid officers are outraged until Milo opens his books and shows, "the tremendous profit" that has been made.[52]

Early in the story, Yossarian tells the doctor that he has gone crazy and must be grounded. The doctor explains "Catch-22," the regulation that says, "a concern for one's own safety in the face of dangers" that are "real and immediate" are the process of "a rational mind." Yossarian's desire to be grounded indicates that he is sane, so he must continue flying missions. The colonel keeps raising the number of missions required, more and more men are killed, and emergency supplies are missing because Milo has removed them for his commercial operations. The incident that breaks Yossarian's nerve is not revealed until near the end of the novel. Snowden, a gunner in his plane, is hit. Yossarian tries to bandage a wound on the man's thigh, but seeing a stain above the man's flack suit, he "ripped open the snaps ... and heard himself scream wildly as Snowden's insides slithered down to the floor." Eventually Yossarian refuses to fly any more missions and the colonel agrees to send him home, but it is Catch-22 again. He can go home a hero if he agrees to be a "pal," to say "nice things" about the colonel who wants to be a general, otherwise, he will be court-martialed and the colonel can make it stick because Yossarian went to Rome without a pass. The colonel concludes, "You'd have to be a fool to throw it all away just for a moral principle." Humor has long since left this novel.[53]

This satire on capitalism and American society is so extreme that the novel qualifies as a tall tale, one that can rank with some of Crockett's exploits. Also, the wartime setting recalls the brutality of the American frontier. The message is the opposite of antebellum humor, however, for Crockett was an admired hero while Milo and the colonel are unrelieved villains. Bradbury speaks of the "humour of absurdity" in a book with "no just causes."[54] Heller's hero, the suffering little man, is unable to control his own life because of a system that is fundamentally evil. When Yossarian finally gives up and decides to desert, he explains that he does not see "heaven or saints or angels"; instead, he sees "people cashing in on every decent impulse and every human tragedy."[55] That he could ever have expected to see heaven, saints, or angels suggests that he may once have held some Edenic ideals.

A humorous novel on American society that is refreshingly free of the bitterness of disillusionment so common in American literature is John Updike's *S* (1988). This epistolary novel with a female protagonist is the last of a trilogy linked to Hawthorne's *The Scarlet Letter*.[56] The *S* of the title parallels the *A* for adulteress that Hawthorne's heroine is forced to wear. In *S*, Sarah Worth, an aristocratic New England matron, has abandoned her doctor husband and joined a religious ashram in Arizona. The ashram is near the town of Hawthorne. Sarah speaks of her Prynne ancestors, discusses the house bought from Mrs. Pyncheon, presses advice on her daughter Pearl, and makes frequent reference to things beginning with A, such as A-frames and vitamin A. Unlike the Lewis and Heller novels, humor is sustained throughout *S*.

Updike has various targets for his satire: New England society, the American proclivity for inventing bizarre religions, and the ease with which dishonest activities can be carried on in the United States. All of the letters are written by Sarah, and, except for some taped conversations, no other voice enters the novel. The ashram is headed by a supposed Indian guru, the Arhat, and Sarah claims that her surroundings are a needed contrast to "the atrophied Puritan theocracy" in which she was raised. She resists disillusionment even though the food is bad, the living accommodations are wretched, and they are expected to work twelve hours a day under the Arizona sun. Work is worship, she reports, and her "worship crew ... is pouring cement for the foundation of this building called the Hall of a Millionfold Joys."[57]

Sarah's epistolary skills are soon discovered and put to the service of the ashram. She writes blatantly dishonest but hilarious letters to government officials, newspaper editors, anxious parents of adolescent adherents, and former members trying to get their money back. One such letter is to a Mrs. Blithedale, who has returned to her former Presbyterian church, which Sarah refers to as "a Calvinist sect which presents earthly prosperity as a sign of divine election." Later, she speaks of "our beautiful experiment in non-competitive living," where people "at peace within themselves and non-attached from material things don't steal and don't need laws." Sarah is depositing money in three different secret accounts and battling her husband for her share of the family assets while, ironically, continuing to write about "consumeristic materialistic capitalistic garbage."[58]

The whole thing is a confidence game. The Arhat is really Art Steinmetz, a Jewish Armenian from Watertown, Massachusetts, who is bitter about his deprived childhood and the contempt he received from New England aristocrats. There are some lurid sex scenes, which Sarah records with a tiny tape recorder concealed in her bra. When she confronts Art with his true identity, he tells her about growing up with battling parents and no religion, "*across the line from all those hotsy-totsy bits of ass like you.*" She declines to join him in trying to rebuild the ashram, shouting in haughty outrage, "Shams. That's what men are. Liars."[59] Sarah has learned the con game; when she departs, she is a wealthy woman.

America's humorists have been overwhelmingly male. With few exceptions, their humor consists of political commentaries on the state of the nation. *S*, plus *The Witches of Eastwick* (1984), show Updike's recognition and engagement with the dramatically increased role of women in the mainstream of American culture. His work is more social than political; where he differs from other American humorists is in the absence of that "bitterness of blasted innocence."[60]

3

Social Paradoxes and Subtle Irony in Canada

THE LOYALISTS WERE FAMILIAR with the British tradition of Augustan satire, especially its use as a moral influence on a rising middle class. The burst of writing in early nineteenth-century Nova Scotia contains much satire, used both for moral and political purposes. As a political weapon, satire could be turned against the disorderly enthusiasm of the despised Americans.

Thomas McCulloch's *The Stepsure Letters* was originally published serially in *The Acadian Recorder* from 1821 to 1823 as *Letters of Mephibosheth Stepsure*. This places McCulloch almost fifteen years ahead of Haliburton and roughly contemporary with Smith's Jack Downing letters in the United States. There is a marked difference between McCulloch's and Smith's series. Downing writes home about his adventures with the federal government, while Stepsure comments on conditions in his native town, using ironic names, such as blacksmith "Tubal Thump" and lumberman "Jack Scorem," as well as a sense of place that brings the town itself to life. [61] McCulloch's is social comedy, directed toward encouraging thrift and hard work. This "vision of society" is the reason Frye gives for naming McCulloch the "founder of genuine Canadian humour."[62]

When he first appeared in 1835, Haliburton's Sam Slick became such an instant success that he pushed other comic characters in the United States, England, and the colonies into the shadows. Such worldwide popularity was a first for Canada and an unwitting forerunner of future attempts to ridicule the United States. Slick is paradoxical and not an original creation. V.L.O. Chittick argues that the character was assembled from American books and newspapers and was designed both to satirize Americans and to reprove the Nova Scotians for their lack of industry and inventiveness, the only qualities that Haliburton admired in the Americans.[63] Even though the Americans now dismiss Slick as the creation of a foreign writer and that Canadians consider him outside the nation's humorous tradition that eschews tall tales and braggadocio delivered by wandering unattached males, he has not been relegated to obscurity. Slick

was broadly popular and selections of his tales can still provoke laughter. He
was in such demand that eleven volumes of his stories were published by 1853.

Sam Slick peddles his Connecticut-made clocks throughout Nova
Scotia, accompanied by the usual learned and moral narrator, known only as
the Squire.[64]

Slick and the Squire match wits over the relative merits of American
versus British and colonial ways. Slick is adamant in his defense of the "free
and enlightened citizens" of the United States, who "fairly take the shine off
creation — they are actilly equal to cash." When cornered, Slick begins to
attack the Nova Scotians, who, he says, should have an owl for an emblem and
the motto "*He sleeps all the days of his life*." On one occasion, Slick tells the
Squire that in solving a problem, one should "never go to books ... but go right
off and cipher it out of nature, that's a sure guide." Another time, Slick reports
an argument with an Irish priest over the degree of freedom in a British colony.
Slick claims that being "under a king," the people are not very free. The priest
"checkmate[s]" Slick when he points out that "if you were seen in Connecticut
a-shakin' hands along with a Popish priest, as you are pleased to call me ...
[and] as you now are in the streets of Halifax ... I guess you wouldn't sell a
clock agin in that State for one while."[65] As a character, Sam Slick managed
to please everyone, and it is a measure of Haliburton's skill as a humorist that
he — a diehard Tory — could sustain the character of the garrulous Yankee
democrat for two decades.

Haliburton grew tired of Sam Slick and wanted to publish tales from Nova
Scotia, but his only collection, *The Old Judge* (1849), was not a success. A
group of stories from *The Old Judge*, "The Keeping-Room of an Inn," describes
people from all walks of life who are marooned at an inn during a blizzard.
They tell one another stories to enliven the days of their isolation. Violence
rages outdoors but never enters the inn. One member of the group, Stephen
Richardson, might be called a Canadianized Sam Slick. He is talkative,
opinionated, a principled wearer of "homespun," but he is very much a part of
the group and free of any harsh satire or grandiose illusions.[66] R.E. Watters calls
The Old Judge "a trail-breaker" for "subsequent Canadian satiric humour."[67]

Since *The Old Judge* was not published in Canada until 1968,[68] it was
unknown to Leacock. Robert L. McDougall says that after Haliburton, "nearly

a hundred years were to pass before Canadians took freely to laughter and mockery again. Stephen Leacock was a long way off."[69]

There are significant parallels between Haliburton and Leacock. Both were highly educated professional men — Haliburton, a lawyer and judge and Leacock, a professor of political economy — so humor was a sideline. Both achieved immediate worldwide fame with their first humorous publications, both were intensely devoted to the British Empire, and both were alternately fascinated with and repelled by the dynamic world of American humor. The English-American dichotomy that pervaded early English Canada was undoubtedly the spice that gave their works such wide appeal. Neither made any attempt to create an Uncle Sam or a John Bull for Canada.

Leacock took little interest in Haliburton's writings, but there are similarities in their works. Plot and character tend to be static and the best works of both are anecdotal, with much stress on social comedy. Neither was an embryo novelist, although Leacock's *Sunshine Sketches of a Little Town* has such unity of place that it is often treated like a novel. Robertson Davies says that *Sunshine Sketches* is as "Canadian as any book that was ever written," although Leacock was "British by birth and American by adoption."[70] Davies had the benefit of hindsight and familiarity with a now-established Canadian humorous tradition.

It is doubtful that Leacock knew what tradition he was following. He came to Canada from England at the age of six, the third son of impoverished rural gentry. His mother was determined that her sons would be gentlemen, and Leacock made much of his struggles to become educated and established. After years as a teacher and undergraduate, he went to the University of Chicago where he studied under Thorstein Veblen. Veblen's theories of the leisure class added to Leacock's sense of poverty, and left him generally hostile to the wealthy while still striving to join their ranks. As a professor at McGill University, he shared the typical academic's disdain for the businessman. The success of his first books and his admiration for Mark Twain left him vulnerable to American enticements.

In *Sunshine Sketches,* the town of Mariposa is described with affectionate irony, a place that is not damaging to the individual. The narrator introduces a newcomer to the town and laughingly notes that if you come to the town from New York, your "standard of vision is all astray." He then lists activities such as "the Fireman's Ball every winter and the Catholic picnic every summer," and assures the newcomer that after a few months he will find the place a "mad round of gaiety." The town has some creative minds and quite a few eccentrics. Josh Smith, owner of Smith's Hotel, weighs two-hundred-and-eighty pounds and wears a "chequered waistcoat" and "plaid trousers" that make him look "like an over-dressed pirate." The Reverend Mr Drone, Dean of the Anglican Church, spends his leisure time reading Theocritus in Greek. He is also fond of machinery; the narrator thinks he never heard Rev. Drone "preach a better sermon than the one on Aeroplanes (Lo, what now see you on high Jeremiah Two)."[71]

The people of Mariposa are impressed by anything British. An election turns on issues of tremendous importance, such as "whether or not Mariposa should become part of the United States, and whether the flag ... should be trampled under the hoof of an alien invader, and whether Britons should be slaves, and whether Canadians should be Britons." Josh Smith wins the Conservative nomination, hoists the Union Jack, decorates his hotel with pictures of the King, and tells his desk clerk: "Take them signs 'American Drinks' out of the bar. Put up noo ones with 'British Beer at all Hours.'" Bagshaw, the Liberal candidate, makes an ill-considered speech in his campaign for reelection, saying, "I am an old man now ... and the time must soon come when I must not only leave politics, but must take my way towards that goal from which no traveller returns." The audience responds with a deep hush for it was "understood to imply that he thought of going to the United States." Smith wins the election.[72]

Leacock sounds more like an American humorist in *Arcadian Adventures with the Idle Rich.* The stories in this book are set ostensibly in an American city — a thinly disguised Montreal — in which he satirizes the amoral, mercenary world of the plutocrat and a number of social institutions. In this book, Leacock comes as close as he would ever come to expressing the bitterness so common in American humor, but harsh satire was not his *métier.* The outraged reaction of the residents of Orillia, Ontario to *Sunshine Sketches* hurt Leacock deeply. Davies argues that Leacock "wanted to be liked, and that is a serious weakness in an artist."[73] In his essay, "Humour as I See It," Leacock insists that humor must be "without harm or malice," and defines it as "the kindly contemplation of the incongruities of life and the artistic expression thereof."[74] He never seriously deviated from that principle. He set the stage for Canadian humor with *Sunshine Sketches* and, since his death in 1944, Canadian humor has poured forth, the vast majority of it compatible with his principles.

Leacock was a great humorist, and his contribution to Canadian culture can hardly be overemphasized. How much influence he had in solidifying a sense of national identity is harder to assess. James Steele writes of his "trinational persona;" Leacock's characters and settings are variously but unmistakably Canadian, American, or British.[75] Even before his death, Canadian literature began building up steam for the explosion that occurred in the 1950s and 1960s. Some of the earliest productions of this new era are works of humor, recognizably following the trail he broke. Comic situations aimed at various forms of pretentiousness and highlighting life's incongruities tend to be lasting forms of humor because they rarely deal with current events. Canadians still read and laugh at Leacock.

The Stephen Leacock Memorial Medal for Canadian humor was established after his death, and the first one awarded in 1947. An early winner was Paul Hiebert for *Sarah Binks* (1947), an excellent example of the type of humor encouraged by Leacock. Sarah Binks, the "Sweet Songstress of Saskatchewan," is a fictional character, but nothing in the book's introduction and acknowledgements gives this away. Sarah is born and raised on a Saskatchewan farm in the early twentieth century, a period in Canada's "fairest and flattest" province that the naive narrator compares to the golden ages of Pericles and Elizabethan England, although on "a small scale." Her family prospers and is able to replace their sod hut with a frame dwelling "faced with the best quality tar paper." Sarah's poems pepper the novel — poems full of misused words, clumsy meter, and tortured rhymes. The narrator tells the reader that Sarah's "love for the animal life is deep and abiding," as seen in her poem, "The Goose":

> The goose, a noisome bird to chatter,
> But handsome on a garnished platter,
> A loathsome brute to toil among,
> But caught and killed and cooked and hung,
> Before a crackling fire,
> A songster to admire.[76]

Sarah's "Song of the Sea" is read by retired Admiral Saltspit, who comments that she "charts her way through the shoals and intricacies of metre in a way that makes us all feel four sheets in the wind." Sarah has never seen the sea, nor does she know any German, but she translates some German hymns. The result — "praying that God you preserve, / So swell, so clean, and good" — is, the narrator admits, "too literal." The brunt of this comic satire is the narrator, who speaks of such things as a monument erected in Sarah's memory, "Binksian" societies and collections, and studies of her work done by learned professors. Thus, it does not matter whether the reader recognizes that Sarah is fictional, for it is the unnamed "scholar" taking her work seriously who is so laughable.[77]

In his Afterword to *Sarah Binks*, Charles Gordon calls the novel "quintessentially Canadian." His reasons are threefold: the work is "damned funny" but is "understated," the "hero [is] cut down to size," and Paul Hiebert never received the acclaim that Gordon believes he deserved.[78]

Over the years, the Leacock Medal has been awarded to a number of journalists who have excelled with humorous columns in newspapers, although none have had the bite of the American comic figure, Mr. Dooley. Frequently, however, the award has gone to poets, novelists, or academics whose main occupations are outside the genre of humor, such as Pierre Berton, Farley Mowat, W.O. Mitchell, Ernest Buckler, and Earle Birney. Birney's comic novel *Turvey* (1949) is a picaresque novel of a Canadian private in World War II. It was written about the same time as *Catch-22* and therefore provides a useful contrast. Private Turvey has as many frustrations with superior officers as Heller's Yossarian. In *Turvey,* the officers are equally frustrated for there are no evil characters in the novel, merely fallible humans trying to cope with the cumbersome mechanisms of a nation at war. Turvey is a simple man who has little education, is accident-prone, and is misplaced and shifted around like a badly addressed parcel. Initially rated subnormal, he reaches genius status after taking the same intelligence test eleven times.

Birney is particularly good with accents. A sergeant with a voice like "a file at work on the teeth of a crosscut" yells at the new arrivals: "Allri unbuttonyahtrousehs ... allawaydown." In England, Turvey and a friend accidentally walk through a minefield in the dark. Turvey throws a rock at a noisy crow and the rock explodes, then daylight reveals where they are. They ask an old man on the other side of a barbed-wire fence for help, and he asks, "You fellers Canide-yins?" then walks on mumbling, "Tryin to lead me up the gahden." Eventually they are rescued by a tank and charged with "being fifteen hours, twenty-three minutes Absent Without Leave ... entering a forbidden area ... [and] illegal discharge of a weapon."[79]

Turvey wants to go to London because he "aint ever seen a nair-raid, or— or ... or the Bloody Tower." A fellow soldier explodes: "Always thinking *violently*. Blood and bombs and things. You should realize its our *duty* as Canadian soldiers to—to *channel* our aggressions." In London, Turvey gets into trouble with the military police but is rescued by his pal, MacGillicuddy, who is wearing civilian clothes. Quick thinking Mac turns to the police: "I say, sawjnt, I hope my friend Tuhvey hasnt been doing anything he shouldnt ... Shall I take cah of him faw you? I'm Gledstone-Hetherington, Waw Office, you know."[80] Turvey has been trying unsuccessfully to join Mac in the Kootenay Highlanders. Birney says that Turvey is like Sancho Panza and Mac like a romantic Quixote.[81]

Earle Birney served overseas in World War II both in the ranks and as an officer, and probably saw as much action as Joseph Heller, yet *Turvey* expresses none of the outrage expressed in *Catch-22*. Unlike Yossarian, Turvey is trying to get to the front to fight the Nazis but is repeatedly frustrated by a cumbersome bureaucracy. George Woodcock says that *Turvey* is "a novel about Canada and Canadians written in a variety of Canadian dictions and exposing with a telling modicum of exaggeration what happens when a still youthful democracy finds itself rather bewilderingly caught in the *melée* of total war."[82]

As we have seen, much of the humor in the United States has become a means of expressing outrage, whereas in Canada, it tends toward the national need to define itself, to locate that elusive Canadian image. In the scramble to find the "Canadian identity," humor has all too often been overlooked, yet Canadian literature abounds with comic characters and comic situations. French-Canadian writers are particularly good with comic situations, especially those concerned with the Quiet Revolution.

Gérard Bessette's novel *Not For Every Eye* (1960)[83] was published just before the Quiet Revolution began. Instead of the bitterness against the Catholic Church shown in Blais's *A Season in the Life of Emmanuel*, Bessette presents a comic situation from the days when the church censured literature. The narrator, Hervé Jodoin, has a mysterious past. He is clearly an intellectual whose career has been destroyed, probably by defying the church, so he has largely withdrawn from society, which he views with sardonic detachment. He is pleased to be considered "a cynical oddball," for it gives him the pleasure of insulting others "with impunity." Jodoin prefers to spend his life doing nothing but drinking. However, he runs out of money, so takes a job as clerk in a bookstore in a small town outside Montreal. The owner of the store keeps censured books in a padlocked room at the back, telling Jodoin that he is only to sell these books to "serious purchasers." One day a student from a local boys' school comes in and asks for the *Essay on Morals and Manners* by Voltaire, a forbidden book. Jodoin pretends ignorance, but is curious about what might happen and sells him the book. The book is discovered, the local priest comes in to grill the suspected culprit, and soon the entire town knows that he is in the midst of a scandal.[84]

Jodoin is proud of his exchange with the priest, finds the whole thing laughable, and is prepared to wait it out, but M. Chicoine, the owner of the bookstore, is terrified. Because he is "a snivelling weakling, disembowelled with fear," Jodoin agrees to a scheme to pack up the censured books in the middle of the night and disappear for a sum of $500. Instead of delivering the censured books to M. Chicoine's hideout, Jodoin takes them to Montreal and sells them. He is elated. He has "outwitted the bigwigs" of the town, "taken in that gutless Pharisee Chicoine," and has cleared "twelve hundred-odd dollars," enough for him to live comfortably for about a year.[85]

The timing of Bessette's novel is ironic. He was unable to find a French-Canadian publisher, so the book was published in Paris in 1960, just as the Quiet Revolution was about to begin. Later it was judged by the Grand Jury des Lettres of Montreal to be one of the ten best French-Canadian novels published between 1945 and 1960.

Social paradoxes are fundamental to Canadian humor. Mordecai Richler is best known for his comic novels set in the Jewish community of Montreal where he grew up. His satires are sufficiently biting that he has ironically but repeatedly been accused of anti-Semitism. Richler drew on a rich Yiddish tradition that he has applied to the unusual world of French-English Montreal.

His humor is particularly effective in scenes of Jewish mothers with Yiddish accents trying to outdo one another with stories of their sons' accomplishments. Robertson Davies is the real heir of Stephen Leacock; he picked up where Leacock left off and accomplished what the earlier humorist could never have hoped for. Davies' early career as actor, journalist, and playwright included a series of newspaper columns about a comic character named Samuel Marchbanks, and so when he began writing novels he was known as a newspaper funnyman and not taken seriously as a novelist. This skeptical attitude toward the humorist is common enough everywhere, and the Canadian public and literati were no exception. Davies's first three novels, later grouped as the Salterton Trilogy,[86] were extremely popular, but were rarely considered "Canadian literature."

While writing the Deptford trilogy,[87] Davies discovered that he was emerging as "a moralist," not any kind of proselytizer, as he hastens to add, but "one who looks at human conduct with as clear an eye as he can manage," and who is "compassionate" but "strives not to be deluded." Clearly he saw much that was amusing in Canadian life, but in another essay he warns his audience to "[n]ever be deceived by a humorist, for if he is any good he is a deeply serious man."[88] It took English and American acclaim for *Fifth Business* (1970) before Canadian critics would cast a serious critical eye on his works. W.J. Keith claims that "Davies's popularity and humor have led Canadian critics to underestimate" his importance as a writer.[89]

The Rebel Angels (1981) is arguably the most hilarious of Davies' works. Woodcock thinks more highly of this book than any of the Deptford novels. He argues that the limited setting allows the author to make effective use of "grotesqueries of character and action."[90] The relative unity of time and place, the university setting, the dramatic and visual nature of many of the scenes, and the prominence of irony and farce recall Davies's earlier novel *Leaven of Malice* (1954), but *The Rebel Angels* is a far more sophisticated novel, in which social institutions, the past, and religion are of paramount importance.

There are a number of eccentric (even grotesque) characters, including the heroine's Gypsy mother, Mamusia, and a philosopher turned Anglican monk named Parlabane. Mamusia has returned to Gypsy ways since the death of her husband, much to the distress of her daughter, Maria, who wants to pursue an academic career and would like to reject her Gypsy past. Their beautiful home has been converted into ten apartments, and become "a drunken, debauched, raped house" that "stank." Mamusia has also become an expert shoplifter, and dresses in gaudy clothes with much jangling gold jewelry. When she learns that Maria is in love with one of her professors, Mamusia decides to give a dinner party. Professors Holier and Darcourt are invited and sit down to a dinner table that "could have appeared in a pageant of the Seven Deadly Sins as an altar to ... Gluttony." The evening ends in a fight when Maria discovers that her mother has put a love potion of ground apple seeds and Maria's menstrual blood into the coffee of her intended suitor. Of course, the spiked coffee gets passed to the wrong professor.[91]

Excrement is a recurring symbol in the novel. Scientific studies with human feces are expected to win a Nobel Prize for a professor, Mamusia revitalizes old violins by sealing them in copper cylinders with horse manure, Holier is studying the filth therapy of the middle ages, and Parlabane talks of the "shit" that nourishes the tree of life.[92] Davies is playful with fads and has often commented in his critical writings about something being in or out of fashion.[93] All of this attention to excrement recalls an earlier scatological period, the age of Rabelais and the subject of Maria's graduate studies. She is searching for wisdom, and the novel's other protagonist, Professor the Reverend Simon Darcourt, recipient of the spiked coffee, thinks he is the teacher who can guide her. As he falls agonizingly in love with her, he idealizes her as Sophia, "the feminine personification of God's wisdom," and a salve to his distress over "the lack of a feminine presence in Christianity."[94]

Parlabane writes a novel, which he calls *Be Not Another*, and announces that it is certain to be a classic. The novel is another vehicle for Davies to poke fun at literary fashions — in this case the interior monologue. No professor will take the time, so Maria is told to read the novel. She complains that "he hasn't a scrap of humour in it" and that "everything is seen from the inside, so microscopically that there's no sense of narrative; it just belly flops along, like a beached whale."[95] Parlabane is unable to find a publisher, so he arranges a bizarre murder-suicide in an effort to generate publicity for the novel that he hopes will give him immortality. *The Rebel Angels* is awash with social incongruities and bizarre situations.

Jack Hodgins' fictions are set almost exclusively on Vancouver Island and
populated with numerous eccentric characters and considerable fantasy.
Woodcock writes that Hodgins' vision is "essentially a pastorally comic one"
and the "real hero" of much of his work is "the *community*."[96] Keith says that
Hodgins is a "regional writer" who "transforms his local backyard into an
image of the whole creative universe."[97] As a humorist, Hodgins is "deeply
serious," but there is a *joie de vivre* about his characters and situations that is
exuberant and offers a "fundamentally positive attitude to life." Families are at
least as vibrant as his communities, with intricate relationships that transcend
individual lives.[98]

The Machen Charm (1995) concerns a bizarre family and the events that
follow the suicide of Glory, wife of the youngest member of the family, Toby.
The time is 1956 and the family, as in so many of Hodgins' fictions, is "a pack
of crazies."[99] To be dubbed the "black sheep" of this family is a "major
achievement," and Toby, the black sheep of his generation, is indulged by the
family. However, being his wife is not an enviable position. The family
members were fond of the dead girl and feel guilty about not having done more
to help her. After the funeral, they decide to repair and finish Toby's shack, to
fix "it up for Glory," and end up rebuilding an old hotel, all in about twenty-
four hours. This is a direct slap in the face to Toby, the family daredevil, who
climbs flagpoles and tall buildings, but could never get around to providing a
decent place for his wife to live.[100]

On the day of the funeral, every family member wonders "*[w]hat would
Toby do?*" Toby had been proud of Glory and is noted for responding to crises
with ever more outrageous acts. Toby stays true to form. He drinks from a
pocket flask during the funeral, blocks traffic and climbs the rafters of a bridge,
and has to be rescued from a glacier in the middle of the night. When he is
driven home and sees the finished house and rebuilt hotel, he is deeply
humiliated and tries to run, but he is surrounded. "He's wondering if he's Rip
Van Winkle," says one family member.[101]

The story is narrated by Rusty, the eldest member of the second
generation, who is only slightly younger than Toby, whom he has always
admired. Flashbacks reveal Rusty's gradual disillusionment with his hero.
When he finds Toby in the crevice of the glacier with a broken arm, Rusty

shouts, "Maybe it's about time you bloody-well grew up." Rusty has a hidden reason for feeling guilty about Glory's death. He and Glory had fought against loving each other until she decided to leave Toby and go to Vancouver. Rusty would be at the university there and she offered to be his "*pal*" and to help him realize his dream of becoming a filmmaker. He had refused, family loyalty getting the better of his personal wishes.[102]

Rusty's anger at Toby and comfort from his understanding mother eases his guilt. He imagines making a movie of "Glory's funeral (in CinemaScope and Technicolor)," which would open with a series of family scenes: Buddy and Grace "bickering in their canary-yellow house"; "cowboy music wailing" from the radio of Aunt Kitty and Uncle Reg; "Avery milking his docile cow"; and Aunt Nora "angry and disapproving even before she remembered what day it was." The final scene "would have to be a helicopter shot" of "crowds of Machens looking up" as Toby, one arm in a sling, climbs to the top of the rebuilt hotel to install a tablecloth as a flag.[103]

Keith speaks of the "Canadian tradition of the tall tale," in connection with fictions by W.O. Mitchell, Davies, and Hodgins. It may be that tall tales are found in all pioneering societies; also, the West Coast of North America draws the most high-spirited of the populace. Hodgins insists on "the authenticity of his apparently fantastic characters." Like those of Davies' in *The Rebel Angels*, Hodgins' characters are within the bounds of possibility.[104] The same cannot be said for the exploits of Davy Crockett. The American tall tale, at least in the nineteenth century, stands alone and cannot be matched by anything devised by a Canadian writer.

4

Conclusion

IN THE DEVELOPMENT OF A NATIONAL LITERATURE, humor is not an early priority. "Serious literature," that will make the outside world sit up and take notice, is rarely sought in the work of those who write comedy. One reason is that humor is time-sensitive, so comic writings rarely seem amusing to a later generation. It is not surprising that Twain was seen as little more than a funnyman for many years. *Huckleberry Finn* was considered a child's story, even though the hero — who did not want to go to Sunday School — was such a poor role model for the nation's children that the book was often banned from schools and libraries. By the time Twain was acknowledged to be an important American writer, his humor was dwindling. Perhaps the ending of *A Connecticut Yankee* was amusing in the nineteenth century, but there is nothing in his last novel *The Mysterious Stranger* (1916), that could cause laughter at any time. Full recognition of Twain's importance to American literature took a degree of hindsight.

Canada's two important early humorists appeared before the nation's literature was well developed, but they are of enormous importance historically. Beverley Rasporich notes that "humour is often an expression of culture," and that American studies, like those by Rourke and Yates, treat humor as "articulations of their society."[105] Haliburton's *The Old Judge* is now being read in such a light, while Leacock has long been recognized for his insight into Canadian life. Writer Guy Vanderhaeghe calls Leacock "one of the great interpreters of this country." Vanderhaeghe grew up in small-town Saskatchewan with grandfathers who were both immigrants of a sort: one came from Belgium and one from Ontario. The one from Ontario was the strangest, but Vanderhaeghe understood him once he read *Sunshine Sketches*.[106] Haliburton and Leacock did not develop into literary artists, and their designations as the "father of American humor" and the "Canadian Mark Twain" are laughable today. If there is such a thing as a Canadian counterpart to Mark Twain, at least as a humorist, it is certainly Robertson Davies.

Deeply felt anger tends to lead to unsophisticated humor. Thus, in the early days of the United States, resentment of the British led directly to the development of comic characters lacking in subtlety. Similarly, in Canada, bitterness over the outcome of the American Revolution led to Sam Slick and some satirically depicted Americans in Susanna Moodie's *Roughing It in the Bush*. Moodie is not known as a humorist, but when her ire was raised, she could be witty. Arriving at their first farm, the Moodies meet a disreputable-looking girl who offers to loan them a whiskey decanter. They have no use for the decanter, and when Mrs. Moodie addresses her as "My good girl," the young woman bristles: "Now, don't go to call me 'gal'—and pass off your English airs on us. We are *genuine* Yankees, and think ourselves as good—yes, a great deal better than you."[107] Such humor can still be found in Canada, as satirizing Americans has never lost its appeal. Canadian humor at the expense of an American stereotype is mild, however, compared to what American writers often do to themselves. Rourke's comment about the American "quarrel with America" steadily gained strength during the twentieth century, leading to such monsters as those in Barth's colonial Maryland and Heller's senior officers. Barely laughable, at least they are recognizably villains — a great improvement over the criminals given heroic status in the nineteenth century.

A notable comic parallel between the two countries emerged in the 1980s and was still popular at the end of the twentieth century. Garrison Keillor's Lake Wobegon series in the United States and Dan Needles' Walt Wingfield plays in Canada are episodic and dramatic, and both are hilarious commentaries on rural life.[108] Keillor's Lake Wobegon began as a radio series, and falls into the American tradition of disparaging life in small towns. Meanwhile, the Wingfield plays, which began as newspaper columns, tell of an urban broker who buys a farm and is laughably ignorant of country life. It is the local farmers who instruct and often rescue this city slicker.

Canada has not found its comic image of the nation and probably never will; at least not until French-English differences are resolved. The Mountie became a mildly comic character in the television show *Due South*, but is too historically heroic to be a major object of humor. In the meantime, French and English Canada are plentifully supplied with humorists, and if they do not speak much to each other, they still have much in common.

Notes

1 Constance Rourke, *American Humour: A Study of the National Character* (New York: Harcourt Brace Jovanovich, 1959), 15.

2 During the long conflict between the northern and southern states of the Union, Yankee was unmistakably a northerner. Southern soldiers who went overseas in World War I were offended by the song, "Over There," with its assertion that "The Yanks are coming."

3 T.C. Haliburton, *Traits of American Humour by Native Authors* (1852) and S. Leacock, *The Greatest Pages of American Humor* (1916).

4 Led and inspired by the comedy team of Wayne and Shuster, who appeared on the Ed Sullivan Show a record breaking fifty-eight times in the late fifties and early sixties, Canada is currently providing comedians to the North American market out of all proportion to its percentage of the population. Martin Short, Jim Carrey, Dan Ackroyd, John Belushi, Bill Murray, and Mike Myers represent the tip of an iceberg.

5 Robertson Davies, *One Half of Robertson Davies* (Markham, ON: Penguin Books, 1978), 272.

6 This motto was inaugurated by the separatist *Parti Québécois,* which objected to the former motto, *La belle provence,* since it labeled Quebec a province rather than a nation.

7 New, *Borderlands,* 43–4.

8 See Stanley Burke and Roy Peterson, *Frog Fables and Beaver Tales* (Toronto: James Lewis & Samuel, 1973).

9 Frye, *Garden,* 220.

10 Geoff Pevere and Greig Dymond, *Mondo Canuck: A Canadian Pop Culture Odyssey* (Scarborough ON: Prentice Hall Canada, 1996), Introduction.

11 Ibid., 195, 121, 4. Pevere and Dymond claim that the "backbone" of the Canadian comic "tradition" has been "sketch comedy ... directed at some readily identifiable target outside itself." They also point out that there have been so many skilled cartoonists and animators that in 1995 Disney opened studios in Vancouver and Toronto because there are "a substantial number of creative people who don't want to leave Canada."

12 Rourke, 29.

13 Norris W. Yates The American Humorist: Conscience of the Twentieth Century (New York: The Citadel Press, 1965), 21–22. Yates lists five characteristics of the crackerbox philosopher: rural; "just folks," who is "shy on book l'arnin but long on common sense"; teller of tall tales; prone to overstatement; and often plays the "wise fool."

14 Rourke, 36–7.

15 Yates, 257.

16 David M. Legate, *Stephen Leacock: A Biography* (Toronto: Doubleday Canada, 1970), 51.

17 H. Northrop Frye, Introduction, *The Stepsure Letters,* by Thomas McCulloch (Toronto: McClelland & Stewart, 1960), ix. Again, Frye is not quite right, since parodying the Americans has become a major industry in Canada.

18 Malcolm Bradbury, Introduction, *The Sketch Book of Geoffrey Crayon, Gent.* by Washington Irving (London: J.M. Dent, 1993), xx–xxi.

19 *Ibid.*, xxxiii.

20 Irving, "Rip Van Winkle," *The Sketch Book*, 36.

21 Irving, "The Legend of Sleepy Hollow," *The Sketch Book*, 302, 293, 298

22 Lynn, 85.

23 Slotkin, *Fatal Environment*, 127–28.

24 Lynn, 79.

25 Rourke, 82, 86–87.

26 *Ibid.*, 131.

27 H.M. Jones, Forward, *Davy Crockett: American Comic Legend*, ed. Richard M. Dorson (New York: Arno Press, 1977), xv–xvi.

28 Lynn, 197, 194.

29 Richard M. Dorson, ed. *Davey Crockett*, 16–17.

30 *Ibid.*, 41–42.

31 Slotkin, *Regeneration*, 5.

32 *Whitman*, I: 169.

33 Qtd by Reynolds, 489.

34 Emerson, *Emerson*, 6.

35 Reynolds, 470.

36 *Ibid.*, 453, 551, 540.

37 *Ibid.*, 470.

38 Lynn, 307.

39 Mark Twain, *Life on the Mississippi* (New York: Signet Classics, 1961), 25–29.

40 Rourke, 264.

41 F. Bret Harte, "Muck A Muck: An Indian Novel after Cooper," *Condensed Novels and Other Papers* (New York: G.W. Carleton, 1867), 11–20.

42 Fiedler, *Return*, 122–23.

43 Lynn, 404, 412, 414–15.

44 Yates, 141.

45 E.B. and Katherine S. White, Introduction, *A Subtreasury of American Humor* (New York: The Modern Library, 1941), xvi.

46 Sinclair Lewis, *Babbitt* (New York: Bantam Books, 1998), 15; Ch 2, 31; Ch 3.

47 John Wickersham, Introduction, *Babbitt*, by Lewis, xiii, xiv.

48 Lewis, *Babbitt*, 188–89; Ch 14, 77; Ch 6, 24; Ch 3, 76, 86, 88; Ch 6.

49 *Ibid.*, 29; Ch 3, 45–6; Ch 4, 186; Ch 14.

50 Joseph Heller, *Catch-22* (New York: Dell Publishing, 1968), 219; Ch 21.

51 *Ibid.*, 14; Ch 1, 33; Ch 4.

52 *Ibid.*, 265–66; Ch 24.

53 *Ibid.*, 47; Ch 5, 449; Ch 41, 436–37; Ch 40.

54 Bradbury, *American Novel*, 212.

55 Heller, 455; Ch 42.

56 The other two are *A Month of Sundays* (1975) and *Roger's Version* (1986). Unlike the author's Rabbit series, these novels have different characters and are only linked by allusions to *The Scarlet Letter.*

57 John Updike, *S* (New York: Fawcett Crest, 1989), 111, 32–33.

58 *Ibid.*, 70, 102–3, 121.

59 *Ibid.*, 241, 248.

60 Yates, 141.

61 Thomas McCulloch, *The Stepsure Letters* (Toronto: McClelland & Stewart, 1960), 17.

62 Northrop Frye, Introduction, *The Stepsure Letters*, by McCulloch, ix.

63 V.L.O. Chittick "The Gen-U-ine Yankee," *On Thomas Chandler Haliburton,* ed. Richard A. Davies (Ottawa: The Tecumseh Press, 1979), 140.

64 In his essay, "No Name is My Name," *The Forty-Ninth and Other Parallels*, ed. David Staines (Boston: University of Massachusetts Press, 1986), Kroetsch speaks of the Squire as one of several nameless characters in Canadian literature (118–19), leading him to the conclusion that remaining incognito is in some sense a Canadian characteristic. The learned and moral narrator in early American humorous writings normally remains nameless.

65 Thomas Chandler Haliburton, *The Clockmaker* (Toronto: McClelland & Stewart, 1993), 94, 67, 111, 150.

66 Haliburton, *Judge*, 163.

67 R.E. Watters, "The Old Judge," *Haliburton* ed. Davies, 230.

68 The 1968 Clarke Irwin edition is abridged. The complete text was finally published in Canada by Tecumseh Press in 1978.

69 Robert L. McDougall, Afterword, *The Clockmaker*, by Haliburton 220.

70 Robertson Davies, Introduction, *A Feast of Stephen: A Leacock Anthology* (Toronto: McClelland & Stewart, 1974), 43.

71 Stephen Leacock, *Sunshine Sketches of a Little Town* (Toronto: McClelland & Stewart, 1989), 15, 18–19, 75.

72 *Ibid.*, 153, 165, 170.

73 Davies, *Stephen*, 19.

74 Stephen Leacock, "Humour as I See It," *Stephen*, ed. Davies, 137–44.

75 James Steele, "Imperial Cosmopolitanism, or the Partly Solved Riddle of Leacock's Multi-National Persona," *Stephen Leacock; A Reappraisal*, ed. David Staines (Ottawa: University of Ottawa Press, 1986), 61.

76 Paul Hiebert, *Sarah Binks* (Toronto: McClelland & Stewart, 1995), 7, 9, 22, 27–28.

77 *Ibid.*, 35, 40–41, 12–13.

78 Charles Gordon, Afterword to *Sarah Binks*, 170–71

79 Earle Birney, *Turvey* (Toronto: McClelland & Stewart, 1989), 61; Ch 5, 109; Ch 7.

80 *Ibid.*, 113; Ch 8, 125; Ch 9.

81 Earle Birney, *The Creative Writer* (Toronto: Canadian Broadcasting Corp., 1966), 41.

82 George Woodcock, Introduction, *Turvey,* by Birney (Toronto: McClelland & Stewart, 1969), x.

83 Gérard Bessette, *Not For Every Eye*, trans. Glen Shortliffe (Toronto: Exile Editions, 1994), originally published in French *as Le Libraire* (Paris: René Julliard, 1960).

84 *Ibid.*, 9, 28, 40–41.

85 *Ibid.*, 85, 91.

86 *Tempest Tost* (1951), *Leaven of Malice* (1954), and *A Mixture of Frailties* (1958).
87 *Fifth Business* (1970), *The Manticore* (1972), and *World of Wonders* (1975). As with the Salterton novels, Davies did not set out to write a trilogy.
88 Davies, *Half*, 16 133.
89 Keith, *Stance*, 175.
90 George Woodcock, *George Woodcock's Introduction to Canadian Fiction* (Toronto: ECW Press, 1993), 89.
91 Robertson Davies, *The Rebel Angels* (Markham, ON: Penguin Books, 1983), 136; Ch 4:2, 216; Ch 5:4.
92 *Ibid.*, 198; Ch 5:1.
93 See Robertson Davies, *A Voice from the Attic* (Toronto: McClelland & Stewart, 1972), 7, and *One Half of Robertson Davies*, 182.
94 Davies, *Angels*, 235; Ch 5:1.
95 *Ibid.*, 274; Ch 6:2.
96 Woodcock, *Introduction to Canadian Fiction*, 165.
97 Keith, *Stance*, 262
98 *Ibid.*, 269. Keith compares these "familial relationships" to Faulkner's tangled families and notes that Hodgins found Faulkner a "major, and initially crippling influence." Faulkner's dark vision seems a glaring contrast to Hodgins's exuberance.
99 *Ibid.*, 262.
100 Jack Hodgins, *The Machen Charm* (Toronto: McClelland & Stewart,1995), 29; Ch 2, 238; Ch 13.
101 *Ibid.*, 23; Ch 1, 275; Ch 16.
102 *Ibid.*, 271; Ch 15, 217; Ch 12.
103 *Ibid.*, 20; Ch 1, 294; Ch 16.
104 Keith, *Stance*, 101, 102.
105 Beverley Rasporich, "Stephen Leacock, Humorist: American by Association," *Leacock* ed. Staines, 69.
106 Guy Vanderhaeghe, "Leacock and Understanding Canada," *Leacock* ed. Staines, 17–18.
107 Moodie, *Bush*, 94.
108 Garrison Keillor, *Lake Wobegon Days* (New York: Penguin Books, 1986) and *Wobegon Boy* (New York: Penguin, 1990). Dan Needles' plays are *Letter From Wingfield* Farm (1984), *Wingfield's Progress* (1987), *Wingfield's Folly* (1990), *Wingfield Unbound* (1997), and *Wingfield on Ice* (2000). At the end of the twentieth century, the Wobegon series continued as a radio show, "The Prairie Home Companion," while the Wingfield plays continued to tour Canada, as popular as ever.

Chapter
Nine

The Tenacity of National Myths

ONE OF THE MOST STRIKING THINGS about the literary works discussed in this study is how many of them could serve as illustrations in three or more chapters. An example from each nation illustrates the point: Mark Twain's *The Adventures of Huckleberry Finn* and Alistair MacLeod's *No Great Mischief*. *Huckleberry Finn*, discussed at length in chapter four, "A Sense of Place," could have been discussed at equal length in the chapters "Nature," "Gender, Ethnicity, and Class," "Violence," and "Humor." In Canada, *No Great Mischief*, used in chapter four, "A Sense of Place," would be suitable material for the chapters "A Sense of the Past," "Nature," "Gender, Ethnicity, and Class," and "Violence." A nation's myths are indeed peppered throughout its literature.

The characteristics of Canada and the United States that have been examined show a tendency for the two nations to become more alike, at least superficially. Both Americans and Canadians are increasingly gripped by the past, and they are equally concerned about wilderness areas and endangered species. Both nations have become more secularized, and the North American Free Trade agreement and the Canadian Charter of Rights and Freedoms — which looks much like the American Bill of Rights and grants the courts greater influence — make the two countries appear even more similar.

Looks aside, however, the two nations will likely never become one. The fundamental differences between Canada and the United States — their different forms of government, the French-English dichotomy in Canada, and perhaps the ubiquity of violence in American society — as well as their different myths make this virtually certain. Canada's French-English division is unlike anything the United States has experienced, and it is doubtful that American law could ever accommodate Quebec. Violence is still the most noticeable difference between the two nations. Americans show little interest in taking handguns from private citizens, while Canadians remain much less tolerant of violence in their country.

Different national myths can be just as divisive as political and legal differences. The more strongly a myth is held in the minds of the people, the more able it is to adapt to changed conditions and remain part of the unexamined life. When challenged, it stirs automatic resistance. Whatever coming together has occurred in the latter half of the twentieth century, American and Canadian myths remain distinctive. The differences ultimately derive from the fact that English and French Canada both have stronger conservative traditions than the United States. That is, conservative in the Burkean sense of viable institutions in which the people have confidence, and an evolutionary rather than revolutionary approach to change — although more radical movements have played a role in Quebec. If they no longer appear so deferential to authority, Canadians still largely trust that their institutions are functional and assume that those elected to public office are at least trying to discharge their responsibilities. The Washington-type scandals that have punctuated American history could happen in Canada, but would likely be tepid in comparison. The populace seems too cautious, perhaps still of the opinion that private lives should be respected. Also, there is no evidence that Canadians are any more willing to join the United States than they have ever been.

It should not be forgotten that both countries were founded on what have been called "shotgun marriages" — an exaggerated image as all parties to the agreements entered voluntarily. French and English Canada agreed to form a confederation, while the northern states accepted a guarantee of slavery in the southern states in order to form a nation. A "marriage of convenience" might be a more appropriate metaphor, but the shotgun image is kept alive through continuing doubt among segments of both populations that the decisions made at the beginning were the correct ones. And the myths and ideals that each side carried into the agreements between French and English Canada, and between northern and southern states, have had a lingering effect.

The old cliché about the United States being a melting pot and Canada a multicultural mosaic is not just an oversimplification; it is wrong. Victor Goldbloom notes that "the American melting pot has never melted down the black, the Asiatic, the Native American," and melting the Irish was a long, painful process. On the other side of the border, Canada, some years ago, "defined itself as a multicultural country." [1] Much like the early days when settlers were encouraged to settle in homogeneous blocks, today sections of some cities are identified by the ethnic origins of the inhabitants, with street names in both the ethnic group's language and English. But other people have moved into these neighborhoods, and second and third generation immigrants have spread out and blended in. The French vowed from the beginning never to be assimilated into the English majority, but there have always been intermarriages and there are more bilingual Canadians than ever before. Canada has been more of a melting pot than the United States, partly because its parliamentary government has had more authority to protect minorities than the American constitutional system. The twenty-first century may even the score.

The dramatic increase in the number of outstanding women writers in the United States since World War II heralded a cultural shift that, at the end of the twentieth century, was still in process. Feminist critics continue to comb American literary history in search of overlooked women writers. Whatever the final count, the overall picture shows that an aversion to perceived effeminacy dominated American thinking through most of its history. Today there are numerous outstanding women writers — none more important than Toni Morrison — who are lighting the way toward a more balanced approach to literary interpretation of American culture. Canadian writers Margaret Atwood, Alice Munro, and Carol Shields — well-known in the United States — may be hastening the process.

Toni Morrison claims that race in the United States has become "metaphorical" and "metaphysical," but whatever its form, "racism is as healthy today as it was in the Enlightenment." She points out that the presence of Black people is evident in every one of the nation's major struggles — including the "framing of the Constitution," the construction of "a free and public school system," "the balancing of representation in legislative bodies," "legal definitions of justice," "theological discourse," and "the concept of manifest destiny." Morrison concludes that "the metaphorical and metaphysical uses of race occupy definitive places in American literature, in the 'national' character, and ought to be a major concern of ... literary scholarship." Race is a factor, at least by implication, in most of the American literature examined in this study, but the concept of Manifest Destiny and Morrison's definition of racism leave some unanswered questions.[2]

Racism in the United States today does not take the form it took at the time of the Enlightenment — or, indeed, any succeeding period up to the 1950s. Many American writers are concerned with race relations in the United States, but a close examination of the nation's past is so painful that they appear to vie with each other to create the most imaginative versions of an American hell. Twain's and Adams' dystopian visions were not directed at the United States so much as at mankind for not measuring up to American expectations. Nathanael West directed his anger at the nation — an early example of the American quarrel with America — so that, gaining steam after World War II, such works look more like self-hatred. Malcolm Bradbury speaks of a "pervasive feeling of the absurdity of American history itself" in the 1960s that was so strong that it instilled a sense of unreality. He argues that "[n]ovelists increasingly saw around them a contemporary American history of vast plots and powers, which shrivelled, drained, and programmed the self."[3] This was not just the experience of novelists. Allen Ginsberg's poem "America" speaks to the nation with words of advice, such as "Go fuck yourself with your atom bomb," but adds another dimension with the accusation, "You made me want to be a saint."[4] No Canadian would ever make such an accusation. Bradbury quotes Philip Roth on "American realities" becoming so "absurd and incredible" that writers "began exploring the unreliable borders between the outward world of history and the imaginary life of fiction." The resulting fascination with postmodernism was so intense that Bradbury claims "it appeared entirely American."[5]

One would think that Gore Vidal, who has written so many acclaimed novels set in the American past and who is interested in history for its own sake, would be an exception to Bradbury's generalization. Such is not the case. Vidal chooses to live in Italy, because "it's not America." Noting that the average American watches six hours of television a day, Vidal asks how they can "defend their liberties when they're busy watching 'The Gong Show,'" an ironic reminder of Jefferson's Little Rebellion. Vidal claims that he wants to "subvert" American society, for the American "system does not work."[6] A major exception to Bradbury's concerns is the view of John Updike, who grew up in the small town of Shillington, Pennsylvania. His father was a high school teacher and his mother a failed writer, an upbringing that instilled in him "earthly insecurity."

During the Vietnam War, he lived in Massachusetts as a member of the New England intelligentsia, and found himself alone in his defense of the United States. "I wanted to keep quiet but could not," he says, for "[g]orge-deep principles of fairness and order were at issue." He found that to the young people of the day, authority was "Amerika, a blood-stained bugaboo to be crushed at any cost. To me, authority was the Shillington High School faculty, my father and his kindly and friendly, rather wan and punctilious colleagues."[7]

A chapter in Updike's memoirs, "A Letter to My Grandsons," is to his daughter's two boys, who have an African father. As he discusses his relatives and his genealogy, he does not evade the subject of race. Formerly assuming that the boys would be treated better in Ghana than in the United States, he is no longer so sure. He writes, "An ideal colorblind society flickers at the forward edge of the sluggishly evolving one ... America is slowly becoming yours, I want to think."[8]

The disastrous consequences of a partnership between an Edenic myth and slavery might have been recognized earlier had the myth not had so much substance. The United States has truly been a land of milk and honey for millions of the world's poor and has retained a vivacity that cannot be denied. Before the middle of the twentieth century, few immigrants who could afford the United States would have chosen to live in Canada. David Staines describes the odd Canadian who turns up in American literature as a "dispassionate witness" who observes "the dreams and the disintegration of the United States."[9] Canadians have been too close to the United States to ever be completely dispassionate, but the attitudes of Canadian literary characters depend largely on whether they are created by American or Canadian authors. American writers — most of whom know little about Canada — are inclined to depict Canadians as dispassionate,[10] while Canadian authors are all too often happy to dwell on the horrors of the American past, which, by implication, gives Canadians moral superiority. For example, Poulin's *Volkswagen Blues* repeatedly points out how the Native peoples were victims of American aggression.

In 1947, Canadians at last ceased being classified as British subjects. George Woodcock claims that World War II "increased the Canadian sense of existing as a separate nation, finally detached from the old imperial links with Britain and anxious to defend itself from being absorbed into a continental culture in North America."[11] In 1960, "Quebec made its belated, dramatic, whirlwind entry into the twentieth century ... impatient to ride off, like Stephen Leacock's horseman, madly in all directions."[12]

Beverley Rasporich remarks on the irony of Leacock creating a Canadian voice while insisting on "there being no such thing as Canadian literature or Canadian humour."[13] Leacock was an imperialist, affected by the Social Darwinism of his day. He believed that the British Empire offered mankind the basis for an effective world organization, an enterprise to be undertaken jointly with "the emerging empire of the United States." True "world peace was to be gradually and securely established ... by the forcible expansion of Anglo-American imperial rule." Canada was to be the core of this "hegemonic iron fist," for with its mineral wealth and inaccessible northland, it could produce "armaments and munitions in places so safeguarded by natural obstacles that no war could impede their manufacture ... All hell can be raised in the bowels of northern Canada," he concluded.[14] In the 1940s Hugh MacLennan insisted that "the colonial understanding was the identity of his country," and that Canadians were "a combination of the British and the American ... the best of both nationalities."[15] In the light of such sentiments, French Canada's preoccupation with the "conquest" of France in North America appears to have considerable justification.

Canada's late blooming has been advantageous in a number of ways. Living so close to the United States with one-tenth the population and a somewhat larger land mass, Canadians have been able to learn from American experience — primarily what not to do and when to do things differently. The most obvious example of this lesson is Canada's development of its West. A more recent example concerns the preservation of cities. Jane Jacobs's book *The Death and Life of Great American Cities* (1961) made a strong impression in North America. She argued that expressways funneling traffic into the heart of a city were detrimental to its life and development. Vancouver has not allowed any such invasion, but work had already begun on a northwest artery into Toronto when a halt was ordered. There it sits to this day, a piece of an expressway that goes a few blocks toward the city center, then leaves drivers to struggle onward through city streets. All over Canada, Los Angeles was seen as a model *not* to be emulated.

That piece of expressway can stand as an ironic symbol of the pride and affection that Canadians have for their cities. It is only a slight exaggeration to say that "making it" in Canada is being able to live in the heart of the city, not necessarily in the suburbs. While New Yorkers live just as happily and expensively in their city, and while there are luxurious homes in Canadian suburbs, a critical difference is that fewer Canadians have felt the need to flee to the suburbs because of crime or poor schools. Canada's cities, as they increasingly appear in the nation's literature, are so vital that they challenge the characters, and are as memorable as the rural communities that were so prominent in early writings. The pasts of these cities are now being immortalized in the nation's literature — for example, Michael Ondaatje's *In the Skin of a Lion* (1987) and Carol Shields' *The Republic of Love* (1992).

The realization that civil society has been preserved better in Canada than in the United States has helped to give Canada's creative artists a new sense of confidence and has enabled them to interpret their own culture without worrying about being behind the times or out of fashion. Writers now see new possibilities for recreating the past without imposing guilt on the present, bringing places to life so that characters blend into the environment, or writing page-turning novels without violent encounters.

The vitality and resilience of the United States should never be underestimated. America, having suffered from the malady expressed by Twain and Adams at the beginning of the twentieth century, has had a long and fearful convalescence but shows signs of recovery. The test is surely the emergence of an ability to treat the past with honesty, to recognize the nation's strengths as well as the dilemmas inherent in a revolutionary past, and to evaluate the present in a constructive rather than a destructive manner. Such contemporary writers as Saul Bellow, John Updike, and Anne Tyler have been creating an America that is alive and robust, that is neither especially good nor unusually evil, and that produces characters who live in a recognizable place and time. All three authors demonstrate a sophisticated humor that bears little resemblance to the biting satire so conspicuous in much American literature. Toni Morrison's writing — *Song of Solomon* (1977) and *Jazz* (1992) are notable — recognizes the warmth and humor that existed in American Black communities of the past.

And yet the myths remain. Road novels continue to pour forth, violence is largely unabated, and the American past is still treated with authorial outrage. Frye was hardly exaggerating when he referred to the Declaration of Independence as "America's book of Genesis." Canada and the United States will not only never be one, they will also never be the same.

At the end of *Continental Divide,* Lipset asks a hypothetical question: What if the British government had shown sounder judgment and the American Revolution had failed or never taken place? Lipset limits himself to political and social matters, but larger questions arise. Disputes over slavery, religion, and language would undoubtedly have occurred, and the northern and southern colonies might have developed as different nations. The slave states would have been forced to face up to emancipation sooner, and the Civil War might have been avoided.

American society, still vigorous and flexible, has been such rich ground for the arts, as well as for popular culture, that it should be able to solve its social problems. The persistent presence of violence and a reluctance to learn from other peoples' experiences may be the greatest obstacles. As long as people see, or demand to see, their nation as a utopia or its polar opposite, no lessons can be learned from outside, even from a neighbor who has a similar heritage and has encountered similar problems. The global economy, free trade agreements, and open borders leave people feeling vulnerable. Yet such openness may stimulate the artists in both countries to develop another kind of border, based on a sense of self, and manifested in superior artistic works that speak for their nations.

Notes

1   Victor C. Goldbloom, "Canada: The Challenge of Coexistence," *Forty-Ninth,* ed. Staines, 16–17.
2   Morrison, *Dark,* 63, 65.
3   Bradbury, *American Novel,* 199.
4   Allen Ginsberg, "America," *Poetry in English,* ed. Rosenthal, 1061–2.
5   Bradbury *American Novel,* 199, 206.
6   Vidal, *Views,* 284, 252, 247–48.
7   John Updike, *Self-Consciousness: Memoirs* (New York: Fawcett Crest, 1990), 130–31, 133.

8   Updike, *Memoirs*, 205.

9   Staines, *Provinces*, 37.

10 According to Staines, Shreve McCannon, in Faulkner's *Absalom, Absalom* (1936), is a "fully realized" Canadian character as "dispassionate witness." Staines, *Provinces*, 50–51.

11 Woodcock, *Spring*, 12.

12 Goldbloom, 13.

13 Rasporich, 81.

14 Qtd by Steele, 64–66.

15 Qtd by Staines, *Provinces,* 15.

Bibliography

Adams, Henry. *The Education of Henry Adams*. Ed. Ernest Samuels. Boston: Houghton Mifflin Co.,1974.

———. *The United States in 1800*. Ithaca: Cornell University Press, 1955.

Allen, Richard. "Providence to Progress: The Migration of an Idea in English Canadian Thought." *Canadian Issues/Themes Canadiens*. Vol. VI, *Religion/Culture*. Association for Canadian Studies (1985): 33–46.

Anderson, Quentin. *The Imperial Self*. New York: Random House, 1971.

Atwood, Margaret. *Alias Grace*. Toronto: Seal Books, 1997.

———. *The Handmaid's Tale*. Toronto: Seal Books, 1986.

———. *Surfacing*. New York: Simon and Shuster, 1972.

———. *Survival*. Toronto: House of Anansi, 1972.

Aubert de Gaspé, Philippe-Joseph. *Canadians of Old*. Trans. Jane Brierley. Montreal: Véhicule Press, 1996.

Ball, Edward. *Slaves in the Family*. New York: Ballantine Books, 1999.

Banks, Russell. *Cloudsplitter*. Toronto: Vintage Canada, 1998.

Barth, John. *The Sot-Weed Factor*. New York: Grosset and Dunlop, 1966.

Becker, Carl. L. *The Declaration of Independence: A Study in the History of Political Ideas*. New York: Vintage Books, 1958.

Beloff, Max, ed. *The Debate on the American Revolution, 1761–1783: A Sourcebook*. New York: Harper Torchbooks, 1963.

Bennett, Donna. "Conflicted Vision: A Consideration of Canon and Genre in English Canadian Literature." Lecker, *Canadian Canons*. 131–149.

Bercovitch, Sacvan. *The Puritan Origins of the American Self*. New Haven: Yale University Press, 1975.

———. "The Rites of Assent: Rhetoric, Ritual, and the Ideology of American Consensus." *The American Self: Myth, Ideology, and Popular Culture*. Ed. Sam B. Girgus. University of New Mexico Press, 1981. 5–42.

Berger, Carl. *The Writing of Canadian History: Aspects of English-Canadian Historical Writing since 1900*. 2nd ed. Toronto: University of Toronto Press, 1986.

Bessette, Gérard. *Not For Every Eye*. Trans. Glen Shortcliffe. Toronto: ExileEditions, 1994.

Birney, Earle. *Turvey*. Toronto: McClelland & Stewart, 1989.

Bissell, Claude. "Haliburton, Leacock, and the American Humorous Tradition." *Canadian Literature* 39 (1969): 5–19.

———. Introduction. *The Imperialist*. By Sara Jeanette Duncan. Toronto: McClelland & Stewart, 1971. v–ix.

Blais, Marie-Claire. *A Season in the Life of Emmanuel*. Trans. Derek Coltman. Toronto: McClelland & Stewart, 1992.

Blake, W.H. Introduction. *Maria Chapdelaine*. By Louis Hèmon. Toronto: Macmillan of Canada, 1973. v–xiii.

Bloom, Harold. *The American Religion: The Emergence of the Post-Christian Nation*. New York: Simon and Schuster, 1992.

———. *How to Read and Why*. New York: Scribner, 2000.

Bodsworth, Fred. *Last of the Curlews*. Toronto: McClelland & Stewart, 1963.

Bradbury, Malcolm. *Dangerous Pilgrimages: Trans-Atlantic Mythologies and the Novel*. London: Penguin Books, 1995.

———. Introduction. *The Sketch Book of Geoffrey Crayon, Gent*. By Washington Irving. London: J.M. Dent, 1993. xix–xxxix.

———. *The Modern American Novel*. New Edition. Oxford: Oxford University Press, 1992.

Bratton, Daniel L. *Thirty-two Short Views of Mazo de la Roche*. Toronto: ECW Press, 1996.

Brooke, Frances, *The History of Emily Montague*. Toronto: McClelland & Stewart, 1961.

Brooks, Cleanth. Introduction. *Light in August*. By William Faulkner. New York, The Modern Library, 1968. v–xxv.

Brossard, Nicole. Afterword. *A Season in the Life of Emmanuel*. By Marie Claire Blais. Toronto: McClelland & Stewart, 1992. 134–138.

Buckler, Ernest. *The Mountain and the Valley*. Toronto: McClelland & Stewart, 1991.

Burke, Edmund. *A Philosophical Enquiry into the Origin of Our Ideas of the Sublime and Beautiful*. Ed. J. T. Boulton. Notre Dame: University of Notre Dame Press, 1968.

Burke, Stanley and Roy Peterson. *Frog Fables and Beaver Tales*. Toronto: James Lewis and Samuel, 1973.

Byatt, A.S. "Alice Munro: One of the great ones." Rev. of *Selected Stories*, by Alice Munro. *The Globe and Mail*, 2 November 1996: D18+.

Cappon, Lester J., ed. *The Adams-Jefferson Letters*. 2 vols. Chapel Hill: University of North Carolina Press, 1959.

Careless, J.M.S. *Canada: A Story of Challenge*. Third Edition. Toronto: Macmillan of Canada, 1974.

———. ed. *Colonists and Canadiens:1760–1867*. Toronto: Macmillan of Canada, 1971.

Carrier, Roch. *La Guerre, Yes Sir!* Trans. Sheila Fischman. Toronto: Anansi, 1970.

Chandler, Raymond. *The Big Sleep*. New York: Vintage Books, 1992.

Charters, Ann. Introduction. *On the Road*. By Jack Kerouac. New York: Penguin Books, 1991. vii–xxx.

Chittick, V.L.O. "The Gen-U-ine Yankee." *On Thomas Chandler Haliburton*. Ed. Richard A. Davies. Ottawa: The Tecumseh Press, 1979. 140–47.

Clift, Dominique. *The Secret Kingdom: Interpretations of the Canadian Character*. Toronto: McClelland & Stewart, 1989.

Clines, Frances X. "They See America Rolling." *The New York Times Book Review*, May 9, 1993: 1+.

Comer, Krista. *Landscapes of the New West: Gender and Geography in Contemporary Women's Writing*. Chapel Hill: University of North Carolina Press, 1999.

Connor, Ralph. *Black Rock: A Tale of the Selkirks*. Chicago: M. A. Donahue, n.d.

———. *Glengarry School Days*. Toronto: McClelland & Stewart, 1975.

———. *The Man from Glengarry*. Toronto: McClelland & Stewart, 1993.

Cook, Eleanor. "A Seeing and Unseeing of the Eye: Canadian Literature and the Sense of Place." *Daedalus* 117: 4 (1988): 215–35.

Cooper, James Fenimore. *The Deerslayer*. New York: Penguin Books, 1987.

———. *The Last of the Mohicans*. Oxford: Oxford University Press, 1990.

———. *The Pioneers*. New York: Penguin Books, 1988.

Cox, James M. "Southwestern Vernacular." Simpson, 82–94.

Craig, G.M. "The 1830s." Careless, *Colonists*. 173–99.

Crawford, Isabella Valancy. "Malcolm's Katie." Sinclair, 157–190.

Cross, Michael. "The 1820s." Careless, *Colonists*. 149–72.

Curry, Ralph L. Introduction. *Arcadian Adventures with the Idle Rich*. By Stephen Leacock. Toronto: McClelland & Stewart, 1969. vii–xi.

Daniels, Roy. Introduction. *As For Me and My House*. By Sinclair Ross. Toronto: McClelland & Stewart, 1960. v–x.

Davies, Richard A., ed. *On Thomas Chandler Haliburton*. Ottawa: The Tecumseh Press, 1979.

Davies, Robertson. Introduction. *Feast of Stephen: A Leacock Anthology*. Toronto: McClelland & Stewart, 1974. 1–45.

———. *Fifth Business*. New York: Signet Books, 1971.

———. *Leaven of Malice*. Toronto: Clarke Irwin, 1964.

———. *The Manticore*. New York: Curtis Books, 1972.

———. *A Mixture of Frailties*. Markham ON: Penguin, 1980

———. *One Half of Robertson Davies*. Markham ON: Penguin, 1978.

———. *The Rebel Angels*. Markham ON: Penguin, 1983.

———. *Tempest-Tost*. Markham ON: Penguin, 1980.

———. *A Voice From The Attic*. Toronto: McClelland & Stewart, 1972.

———. *World of Wonders*. Markham ON: Penguin, 1977.

Denham, Paul and Mary Jane Edwards. Introduction. *Canadian Literature in the 70s*. Toronto: Holt, Rinehart and Winston, 1980. xi–xxiv.

de Crèvecoeur, Hector St. John. *Letters from an American Farmer*. New York: Fox, Duffield and Co., 1904.

de la Roche, Mazo. *Jalna*. Toronto: Macmillan of Canada, 1947.

———. *The Whiteoaks of Jalna*. Toronto: Macmillan of Canada, 1929.

———. *Whiteoak Harvest*. Toronto: Macmillan of Canada, 1948.

DeLillo, Don. *Underworld*. New York: Scribner, 1998.

de Tocqueville, Alexis. *Democracy in America*. 2 vols. Trans. Henry Reeve. New York: Schocken Books, 1961.

Dickinson, Emily. *Final Harvest: Emily Dickinson's Poems*. Ed. Thomas H. Johnson. Boston: Little Brown,1967.

Dickstein, Morris. Introduction. *Main Street*. By Sinclair Lewis. New York: Bantam Classic, 1996. vii–xix.

Doctorow, E.L. *Billy Bathgate*. New York: Harper and Row, 1990.

Dorson, Richard M. ed. *Davy Crockett: American Comic Legend*. New York: Arno Press, 1977.

Dreiser, Theodore. *An American Tragedy*. Cleveland: The World Publishing Co, 1948.

Duffy, Dennis. *Gardens, Covenants, Exiles: Loyalism in the Literature of Upper Canada/Ontario*. Toronto: University of Toronto Press, 1982.

———. *Sounding the Iceberg: An Essay on Canadian Historical Novels*. Toronto: ECW Press, 1986.

———. *A World Under Sentence: John Richardson and the Interior*. Toronto: ECW Press, 1996.

Duncan, Sara Jeanette. *The Imperialist*. Toronto: McClelland & Stewart, 1990.

Edman, Irwin. Introduction. *Emerson's Essays*. New York: Thomas Y. Crowell, 1951. v–x.

Eliot, T.S. *The Waste Land*. Rosenthal, 888–900.

———. *Four Quartets*. London: Faber and Faber, 1970.

Ellison, Ralph. *Invisible Man*. New York: Vintage Books, 1990.

Emerson, Ralph Waldo. *The Complete Works of Ralph Waldo Emerson*. 12 vols. Boston: Houghton, Mifflin, 1904.

———. *Ralph Waldo Emerson*. Ed. Richard Poirier. Oxford: Oxford University Press, 1990.

Erdrick, Louise. *The Beet Queen*. New York: Bantam Books, 1987.

———. *Tales of Burning Love*. New York: Harper Perennial, 1997.

Faulkner, William. *The Bear. Three Famous Short Novels by William Faulkner*. New York: Vintage Books, 1961. 185–316.

———. *Light in August*. New York: The Modern Library, 1968.

Fiedler, Leslie. *The Return of the Vanishing American*. New York: Stein and Day, 1968.

Fitzgerald, F. Scott. *The Great Gatsby*. New York: Charles Scribner's Sons, 1953.

Fogel, Stanley. *A Tale of Two Countries: Contemporary Fiction in Canada and the United States*. Toronto: ECW Press, 1984.

Ford, Henry. Interview with Charles N. Wheeler. *Chicago Tribune*. May 25, 1916.

Franklin, Benjamin. *The Autobiography and Other Writings*. New York: Signet Classics, 1961.

Friedenberg, Edgar Z. *Deference to Authority: The Case of Canada*. White Plains, NY: M.E. Sharpe, 1980.

Frost, Robert. *Complete Poems of Robert Frost*. New York: Henry Holt, 1949.

Frye, Northrop. *The Bush Garden: Essays on the Canadian Imagination*. Toronto: Anansi, 1971.

———. *Divisions on a Ground: Essays on Canadian Culture*. Toronto: Anansi, 1982.

———. Introduction. *Collected Poems: E.J. Pratt*. 2nd edition. Toronto: Macmillan, 1960. xiii–xxviii.

———. Introduction. *The Stepsure Letters*, by Thomas McCulloch. iii–ix.

———. "Levels of Cultural Identity." *The Eternal Act of Creation: Essays, 1979 – 1990*. Ed Robert D. Denham. Bloomington: Indiana University Press, 1993: 168–182.

Gelpi, Albert J. *Emily Dickinson: The Mind of the Poet*. New York: W.W. Norton, 1971.

Ginsberg, Allen. "America." Rosenthal, 1061–63.

Godfrey, Stephen. "I really feel I took a lot of risks in this one." *The Globe and Mail*. 11 August 1989: C9.

Goldbloom, Victor C. "Canada: The Challenge of Coexistence." Staines, *Forty-ninth*. 9–18.

Grace, Sherrill E. "Comparing Mythologies: Ideas of West and North." Lecker, *Borderlands*. 243–262.

Granatstein, J.L. *Who Killed Canadian History?* Toronto: Harper Perennial, 1998.

———. *Yankee Go Home: Canadians and Anti–Americanism*. Toronto: Harper Collins, 1996.

Greeley, Horace. *An Overland Journey*. Readex Microprint Corporation, 1966.

Grove, Frederick P. *Settlers of the Marsh*. Toronto: McClelland &Stewart, 1989.

Gunners, Kristjana. Afterword. *Settlers of the Marsh*, by Frederick Grove. 267–275.

Haliburton, Thomas Chandler. *The Clockmaker*. Toronto: McClelland & Stewart, 1993.

———. *The Old Judge or Life in a Colony*. Ottawa: The Tecumseh Press, 1978.

Hammett, Dashiell. *The Maltese Falcon*. New York: Vintage Books, 1992.

Handy, Robert T. "Protestant Patterns in Canada and the United States: Similarities and Differences." *In the Great Tradition: In Honor of Winthrop S. Hudson, Essays on Pluralism, Volunteerism and Revivalism*. Ed. J.D. Ban and Paul R. Dekar. Valley Forge, Pa: Judson Press, 1982. 33–51.

Harrison, Dick, ed. *Crossing Frontiers: Papers in American and Canadian Western Literature*. Edmonton: University of Alberta Press, 1979.

———. *Unnamed Country: The Struggle for a Canadian Prairie Fiction*. Edmonton: University of Alberta Press, 1977.

Harte, F. Bret. "Muck A Muck: An Indian Novel, after Cooper." *Condensed Novels and Other Papers*. New York: G.W. Carleton, 1867. 11–20.

Hatch, Nathan O. *The Democratization of American Christianity*. Yale UP, 1989.

Hawthorne, Nathaniel. *Hawthorne's Short Stories*. New York: Vintage Books, 1946.

———. Introduction. *The House of the Seven Gables: A Romance*. New York: Signet Classics, 1961. vii–ix.

———. *Letters of Hawthorne to William D. Ticknor, 1851–1864*. Vol. I. Newark, NJ: The Carteret Book Club, 1910.

———. *The Marble Faun*. New York: Signet Classics, 1961.

———. *The Scarlet Letter*. New York: Signet Classics, 1999.

Hébert, Anne. *Kamouraska*. Toronto: General Publishing, 1982.

Heller, Joseph. *Catch–22*. New York: Dell Publishing, 1968.

Hemingway, Ernest. *The Old Man and the Sea*. New York: Collier Books, 1980.

———. *The Sun Also Rises*. New York: Charles Scribner's Sons, 1954.

Hémon, Louis. *Maria Chapdelaine*. Trans. W.H. Blake. Toronto: Macmillan of Canada, 1973.

Hiebert, Paul. *Sarah Binks*. Toronto: McClelland & Stewart, 1999.

Hodgins, Jack. *The Machen Charm*. Toronto: McClelland & Stewart, 1995.

Hofstadter, Richard. *America at 1750: A Social Portrait*. New York: Alfred A. Knopf, 1971.

———. *Anti-intellectualism in American Life*. New York: Vintage Books, 1973.

Howe, Irving. Introduction. *The Bostonians*, by Henry James. New York: The Modern Library, 1956. v–xxviii.

Howe, Joseph. "Acadia." Sinclair, 17–41.

Howells, William Dean. *A Hazard of New Fortunes*. New York: Signet Classic, 1965.

———. *The Rise of Silas Lapham*. New York: Oxford University Press, 1996.

Innis, Harold A. *The Fur Trade in Canada: An Introduction to Canadian Economic History*. Toronto: University of Toronto Press, 1970.

Irving, Washington. *The Sketch Book of Geoffrey Crayon, Gent*. Ed. Malcolm Bradbury. London: J.M. Dent, 1993.

Jackson, Shirley. "The Lottery." *The Small Town in American Literature*. 2nd ed. Ed. David M. Cook and Craig G. Swauger. New York: Harper and Row, 1977. 218–25.

Jacobs, Jane. *Death and Life of Great American Cities*. Toronto: Random House Canada, 1992.

James, Henry. *The American*. New York: Holt, Rinehart and Winston, 1949.

———. *The Art of the Novel*. New York: Charles Scribner's Sons, 1934.

———. *The Bostonians*. New York: The Modern Library, 1956.

———. *Hawthorne*. New York: AMS Press, 1968.

———. *The Portrait of a Lady*. New York: Modern Library, 1951.

———. *The Wings of the Dove*. New York: Modern Library, 1937.

Jameson, Anna Brownell. *Winter Studies and Summer Rambles in Canada*. Selections. Toronto: McClelland & Stewart, 1965.

Jefferson, Thomas. *The Portable Thomas Jefferson*. Ed. Merrill D. Peterson. New York: Penguin Books, 1975.

Johnson, J. Lee and John H. Johnson. "Ralph Connor and the Canadian Identity." *Queen's Quarterly* 79 (Summer 1972).

Johnston, Wayne. *The Colony of Unrequited Dreams*. Toronto: Vintage Canada, 1999.

Jones, H.M. Forword. Dorson, xi–xxvi.

Kaye, Francis W. "Canadian-American Prairie-Plains Literature in English." Lecker, *Borderlands,* 222–242.

Kaplan, Justin. Introduction. *A Connecticut Yankee in King Arthur's Court*. By Mark Twain. New York: Penguin Books, 1986. 9–23.

Kazin, Alfred. *God and the American Writer*. New York: Vintage Books, 1998.

———. Introduction. *The Day of the Locust*. By Nathanael West. New York: Penguin, 1983. v–xvii.

Keillor, Garrison. *Lake Woebegon Days*. New York, Penguin,1986.

Keith, W.J. *An Independent Stance: Essays on English Canadian Criticism and Fiction*. Erin, ON: The Porcupine's Quill, 1991.

———. *Charles G.D. Roberts*. Toronto: The Copp Clark Publishing Co., 1969.

———. *Epic Fiction: The Art of Rudy Wiebe*. Edmonton: The University of Alberta Press, 1981.

———. Ed. *A Voice in the Land: Essays By and About Rudy Wiebe*. Edmonton: NeWest Press, 1981.

Kerans, R.P. "Two Nations Under Law." D. Thomas, 215–233.

Kerouac, Jack. *On the Road*. New York: Penguin Books, 1991.

Kingsolver, Barbara. *Pigs in Heaven*. New York: Harper Perennial, 1994.

Kirby, William. *The Golden Dog*. Toronto: McClelland & Stewart, 1969.

Kirn, Walter. "The Wages of Righteousness." Rev. of *Cloudsplitter.* By Russell Banks. *The New York Times Book Review.* 22 February 1998, 9.

Krieger, Murray. Afterword. *The Marble Faun*. By Nathaniel Hawthorne. New York: Signet Classics, 1961. 335–346.

Kroetsch, Robert. *Badlands*. Toronto: General Publishing, 1976.

———. *Gone Indian*. Nanaimo, BC: Theytus Books, 1981.

———. *The Lovely Treachery of Words: Essays Selected and New*. Toronto: Oxford University Press, 1989.

———. "No Name is My Name." Staines, *Forty-ninth.* 116–128.

Kroetsch, Robert and Reingard M. Nischik, eds. *Gaining Ground: European Critics on Canadian Literature*. Edmonton: NeWest Press, 1986

Lamar, Howard R. "The Unsettling of the American West: The Mobility of Defeat." Harrison, *Frontiers,* 35–54.

Laurence, Margaret. *The Diviners.* Toronto: McClelland & Stewart, 1975

Lawrence, D.H. *Studies in Classic American Literature*. New York: The Viking Press, 1961.

Leacock, Stephen. *Arcadian Adventures with the Idle Rich*. Toronto:
    McClelland & Stewart, 1989.
———. "My Financial Career." *Literary Lapses*. Toronto: McClelland &
    Stewart, 1957. 1–4.
———. *Sunshine Sketches of a Little Town*. Toronto: McClelland &
    Stewart,1989.
Lecker, Robert, ed. *Borderlands: Essays on Canadian-American Relations*.
    Toronto: ECW Press, 1991.
———. ed. *Canadian Canons: Essays in Literary Value*. Toronto: University
    of Toronto Press,1991.
Lee, Harper. *To Kill a Mockingbird*. Toronto: Popular Library, 1962.
Legate, David M. *Stephen Leacock: A Biography*. Toronto: Doubleday
    Canada, 1970.
Le Gates, Marlene. *In Their Time: A History of Feminism in Western Society*.
    New York: Routledge, 2001.
Leithauser, Brad. Introduction. *The Grapes of Wrath*. By John Steinbeck.
    New York: Everyman's Library, 1993. v–xvi.
LePan, Douglas. "Canoe Trip." A.J.M. Smith, 86.
Lewis, R.W.B. *The American Adam: Innocence, Tragedy, and Tradition in
    the Nineteenth Century*. Chicago: Phoenix Books, 1958.
Lewis, Sinclair. *Babbitt*. New York: Bantam Books, 1998.
———. *Elmer Gantry*. New York: Signet Classics, 1980.
———. *Main Street*. New York: Bantam Books, 1996.
Lipset, Seymour Martin. *American Exceptionalism: A Double-Edged Sword*.
    New York: W.W. Norton, l996.
———. *Continental Divide: The Values and Institutions of the United States
    and Canada*. New York: Routledge, 1990.
Lovejoy, Arthur O. *The Great Chain of Being: A Study of the History of An
    Idea*. New York: Harper & Row, 1960.
Lucas, Alec. Introduction. *Wild Animals I Have Known*. By Ernest Thompson
    Seton. Toronto: McClelland & Stewart, 1977. vii–xii.
Lynn, Kenneth S., ed. *The Comic Tradition in America*. New York:
    Doubleday Anchor, 1958.
McCarthy, Cormac. *All the Pretty Horses*. Vol. 1 of *The Border Trilogy*. New
    York: Vintage Books, 1993.
———. *The Crossing*. Vol. 2 of *The Border Trilogy*. New York: Vintage
    Books, 1995.
———. *Cities of the Plain*. Vol. 3 of *The Border Trilogy*. New York: Vintage
    Books, 1999.
McCulloch, Thomas. *The Stepsure Letters*. Toronto: McClelland &
    Stewart, 1960.

Macdonald, John A. Unpublished letter from John A. Macdonald to Sir
  Henry James Sumner Maine in Calcutta, April 9, 1867. National
  Archives of Canada.
MacDonald, Mary Lu. "The Natural World in Early Nineteenth-Century
  Canadian Literature," *Canadian Literature* 91 (1981): 48–65.
McDougall, Robert L. Afterword. *The Clockmaker*. By T.C. Haliburton.
  Toronto: McClelland & Stewart, 1993. 211–220.
Macintyre, Linden. "All the News That's Fit to Sell." *Queen's Quarterly*. 22
  108.1 (Spring 2001) 37–44.
MacLennan, Hugh. *Return of the Sphinx*. Toronto: Macmillan of Canada, 1976.
———. *Two Solitudes*. Toronto: Macmillan of Canada, 1967.
———. *Each Man's Son*. Toronto: Macmillan of Canada, 1974.
MacLeod, Alistair. *No Great Mischief*. Toronto: McClelland & Stewart, 1999.
MacLulich, T.D. "Our Place on the Map: The Canadian Tradition in Fiction."
  University of Toronto Quarterly 52.2 (1982/3): 191–208.
Maier, Pauline. *American Scripture: Making the Declaration of
  Independence*. New York: Vintage Books, 1998.
Mandel, Eli, ed. *Contexts of Canadian Criticism: A Collection of Critical
  Essays*. Toronto: University of Toronto Press, 1977.
McMullen, Lorraine. *Twentieth Century Essays on Confederation Literature*.
  Ottawa: The Tecumseh Press, 1976.
McNaught, Kenneth, with John C. Ricker and John T. Saywell. *Manifest
  Destiny: A Short History of the United States*. Toronto: Clarke, Irwin, 1963.
Magee, William H. "Local Colour in Canadian Fiction." McMullen, 77–92.
Martin, Sandra. "I think you carry a landscape within you." *The Globe and
  Mail* 27 April 2000: D9.
Marx, Leo. *The Machine in the Garden: Technology and the Pastoral Ideal in
  America*. New York: Oxford University Press, 1967.
———. *The Pilot and the Passenger: Essays on Literature, Technology, and
  Culture in the United States*. New York: Oxford University Press, 1988.
May, Henry F. *The End of American Innocence: A Study of the First Years of
  Our Own Time: 1912–1917*. Oxford: Oxford University Press, 1979.
Melville, Herman. *Billy Budd, Foretopman. The Shorter Novels of Herman
  Melville*. Ed. Raymond Weaver. Greenwich, CT: A Fawcett Premier
  Book, 1967. 198–272.
———. *The Confidence Man*. New York: Oxford University Press, 1991.
———. *Moby Dick*. New York: W.W. Norton, 1967.
———. *Pierre or, The Ambiguities*. New York: Signet Classics, 1964.
Menand, Louis. *The Metaphysical Club*. New York: Farrar, Straus and
  Giroux, 2002.
Meyers, Roy W. *The Middle Western Farm Novel in the Twentieth Century*.
  Lincoln: University of Nebraska Press, 1965.

Miller, John C. *The Federalist Era: 1789–1801*. New York: Harper Colophon Books, 1960.

Miller, Perry. *Errand into the Wilderness*. Cambridge: Harvard University Press, 1956.

———. *Jonathan Edwards*. New York: Meridian Books, 1959.

———. *The Life of the Mind in America: From the Revolution to the Civil War*. New York: Harcourt, Brace and World, 1965.

———. *Nature's Nation*. Cambridge: Harvard University Press, 1967.

Millstein, Gilbert. Rev. of *On the Road*. By Jack Kerouac. *The New York Times*, 4 September 1957.

Mitchell, W.O. *Who Has Seen the Wind*. Toronto: Macmillan, 1974.

Montgomery, Lucy Maud. *Anne of Green Gables*. Toronto: McClelland & Stewart, 1992.

Moodie, Susanna. *Life in the Clearings*. Ed. Robert L. McDougall. Toronto: Macmillan of Canada, 1976.

———. *Roughing It in the Bush*. Toronto: McClelland & Stewart, 1989.

Moore, Brian. *Black Robe*. Markham ON: Penguin Books, 1987.

Morison, S. E., ed. *Sources and Documents illustrating the American Revolution, 1764–1788*. London: Oxford University Press, 1951.

Morrison, Toni. *Beloved*. New York: New American Library, 1988.

———. *Jazz*. New York: Alfred A. Knopf, 1992.

———. *Paradise*. New York: A Plume Book, 1999.

———. *Playing in the Dark: Whiteness and the Literary Imagination*. Harvard University Press, 1992.

———. *Song of Solomon*. New York: Signet Classic, 1978.

Morton, W.L. *The Canadian Identity*. 2nd ed. Toronto: University of Toronto Press, 1972.

Moss, John. *A Reader's Guide to the Canadian Novel*. Toronto: McClelland & Stewart, 1981.

———. *Sex and Violence in the Canadian Novel: The Ancestral Presence*. Toronto: McClelland & Stewart, 1977.

Munro, Alice. "A Wilderness Station." *Open Secrets*. Toronto: McClelland & Stewart, 1994. 190–225.

New, W.H. *Borderlands: How We Talk About Canada*. Vancouver: University of British Columbia Press, 1998.

North, Sterling. *The Writings of Mazo de la Roche*. Boston: Little Brown and Co, n.d.

Oates, Stephen B. *The Approaching Fury: Voices of the Storm, 1820–1861*. New York: Harper Collins, 1997.

O'Connor, Flannery. *Three By Flannery O'Connor*. New York: Signet Books, 1962.

Ondaatje, Michael. *In the Skin of a Lion*. Toronto: Penguin Books, 1988.

Ostenso, Martha. *Wild Geese*. Toronto: McClelland & Stewart, 1971.

Pache, Walter. "The Fiction Makes Us Real: Aspects of Postmodernism in Canada." Kroetsch and Nischik, 64–77.

Padover, Saul K. *Jefferson*. New York: The New American Library, 1952.

Parker, Gilbert. *The Seats of the Mighty*. Toronto: McClelland & Stewart, 1985.

Pearce, Richard. Introduction. *Critical Essays on Thomas Pynchon*. Boston: G.H. Hall, 1981.

Pease, Donald E. Introduction. *The Deerslayer*. By James Fenimore Cooper. New York: Penguin Books, 1987. vii–xxv.

Peterson, Merrill D., ed. *The Portable Thomas Jefferson*. New York: Penguin Books, 1975.

Pevere, Geoff and Greig Dymond. *Mondo Canuck: A Canadian Pop Culture Odyssey*. Scarborough ON: Prentice-Hall Canada, 1996.

Pincott, Jennifer. "The Inner Workings: Technoscience, Self, and Society in DeLillo's *Underworld*." *Undercurrent: An Online Journal for the Analysis of the Present*. Number 7, Spring 1999.

Poe, Edgar Allan. *Selected Writings of Edgar Allan Poe*. Ed. Edward H. Davidson. Boston: Houghton Mifflin, 1956.

Poirier, Richard. Introduction. *Emerson*. Oxford: Oxford U.P., 1990. ix–xx.

———. *Trying It Out in America: Literary and Other Performances*. New York: Farrar, Strauss and Giroux, 1999.

Polk, John. "Lives of the Hunted." McMullen, 102–110.

Poulin, Jacques. *Volkswagen Blues*. Trans. Sheila Fischman. Toronto: McClelland & Stewart, 1988.

Powe, Bruce. *A Climate Charged*. Oakville, ON: Mosaic, 1984.

Pratt, E.J. *The Collected Poems of E.J. Pratt*. 2nd ed. Toronto: The Macmillan Company of Canada, 1962.

Prentice, Alison, Paula Bourne, Gail Cuthbert Brandt, Beth Light, Wendy Mitchinson, and Naomi Black. *Canadian Women: A History*. Toronto: Harcourt Canada, 1996.

Proulx, E. Annie. *The Shipping News*. New York: Touchstone, 1993.

Puzo, Mario. *The Godfather*. Greenwich CT: Fawcett Crest, 1969.

Pynchon, Thomas. *The Crying of Lot 49*. Toronto: Bantam, 1980.

Rasporich, Beverley. "Stephen Leacock, Humorist: American by Association." Staines, *Leacock*. 69–82.

Reynolds, David S. *Beneath the American Renaissance: The Subversive Imagination in the Age of Emerson and Melville*. New York: Alfred A. Knopf, 1988.

Richardson, John. *Wacousta or The Prophecy*. Toronto: McClelland & Stewart, 1967.

Richler, Mordecai. *The Apprenticeship of Duddy Kravitz*. Toronto: McClelland & Stewart, 1974.

———. *Solomon Gursky Was Here*. Markham, ON: Viking, 1989.

———. *Son of a Smaller Hero*. Toronto: McClelland & Stewart, 1966.

Ringe, Donald A. Introduction. *The Pioneers*. By James Fenimore Cooper. New York: Penguin Books, 1988. vii–xxii.

Ringuet. *Thirty Acres*. Trans. Felix and Dorothea Walters. Toronto: McClelland & Stewart, 1989.

Roberts, Charles G.D. *The Kindred of the Wild: A Book of Animal Life*. Toronto: Copp Clark, 1902.

———. *The Last Barrier and Other Stories*. Toronto: McClelland & Stewart, 1970.

Rosenthal, M.L. *Poetry in English: An Anthology*. Toronto: Oxford University Press, 1987.

Ross, Malcolm, ed. *Poets of the Confederation*. Toronto: McClelland & Stewart, 1960.

Ross, Sinclair. *As For Me and My House*. Toronto: McClelland & Stewart, 1989.

Rossiter, Clinton, ed. *The Federalist Papers: Alexander Hamilton, James Madison, and John Jay*. New York: New American Library, 1961.

Roth, Philip. *The Human Stain*. New York: Vintage Books, 2001.

Rourke, Constance. *American Humor: A Study of the National Character*. 1931 rpt; New York: Harcourt Brace Jovanovich, 1961.

Roy, Gabrielle. *Windflower*. Trans. Joyce Marshall. Toronto: McClelland & Stewart, 1991.

Ruland, Richard. Introduction. *Twentieth Century Interpretations of Walden*. Englewood Cliffs, NJ: Prentice Hall, 1968. 1–6.

Safire, William. *Scandalmonger*. New York: Harcourt, 2000.

Schäfer, Jürgen. "A Farewell to Europe: Rudy Wiebe's *The Temptations of Big Bear* and Robert Kroetsch's *Gone Indian*." Kroetsch and Nischik, 79–90.

Schorer, Mark. Afterword. *Elmer Gantry*. By Sinclair Lewis. New York: Signet Classics, 1980. 419–30.

———. Afterword. *Main Street*. By Sinclair Lewis. New York: Signet Classics, 1961. 433–39.

Scott, Winfield Townley. Rev. of *Collected Poems of E.J. Pratt. Poetry*, September 1945: 332.

Seelye, John. Introduction. *The Adventures of Huckleberry Finn*. By Mark Twain. New York: Penguin Books, 1986. vii–xxviii.

Seton, Ernest Thompson. *Wild Animals I Have Known*. Toronto: McClelland & Stewart, 1977.

Shields, Carol. *The Republic of Love*. Toronto: Fawcett Crest, 1992.

———. *The Stone Diaries*. Toronto: Vintage Books, 1993.

Shorer, Mark. Afterword. *Main Street*. By Sinclair Lewis. New York: New American Library, 1961. 433–39.

Simon, James F. *What Kind of Nation: Thomas Jefferson, John Marshall, and the Epic Struggle to Create a United States*. New York: Simon & Schuster, 2002.

Simpson, Claude M., ed. *Twentieth-Century Interpretations of Huckleberry Finn*. Englewood Cliffs, NJ: Prentice-Hall, 1968.

Sinclair, David, ed. *Nineteenth-Century Narrative Poems*. Toronto: McClelland & Stewart, 1972.

Sirois, Antoine. Afterword. *Thirty Acres*. By Ringuet. Toronto: McClelland & Stewart, 1989. 301–306.

Slotkin, Richard. *The Fatal Environment: The Myth of the Frontier in the Age of Industrialization, 1800–1890*. Norman: University of Oklahoma Press, 1985.

———. *Gunfighter Nation: The Myth of the Frontier in Twentieth-Century America*. Norman: University of Oklahoma Press, 1998.

———. *Regeneration Through Violence: The Mythology of the American Frontier, 1600–1860*. Norman: University of Oklahoma Press, 1973.

Smith, A.J.M., ed. *The Oxford Book of Canadian Verse in English and French*. Toronto: Oxford University Press, 1965.

Smith, Henry Nash. *Democracy and the Novel: Popular Resistance to Classic American Writers*. Oxford: Oxford University Press, 1981.

———. *Mark Twain: The Development of a Writer*. New York: Atheneum, 1972.

———. *Virgin Land: The American West as Symbol and Myth*. New York: Vintage Books, 1957.

Smith, Tamara Palmer. "Melting Pot and Mosaic: Images and Realities." D. Thomas, 303–325.

Spiller, Robert E. Afterword. *The Pioneers*. By James Fenimore Cooper. New York: Signet Classics, 1964. 437–44.

Staines, David. *Beyond the Provinces: Literary Canada at Century's End*. Toronto: University of Toronto Press, 1995.

———. ed. *The Forty-Ninth and Other Parallels*. University of Massachusetts Press, 1986.

———. ed. *Stephen Leacock: A Reappraisal*. Ottawa: University of Ottawa Press, 1986.

Stead, Robert J.C. *Grain*. Toronto: McClelland & Stewart, 1969.

Steele, James. "Imperial Cosmopolitanism, or the Partly Solved Riddle of Leacock's Multi-National Persona." Staines, *Leacock*. 59–68.

Stegner, Wallace. *Wolf Willow: A History, A Story, and a Memory of the Last Plains Frontier*. New York: Viking, 1963.

Steinbeck, John. *The Grapes of Wrath*. New York: Everyman's Library, 1993.

Stevenson, Winona. "Colonialism and First Nations Women in Canada." *Scratching the Surface: Canadian Anti-Racist Feminist Thought*. Ed. Enakshi Dua and Angela Robertson. Toronto: Women's Press, 1999. 49–80.

Stewart, Gordon and George Rawlyk. *A People Highly Favoured of God: The Nova Scotia Yankees and the American Revolution*. Toronto: Macmillan of Canada, 1972.

Stewart, Walter. *True Blue: The Loyalist Legend*. Toronto: Collins, 1985.

Stowe, Harriet Beecher. *Uncle Tom's Cabin*. London: J.M. Dent & Sons, 1961.

Styron, William. *The Confessions of Nat Turner*. New York: Signet Books, 1968.

Sullivan, Rosemary. "Summing Up." Harrison, *Frontiers*. 144–57.

Surette, Leon. "Creating the Canadian Canon." Lecker, *Canons*. 17–29.

Sutherland, Ronald. *Second Image: Comparative Studies in Quebec/Canadian Literature*. Don Mills, ON: Newpress, 1971.

Tallman, Warren. "Wolf in the Snow." Mandel, *Contexts*. 232–53.

Tanner, Tony. *City of Words: American Fiction 1950–1970*. New York: Harper and Row, 1971.

————. "The Lost America — The Despair of Henry Adams and Mark Twain." *Twentieth Century Views: Mark Twain*. Englewood Cliffs, NJ: Prentice-Hall, 1963. 159–74.

Tate, Allen. "Emily Dickinson," *Interpretations of American Literature*. Ed. Charles Feidelson, Jr. and Paul Brodtkorb, Jr. New York: Oxford University Press, 1959. 197–211.

Thomas, Clara. Preface. *Canadians of Old*. By Aubert de Gaspé. Toronto: McClelland & Stewart, 1974. vii–xii.

————. Introduction. *Winter Studies and Summer Rambles in Canada*. By Anna Brownell Jameson. ix–xiv.

Thomas, David, ed. *Canada and the United States: Differences that Count*. Peterborough ON: broadview press, 1993

Thoreau, Henry David. *Walden and Other Writings*. Ed. Brooks Atkinson. New York: The Modern Library, 1992.

————. *A Week on the Concord and Merrimack Rivers. The Writings of Henry David Thoreau*. Vol I. Boston: Houghton Mifflin, 1906.

————. *A Yankee in Canada. The Writings of Henry David Thoreau*. Vol V. *Excursions and Poems*. Boston: Houghton Mifflin, 1906.

Thorner, Thomas, ed. *"a country nourished on self-doubt": Documents in Canadian History, 1867–1980*. Peterborough ON: broadview press, 1998.

Thurber, James. *James Thurber: 92 Stories*. New York: Wings Book, 1994.

Traill, Catharine Parr. *The Backwoods of Canada*. Toronto: McClelland & Stewart, 1989.

Trueheart, Charles. "Strangers in a not-so-strange land." *The Globe and Mail* 5 October 1996: D3.

Turner, Frederick Jackson. *Frontier and Section: Selected Essays of Frederick Jackson Turner*. Englewood Cliffs, NJ: Prentice-Hall, 1961.

Twain, Mark. *The Adventures of Huckleberry Finn*. New York: Penguin Books, 1986.

———. *The Adventures of Tom Sawyer*. New York: Penguin, 1986.

———. *A Connecticut Yankee in King Arthur's Court*. New York: Penguin Books, 1986.

———. *Life on the Mississippi*. New York: Signet Classics, 1961.

———. *The Mysterious Stranger and Other Stories*. New York: Dover Publications, 1972.

Tyler, Anne. *Saint Maybe*. Toronto: Penguin Books, 1992.

Updike, John. *Hugging the Shore: Essays and Criticism*. New York: Vintage Books, 1984.

———. *In the Beauty of the Lilies*. New York: Fawcett Columbine, 1997.

———. "Magnetic North." Rev. of *Selected Stories*. By Alice Munro. *The New York Times Book Review*, 27 October 1996: 11+.

———. *Memories of the Ford Administration*. New York: Fawcett Crest, 1993.

———. *A Month of Sundays*. New York: Fawcett Columbine, 1976.

———. *Rabbit is Rich*. New York: Fawcett Crest, 1982.

———. *Rabbit Redux*. New York: Fawcett Crest, 1972.

———. *Rabbit at Rest*. New York: Fawcett Crest, 1991.

———. *Rabbit Run*. Greenwich, CT: Fawcett Crest, 1960.

———. *Roger's Version*. New York: Fawcett Crest, 1987.

———. *S.* New York: Fawcett Crest, 1989.

———. *Self-Consciousness: Memoirs*. New York: Fawcett Crest, 1990.

———. *The Witches of Eastwick*. New York: Alfred A. Knopf, 1984.

Vanderhaeghe, Guy. "Leacock and Understanding Canada." Staines, *Leacock*. 17–22.

Vidal, Gore. *Burr*. Toronto: Bantam, 1974.

———. *1876*. New York: Ballantine, 1976.

———. *Empire*. New York: Ballantine, 1987.

———. *Hollywood*. New York: Ballantine, 1991.

———. Interview with Michael Anderson. *The New York Times Book Review*, 30 August 1992: 27.

———. *Lincoln*. New York: Random House, 1984.

———. *Views From a Window: Conversations with Gore Vidal*. Ed. Robert J. Stanton and Gore Vidal. Secaucus NJ: Lyle Stuart, 1980.

———. *Washington, D.C.* New York: Ballantine, 1976

Walcutt, Charles Child. "The Range of Interpretations — *The Scarlet Letter* and Its Modern Critics," *Twentieth Century Interpretations of The Scarlet Letter*. Ed. John C. Gerber. Englewood Cliffs NJ: Prentice-Hall, 1968. 71–81.

Watson, Sheila. *The Double Hook*. Toronto: McClelland & Stewart, 1969.

Watters, R.E. "The Old Judge." R. A. Davies, 216–31.

West, Nathanael. *The Day of the Locust*. New York: Penguin, 1983.

314 CANADIANS ARE NOT AMERICANS

White, E.B. and Katherine S. *A Subtreasury of American Humor*. New York: The Modern Library, 1941.

Whitman, Walt. *The Complete Poetry and Prose of Walt Whitman*. 2 vols. New York, Pellegrini and Cudahy, 1948.

Wickersham, John. Introduction. *Babbitt*, By Sinclair Lewis. New York: Bantam, 1998. vii–xx.

Wiebe, Rudy. "Bear Spirit in a Strange Land." Keith, *Voice*. 143–49.

———. "On the Trail of Big Bear." Keith, *Voice*. 132–42.

———. *The Scorched Wood People*. Toronto: McClelland & Stewart, 1977.

———. *The Temptations of Big Bear*. Toronto: McClelland & Stewart, 1976.

Winters, Ivor. "Emily Dickinson and the Limits of Judgment," *Maule's Curse: Seven Studies in the History of American Obscurantism*. Norfolk, CT: New Directions, 1938. 149–65.

Wise, S.F. "The 1790s." Careless, *Colonists*. 62–94.

Wollstonecraft, Mary. *A Vindication of the Rights of Woman. Woman in Western Thought*. Ed. Martha Lee Osborne. New York: Random House, 1979.

Woodcock, George. *George Woodcock's Introduction to Canadian Fiction*. Toronto: ECW Press, 1993.

———. Introduction. *Turvey*. By Earl Birney. Toronto: McClelland & Stewart, 1969. ix–xv.

———. *Northern Spring: the Flowering of Canadian Literature*. Vancouver: Douglas and McIntyre, 1987.

Yates, Norris W. *The American Humorist: Conscience of the Twentieth Century*. New York: The Citadel Press, 1965.

Credits

Penguin Canada

From *The Rebel Angels* by Robertson Davies. Copyright © 1981. Used by permission of Pearson Penguin Canada Inc.

From *Mondo Canuck: A Canadian Pop Culture Odyssey* by Geoff Pevere and Greig Dymond. Copyright © 1996. Used by permission of Pearson Penguin Canada Inc.

From *Solomon Gursky Was Here*. Copyright © 1989 by Mordecai Richler. Used by permission of Pearson Penguin Canada Inc.

From *Saint Maybe* by Anne Tyler. Copyright © 1991. Used by permission of Pearson Penguin Canada Inc.

The Porcupine's Quill

From *An Independent Stance: Essays on English-Canadian Criticism and Fiction* by W.J. Keith. Copyright © 1991. Used by permission of The Porcupine's Quill.

Random House Canada

Extracted from *The Colony of Unrequited Dreams* by Wayne Johnston. Copyright © 1998 by Wayne Johnston. Reprinted by permission of Alfred A. Knopf Canada.

Extracted from *The Stone Diaries* by Carol Shields. Copyright © 1993 by Carol Shields. Reprinted by permission of Random House Canada.

Random House

From *The Declaration of Independence: A Study in the History of Political Ideas* by Carl L. Becker, copyright © 1970 renewed. Reprinted by permission of Random House Inc.

From *Invisible Man* by Ralph Ellison. Copyright © 1980 renewed. Reprinted by permission of Random House Inc.

From *Light in August* by William Faulkner. Copyright © 1932, renewed 1959 by William Faulkner. Copyright 1968 by Random House Inc. Reprinted by permission of Random House Inc.

From *God and the American Writer* by Alfred Kazin. Copyright © 1997. Reprinted by permission of Vintage Books, division of Random House Inc.

From *Babbitt* by Sinclair Lewis. Copyright © 1950 renewed. Reprinted by permission of Random House Inc.

From *American Scripture: Making the Declaration of Independence* by Pauline Maier. Copyright © 1997. Reprinted by permission of Vintage Books, division of Random House Inc.

From *Beneath the American Renaissance: The Subversive Imagination in the Age of Emerson and Melville* by David S. Reynolds. Copyright © 1988. Reprinted by permission of Alfred A. Knopf, division of Random House Inc.

Index